STRATEGIC ASIA

STRATEGIC ASIA

RESHAPING ECONOMIC INTERDEPENDENCE
in the Indo-Pacific

Edited by

Ashley J. Tellis, Alison Szalwinski, and Michael Wills

With contributions from

Victor A. Ferguson, Benjamin Herscovitch, Hyo-young Lee,
Darren J. Lim, Syaru Shirley Lin, Vikram Nehru, William J. Norris,
Gulshan Sachdeva, Yul Sohn, Ashley J. Tellis, and Kristin Vekasi

THE NATIONAL BUREAU *of* ASIAN RESEARCH
Seattle and Washington, D.C.

THE NATIONAL BUREAU *of* ASIAN RESEARCH

Published in the United States of America by
The National Bureau of Asian Research, Seattle, WA, and Washington, D.C.
www.nbr.org

Copyright © 2023 by The National Bureau of Asian Research

All rights reserved. No part of this publication may be reproduced, stored in a retrieval system, or transmitted in any form or by any means, electronic, mechanical, photocopying, recording, or otherwise, without prior permission of the publisher.

ISBN (print): 978-1-939131-80-5
ISBN (electronic): 978-1-939131-81-2

Cover images
 Front: Paper folding ship of dollar and yuan currency © Hakule
 Back (left to right): © Tryaging; © Pixnio; © Moerschy; and © Pixabay

Design and publishing services by The National Bureau of Asian Research.

Cover design by Stefanie Choi.

Publisher's Cataloging-In-Publication Data
(Provided by Cassidy Cataloguing Services, Inc.)

Names:	Tellis, Ashley J., editor.	Szalwinski, Alison, editor.	Wills, Michael, 1970- editor.	Ferguson, Victor A., contributor.	National Bureau of Asian Research (U.S.), publisher, sponsoring body.
Title:	Reshaping economic interdependence in the Indo-Pacific / edited by Ashley J. Tellis, Alison Szalwinski, and Michael Wills ; with contributions from Victor A. Ferguson [and 10 others].
Other titles:	Strategic Asia
Description:	Seattle ; Washington, D.C : The National Bureau of Asian Research, [2023]	Includes bibliographical references and index.
Identifiers:	ISBN: 978-1-939131-80-5 (print)	978-1-939131-81-2 (electronic)
Subjects:	LCSH: Indo-Pacific Region--Foreign economic relations--21st century.	Indo-Pacific Region-- Strategic aspects.	Indo-Pacific Region--Foreign economic relations--China.	China--Foreign economic relations--Indo-Pacific Region.	Indo-Pacific Region--Politics and government--21st century.
Classification:	LCC: DS341 .R47 2023	DDC: 327.5--dc23

Printed in the United States.

The paper used in this publication meets the minimum requirement of
the American National Standard for Information Sciences—Permanence
of Paper for Printed Library Materials, ANSI Z39.48-1992.

Contents

Preface vii
Alison Szalwinski and Michael Wills

Interdependence Imperiled?
Economic Decoupling in an Era of Strategic Competition 3
Ashley J. Tellis
    This chapter assesses the changes to the international economic landscape fueled by China's rise and examines how the United States is navigating this challenge.

The Future of China's Economic Power 35
William J. Norris
    This chapter examines recent strategic developments in China's foreign economic relations with an eye toward their implications for broader geopolitical dynamics.

Japan's Approach to Economic Security and Regional Integration 69
Kristin Vekasi
    This chapter examines the systematic efforts by the Japanese government to minimize security vulnerabilities from economic dependence on China and finds scarce evidence for broad decoupling.

South Korea's Economic Statecraft: Between Interdependence
and National Security 99
Yul Sohn and Hyo-young Lee
    This chapter examines how weaponized interdependence and pressures to decouple have affected South Korea's foreign policy.

Taiwan: Walking the Tightrope between the United States and China . . 129
Syaru Shirley Lin
> This chapter examines the implications of U.S.-China decoupling for Taiwan's integration with the Chinese and world economies and explores how this economic fragmentation is shaping the context in which the Taiwanese are determining their island's future.

India's Reluctant Participation in the Evolving
Indo-Pacific Economic Architecture 165
Gulshan Sachdeva
> This chapter examines how India, contrary to its ambition to be an important strategic player in the Indo-Pacific, has been a reluctant participant in the region's emerging economic architecture and argues that decoupling from China could be harmful for the Indian economy.

U.S.-China Economic Rivalry in Southeast Asia
and Its Implications 201
Vikram Nehru
> This chapter examines how Southeast Asian economies have been affected by U.S.-China rivalry, how the region's economic policies have responded, and how the United States should reconsider its economic policies toward the region.

Australia's Reassessment of Economic Interdependence with China . . 237
Darren J. Lim, Benjamin Herscovitch, and Victor A. Ferguson
> This chapter examines how Australia is grappling with the trade-offs of deep economic interdependence with China and the real—albeit so far limited—impacts that emerging national security concerns are having on how policymakers and economic actors think about and manage bilateral exchange.

About the Contributors 277

About Strategic Asia 283

Index 287

Preface

Alison Szalwinski and Michael Wills

In April 2023, the United States adopted European Commission president Ursula von der Leyen's framing for its declared economic strategy toward China. In the aftermath of speeches by National Security Advisor Jake Sullivan and Treasury Secretary Janet Yellen outlining the U.S. approach, popular attention was focused on perceived divergences in levels of hawkishness between the two.[1] However, these differences obscured a notable rhetorical agreement: both speeches roundly rejected the idea of U.S.-China "decoupling," instead preferring von der Leyen's "de-risking" approach. During her August 2023 trip to Beijing, Commerce Secretary Gina Raimondo noted that "the vast majority of [the U.S.-China] trade and investment relationship" is not connected to national security, and she committed the United States to "promoting trade and investment" in these areas—a pledge that aligns with a strategy of targeted de-risking rather than broad decoupling.[2]

The rhetorical alignment behind de-risking was the culmination of a process that began in the summer of 2018, when the Trump administration began implementing a series of policies that pointed in the direction of broad-based decoupling. While the concept of full decoupling was only ever overtly supported by the most ardent hawks,[3] measures such as imposing tariffs on the majority of Chinese exports to the United States were squarely aimed at restricting the bilateral economic relationship. Furthermore, the

---

[1] "The Fault Lines in America's China Policy," *Economist*, May 16, 2023.

[2] Gina M. Raimondo, "U.S. Secretary of Commerce Gina Raimondo Delivers Remarks Ahead of Bilateral Meeting with PRC Minister of Commerce Wang Wentao," U.S. Department of Commerce, August 28, 2023, https://www.commerce.gov/news/speeches/2023/08/us-secretary-commerce-gina-raimondo-delivers-remarks-ahead-bilateral-meeting.

[3] "Economic Security as National Security: A Discussion with Dr. Peter Navarro," Center for Strategic and International Studies, November 13, 2018, https://www.csis.org/analysis/economic-security-national-security-discussion-dr-peter-navarro.

Trump administration's approach toward technology—which included an initial effort to choke out Chinese telecommunications provider ZTE, followed by the longer-lasting campaign against Huawei—culminated in an attempt to completely excise Chinese companies and supply chains from the full scope of U.S. and allied telecom networks.[4]

Despite these initial steps in the direction of decoupling, as the economic costs became clear, a consensus solidified around a limited form of decoupling—a partial disengagement between the U.S. and Chinese economies in critical sectors.[5] While partial disengagement is more realistic than full decoupling, it poses the policy challenge of defining the boundaries of "partial." Under the "Sullivan doctrine," for instance, U.S. export controls should be used to cut off China from semiconductor manufacturing equipment to maintain "as large of a lead as possible,"[6] but simultaneously should be confined to a "small yard, high fence" approach.[7] Suffice it to say that many U.S. allies and partners—especially in Europe—were concerned with the scope of U.S. partial disengagement policies.[8] Therefore, when President von der Leyen ascribed the moniker of "de-risking" to the European approach, identifying "China's economic and security ambitions" as one such risk, U.S. policymakers seized on this opportunity to rebrand their expansive view of partial disengagement as proportional to their perception of the risks posed by China.

The policy parameters of the U.S. de-risking approach, however, do not seem fundamentally different from the earlier partial disengagement era. The trade relationship has not fundamentally changed in scale or intensity, despite the persistence of many of the Trump administration's tariffs. The Biden administration's lack of interest in reopening the trade war reflects a rejection of decoupling, but its lack of interest in removing the tariffs,

---

[4] "Building a Clean Network: Key Milestones," U.S. Department of State, https://2017-2021.state.gov/building-a-clean-network-key-milestones.

[5] See Charles W. Boustany and Aaron L. Friedberg, "Partial Disengagement: A New U.S. Strategy for Economic Competition with China," National Bureau of Asian Research, NBR Special Report, no. 82, November 2019, https://www.nbr.org/publication/partial-disengagement-a-new-u-s-strategy-for-economic-competition-with-china.

[6] Jake Sullivan, "Remarks by National Security Advisor Jake Sullivan at the Special Competitive Studies Project Global Emerging Technologies Summit," White House, September 16, 2022, https://www.whitehouse.gov/briefing-room/speeches-remarks/2022/09/16/remarks-by-national-security-advisor-jake-sullivan-at-the-special-competitive-studies-project-global-emerging-technologies-summit.

[7] Jake Sullivan, "Remarks by National Security Advisor Jake Sullivan on the Biden-Harris Administration's National Security Strategy," White House, October 12, 2022, https://www.whitehouse.gov/briefing-room/speeches-remarks/2022/10/13/remarks-by-national-security-advisor-jake-sullivan-on-the-biden-harris-administrations-national-security-strategy.

[8] Christina Lu, "Washington Doesn't Want You to Call It Decoupling," *Foreign Policy*, April 27, 2023, https://foreignpolicy.com/2023/04/27/us-china-economy-technology-sullivan-yellen.

even though most cover nonstrategic goods, suggests that the shift toward de-risking is principally about branding. U.S. investment screening and export control policies—while expansive relative to a pre-Trump baseline—remain targeted toward a small number of cutting-edge technologies, including next-generation information and communications technology infrastructure, leading-edge semiconductors, and artificial intelligence (AI). The only new initiative thus far is the Biden administration's executive order on outbound investment screening. However, this measure is narrowly scoped and was already in the works prior to the adoption of de-risking as a descriptor of U.S. policy.

As the United States seeks to clarify where it stands on de-risking, so too do U.S. allies and partners. As seen throughout this *Strategic Asia* volume, the scale and nature of these measures are largely dependent on each country's experiences with the risks of economic engagement with China. Despite the different sources of risk, one common thread emerges: each country's efforts at de-risking are caveated by a cold statistical reality—bilateral trade with China has not significantly decreased, and in many cases has even increased. Much like the United States, U.S. allies and partners acknowledge the unfeasibility of broad decoupling and have crafted their policies accordingly.

The debate regarding the risks of integration between China and liberal democracies has followed quite a different trajectory in China itself. First, it began significantly earlier. Indeed, fears of overdependence on a technologically superior foreign rival are ingrained in the DNA of the Chinese Communist Party (CCP)—dating back to the era of the Sino-Soviet split.[9] Despite the wishful thinking of some foreign observers, the intention of the CCP's reform and opening was not to integrate China's economy with global supply chains but rather to enhance the country's capacity to be economically self-reliant.[10] While these strains of thought were not dominant in the Deng Xiaoping and Jiang Zemin eras, they became increasingly prevalent as early as the Hu Jintao era—well before the emergence of similar views in the West—through the concept of "indigenous innovation" introduced in the National Medium- and Long-Term Program for Science and Technology Development (2006–2020). These efforts have only escalated under Xi Jinping, with the 2015 rollout of the Made in China 2025 plan and his efforts to place the "commanding heights" of advanced

---

[9] David Kerr, "Has China Abandoned Self-Reliance?" *Review of International Political Economy* 14, no. 1 (2007): 77–104.

[10] Ibid.

technology and security-critical economic sectors under tighter party-state control.[11]

A second critical difference between the Chinese and Western views on de-risking is that Chinese leaders—especially recently—have adopted a significantly more expansive view of risk than that of the United States, let alone the United States' Asian or European partners. The "dual circulation" strategy reflects an effort to expand self-reliance beyond high-tech or strategic sectors to the economy as a whole—that is, to insulate the Chinese economy against the perceived risk of shocks emerging from foreign efforts at decoupling, no matter how implausible those fears may actually be.[12]

Based on the nominally straightforward principles of de-risking—namely, identify where external dependencies pose risks and then implement trade restrictions, industrial policies, or other measures to mitigate those risks—countries are now striking out on the path toward de-risking in practice. However, unwinding or reshaping the trillions of decisions made over the course of decades by individual companies and consumers—the ultimate building blocks of globalization—poses complications on a scale that is difficult to comprehend. These complications have even bedeviled China's efforts. Stubbornly anemic domestic consumer spending has undermined the shift toward dual circulation,[13] while attempts to transition government and state-owned enterprises away from reliance on Western technology demonstrate that large-scale decoupling is beyond even the immense domestic power of the CCP to enforce.[14] The challenge is still greater in countries that must attempt to balance government intervention to shift incentives in support of de-risking with an ideological commitment to the principles of a free-market economic system. Coupled with atrophied state capacity to implement industrial policy after nearly three post–Cold War decades of unchecked economic liberalism, meaningfully shifting economic dependencies will be a long, arduous process.

These challenges reflect the fact that a strategy of de-risking, though warranted given the realities of long-term, high-intensity, peer-to-peer strategic competition, is a departure from an idealized vision of an integrated global economy. As Ashley Tellis notes in his introduction to this volume,

---

[11] Nadège Rolland, *China's Eurasian Century? Political and Strategic Implications of the Belt and Road Initiative* (Seattle: NBR, 2017), 102.

[12] Alicia Garcia Herrero, "What Is Behind China's Dual Circulation Strategy," *China Leadership Monitor*, September 1, 2021, https://www.prcleader.org/post/what-is-behind-china-s-dual-circulation-strategy.

[13] Damien Ma and Houze Song, "China's Consumption Conundrum: Can Xi Get Chinese Citizens to Stop Saving and Start Spending?" *Foreign Affairs*, March 16, 2023.

[14] Tobias Mann, "China Rallies Support for Kylin Linux in War on Windows," *Register*, July 3, 2022, https://www.theregister.com/2022/07/03/china_openkylin.

this strategy requires a shift from a focus on absolute gains to one in which states seek to maximize their relative economic power (p. 5). This has led to the emergence of heterodox views challenging the elite consensus around the merits of partial economic and technological disengagement from China. From some there are calls to abandon the de-risking approach as unfeasible or escalatory.[15] But as long as great-power competition persists—and as long as the parties to that competition recognize the numerous times in which economic and technological dependencies have been leveraged toward grand strategic ends—such a reversal is strategically and politically unviable. Another group of voices calls for the establishment of a new set of organizing principles for globalization. Some advocates of this view are countries that desire to play a greater role in economic rulemaking.[16] Others wish to see a new form of globalization emerge to meet challenges relating to climate change, the post-pandemic environment, and other transnational threats.[17]

As the chapters in this volume show, the long process of de-risking is beginning across the Indo-Pacific. Governments are embracing gradualism, reluctant to make large-scale, perhaps irreversible, changes to the prevailing strategic trade policy. For instance, Sullivan doctrine–era U.S. export controls remain narrowly targeted at aspects of China's semiconductor and AI ecosystems and have maintained exemptions for South Korean and Taiwanese companies, thus precluding tough decisions about the disposition of their risky existing investments in China.[18] While governments may welcome the flexibility that these approaches provide, policy uncertainty and unpredictability are anathema to global businesses. Many have begun pursuing their own approaches to de-risking—not just from the strategic and macro risks that governments would recognize in their own de-risking

---

[15] James Crabtree, "U.S.-China De-Risking Will Inevitably Escalate," *Foreign Policy*, August 20, 2023, https://foreignpolicy.com/2023/08/20/derisking-decoupling-us-china-biden-economy-trade-technology-semiconductors-chips-supply-chains-ai-geopolitics-escalation; Elliot Smith, "Dimon Calls for Washington-Beijing Engagement in First China Visit since 2021 Controversy," CNBC, May 31, 2023, https://www.cnbc.com/2023/05/31/dimon-calls-for-washington-beijing-engagement-in-first-china-visit-since-2021-controversy.html; and Michael D. Swaine and Andrew Bacevich, "A Restraint Approach to U.S.-China Relations: Reversing the Slide Toward Crisis and Conflict," Quincy Institute, Quincy Paper, no. 11, April 18, 2023, https://quincyinst.org/report/u-s-relations-with-china-a-strategy-based-on-restraint.

[16] Sanjana Joshi and Samridhi Bimal, "India's Engagement with the Global Economic Order," *UNISCI Journal*, no. 49 (2019): 63–78, https://www.unisci.es/wp-content/uploads/2019/01/UNISCIDP49-4SANJANA.pdf; and "Homeland Economics," *Economist*, October 7, 2023, https://www.economist.com/special-report/2023-10-07.

[17] Ngozi Okonjo-Iweala, "Why the World Still Needs Trade," *Foreign Affairs*, June 8, 2023.

[18] John Liu, "South Korean Chip Makers Get U.S. Waivers from China Export Rules," *New York Times*, October 9, 2023, https://www.nytimes.com/2023/10/09/business/samsung-sk-hynix-us-chip-export-controls.html.

framework, but also from the risk that their operations get caught up in the fallout from geopolitical de-risking.

The key question for businesses, therefore, is how the growing push toward de-risking shapes the environment in which they operate. For decades, businesses have benefited from a consistent and increasingly frictionless global landscape. They have based their investment, supply chain, and market decisions on the presumption that these trends would persist. These assumptions underpinned the rise of multinational companies largely untethered to their nominal headquarters—a phenomenon that may struggle to survive in an era of intensifying strategic competition where the economic domain is an arena for contestation. Companies will therefore have to examine whether their multinational nature can be maintained or leveraged against these trends, or whether steps such as fragmentation or more firmly aligning with one great power and becoming, if not a "national champion," at least a national actor are necessary.

While governments may welcome the opportunity to shift the broad trajectory of the private sector with de-risking signals, this also raises questions for policymakers regarding the scope of de-risking and the potential for self-reinforcing trends and cycles of escalatory disengagement. The interaction between incipient consensus around the need for de-risking and political positioning on China in the 2024 U.S. election cycle increases the possibility of such trends affecting U.S. policy. These cycles—especially if they emerge from the United States—could potentially lead to the establishment of Cold War–style economic blocs, within which trade and investment are broadly open but between which economic interactions are limited. The fact that this outcome is closer to the full decoupling that we have previously identified as unfeasible suggests that governments must clearly delineate the bounds of the risks that they seek to contain, or face the possibility of businesses being incentivized to make decisions that impose what are generally agreed to be unacceptably high economic costs. The logic of escalatory disengagement, however, poses an even greater risk: that eventually perceptions of risk spiral to such a point that countries feel the need to—either collectively or individually—pursue policies that resemble 1930s-era autarky. For instance, recent CCP statements and activities, including targeted raids on and security investigations into economic consultants and researchers, appear designed to crack down on the gathering of even basic economic information by foreigners.[19] This would represent a step toward cutting off or regarding as inherently suspicious full classes of economic transactions in a manner that points toward a broad decoupling.

---

[19] David Pierson and Daisuke Wakabayashi, "China's Raids of Foreign Firms Have Roots in National Security," *New York Times*, May 10, 2023.

These concerns remain hypothetical, as de-risking—at least outside of China—is still in its infancy. There are many uncertainties about how this process will evolve. For the United States, the fact that both the Biden and Trump administrations committed to a similar strategy of partial disengagement, despite adopting wildly different tactics in pursuit of their objectives, suggests that it will remain in the mainstream of both U.S. political parties' thinking for the foreseeable future.

Likewise, the fact that U.S. allies and partners—while often resistant to specific U.S. policies that harm their or their companies' interests—have adopted a similar approach suggests that the move toward de-risking represents a global trend. De-risking will also not be one-sided. Chinese policy has—for far longer than U.S. or like-minded governments—identified greater risks in international economic engagement and erected stronger, broader barriers to this engagement. The connection of this policy to long-standing ideological predilections surrounding self-sufficiency, as well as the fundamental imperative of the CCP toward retaining control over any force—economic and foreign ones particularly—that could challenge its hold on power, means that the de-risking within Chinese strategy is far more assured than in any other country. While the degree to which policies aimed at disengagement on both sides of strategic competition will mutually reinforce each other is uncertain, the findings of this *Strategic Asia* volume clearly show that de-risking is now sufficiently embedded into the political logic of key Indo-Pacific actors to ensure that it will continue to shape the global economic order through this decade and beyond.

Alison Szalwinski
Vice President of Research
NBR

Michael Wills
Executive Vice President
NBR

STRATEGIC ASIA

EXECUTIVE SUMMARY

This chapter assesses changes to the international economic landscape fueled by China's rise and examines how the U.S. is navigating this challenge.

MAIN ARGUMENT

The intensification of globalization in the post–Cold War era has contributed to deep economic integration with China. China's entry into the World Trade Organization made it a linchpin of global trade, and its impressive ensuing growth has enabled it to challenge U.S. hegemony. The rising rivalry with Beijing in recent years has driven Washington to pursue trade diversification, expand domestic manufacturing, and lessen dependency on China. While the Trump administration inchoately sought to decouple from China, the Biden administration has emphasized "de-risking" to protect critical supply chains while vigorously competing with China through various restrictive trade and industrial policies. Driven by this competition and their own problems with Beijing, key Indo-Pacific states are also struggling to diversify from China without cutting off any of the existing linkages that provide them with significant economic and strategic benefits.

POLICY IMPLICATIONS

- Large-scale economic decoupling from China is unlikely for the U.S. and Indo-Pacific nations given the importance of the absolute gains from trade. Consequently, narrow trade diversification may be the only outcome within reach.

- U.S.-China competition threatens globalization, even as China's diminishing trade linkages with the U.S. potentially increase its own strategic autonomy.

- Although U.S. de-risking might limit the dangers posed by Beijing to critical supply chains, China's strong trade ties with U.S. partners and others will advance both its domestic and strategic ambitions, thus undermining U.S. efforts to limit China's rising power.

Overview

Interdependence Imperiled? Economic Decoupling in an Era of Strategic Competition

Ashley J. Tellis

For a few years now, the United States and other nations in the Indo-Pacific region have faced increasing pressures to reconfigure their economic ties with China. The deep commercial linkages that reciprocally bind China and its trading partners have arisen due to globalization, the historical process centered on the growing interconnectedness of national economies because of the vastly increased cross-border exchange of goods and services, finance, technology, people, and data. These expanding ties, which intensified after the Cold War, have undoubtedly benefited all the states involved, at least in the aggregate, even if the resulting gains have not always been symmetrically shared either among or within them. In fact, the history of the last several decades suggests that all the states in the Indo-Pacific seemed willing to live with the differences in gains arising from their trade with China as long as the absolute benefits were positive and Beijing did not pose any significant threat to their security.

Until the advent of Xi Jinping as China's supreme leader, both conditions seemed to obtain—to the advantage of China as well as its trading partners. Unfortunately, the assertiveness that incipiently manifested first under Hu Jintao only intensified under Xi, thus raising the question of whether Beijing's partners, most importantly the United States, could live with the risks of their deepened economic dependence on China if it became a danger to their interests. These risks were seen to emerge from multiple directions.

Ashley J. Tellis is the Tata Chair for Strategic Affairs and a Senior Fellow at the Carnegie Endowment for International Peace. He is also Research Director of the Strategic Asia Program at the National Bureau of Asian Research. He can be reached at <atellis@ceip.org>.

China's asymmetric gains from trade, some of which derived from its exploitative trade practices and which previously could be ignored, could not now be disregarded if they contributed toward the enlargement of its already massive and increasingly threatening military capabilities. Furthermore, China's willingness to constrict critical raw materials exports or access to its markets as a form of coercion raised questions about its commitment to mutually beneficial interdependence in the face of various political disputes. Finally, the growing recognition that China had become the locus of excessive concentration in the international economy for everything from electronics to pharmaceuticals—even if for entirely legitimate reasons—accentuated fears that it had come to enjoy unacceptable leverage vis-à-vis the rest of the international system.

None of these issues mattered much when China's international behavior was benign, as was consciously the case when Deng Xiaoping's policy of "hide and bide" guided the country's external conduct. But the rising Chinese forcefulness under Xi has intensified the threats perceived as emanating from China not only in neighboring countries and the United States but increasingly in Europe as well. Those nations most directly threatened by Chinese military power have consequently embarked on increased efforts at internal and external balancing. Internal balancing generally entails mobilizing greater domestic resources for security (usually manifested through larger defense budgets) and improving a nation's military forces to cope with the anticipated threats. External balancing, in contrast, involves doubling down on preexisting alliances where available or forming strategic partnerships of various kinds to parry the emerging dangers posed by China. Even when external balancing is possible, all countries that are unnerved by Chinese power—including the United States, its Asian allies, and various neutral powers in the Indo-Pacific—have concentrated on internal balancing as their primary instrument of defense. Such responses are to be expected whenever new threats surface in the unruly world of international politics.[1]

The resulting competition between China and its rivals, however, is occurring amid novel historical conditions: the deep economic interdependence produced by globalization. Unlike the Cold War, when the competing antagonists—the United States and the Soviet Union, together with their affiliates—had no meaningful commercial linkages with one another, China and its opponents today are bound together by deep economic ties along different dimensions. This new reality poses discomfiting dilemmas

---

[1] For a useful overview of balancing and its internal and external facets, see William C. Wohlforth, Stuart J. Kaufman, and Richard Little, "Introduction: Balance and Hierarchy in International Systems," in *The Balance of Power in World History*, ed. Stuart J. Kaufman, Richard Little, and William C. Wohlforth (New York: Palgrave Macmillan, 2007), 1–21.

on all sides and raises the question of whether the states threatened by China will respond by diminishing their economic engagement with Beijing both in order to limit its increases in power and as a form of insurance against excessive dependency on China.

This issue is of interest for both theoretical and policy reasons. The pursuit of strategies focused on limiting economic engagement with China or diversifying away from it despite the higher costs entailed would suggest that the threatened states are willing to limit the absolute gains deriving from trade to concentrate on meeting the dangers to their security. This emphasis on relative over absolute gains would be consistent with the expectations of various realist theories of international politics.[2] The policy implications of such a shift are just as important: any concerted effort to consciously alter the existing patterns of trade, which hitherto were shaped mainly by market forces, creates opportunities for developing new strategic partnerships among states that may not have had tight economic linkages. Such a development not only would test the relative strength of state power over societal forces but also could boost the prospects for creating new "soft balancing" coalitions against China through economic ties as a complement to (or even as a substitute for) strategic affiliations.[3] The United States, in particular, as the hegemonic power most directly affected by China's rise as a new systemic rival, could be expected to display an inordinate interest in such developments, even encouraging them as a means of correcting the evolving shift in the balance of power with China.

This volume in the *Strategic Asia* series, *Reshaping Economic Interdependence in the Indo-Pacific*, examines whether there are fundamental changes occurring in the physical, financial, and virtual realms of the Asian trading system because of intensifying U.S.-China competition and China's rising political problems with many of its neighbors. Through a series of studies focused on key countries and the Southeast Asian subregion, the book investigates whether decoupling from China is underway in merchandise trade, service and investment flows, labor movements, and the digital economy and data governance (to the degree that each of these is significant for the countries in focus). To do so, each chapter describes the political challenges facing the nation (or nations) involved and the composition and direction of trade in order to assess whether any significant shift toward limiting the economic exposure to China is occurring and,

---

[2] For a summary overview of the issues involved, see Joseph Grieco, Robert Powell, and Duncan Snidal, "The Relative-Gains Problem for International Cooperation," *American Political Science Review* 87, no. 3 (1993): 729–43.

[3] This concept receives extended discussion in T.V. Paul, *Restraining Great Powers: Soft Balancing from Empires to the Global Era* (New Haven: Yale University Press, 2018).

if so, the prospects for success. The entire volume is thus unified by an interest in examining the evidence for decoupling from China by various Indo-Pacific states and what the consequences of such a development might be for regional and global politics.

The headline conclusion is that, despite the growing dangers posed by Beijing, the regional states still value the gains from trade with China. They are loath to restrict their commercial ties because the absolute gains accruing are desirable both to fulfill domestic political objectives and to effectively support the internal balancing necessary to cope with Chinese assertiveness. To the degree that decoupling is contemplated, it is highly narrow and by no means universal. Most nations prefer to diversify some elements of their trade beyond China, but without cutting off any of the existing linkages with the Chinese production system. This suggests that geopolitical competition under globalization will remain a complicated endeavor: those states that gain a strategic advantage will not be those that restrict ties with their rivals as a rule but rather exploit the economic interdependence that binds them to their competitors, as well as to other bystanders, to buttress their own efforts at internal balancing. That, at any rate, seems to be the first-best strategy. A fallback approach centers on constricting trade with China in the narrowest ways—principally to protect national defense capabilities—while expanding economic links through high-quality agreements with a targeted set of friends and partners.[4]

This chapter sets the context for this conclusion and is divided into three sections. The first section examines how globalization arose and how it created the conditions for China's dominant presence in the global production chains that have propelled its international ascendancy. The second section describes how Washington began to push back against China's rise as a strategic rival by utilizing various instruments of statecraft to reconfigure its post–Cold War commercial ties with Beijing in order to protect U.S. hegemony. The third section summarizes the key insights emerging from the chapters in this volume, which illuminate the larger conclusion that decoupling, even in soft forms, is proving to be difficult in the Indo-Pacific, although many states persist in their efforts to limit their vulnerability to Chinese power. The conclusion summarizes the implications for future great-power competition between the United States and China.

---

[4] This conclusion is based on the insight originally detailed in Duncan Snidal, "Relative Gains and the Pattern of International Cooperation," *American Political Science Review* 85, no. 3 (1991): 701–26. For further discussion, see Ashley J. Tellis, *Balancing Without Containment: An American Strategy for Managing China* (Washington, D.C.: Carnegie Endowment for International Peace, 2014); and Ashley J. Tellis, "The Geopolitics of the TTIP and the TPP," in *Power Shifts and New Blocs in the Global Trading System*, ed. Sanjaya Baru and Suvi Dogra, Adelphi Series 450 (London: International Institute for Strategic Studies, 2015).

The Rise of Globalization and Its Consequences

When viewed over the long arc of modern history, the postwar period has witnessed the most dramatic upsurge in economic interdependence. If the modern era is dated as beginning in 1492, the extent of trade openness—defined as the sum of global exports and imports divided by global GDP—never exceeded 10% before the early nineteenth century.[5] The first wave of globalization that began thereafter saw a dramatic spike, reaching a high of around 30% early in the twentieth century, but this expansion collapsed with the onset of World War I, and the downturn persisted throughout the interwar period and into World War II.[6]

The triumph of American hegemony in the aftermath of that catastrophic conflict breathed fresh life into global trade as the new superpower consciously set about recreating an open trading system that was intended to, *inter alia*, rebuild the war-torn states in order to buttress their stability and thereby strengthen the various U.S.-led alliances in their struggles against global Communism.[7] This new regime, which would launch the second wave of globalization, had to overcome significant domestic and international preferences for protectionism. It was finally institutionalized through the General Agreement on Tariffs and Trade (GATT). The GATT enshrined the United States' postwar conviction that free markets at home, when married to increasingly freer trade abroad, remained the most efficient device not only for accelerating economic growth and expanding national power but also for producing peace and stability—which would inevitably result from the deepened economic interdependence produced by the progressive elimination or reduction of quotas, tariffs, and subsidies among the participating states.

This vision proved eminently successful. By 1995, when the GATT had evolved into its successor entity, the World Trade Organization (WTO), the original 23 signatories had expanded to 125 countries, with their economic interactions covering about 90% of global trade.[8] Not surprisingly, trade openness in the international system had then reached an all-time high at a little over 43%.[9] This outcome was clear evidence of the success of U.S.

---

[5] Antoni Estevadeordal, Brian Frantz, and Alan M. Taylor, "The Rise and Fall of World Trade, 1870–1939," *Quarterly Journal of Economics* 118, no. 2 (2003): 359–407.

[6] Mariko J. Klasing and Petros Milionis, "Quantifying the Evolution of World Trade, 1870–1949," *Journal of International Economics* 92, no. 1 (2014): 185–97.

[7] For the history of this effort, see Thomas W. Zeiler, *Free Trade, Free World: The Advent of GATT* (Chapel Hill: University of North Carolina Press, 1999).

[8] "General Agreement on Tariffs and Trade," *Encyclopedia Britannica*, August 1, 2023, https://www.britannica.com/topic/General-Agreement-on-Tariffs-and-Trade.

[9] Drawn from World Bank, "Trade (% of GDP)," World Development Indicators, https://datacatalog.worldbank.org/indicator/f22f8e24-c0ce-eb11-bacc-000d3a596ff0/Trade----of-GDP.

policy. Since the end of World War II, Washington had consistently pushed for expanded international trade through eight rounds of GATT negotiations. Each one built on the achievements of its predecessors to reduce quantitative barriers and institutionalize the idea of trade without discrimination—codified in the "most favored nation" principle—while creating new mechanisms for arbitrating interstate commercial disputes and setting the pattern for complex future multilateral negotiations.

Even as the United States exhibited leadership on trade expansion, its vast military capabilities—despite concurrently competing with Soviet power—provided the systemic guarantees that the physical movement of goods across the commons would proceed unhindered. Simultaneously, U.S. military prowess ensured that the inequalities in relative gains that inevitably arise in all trading relationships would not be exploited by some of the participating states to threaten the security of other key actors within the trading network.[10]

The GATT years (1947–95) thus witnessed the progressive expansion of globalization that had first begun in the nineteenth century, with beneficial effects for international economic growth and the progressive revitalization of those countries destroyed by World War II. While the lowering of trade barriers and the asymmetric opening of the U.S. market to U.S. allies and less-developed countries had an important role to play in producing these outcomes, advancements in technology also made a huge difference. The remarkable transformations in transportation, especially road and rail networks, shipping, and aviation, that had long been underway—when married to the differences in national factor endowments—now permitted the large-scale decoupling of the production and consumption nodes that gradually became visible during the Cold War era. The advanced economies in North America, Europe, and eventually Northeast Asia exploited the fruits of industrialization to create lucrative production clusters in their home regions. This clustering permitted the fabrication of complex commodities by reducing the costs of coordination required to produce these goods. Due also to the diminishing costs of transportation, huge numbers of high-quality finished products could now be delivered easily throughout the developed world and to developing countries.[11]

The emergence of these early global value chains, which defined the character of the postwar economic system prior to the rise of China, created a striking divergence in international incomes between the developed

---

[10] Michael C. Webb and Stephen D. Krasner, "Hegemonic Stability Theory: An Empirical Assessment," *Review of International Studies* 15, no. 2 (1989): 183–98.

[11] Richard Baldwin, "Global Supply Chains: Why They Emerged, Why They Matter, and Where They Are Going," in *Global Value Chains in a Changing World*, ed. Deborah K. Elms and Patrick Low (Lausanne: WTO Publications, 2013), 13–59.

and developing countries. The former were marked by the capacity for technological innovation, manufacturing specialization, production at scale, and remunerative exports, while the latter—most of which were still poor and recovering from the legacies of colonialism—were unable to compete either in large-scale industrialization or in technological innovation. (The Soviet bloc, which chose to sit out of the economic integration occurring among its rivals, attempted to ape both their industrialization and their innovation but came out a poor second.) As a result, the GATT era was characterized by a striking increase in the wealth accruing to the industrialized economies of the "first world." Although the less industrialized states of the developing "third world" also grew as a result of their connectivity to the open trading system, their income gains were less pronounced. As Lant Pritchett summarized, "The growth rates of [developing] countries have been, on average, slower than the richer countries, producing divergence in relative incomes."[12]

The advent of the WTO era, however, would transform these dynamics dramatically. At the highest level of generalization, the second wave of globalization that began after World War II and gathered steam during the GATT period has been sustained to this day. The level of trade openness, which had grown to over 43% by 1995, has risen even further since: it peaked at almost 61% in 2008, just before the global financial crisis hit, recovering to slightly under 57% in 2021.[13] World trade has undoubtedly grown more slowly than GDP since the financial crisis—a reality that the *Economist* has dubbed "slowbalisation"[14]—but, as one other survey concluded, "the globe [still] remains deeply interconnected, and [trade] flows have proved remarkably resilient [even] during the most recent turbulence."[15] This study, in fact, notes that "trade in manufactured goods reached a record high in 2021 despite [the] new disruptions to supply chains" caused by the U.S.-China trade war and the Covid-19 pandemic, and "the fastest-growing flows are now data, services, intellectual property (IP), and international students."[16] All this data suggests that globalization endures despite countervailing pressures.

The fact that economic connectivity has increased since the WTO came into existence, however, should not obscure the critical changes that have occurred since the end of the GATT era. The earliest phase of postwar globalization brought about by the GATT system was distinguished by the manufacturing dominance enjoyed by the advanced economies and their

---

[12] Lant Pritchett, "Divergence, Big Time," *Journal of Economic Perspectives* 11, no. 3 (1997): 3–17.

[13] Drawn from World Bank, "Trade (% of GDP)."

[14] "The Steam Has Gone Out of Globalisation," *Economist*, January 24, 2019.

[15] Janet Bush, ed., "Global Flows: The Ties That Bind in an Interconnected World," McKinsey Global Institute, November 2022, iv.

[16] Ibid., 4.

export gains arising out of the maturing revolutions in transportation. With the steady integration of developing countries into the global trading system (especially China, which joined the WTO in 2001), further shifts were underway. For one thing, the legacies of colonialism had increasingly receded into the past, and most of the third world was now populated by a variety of developmental states. The most capable nations, such as China, had favorable factor and social endowments that positioned them to exploit the emerging technological revolutions that were beginning to unfold. The ensuing transformations in the international economic system would be propelled this time around not by local clustering and lowered transportation costs—the drivers of change during most of the GATT era—but rather by the interaction of labor cost differentials and the emergence of the information and communications technology (ICT) revolution.[17]

These new variables amplified the benefits previously produced by industrial growth, such as urbanization, the upskilling and education of the workforce, and the local production of medium-complexity goods, but also created new effects. The availability of a huge pool of skilled low-cost labor in China (and to a lesser degree in Southeast Asia) induced multinational firms from developed countries to move their manufacturing operations to these locales, where Western technology, management skills, and finance were married to indigenous labor to produce advanced manufactured goods on a large scale for export to the world at large. The arrival of the ICT revolution enabled a radical desegregation of the manufacturing process: it made possible the supervision of "complexity at distance,"[18] such that each component of the finished product could be fabricated in different national locations based on their cost advantages. The persisting gains in lower transportation costs that were first realized during the GATT era, then, permitted these components to be exported and re-exported as necessary across borders before being finally assembled into end products in China prior to their eventual sale to the wider world.

China's large size, its huge reserves of savings, its low-cost yet skilled manpower, the remarkable industriousness and entrepreneurism of its people, and its purposeful state-controlled economic liberalization thus made it a conspicuous beneficiary of this latest evolution of globalization. In time, the consolidation of this pattern enabled China to develop a vast production system (a "global value chain") centered on itself, integrating thousands of component suppliers (mainly in Northeast and Southeast Asia but also, when necessary, in Europe and the Americas) who produced intermediate goods

---

[17] Baldwin, "Global Supply Chains," 16–24.

[18] Ibid., 16.

for the finished products that were finally manufactured in China either for domestic consumption or for export.[19]

Thanks to this progression in globalization, China became the "new workshop of the world,"[20] one that currently produces close to 30% of the world's manufacturing output and dominates the global trading system, with close to a 15% share of global exports (almost double that of the United States in the second spot) and an 11.5% share of global imports (second only to the United States) in 2020.[21] This outcome was a natural product of the success of market capitalism as it crossed national boundaries. Once the overarching framework of economic cooperation was constructed through state action, private actors from the developed world in search of profit moved technological, managerial, and financial resources to China, which were married to its cheap and skilled labor to create allocative efficiency on a scale that was previously beyond reach.[22] This transformation, in turn, produced three critical consequences that would have an important bearing on the future of interdependence.

For starters, the rise of China and the concomitant rise of Asia resulting from the WTO era of globalization undermined the industrial dominance of the developed world that was the distinguishing characteristic of the GATT period. Today, deindustrialization marks the developed West in conspicuous ways as a small number of developing countries—mostly centered on the Chinese production system—have eclipsed the older and previously established centers of mass manufacturing, often creating new economic and political problems in these countries as a result.[23] As this process has unfolded, the income differences between the developed and developing world are also diminishing. While the gap between the two is still significant, the income divergence that marked the GATT era is eroding as

---

[19] Alicia Garcia Herrero, "China and the Transformation of Value Chains," Bruegel, November 2019, https://www.bruegel.org/sites/default/files/wp-content/uploads/2019/11/Presentation-by-Alicia-Garcia-Herrero.pdf.

[20] "A New Workshop of the World," *Economist*, October 10, 2002, https://www.economist.com/asia/2002/10/10/a-new-workshop-of-the-world.

[21] "Top 10 Manufacturing Countries in the World," Safeguard Global, December 20, 2022, https://www.safeguardglobal.com/resources/blog/top-10-manufacturing-countries-in-the-world; Alessandro Nicita and Carlos Razo, "China: The Rise of a Trade Titan," UN Conference on Trade and Development, April 27, 2021, https://unctad.org/news/china-rise-trade-titan; and General Administration of Customs of the People's Republic of China, "Review of China's Foreign Trade in 2020," January 14, 2021, http://english.customs.gov.cn/Statics/436edfa3-b30d-45cd-8260-7d5baf34a5a8.html.

[22] For details, see Mona Haddad, "Trade Integration in East Asia: The Role of China and Production Networks," World Bank, Policy Research Working Paper, no. 4160, March 2007, https://documents1.worldbank.org/curated/en/934051468236684868/pdf/wps4160.pdf.

[23] Khuong Vu, Nobuya Haraguchi, and Juergen Amann, "Deindustrialization in Developed Countries amid Accelerated Globalization: Patterns, Influencers, and Policy Insights," *Structural Change and Economic Dynamics* 59 (2021): 454–69.

the share of global GDP produced by the developed world steadily contracts. The International Monetary Fund estimates that when GDP is measured in terms of purchasing power parity, the emerging and developing world already contributes more to global GDP than the advanced economies and has done so since around 2007.[24]

Furthermore, although the power of the advanced economies still lies in their possession of superior technology and scientific knowledge—as embodied in IP—the globalization of production chains has resulted in the diffusion of critical technologies to the new producers of intermediate and final goods in the developing world.[25] Because international production chains require high-quality components from numerous sources, the Western owners of IP invariably seek to nurture long-term business relationships with various manufacturing units, which often take the form of joint ventures with local firms in key emerging economies. This, in turn, often entails capital expenditures to create advanced production facilities, training for the native labor force, the inculcation of managerial expertise, and the transfer of technology to meet the quality standards expected of these products manufactured overseas.[26]

In a country like China, which boasts both a calculating state that is determined to transform its technology base and a highly skilled labor force that can absorb many advanced technologies received from abroad, the diffusion of IP to the progressive disadvantage of its creators is inevitable—even if the more egregious possibilities of coercive transfers and outright theft are disregarded. Given the predictability of this outcome, IP holders from the developed world invariably aim to utilize the profits recovered from overseas manufacturing to fund further advancements in technology so as to ensure their continued dominance. Although risky, the successes of globalization leave them with few better choices, even if the technological leavening of the recipients eventually contributes to expanding the strength of their home countries.

Finally, the growing economic power of the developing world and its increasing technological competency due to the successful globalization witnessed in the WTO era have produced shifts in the geopolitical balance of power, with the rise of China only being the most striking example of

---

[24] International Monetary Fund (IMF), "GDP Based on PPP, Share of World," https://www.imf.org/external/datamapper/PPPSH@WEO/OEMDC/ADVEC/WEOWORLD.

[25] For more on this dynamic, see IMF, *World Economic Outlook: Cyclical Upswing, Structural Change* (Washington, D.C.: IMF, 2018), 173–214.

[26] For an insightful overview of the process, see Fukunari Kimura, "How Have Production Networks Changed Development Strategies in East Asia?" in Elms and Low, *Global Value Chains in a Changing World*, 361–83.

this phenomenon.[27] Any shift in the underlying distribution of material capabilities has geopolitical impact, and the history of the postwar period is no exception to this rule. But the two previous alterations that occurred under the aegis of U.S. hegemony had minimal disruptive impact because the early revival of war-torn Europe and the later regeneration of the East Asian economies, such as Japan, South Korea, Taiwan, and Singapore, all involved small nations that had either alliance ties or close affinities with the United States. The rise of China, however, is different for several reasons. China is a large, continental-sized country that rivals the United States in potential power. It has prospered greatly because of its participation in the U.S.-led trading order, yet it increasingly poses a persistent and dangerous military threat to the guardian of that system, the United States, as well as to U.S. allies. Moreover, Beijing has sharp political and ideological differences with Washington, which have made it Washington's most consequential rival since the end of the Cold War marked the demise of the Soviet Union.[28] The deepening antagonisms between the United States and China are thus not surprising: they mirror the problems witnessed endlessly when power distributions threaten to shift in the international system.[29]

What makes the U.S.-China competition in the postwar period unique, however, is that it is deeply embedded within the economic interdependence that has been produced by the very globalization fostered by the United States. The economic linkages between the two countries are so deep that they have been aptly described as in "codependency."[30] Yet the ties that bind have also begun to chafe as Washington and Beijing now struggle to advance their own competitive geopolitical interests. China's assertive behaviors in various parts of the Indo-Pacific have created similar challenges for its other economic partners—Japan, South Korea, Taiwan, the Philippines, and India, to name a few. All these states have strong trade ties with Beijing, but their persistent political problems with

---

[27] For a rich history that illuminates the past, see George Modelski and William R. Thompson, *Leading Sectors and World Powers: The Coevolution of Global Economics and Politics* (Columbia: University of South Carolina Press, 1996). For a specific application to China, see Michael D. Swaine and Ashley J. Tellis, *Interpreting China's Grand Strategy: Past, Present, and Future* (Santa Monica: RAND Corporation, 2000), 151–229.

[28] Ashley J. Tellis, "Power Shift: How the West Can Adapt and Thrive in an Asian Century," German Marshall Fund and Legatum Institute, Asia Paper Series, January 2010.

[29] Robert Gilpin, *War and Change in World Politics* (Cambridge: Cambridge University Press, 1981); and Karen A. Rasler and William R. Thompson, *The Great Powers and Global Struggle, 1490–1990* (Lexington: University Press of Kentucky, 1994).

[30] Stephen Roach, *Unbalanced: The Codependency of America and China* (New Haven: Yale University Press, 2014).

China have resulted in "hot economics, cold politics" increasingly defining the nature of their overall relationship.[31]

The U.S. Pushback Against China

Given these developments, the United States has attempted to extricate itself from the constraints imposed by economic interdependence with China by toying with the idea of "decoupling"—that is, by limiting economic engagement with Beijing in order to either correct U.S. economic losses or restore Washington's freedom of action in the arena of international politics.[32] Whatever the motivations, the notion of decoupling is aimed at consciously reducing U.S. dependency on China, which, if taken to its limit, would imply the recreation of entirely separate global production chains that have no (or at best minimal) reliance on Chinese materials, technology, or production facilities. If such an outcome could be engineered, it would effectively result in a fragmented globalization, where relatively independent production networks—each incorporating separate supply chains and possibly different technical standards, business models, and legal and regulatory frameworks—would come into being and coexist unhappily.[33]

An evolution of this sort would be extraordinary on multiple counts. Any significant restructuring now between major trading partners such as the United States and China would be distinctive in the first instance because it would have occurred in peacetime. In the past, war has been the main precipitant for radical dislocations in commercial exchanges across national borders.[34] Such a development, to the degree that it was precipitated by U.S. political decisions, would also be ironic in that Washington would finally have mimicked Beijing's "desire for a kind of managed integration that enhances China's development progress, while building national champions and mitigating the risks associated with a full merging with the global economy."[35] This evolution would be enormously consequential as well. Because the

---

[31] Ji Siqi and Ralph Jennings, "China, Philippines Cautiously Flip Trade Dip as 'Hot Economics, Cold Politics' Define Relations," *South China Morning Post*, August 9, 2023, https://www.scmp.com/economy/china-economy/article/3230537/china-philippines-cautiously-flip-trade-dip-hot-economics-cold-politics-define-relations.

[32] Keith Johnson and Robbie Gramer, "The Great Decoupling," *Foreign Policy*, May 14, 2020, https://foreignpolicy.com/2020/05/14/china-us-pandemic-economy-tensions-trump-coronavirus-covid-new-cold-war-economics-the-great-decoupling.

[33] "Economic Decoupling: Our New Reality?" American Chamber of Commerce in France, December 2021, https://amchamfrance.org/wp-content/uploads/2021/12/Economic-Decoupling-Our-New-Reality.pdf.

[34] Johnson and Gramer, "The Great Decoupling."

[35] "Decoupling—Severed Ties and Patchwork Globalisation," European Union Chamber of Commerce and MERICS, 2021, 10, https://merics.org/en/report/decoupling-severed-ties-and-patchwork-globalisation.

United States is the principal underwriter of the open trading system, any major shift by Washington toward protectionism would constitute not a modest erosion but a fundamental rewriting of the rules of the game. Unlike China's parasitic integration into the global trading system—an outcome that, however corrosive, was tolerable because, when all is said and done, Beijing is still more a beneficiary of the regime than its guarantor—U.S. policies on international trade remain the cornerstone on which its continued health, not to mention liberalization, depends.[36] As such, even purely national decisions taken by Washington have extranational effects.

That the structural disruption of trade flows ensuing from the pursuit of decoupling would undermine the postwar U.S. vision of global economic integration goes without saying. But it would also do more. It would subvert the greatest achievements of globalization hitherto: the increases in allocative efficiency and, by extension, the improvements in aggregate growth and welfare, as well as technological innovation, which have increased the overall prosperity of the developed world even as they have raised incomes and lifted millions out of poverty in developing countries. The danger of putting these gains at risk is well understood in the United States, but the pressures to decouple from China nonetheless have deep roots in two sources.

For starters, national security elites fear that the rise of China has diminished the relative power of the United States. This weakening of U.S. hegemony not only erodes its capacity to protect the larger Western international order but also weakens, in the language of Mancur Olson, its standing as a "privileged" actor, meaning its ability to make those supernormal contributions necessary to maintain the open trading system as a collective good.[37] Rectifying the loss in relative power requires the United States to consider, among other things, some sort of decoupling from China that holds the promise of limiting its ascendancy.[38] If the United States can recover its relative advantages as a result, it could—in the most optimistic conception—continue underwriting the open trading system with fewer burdens than might be possible in the face of progressive (relative) decline.

Furthermore, the threats posed to the United States and its partners by Beijing's growing military and technological capabilities often provide sufficient reason for Washington to consider decoupling from China as a means of arresting its growth. Such decoupling is arguably even

---

[36] The relationship between trade openness and hegemonic power remains the foundation of hegemonic stability theory, which received its classic formulation in Charles Kindleberger, *The World in Depression, 1929–1939* (Berkeley: University of California Press, 1973). Kindleberger emphasized that open trading systems could survive only if there existed a hegemonic power to bear the costs of upholding them.

[37] Mancur Olson, *The Logic of Collective Action* (Cambridge: Harvard University Press, 1965), 48–50.

[38] An extreme version of this argument is offered in Robert Lighthizer, *No Trade Is Free: Changing Course, Taking on China, and Helping America's Workers* (New York: Broadside Books, 2023).

more justified because China has already pursued a strategy of targeted disengagement from the global trading system right from the moment when it began opening up to the world. Consequently, a U.S. response that helped limit China's advantages and thereby improve its relative position globally was necessary to sustain the open trading system over the long term while neutralizing the growing political dangers posed by expanding Chinese military and technological capabilities.[39]

Even as concerns about relative gains and their impact on U.S. participation in the international trading system surfaced, Washington initially responded by attempting to correct the problems through further liberalization of global trade. The Doha round of WTO negotiations sought to expand trade in agriculture and services as well as to protect IP (in addition to other efforts at enlarging market access) with the ambition of securing gains for the United States where it had important comparative advantages. The difficulties attending these negotiations eventually pushed Washington to pursue partial free trade agreements involving selected partners as a substitute for universal trade expansion, a strategy that unfortunately met with only partial success.

While these efforts were underway, the impact of the "China shock" began to be increasingly felt in the United States (and other industrialized nations).[40] Between China's comparative advantages and its structurally unfair trade practices, those U.S. states most exposed to competition from China experienced increased unemployment and reduced wages resulting from dramatic deindustrialization. It has been estimated that China's entry into the WTO accounted for 59.3% of all U.S. manufacturing job losses between 2001 and 2019.[41] Such outcomes should not have been surprising. Although classical trade theory predicted that exchange across borders would leave both partners better off, not all individuals within the trading nations

---

[39] Charles W. Boustany Jr. and Aaron L. Friedberg, "Partial Disengagement: A New U.S. Strategy for Economic Competition with China," National Bureau of Asian Research, NBR Special Report, no. 82, November 2019, https://www.nbr.org/wp-content/uploads/pdfs/publications/sr82_china-task-force-report-final.pdf. See also Aaron L. Friedberg, *Getting China Wrong* (Medford: Polity Press, 2022), which defends a partial free-trade system as the solution to the problems posed by China's asymmetric gains.

[40] David H. Autor, David Dorn, and Gordon H. Hanson, "The China Shock: Learning from Labor Market Adjustment to Large Changes in Trade," National Bureau of Economic Research, NBER Working Paper Series, no. 21906, January 2016, https://www.nber.org/system/files/working_papers/w21906/w21906.pdf.

[41] Autor, Dorn, and Hanson, "The China Shock." The findings of this working paper are summarized in "The China Shock and Its Enduring Effects," Stanford Center on China's Economy and Institutions, SCCEI China Briefs, October 1, 2022, https://fsi9-prod.s3.us-west-1.amazonaws.com/s3fs-public/2022-12/china_shock_enduring_effects_10.1.22.pdf. The longer-term impact of the China shock has been disputed by other studies, which are usefully summarized in Scott Kennedy and Ilaria Mazzocco, "The China Shock: Reevaluating the Debate," Big Data China, October 14, 2022, https://bigdatachina.csis.org/the-china-shock-reevaluating-the-debate.

would benefit equally. Even if the populations at large gained from lowered prices because of trade, groups may be advantaged differently depending on what they consume. Moreover, even if they do benefit where consumption is concerned, these gains might not compensate sufficiently for the employment and wage losses that could come in the wake of expanded trade.[42] When the domestic losers from globalization are concentrated geographically, they can possibly shape political outcomes—using the power of the ballot to correct the losses suffered in the marketplace.

Whether or not this factor was critical to the outcome of the 2016 U.S. presidential election, Donald Trump entered office on a plank aimed at containing China as an economic, and especially as a trading, threat to the United States. In short order, his administration also declared China to be a strategic competitor that was "leveraging military modernization, influence operations, and predatory economics to coerce neighboring countries to reorder the Indo-Pacific region to [its] advantage."[43] This growth in Chinese power, the administration correctly noted, helped underwrite Beijing's massive military modernization, which was aimed at seeking "Indo-Pacific regional hegemony in the near term and displacement of the United States to achieve global preeminence in the future."[44]

Although Trump personally seemed curiously ambiguous about the national security threats posed by China's rise, he nonetheless sought to counter its economic ascendancy. He did so, however, through an erratic and counterproductive campaign of imposing tariffs not only on China but also on many U.S. allies—an approach consistent with his view that the multilateral trade system was disastrous for the United States. Trump's tariffs, unfortunately, proved to be the bigger disaster, costing the U.S. economy dearly in terms of lost wages, jobs, and GDP growth, while doing nothing to correct the structural distortions in China that were the source of its unfair advantages in international trade.[45] In any event, toward the end of Trump's term in office, the disruptions caused by the Covid-19 pandemic only served to remind the world about the dangers of China's domination in global manufacturing and pushed the United States and its partners

---

[42] For a useful summary of the distributional consequences of trade, see Erhan Artuc, "Distributional Effects of International Trade: Facts and Misconceptions," World Bank, Development Research Group, https://thedocs.worldbank.org/en/doc/621581582658115902-0050022020/original/ErhanArtucPolicyResearchTalkTheDistributionalEffectsofInternationalTrade.pdf.

[43] U.S. Department of Defense, "Summary of the 2018 National Defense Strategy of the United States of America," 2018, 2, https://dod.defense.gov/Portals/1/Documents/pubs/2018-National-Defense-Strategy-Summary.pdf.

[44] Ibid.

[45] Erica York, "Tracking the Economic Impact of U.S. Tariffs and Retaliatory Actions," Tax Foundation, July 7, 2023, https://taxfoundation.org/research/all/federal/tariffs-trump-trade-war.

toward contemplating further decoupling from China as a means to increase their national resilience to future shocks. Trump succinctly captured these sentiments when he declared: "We will make America into the manufacturing superpower of the world and will end our reliance on China once and for all. Whether it's decoupling or putting in massive tariffs like I've been doing already, we will end our reliance in China, because we can't rely on China."[46]

The Russian invasion of Ukraine, which began a little over a year after Trump departed office, pushed the European community further in this direction. The costs of being deeply dependent on Russian energy now came to be acutely burdensome, with the result that Europe too finally joined the United States in discovering the merits of decoupling, this time from Russia. The discomfort with globalization, which was manifested early through the United Kingdom's 2016 referendum on Brexit, thus received its final consolidation through the war in Ukraine. The war pushed the United States and Europe—previously the greatest champions of globalization—together on a new course that reflects a marked suspicion of free trade and deeper international integration. This policy shift is striking because it also implicates key Indo-Pacific countries such as Japan and South Korea, which benefited from free trade but are now looking for substitutional solutions because of their own growing problems with China. All told, then, even though globalization itself is not receding, the loss of policy support for its open-ended expansion is a significant change from the optimism that prevailed after the end of the Cold War. As such, this new consensus represents a clear—and potentially dangerous—break from past U.S. trade policy during the postwar era.[47]

Because China, however, has become so central to the global economy, any radical decoupling from it is unlikely to lie within reach during peacetime. Not only would any such effort prove to be utterly chaotic if implemented as a state policy, but it also would result in a striking diminishment of the standards of living, even in the developed world, with disruptive economic and political consequences. The turbulent dislocations would make the disruptions of the Covid-19 pandemic seem trivial in comparison.

Consequently, President Joe Biden's administration has replaced its predecessor's inchoate ambitions about decoupling from China with a more limited goal, now described as "de-risking," which has been defined as "having resilient effective supply chains, and ensuring [that the United

---

[46] "Trump Again Raises Idea of Decoupling Economy from China," Reuters, September 15, 2020, https://www.reuters.com/article/usa-trump-china/trump-again-raises-idea-of-decoupling-economy-from-china-iduskbn25z08u.

[47] For an insightful survey of this issue, see Pinelopi K. Goldberg and Tristan Reed, "Is the Global Economy Deglobalizing? And If So, Why? And What Is Next?" Brookings Institution, Brookings Papers on Economic Activity, Spring 2023, https://www.brookings.edu/wp-content/uploads/2023/03/BPEA_Spring2023_Goldberg-Reed_unembargoed.pdf.

States] cannot be subject to the coercion of any other country."[48] If taken at face value, this description suggests that the United States simply seeks to create a redundancy of supply chains—either through unilateral investments or through cooperative actions with its friends—where certain critical technologies are concerned. Yet even a cursory survey of the administration's actions suggests that this explanation of what de-risking entails is all too modest. On the contrary, the diverse actions undertaken, though intended to exemplify targeted disengagement, actually reflect the larger strategic competition with Beijing. They express the administration's conviction that winning the great-power sweepstakes with China requires not merely parrying its emerging military threats in the Indo-Pacific and globally but also, and more fundamentally, dominating the cycles of innovation—by maintaining "as large of a lead as possible" over China—in order to preserve the hegemonic position of the United States in international politics.[49]

Accordingly, Biden's pushback on China thus far has gone beyond just efforts at minimizing the risks to U.S. supply chains. This is clear from at least six distinct policies pursued by his administration.

First, the administration has retained all of Trump's expansive tariffs on China. Although the Trump tariffs were intended to initially correct the U.S. trade deficit with Beijing and eventually rectify China's structural distortions through the planned "phase two" trade negotiations, the bilateral trade deficit has only further ballooned since Biden took office, with few other gains to show in terms of GDP, wage, or employment growth. Since the Biden administration has also not demonstrated any interest in pursuing trade negotiations with China to address its structural distortions, the value of preserving the inherited tariffs is questionable—except for political signaling. In contrast, the administration's approach to sanctions on Chinese apps and companies has been more sensible. The earlier bans on Chinese apps have been revoked, and the Commerce Department is now vested with the authority to monitor and appropriately control any software applications that may prejudice national security. Similarly, the oversight of Chinese military companies has now been transferred from the Department of Defense to the

---

[48] Eric Martin, "U.S. Wants to 'De-risk,' Not Decouple, from China, Biden Aide Says," Bloomberg, April 27, 2023, https://www.bloomberg.com/news/articles/2023-04-27/us-wants-to-de-risk-not-decouple-from-china-biden-aide-says.

[49] "Remarks by National Security Advisor Jake Sullivan at the Special Competitive Studies Project Global Emerging Technologies Summit," White House, September 16, 2022, https://www.whitehouse.gov/briefing-room/speeches-remarks/2022/09/16/remarks-by-national-security-advisor-jake-sullivan-at-the-special-competitive-studies-project-global-emerging-technologies-summit.

Treasury's Office of Foreign Assets Control so that the sanctions on these entities may be administered more effectively.[50]

Second, the administration has promulgated new restrictions on the export of advanced integrated circuits, electronic components containing advanced integrated circuits, semiconductor manufacturing equipment, and related software and technology to China. The expansion of U.S. export controls and the creation of new rules that constrain third-country activities pertaining to China's semiconductor and supercomputing manufacturing capabilities are intended to limit the threat that Beijing could pose to U.S. national security, especially through the development of advanced weapons.[51] Because technology is central to great-power competition today in a way that industrialization was during the twentieth century, the administration's strategy is prima facie reasonable and has been defended as exemplifying the "small yard and high fence"[52] approach that restricts trade only in regard to a small set of foundational capabilities. Yet the gambit is not without risks. Future controls in other arenas such as quantum technologies, artificial intelligence, biotechnology and biomanufacturing, advanced telecommunications, and advanced materials—which have been identified as critical to the evolving U.S.-China competition—could easily expand the "small yard" in ways that disfigure it beyond recognition. If this were to occur through either bureaucratic momentum or leadership indiscipline (which often accompany such policy shifts once they are initiated), the ambition of maintaining "as large of a lead as possible" over China could itself be subverted because sustaining technological supremacy when international knowledge flows of different kinds are constricted could prove to be daunting in an era of deep economic interdependence.[53]

Third, the administration has persisted with its predecessor's policy of intensively scrutinizing Chinese foreign direct investment into the United States. The Committee on Foreign Investment in the United States (CFIUS), whose review authority was expanded in 2018 with an eye to

---

[50] Brian J. Egan et al., "China Faces Existing and Expanded U.S. Restrictions on Trade, Investment and Technology," Skadden, January 19, 2022, https://www.skadden.com/insights/publications/2022/01/2022-insights/regulation-enforcement-and-investigations/china-faces-existing-and-expanded-us-restrictions.

[51] For details, see "Biden Administration Restricts U.S. Exports of Advanced Computing and Semiconductor Manufacturing Equipment, Software, and Technology to China," Dorsey, November 28, 2022, https://www.dorsey.com/newsresources/publications/client-alerts/2022/11/us-adds-strict-limits-on-technology-exports.

[52] "Remarks by National Security Advisor Jake Sullivan on Renewing American Economic Leadership at the Brookings Institution," White House, April 27, 2023, https://www.whitehouse.gov/briefing-room/speeches-remarks/2023/04/27/remarks-by-national-security-advisor-jake-sullivan-on-renewing-american-economic-leadership-at-the-brookings-institution.

[53] For insightful analysis of the issues involved, see Hugo Meijer, *Trading with the Enemy: The Making of U.S. Export Control Policy toward the People's Republic of China* (New York: Oxford University Press, 2016).

preventing Beijing from acquiring U.S. firms with advanced technology, including those with military implications, continues to keep "China in the crosshairs."[54] The number of reviews has expanded in comparison with other foreign investments in the United States. This enhanced scrutiny of Chinese investments is appropriate because Beijing has often sought to circumvent U.S. export controls pertaining to advanced technology by instead acquiring the U.S. companies that create them. In a similar vein, CFIUS authority has been expanded to include oversight of China's real estate acquisitions in the United States, especially transactions that involve properties located within a certain proximity of important national security installations.[55] And the U.S. Securities and Exchange Commission has increased the disclosure requirements for foreign holding companies as well.

Fourth, the administration has complemented the scrutiny of inward Chinese direct investment with a striking new innovation, namely, the prohibition of certain outward U.S. investments in semiconductors and microelectronics, quantum information technologies, and artificial intelligence capabilities to China. The diffusion of these technologies, which are relevant to military, intelligence, surveillance, or cyberspace operations, is sought to be controlled through new restrictions on the acquisition of equity interests, the provision of debt financing, greenfield investments, and joint ventures involving Chinese nationals.[56] Although passive investments lie outside the purview of these carefully targeted restrictions, they nonetheless represent a novel effort to prevent U.S. entities from aiding the growth of China's technological capabilities. One observer described this initiative "as a major step in setting up a U.S. system of oversight to screen transactions to countries of concern," which could only be "expected to expand in time."[57]

Fifth, the administration has embarked on a "place-based" industrial policy with multiple facets.[58] Born of the conviction that the free-market solutions that drove globalization in previous years failed American workers,

---

[54] Martin Chorzempa, "U.S. Security Scrutiny of Foreign Investment Rises, but So Does Foreign Investment," Peterson Institute for International Economics, September 1, 2022, https://www.piie.com/blogs/realtime-economic-issues-watch/us-security-scrutiny-foreign-investment-rises-so-does-foreign.

[55] Christian C. Davis et al., "CFIUS Expands Jurisdiction Over—and States Restrict Chinese Investment in—Real Estate," Akin, May 19, 2023, https://www.akingump.com/en/insights/alerts/cfius-expands-jurisdiction-overand-states-restrict-chinese-investment-inreal-estate.

[56] Gavin Bade, "Biden Sets New Rules Restricting U.S. Investments in China," Politico, August 9, 2023, https://www.politico.com/news/2023/08/09/biden-investment-rules-hits-chinese-chip-ai-computing-00110488.

[57] Karen Freifeld, "Biden Order Curbing Investment to China Expected Next Week—Sources," Reuters, August 4, 2023, https://www.reuters.com/world/us/biden-order-curbing-investment-china-expected-next-week-sources-2023-08-04.

[58] "The Biden Administration Embraces Place-Based Industrial Policy," Economist, July 27, 2023, https://www.economist.com/united-states/2023/07/27/the-biden-administration-embraces-place-based-industrial-policy.

accelerated U.S. deindustrialization, enabled China's rise, and strengthened China's ability to mount serious military challenges to the United States, the administration's "21st-century industrial strategy" has embarked, inter alia, on a concerted effort to return manufacturing to the United States through the massive provision of government funds to a wide range of industries from clean energy to semiconductor fabrication.[59] The motivations underlying this effort are simultaneously political, economic, and strategic. The administration seeks to strengthen the U.S. middle class (and thereby win its support for U.S. global leadership and perhaps for the Democratic Party), stimulate the technological recrudescence of the U.S. economy (to, among other things, bolster domestic employment and mitigate climate change), and stay ahead of China (by pushing the technology frontier outward in both the civilian and military realms to the advantage of the United States).

These objectives are understandable given current circumstances, but the dangers are not trivial. They include the inconsistent success of industrial policy in the past, the problems associated with increasing costs when investment decisions are freed from the discipline of the market, the risk of stimulating comparable efforts by other states to the detriment of both the nation and the global system as a whole, and the problems of intensifying fissures not just among states but within U.S. alliances themselves.[60] At the end of the day, the real challenge is that successful industrial policy requires a persistent manipulation of incentives and not simply episodic initiatives at the margin. Absent such a commitment—especially when trying to resuscitate a domestic industry with incumbent international competitors—it will be difficult to create a self-sustaining ecosystem that effectively joins labor, capital, and innovation. Moreover, producing such success might end up being even more dangerous if it leads to the large-scale subversion of markets within the U.S. economy as a result of increased state dominance.

Sixth, and finally, the administration—partly in an effort to mitigate the risks of its industrial policy—has declared its support for "friendshoring," which focuses on shifting existing supply chains (or parts thereof) that are currently anchored in China to countries that are either political allies or strategic partners of the United States.[61] If these shifts are narrowly limited to those items that are essential to national security, the policy of friendshoring

---

[59] "Brian Deese on Biden's Vision for 'a Twenty-First-Century American Industrial Strategy,'" Atlantic Council, June 23, 2021, https://www.atlanticcouncil.org/commentary/transcript/brian-deese-on-bidens-vision-for-a-twenty-first-century-american-industrial-strategy.

[60] For an excellent evaluation of Biden's industrial policy, see Robert Kuttner, "Reclaiming U.S. Industry," *American Prospect*, January 24, 2023, https://prospect.org/economy/2023-01-24-biden-american-industrial-policy.

[61] "Remarks by Secretary of the Treasury Janet L. Yellen on Way Forward for the Global Economy," U.S. Department of the Treasury, April 13, 2022, https://home.treasury.gov/news/press-releases/jy0714.

can be defended even if it entails additional costs. But the danger is that if friendshoring gains momentum, various special interests within the United States and elsewhere will find excuses for using state resources to move production across national boundaries without regard for economic viability.[62] At its core, friendshoring essentially involves using state power through either sovereign directives or financial incentives to change the decisions of private actors about where investment and production are located. Unilateral actions by a government toward this end could precipitate emulation by other countries and a destructive race to the bottom.

The success of any friendshoring strategy, accordingly, requires coordination between states—and more. Rarely do exhortations alone—as the Biden administration seems to be invested in—suffice because the costs of moving production against economic logic are often prohibitive. Consequently, financial incentives to private actors are usually necessary, unless these entities choose to move production to less economically attractive locations simply as a response to geopolitical risks. When this is not the case, however, friendshoring could easily run aground because of the unavailability of the requisite subsidies, national competition among states over relocation, increased costs arising from investments shifting to more marginal sites, and, finally, the simple difficulty of moving production because of the limitations associated with many alternative geographies.[63]

This last consideration is not insignificant. Because of differences in factor endowments, there are few alternatives outside China in Asia where manufacturing at comparable scale and quality can be undertaken. Given that private companies have no peers in finding the best settings (and partners) to build their value chains, it would be comical to assume that governments—and the United States is no exception—will be able to induce the relocation of manufacturing activities or the widespread restructuring of global production systems through rhetorical appeals or even through inexpensive selective incentives. Not surprisingly, then, the Biden administration and its international partners thus far have little to show by way of success where friendshoring is concerned.[64]

---

[62] Raghuram G. Rajan, "Just Say No to "Friend-shoring," Project Syndicate, June 3, 2022, https://www.project-syndicate.org/commentary/friend-shoring-higher-costs-and-more-conflict-without-resilience-by-raghuram-rajan-2022-06.

[63] Halit Harput, "The Hidden Costs of Friend-shoring," Hinrich Foundation, November 15, 2022, https://www.hinrichfoundation.com/research/article/trade-and-geopolitics/the-hidden-costs-of-friend-shoring.

[64] The difficulties of engineering successful friendshoring are clearly explicated in "Globalization 2.0: Can the U.S. and EU Really 'Friendshore' Away from China?" Allianz, October 5, 2022, https://www.allianz.com/content/dam/onemarketing/azcom/Allianz_com/economic-research/publications/specials/en/2022/october/2022_10_05_Globalization_AZ.pdf.

Irrespective of how successful each of the elements in the administration's de-risking strategy has been thus far—and this survey has not captured those elements that are entirely internal, such as the increased domestic investments in science and technology or the nurturing of science, technology, engineering, and mathematics talent—the challenge of managing economic dependence on China has become a preoccupation of many states in the Indo-Pacific region. The shift in the U.S. attitude toward globalization, and trade ties with China in particular, has already produced demonstration effects as several Indo-Pacific nations, prompted by their own ongoing problems with China, have moved to implement de-risking strategies of their own, often with Washington's express encouragement. Other states find themselves caught in the middle of what is seen as unwelcome U.S.-China competition. But whatever the various regional attitudes may be, the chapters in this volume indicate that the process of decoupling is fraught and its ultimate success is entirely unclear.

Asian "Decoupling" from China

The chapters that follow suggest that how the Indo-Pacific states respond to the possibilities of decoupling from China depends on many variables, such as (1) the character and the intensity of their competition with China, (2) the history of their bilateral relations, (3) the extent of their interdependence with China and the availability of alternatives, (4) the benefits and costs of altering their existing patterns of trade with China, (5) the character of their state-society relations at home, (6) the relative power differential between themselves and China, and (7) the existence of strategic partnerships (especially alliances) with external powers, particularly the United States, and their influence over national decision-making. The interaction of these factors shapes the different behaviors pertaining to loosening economic ties with China.

When viewed synoptically, the contributions to this volume indicate that despite the myriad concerns about China as a potential—or sometimes even as a growing—strategic threat, the value of maintaining strong trade ties with it has not diminished. Even countries like Japan and India, which are intensely fearful of Chinese aggressiveness, cannot cut ties with China, no matter how desirable such independence may seem. For all nations in the Indo-Pacific, China is simply too big and too important, either as a supplier or as a market, to be divested from. Consequently, diversification from China may be the best that can be achieved, but even this solution has inherent limits where merchandise trade is concerned because China "maintains its manufacturing leadership,"[65] remains a vital supplier of many commodities or raw materials for which there are no economical substitutes, and, thanks to its size and growing prosperity, offers huge markets for goods produced by others at a time when there are few comparable alternatives.

Since this volume focuses on the prospects of decoupling from China, it is perhaps appropriate that the first chapter centers on China itself. William J. Norris considers how China has responded to the threats of decoupling by other countries and highlights a series of paradoxes in this connection. To begin with, China's integration with the global system has always been strategic and deliberately uneven in that Beijing wanted to benefit from external integration but without becoming vulnerable to the outside world. In fact, Beijing has always viewed—and shaped—external linkages with an eye to exploiting others' dependencies on China. That China is now the most important hub for many global supply chains gives it enormous leverage, which many countries, including the United States, will be unable to easily escape from without suffering increased costs. Even as these dependencies remain significant, Norris notes that China's own reliance on foreign trade as an engine of growth is steadily diminishing, with domestic consumption already accounting for more than half of its national product. With Xi Jinping's emphasis on "dual circulation," China's trade-to-GDP ratios could further decline. This suggests that even as many countries continue to be dependent on trade with China for their continued prosperity, China itself will be increasingly liberated from trade- and export-driven growth, thus increasing its strategic autonomy. Its other economic problems still remain significant, but the steady shift away from trade as a driver of growth—a sign of China's maturation as an economy—is noteworthy.

As far as the United States is concerned, bilateral trade with China continues to grow, setting new records (to include ever-increasing U.S. imports from China). But, as other studies have pointed out, this fact obscures important emerging cleavages in U.S.-China trade relations. When eleven major types of flows encompassing trade, capital, information, and people have been examined, the share of U.S. flows involving China has declined for eight types of flows, increasing for only one, with two others remaining somewhat stable (that is, falling by less

---

[65] Yukon Huang and Genevieve Slosberg, "China's Response to the U.S. Trade War," *China Leadership Monitor*, June 1, 2023, 8.

than 5%).⁶⁶ Norris confirms this change when he notes that China is increasingly less important as a source of U.S. imports, which are shifting toward other low-cost Asian producers at China's expense. Despite these changes, however, the United States and China still maintain the largest trading relationship between two nations that do not share a common border, but whether this will suffice to restrain a China that will be increasingly less dependent on the United States for its continued growth remains a disquieting question that Norris flags for further consideration.

Kristin Vekasi's chapter on Japan offers critical insights on the viability of decoupling from China because Japan remains, in principle, the best test case for such a possibility due to several factors: Tokyo increasingly views China as its most dangerous security threat; Japan is an advanced industrial nation that depends heavily on foreign trade; and the United States guarantees Japanese security over and above the protection offered by Japan's own formidable military forces. If any nation can dramatically minimize (or transform) its economic dependence on China at least cost, it should be Japan. Yet Vekasi's analysis indicates that despite Tokyo's strong desire to limit economic linkages with Beijing because of the latter's growing assertiveness, Japanese businesses still view China as indispensable to their economic viability. In an era where Japan's ubiquitous industrial presence is manifested not simply through branded products but by myriad internal (and invisible) components, the importance of supply chains that traverse China, among other countries, has only increased.

Vekasi notes that Japan's patterns of trade are shifting. Consistent with the insights offered by gravitational models of trade, Japan today trades more with Asia than with the United States and Europe. But even as Japan has increased its focus on Southeast Asia as a complement to its trade with China—the essence of its diversification strategy for both economic and strategic reasons—its gross trade and investment with both entities has increased. This confirms that even a country as concerned about Chinese assertiveness as Japan simply cannot—and does not seek to—sever commercial ties with China, even though Tokyo has begun to consciously restrict the export of certain types of high technology to China, secure supply chains in critical sectors, and increase Japan's resilience to security and economic risks more generally. In fact, Japan remains a great example of how even a formidable

---

⁶⁶ Steven A. Altman and Caroline R. Bastian, "DHL Global Connectedness Index 2022," New York University, Stern School of Business, Center for the Future of Management and DHL Initiative on Globalization, 2022, 23–29, https://www.dhl.com/content/dam/dhl/global/delivered/documents/pdf/dhl-global-connectedness-index-2022-complete-report.pdf. In contrast, and more significantly from a geopolitical point of view, when the economic relations between the United States and its partners and China and its partners are examined, the evidence suggests "that the fragmentation of flows between rival blocs of countries is much more limited than decoupling between the U.S. and China, both in terms of the types of flows involved and the magnitude of the changes in flow patterns."

state concerned about intensifying Chinese threats cannot dismiss its societal interests in continued trade with China—without which its own national security preparedness would actually suffer.

Even more than Japan, South Korea too finds itself on the horns of a painful dilemma. South Korea's economic success owes deeply to the country's integration in global trade, which has made China its largest export market. This reality, combined with Seoul's historic desire to avoid alienating Beijing, has made South Korea an unfortunate victim of Chinese intimidation in recent years. The deep political divisions in South Korean society—with progressives focused more on seeking reconciliation with North Korea and preserving ties with China, while conservatives emphasize strengthening the security alliance with the United States and reconciling with Japan to cope with the dangers emerging from both Pyongyang and Beijing—have not made matters easier. As Yul Sohn and Hyo-young Lee's chapter emphasizes, South Korea now struggles to manage its intense dependence on China, which has consistently yielded a trade surplus for Seoul over the years, with its tight security dependence on the United States, which is now locked into a deep confrontation with China.

The integration between China and South Korea is particularly pronounced in the production of semiconductors—the latter's single-largest export item to China. Seoul also remains highly dependent on China for raw materials used in the production of other manufactured goods. Thus, extricating from China, whether or not in response to U.S. pressures, is proving to be difficult at a time when South Korean exports to Southeast Asia—which also depend on Chinese intermediate products—are themselves rising. Because the structure of Chinese–South Korean trade is now essentially intra-industry trade, limiting the trading ties between the two countries is proving to be extremely difficult even when they intensely compete for new markets in places such as Southeast Asia. The fact that Chinese–South Korean, U.S.-Chinese, and South Korean–North Korean ties are frayed simultaneously burdens Seoul immensely. While it has sought to limit these dangers by doubling down on the partnership with Washington, improving ties with Tokyo, and increasing its domestic competitiveness and manufacturing autonomy, Sohn and Lee suggest that any consequential decoupling from China is likely to lie beyond reach for some time to come.

Syaru Shirley Lin's chapter on Taiwan highlights a similar predicament of perhaps even greater intensity. If there is any one country that has borne the brunt of Chinese coercion in recent years, it is Taiwan. Yet Taiwan's most significant contribution to the international economy— semiconductor manufacturing—is inextricably dependent on its commercial and technological integration with China. Even as tensions across the

Taiwan Strait have increased and Xi Jinping's drive to "Make in China" gathers steam for both economic and strategic reasons, the imperative for Taiwanese ICT firms—which contribute around 40% of the nation's GDP— to remain ensconced in China has only intensified. The political problems notwithstanding, Taiwan's trade with China constitutes over 40% of its total trade, with both its bilateral trade and its trade surplus increasing to record levels despite the presence of an autonomy-conscious Democratic Progressive Party government in Taipei that stringently regulates all investments involving strategic industries in China.

The dangers of excessive economic dependence on China are well understood in Taiwan. The Taiwanese government has prevented advanced semiconductor manufacturing from moving to China and has acquiesced to U.S. pressure to create new semiconductor manufacturing facilities in the United States. But the survival of the Taiwanese ICT sector, to include advanced semiconductor fabrication facilities on the island, simply depends on its continued presence in China. As Lin notes succinctly, for all its challenges, "for Taiwanese manufacturers who serve large multinational clients, there seems to be no readily available alternative to China." The fruits of globalization have thus made China the vital gateway for Taiwan even when the latter seeks to expand trade with wider global markets. A failure to adequately appreciate this fact, Lin fears, could result in Washington inadvertently instrumentalizing Taipei in its rivalry with Beijing, with grave consequences for both Taiwan's domestic politics and its security vis-à-vis China.

Unlike China, Japan, South Korea, and Taiwan, whose economic ascendancy has been underwritten by their deep knitting into global trading system, India's rise has been driven largely by the progressive expansion of its domestic market. In the aftermath of its 1991 economic reforms, however, India's trading links with the world, and especially with the Asian economies, have expanded impressively. One outcome of this new orientation has been growing Sino-Indian trade, with China catapulting to within the top two spots on the Indian trading roster, even as political relations between the two neighbors have acutely deteriorated in recent years. For all the impressive gains in bilateral trade, however, the imbalances are also striking: China enjoys a huge trade surplus derived from its export of capital and consumer goods and critical intermediates, which India's exports of raw materials and intermediates cannot match in value. This fact, exacerbated by the meltdown in Sino-Indian relations since 2000, has impelled India to pursue decoupling from China—a goal that has only received a fillip as a result of parallel U.S. efforts in the same direction since at least the Trump administration.

As Gulshan Sachdeva's chapter in this volume describes, New Delhi may be the only outlier in the Indo-Pacific region in that it is deliberately attempting to limit economic connectivity with China, partly to punish Beijing for its aggression on the border and partly to limit India's vulnerabilities to future Chinese coercion. To that end, New Delhi has embarked on a diverse set of initiatives ranging from banning Chinese apps to limiting Chinese FDI in critical sectors to doubling down on Indian manufacturing as a substitute for Chinese imports. For all these efforts, however, autonomy from China is nowhere in sight. Many of the heavily promoted "Make in India" projects, including marquee initiatives such as Apple's manufacture of iPhones in India, still rely heavily on imported Chinese components, as does the otherwise successful Indian pharmaceutical industry, which cannot operate without active pharmaceutical ingredients sourced from China. Furthermore, the economics of much of India's import-substituting manufacturing are controversial, and the ambition to entice production exiting from China has not yet borne significant fruit.[67] When this is coupled with India's still strong reluctance to join major trading agreements such as the Regional Comprehensive Economic Partnership or even the trade pillar of the shallow U.S.-led Indo-Pacific Economic Framework, Sachdeva concludes that there is a real danger that India may end up outside major global supply chains and, as a result, find itself trapped in a low-level equilibrium—to its disadvantage in the evolving competition with China.

Unlike the chapters surveyed thus far—which focus on countries that have approached (or have been compelled to approach) decoupling because of strategic imperatives—Vikram Nehru's chapter on Southeast Asia is distinctive not only because it assesses an entire region rather than just a single country but, more significantly, because this region still remains an unabashed champion of globalization. Because Southeast Asia's success during the past few decades—the fruit of the second wave of U.S.-led globalization in Asia during the postwar period—has been intimately linked to growing international interdependence, all the regional states are determined to protect their extant structure of trade. This structure has witnessed the region's progressive integration into the China-centered production system, while being equally nourished by U.S. and Japanese investment in a virtuous symbiosis that has made Southeast Asia's trade-to-GDP ratio the highest for any region in the world, including the European Union. The prosperity

---

[67] Rahul Chauhan, Rohit Lamba, and Raghuram Rajan, "The PLI Scheme: Sense and Nonsense in the Debate," January 2023, available at https://studylib.net/doc/26054867/the-pli-scheme--sense-and-nonsense-in-the-debate; Rajiv Kumar, "Can We Please Not Judge PLIs by Value Added," *Times of India*, August 29, 2023, https://timesofindia.indiatimes.com/blogs/toi-edit-page/can-we-please-not-judge-plis-by-value-added; Irene Yuan Sun, "The World's Next Factory Won't Be in South Asia," Bloomberg, October 5, 2019, https://www.bloomberg.com/view/articles/2019-10-06/why-factories-leaving-china-aren-t-going-to-india?embedded-checkout=true; and Viswanathan Rajendran and Patrick Van den Bossche, "The Make in India Moment Is Here," *Times of India*, May 5, 2020, https://timesofindia.indiatimes.com/blogs/voices/the-make-in-india-moment-is-here.

that has accrued as a result has made Southeast Asia a vociferous defender of free trade. Not surprisingly, the region is deeply alarmed by the threat of any U.S.-China conflict that threatens to force diverse forms of decoupling, which could destroy the productive regional integration that has benefited all its constituent states.

The geopolitical threats posed by China in Southeast Asia are undoubtedly unsettling, and most of the resident nations hope that U.S. military power will suffice to preserve the peace that has allowed them to prosper. But they fear that the threat of decoupling from China, however labeled, would tear asunder the bonds that could help avert conflict while also destroying the prosperity that has been built up over decades. Consequently, even though the region has actually benefited from the decoupling that has occurred in U.S.-China trade—since most reshoring has resulted in greater investment in Southeast Asia—the dangers of further tariff wars, fragmenting standards, and technological cleavages are viewed as forcing unpalatable choices upon the regional states. Because these nations are minnows in a sea of whales, their ability to shape the outcome of U.S.-China rivalry is admittedly limited. To the degree that they can, however, they have sought to moderate this competition by refusing to become party to any policies aimed at eroding integration while seeking to keep both the United States and China productively enmeshed in Southeast Asia and enticing other major extraregional states such as Japan, South Korea, India, and Taiwan to remain engaged.

The last chapter, Darren Lim, Benjamin Herscovitch, and Victor Ferguson's study of Australia, once again confirms the larger theme running through the volume: that economic engagement with China is critical to national prosperity and that even capitals allied with Washington seek to avert the worst downside of deepening U.S.-China rivalry, even if they have no illusions about the dangers posed by Beijing's ambitions. For many years, Australia invested deeply in its economic ties with China. This was a natural outcome for an open economy that relied heavily on trade—especially exports of agricultural goods, minerals, and energy—for its growth. China's demand for exactly these inputs made the country an important partner for Australia. Accordingly, Canberra sought to protect commercial ties with China, which had become Australia's largest two-way trading partner and an important source of foreign investment. The deindustrialization of the Australian economy, which occurred as a result of domestic market liberalization, made Australia even more dependent on trade in primary goods, especially with the fast-growing economies in Asia.

Chinese aggressiveness during the last decade, however, involving attempts at manipulating Australian domestic politics coupled with a blatant economic coercion campaign, set the stage for Canberra's re-evaluation of its previous conviction that trade relations could be detached from international competition—something the supply vulnerabilities created by the Covid-19 pandemic only reinforced. Recognizing the emergent Chinese threat, Australia soon doubled down on its traditional security alliance with the United States. This involved acquiring new military capabilities through the AUKUS agreement with the United States and the United Kingdom and supporting an enhanced U.S. military presence in Australia and regionally, while strengthening national security by imposing new restrictions on Chinese ICT firms and initiating screening of Chinese investments in sensitive sectors. Canberra simultaneously embarked on its own de-risking strategy by seeking new markets beyond China. Despite all these initiatives—and the loss of optimism about China as an economic partner—Australia still remains intertwined with China. As Lim, Herscovitch, and Ferguson succinctly explain, "the economic opportunities presented by China's internal market in terms of size and price premiums remain unparalleled. Even many of those businesses directly in the firing line of Beijing's sanctions appear to have calculated that the potential risk of politically motivated disruption recurring in the future does not justify the economic costs of a permanent exit from the trading relationship."

Conclusion: Dilemmas Ahoy!

It is indeed tragic that globalization, which has been a vital legacy of the United States' postwar hegemony, has now collided with the exigencies of U.S.-China competition. Yet such an outcome is not surprising because the pressures of geopolitical rivalry inevitably make states sensitive to the problem of relative gains. Consequently, China's economic ascendancy, which derives from the country's integration into the open trading system and was once viewed as a positive benefit for all, is now perceived through more jaundiced eyes as Beijing continues to challenge Washington in the Indo-Pacific and even globally. It is not surprising, then, that the United States seeks to limit the continued rise of Chinese power in a variety of ways.

In the aftermath of recognizing China as a strategic competitor, the United States—and the Biden administration, in particular—has sought to pursue a policy of "de-risking." This policy has been advertised as seeking to limit the vulnerabilities posed by manufacturing concentration in China and its accompanying dominance in those critical supply chains that are vital to the health of all national economies. This more conservative aim, however, intersects with the larger imperatives of U.S.-China competition, which have taken Washington in the direction of not simply reducing overreliance on China for critical goods but attacking its capacity to dominate the "leading sectors" of the emerging global economy and thereby arresting its rise as a genuine peer of the United States.[68]

This objective is understandable—even defensible, from the viewpoint of U.S. interests—but it brings multiple dangers in its trail.[69] Any effort at slowing China's growth through initiatives such as strategic denial and industrial policy will inevitably degrade economic efficiency globally, which will also increase costs and reduce U.S. competitiveness, potentially diminishing U.S. growth as well. These disadvantages may be accepted as tolerable penalties if they burden China more than the United States. This is, after all, the essence of competition involving relative gains. But there is no assurance that Washington will in fact come out enduringly ahead if China can productively sustain its other trade partnerships, as it seems to be doing, at a time when the United States, for domestic political reasons, remains reluctant to join the very agreements, such as the Trans-Pacific Partnership, that it had previously championed.[70] Expanding market access to the successful Asian economies by cementing high-standard trade agreements offers the United States a beneficial way to correct its relative losses vis-à-vis China and is an indispensable complement to the technology controls and state-led industrialization now being implemented.[71]

The Biden administration's Indo-Pacific Economic Framework is, unfortunately, an all-too-poor substitute in this context. Strengthening the multilateral trading system, which the United States itself constructed, is also necessary, at the very least by making a new push for WTO reform to include resuscitating its Appellate Body. Although the United States relies less on trade for its own economic growth than its many partners do, securing their cooperation vis-à-vis China will require greater attentiveness by Washington to the multilateral trading regime, which matters greatly to them. Admittedly, the United States must also do better on several other counts, such as repairing its public finances, reforming its immigration policies, expanding investments in education, and increasing public funding for research and development.[72]

---

[68] An extended discussion of the notion of "leading sectors" can be found in Modelski and Thompson, *Leading Sectors and World Powers*.

[69] For a wider perspective on the risks beyond U.S.-China competition, see Robert B. Zoellick, "Team Biden Wants a Revolution," *Washington Post*, August 15, 2023.

[70] The domestic constraints—including the divisions within the Biden administration—with respect to developing a sensible U.S. trade policy are described in Bob Davis, "Biden Promised to Confront China. First He Has to Confront America's Bizarre Trade Politics," *Politico*, January 31, 2022, https://www.politico.com/news/magazine/2022/01/31/biden-china-trade-politics-00003379.

[71] Tellis, "The Geopolitics of the TTIP and the TPP," 93–112.

[72] For more on the challenges of revitalizing the U.S. economy, see Tellis, *Balancing Without Containment*, 67–84.

These challenges become especially problematic because, as the analyses in this volume suggest, even U.S. allies and partners that are otherwise troubled by Chinese assertiveness have not found any satisfactory way of decoupling from China as a means of limiting its growth in power. Other than doing what is minimally required to buy insurance against overdependence on China in certain narrow areas, they seem intent on sustaining—perhaps even expanding—their trading relationships with China because of the absolute gains they enjoy. Since China already seems intent on further limiting its dependence on the United States for its own reasons, Washington could face the problem of confronting a Beijing that is far more autonomous—because of thinner Sino-U.S. economic linkages—even as strong Chinese trade connectivity with other states (including U.S. allies and partners) pushes them deeper into the crossfire of U.S.-China rivalry.

The challenges of security competition under conditions of economic interdependence are not well understood in regard to their empirical consequences. Consequently, Washington will have to muster extraordinary discipline to ensure that its new attitude toward interdependence with Beijing does not end up undermining U.S. interests—economic and political—more than it does China's ambitions.

EXECUTIVE SUMMARY

This chapter examines recent strategic developments in China's foreign economic relations with an eye toward their implications for broader geopolitical dynamics.

MAIN ARGUMENT

Both China and the U.S. seek to make their respective economies less dependent on each other. The extent to which they will be successful in doing so largely remains to be seen. At this early stage, there is some indication that China's efforts to move toward an economic growth model driven more by domestic consumption than exports are making progress. However, whether China can sustain its economic success in the face of the numerous challenges confronting its economy remains unclear.

POLICY IMPLICATIONS

- Firms (and their microeconomic, self-interested optimization) drive much of the economic dynamics of the Asia-Pacific region. Although analysts and policymakers tend to focus on nation-states when considering the strategic implications of economics, it is more accurate to understand economic statecraft in terms of the government policies shaping the incentive structures for the commercial actors that actually conduct most economic activity.

- De-risking (rather than decoupling) is a more likely outcome for foreign firms as they reconsider their reliance on China. However, important questions remain around how the U.S. and others would implement such de-risking.

- China's "dual circulation" and other strategic economic policies, if successful, will likely reduce its foreign economic dependence even as they foster increased foreign reliance on China. However, there remains a good deal of uncertainty surrounding China's ability to continue its economic success as well as the viability of initiatives like Made in China 2025 in the face of concerted efforts to limit China's access to leading-edge technology with national security implications.

China

The Future of China's Economic Power

William J. Norris

This chapter examines the impact of growing U.S. and regional interest in decoupling from China on the country's economic and strategic interests in Asia and globally. The United States and China are the world's largest and second-largest economies, respectively, and their economies are deeply interconnected. Yet even as the countries' economic ties have grown, geopolitical tensions have risen over the past few years, producing noisy pressures to decouple and disentangle the two economies. This has been most pronounced in the realm of technology. The United States has banned exports to China of materials used to make advanced semiconductors and other advanced technologies with military applications.[1] The war in Ukraine has accelerated China's efforts, in partnership with Russia, to shift the international order away from U.S. dominance. With its currency-swap agreements and efforts to denominate trade in the renminbi, China has sought to provide an alternative that weakens the U.S. dollar's status as the global reserve currency.[2] But how much of the U.S.-China economic relationship has actually changed?

Available data suggests that the economic complementarity and the stickiness of integrated supply chains that have been developed over

---

William J. Norris is an Associate Professor of Chinese Foreign and Security Policy, Director of China Studies, and Director of the Economic Statecraft Program in the Bush School of Government and Public Service at Texas A&M University. He can be reached at <economicstatecraft@tamu.edu>.

[1] Saif M. Khan, "U.S. Semiconductor Exports to China: Current Policies and Trends," Center for Security and Emerging Technology, October 2020, https://cset.georgetown.edu/publication/u-s-semiconductor-exports-to-china-current-policies-and-trends; and Wei Meng, "Fazhan Zhongguo zhudao de xinxing quanqiu bandaoti gongying lian" [Developing a New Global Semiconductor Supply Chain Led by China], *Economic Herald* 12 (2022): 74–77.

[2] Lu Qianjin, "Meiyuan baquan he guoji huobi tixi gaige—jian lun renminbi guoji hua wenti" [U.S. Dollar Hegemony and the Reform of the International Monetary System: On the Issue of RMB Internationalization], *Journal of Shanghai University of Finance and Economics* 12, no. 1 (2010): 61–69; and Gao Xingwei, "Zhong Mei maoyi moca xia renminbi guoji hua zhanlüe yanjiu" [Research on the Internationalization Strategy of RMB under Sino-U.S. Trade Friction], *Economist*, 59–67.

decades have—at least thus far—made decoupling less extensive than may be generally perceived. Outside of a few specifically targeted industries like semiconductors, much of the economic integration seems to remain in place. In the absence of a real and significant disruption, individual firms are still likely to follow the optimization logic that led them to outsource and seek the most efficient production networks over the past four decades. In the absence of any clear and immediately pressing need to change, most companies will simply continue on with "business as usual," despite the shifting geopolitical landscape.

This chapter's central thesis is that while China seeks to reduce its reliance on international economic links as its economy matures, uncertainty surrounds the feasibility of such a strategy. It is clear that consumption is playing a larger role in driving China's economy, but international ties in areas like technology, agriculture, and raw materials still provide critical pieces of the country's continued economic success. Recent frictions may be influencing China's trade at the margins, with significant growth taking place among partners like Russia, Vietnam, Indonesia, and Saudi Arabia, while China's largest sources of imports (Taiwan, South Korea, Japan, and the United States) seem fairly steady, growing roughly in line with its overall economic growth. But ultimately, microeconomic decisions about optimizing supply chains and firm-level risk appetites will prove to be determinative. Government policies meant to prod economies toward decoupling must recognize the centrality of firm-level dynamics in determining the scale and type of economic links that will shape strategic geopolitical dynamics in Asia and beyond.

Rather than decoupling, de-risking may be a more realistic paradigm to guide future developments in this area. De-risking would involve deliberate self-examination at the firm level of the possible exposure to revenue or operational risk that may be present in a particular company's supply chain, business model, or production networks. Firms may then wish to take measures to build additional contingency planning, diversification, or resilience. If change is not required, most companies would prefer not to have to reconfigure their complex production networks.

This chapter is organized into four major sections. The first provides the broad strategic context for China's contemporary economic situation. The second covers important recent developments, including the impact of Covid-19, disruptions in supply chains, and China's "dual circulation" strategy, before moving on to a strategic assessment in the third section. The chapter's conclusion attempts to forecast what these still emerging patterns suggest about China's future political economy, growth rates, and global ambitions.

Strategic Context

There has been a significant shift in the U.S.-China relationship. On the Chinese side, this has been driven by three key dynamics. First, the maturation and changing nature of China's economic model have prompted structural changes that have placed China in a less complementary and more directly competitive position vis-à-vis the United States and other advanced industrial economies. The economic dimension of the U.S.-China relationship had long served as a floor anchoring the political-security rivalry, but China's efforts to move up the value chain, restrict access to its markets, and skirt World Trade Organization requirements have resulted in friction. To understand today's strategic context, one ought to bear in mind China's own economic transformation. In particular, the role of foreign trade has evolved from serving as a primary catalyst driving China's development model.[3] As discussed in more detail below, since the 2008 global financial crisis, investment has been used to compensate for the drop in exports within China's GDP. This structural change was driven by policy changes and active government support to prop up continued economic growth.[4]

This suggests the second major factor driving the shift in China's position: that these organically occurring developments in China's economic maturation have been supported, encouraged, and accelerated by deliberate Chinese policy choices designed to propel the economy forward. Beijing's dual circulation development strategy has sought to move China's economic growth engine toward domestic consumption and further insulate the Chinese economy from foreign dependence.[5] A key component of the dual circulation strategy, as articulated by Chinese leadership and various experts, involves trade diversification and supporting Chinese firms that are moving up international value chains in areas such as 5G deployment and cloud computing. However, efforts to indigenize state-of-the-art technology and move up the value chain have caused friction with China's partners.[6]

---

[3] For a more detailed account of the structural evolution of economics in China's overall grand strategy, see William J. Norris, "China's Post–Cold War Economic Statecraft: A Periodization," *Journal of Current Chinese Affairs* 50, no. 3 (2021): 294–316.

[4] Gallina Andronova Vincelette et al., "China: Global Crisis Avoided, Robust Economic Growth Sustained," World Bank, Working Paper, no. 5435, September 1, 2010, https://openknowledge.worldbank.org/entities/publication/27645dfe-8e44-5cc7-8489-3ab43199729b; and Nicholas R. Lardy, *Sustaining China's Economic Growth: After the Global Financial Crisis* (Washington, D.C.: Peterson Institute for International Economics, 2011).

[5] Wu Shanlin, "'Shuang xunhuan' xin fazhan geju de zhanlüe hanyi" [Strategic Implication of the New Development Pattern of "Dual Circulation"], *Qiushi* 6 (2020): 90–99; and Ming-Hua Liu, Dimitris Margaritis, and Yang Zhang, "The Global Financial Crisis and the Export-Led Economic Growth in China," *Chinese Economy* 52, no. 3 (2019): 232–48.

[6] See Pengbin Yuan et al., "5G quanqiu qushi yu Zhongguo zhanlüe" [Global 5G Trends and China's Strategy], *Global Science, Technology, and Economy Outlook* 9 (2019): 18–22.

China has also taken measures specifically designed to neuter what it believes is foreign extraterritorial overreach, such as the Anti-Foreign Sanctions Law and Blocking Statute. According to Chinese experts, these are designed to "not only thwart the U.S.'s economic and political goals but also contribute to establishing the foundation of China's blocking legislative system, creating political leverage and legal weapons for negotiations."[7] Provisions of the Anti-Monopoly Law exercise jurisdiction over "extraterritorial monopolistic behaviors affecting the domestic market," while the Cybersecurity Law authorizes relevant departments to hold accountable and impose necessary sanctions on institutions, organizations, and individuals from abroad that harm China's critical information infrastructure.[8]

Finally, beyond the realm of economics, China has adopted a more confrontational approach to its foreign relations. Under Xi Jinping, the country has emphasized themes of national rejuvenation and adopted a new style of great-power foreign policy.[9] Chinese domestic politics now loudly reverberate in its foreign policy, and many of its domestic and international policy choices (e.g., regarding Made in China 2025, the Xinjiang detention camps, Covid-19, and Taiwan) have contributed to the deterioration in U.S.-China relations.[10] China's direction (toward greater domestic control, state-driven technological advancement, decreasing external economic reliance, industrial upgrading, and self-serving indigenous innovation) seemed to be reconfirmed by the results of the 20th Party Congress.[11] Notably, China's more assertive "major country/great power" (*daguo*) foreign policy was affirmed.[12]

---

[7] Guang Ma and Qiyang Mao, "Danbian zhicai yu zuduan lifa xia Zhongguo qiye de hegui kunjing yu yingdui celüe" [Compliance Dilemma and Coping Strategies for Chinese Enterprises Under Unilateral Sanctions and Blocking Legislation], *Wuhan University International Law Review* (2023): 17–37.

[8] See, for instance, Article 2 of the Anti-Monopoly Law and Article 75 of the Cybersecurity Law.

[9] Xi Jinping, "Juesheng quanmian jiancheng xiaokang shehui duoqu xin shidai Zhongguo tese shehui zhuyi weida shengli—zai Zhongguo Gongchandang Di Shijiu Ci Quanguo Daibiao Dahui shang de baogao" [Decisive Victory in Building a Moderately Prosperous Society in an All-Around Way and Winning the Great Victory of Socialism with Chinese Characteristics in the New Era—Report at the Nineteenth National Congress of the Communist Party of China], *Party Building*, November 2017, 15–34; and Zhang Zhengguang, "Dang de Ershi Da yu Zhonghua minzu weida fuxing de lishi jincheng" [The 20th National Congress of the Communist Party of China and the Historical Process of the Great Rejuvenation of the Chinese Nation], *Theory Construction* 38, no. 6 (2022): 1–9.

[10] James B. Steinberg, "What Went Wrong? U.S.-China Relations from Tiananmen to Trump," *Texas National Security Review* 3, no. 1 (2020): 118–33; Ryan Hass, "U.S.-China Relations: The Search for a New Equilibrium," Brookings Institution, February 2020, https://www.brookings.edu/articles/u-s-china-relations-the-search-for-a-new-equilibrium; and Deborah L. Swenson and Wing Thye Woo, "The Politics and Economics of the U.S.-China Trade War," *Asian Economic Papers* 18, no. 3 (2019): 1–28.

[11] As is often the case for major policy venues, various communities of Chinese academics subsequently parsed the results of the 20th Party Congress and what it meant for their respective disciplines. For an example of how Chinese industrial economists digested the outcomes of the 20th Party Congress, see Jiang Xiaojuan et al., "Studying and Interpreting the Spirit of the 20th National Congress of the Communist Party of China," *China Industrial Economics*, November 2022, 5–25.

[12] Zhang Qingmin, "Ershi Da yihou de Zhongguo waijiao: Lijie yu sikao" [China's Diplomacy after the 20th Party Congress: Understanding and Reflection], *Foreign Affairs Review* 39, no. 6 (2022): 1–21.

Anytime there is a rapidly rising power in an international system dominated by an incumbent great power, there is likely to be friction. Historically, such dynamics can even lead to war between the great powers. China's economic evolution has been exacerbated by the economic, political, and security policy choices of its leadership over the past two decades. Decisions to prioritize increasing domestic control and security over economic liberalization, provocative (often militarized or para-militarized) assertion of territorial claims, "wolf warrior" diplomacy, united front activities, and party building have all fueled concerns about China's growing power. The result has been the strategic context framing the present state of affairs for China's international situation.

Is This New Era of Friction Shifting China's Economic Patterns?

Recently, China has figured less prominently as a source of U.S. imports. It had grown from accounting for 4% of all U.S. imports in 2000 to 13% in 2010 and 15% in 2018.[13] This trend reversed by 2021, however, when China accounted for only 10%. Due to increasing diversification, the proportion of U.S. imports from China declined, even as Chinese exports to the United States reached record highs in absolute terms. China fell from being the second-largest source of U.S. imports (behind the European Union) in 2018 to the fourth position in 2021 (behind the EU, Mexico, and Canada). Filling this vacuum have been Asia-Pacific partners like Vietnam, Taiwan, South Korea, India, Thailand, and Malaysia. All were among the top-ten exporters gaining market share during 2018–21.[14] These developments might be interpreted as early signs of the fruits of individual firms' de-risking decisions. As countries and businesses seek to hedge against over-reliance on China, many have relocated supply chains or added capacity in other Asia-Pacific host nations.[15]

Yet the United States and China continue to be deeply economically linked. In 2021 a record-setting $530 billion of exports flowed from China to the United States.[16] Supply chains in some of the world's most important

---

[13] "Globalization 2.0: Can the U.S. and EU Really 'Friendshore' Away from China?" Allianz, October 5, 2022, 12, https://www.allianz.com/en/economic_research/publications/specials_fmo/trade-china-globalization.html.

[14] Ibid.

[15] Preetam Basu and Partha Ray, "China-Plus-One: Expanding Global Value Chains," *Journal of Business Strategy* 43, no. 6 (2022): 350–56; Willy C. Shih, "Global Supply Chains in a Post-Pandemic World," *Harvard Business Review* 98, no. 5 (2020): 82–89; and Guiyang Zhu, Mabel Chou, and Christina Tsai, "Lessons Learned from the Covid-19 Pandemic Exposing the Shortcomings of Current Supply Chain Operations: A Long-Term Prescriptive Offering," *Sustainability* 12, no. 14 (2020): 5858.

[16] Observatory for Economic Complexity, "Bilateral Trade Selector: United States and China (2021)," https://oec.world/en/profile/bilateral-country/usa/partner/chn?dynamicBilateralTradeSelector=year2021.

industries continue to be highly integrated across Asia. China's share of the global exports market increased from 5% in 2002 to 9% in 2008 to 13% in 2019 before the outbreak of the pandemic. By 2021, the country accounted for 15% of all global exports.[17] Although international trade and foreign investment continue to play key roles in China's economic success, they are becoming less indispensable than they once were as a driver of its economic growth. In the 1980s, special economic zones and the booming export industries of China's eastern and southern coastal provinces served as economic growth engines for the entire nation's rapid modernization. But as China's economy has now become the world's second-largest, the foundation for continued growth looks to be shifting.

China's Changing Economic Model

Even as China continues to play an increasingly central role in global and regional economic integration, its domestic economic model is becoming less reliant on exports to drive growth. In response to the anticipated drop in exports as a result of the 2008 global financial crisis, Beijing accelerated investment to offset the slack left by lost exports.[18] Investment ballooned to displace a substantial portion of what had been a largely export-oriented growth model. This remains at a stubbornly high level, sustaining GDP growth, but often doing so at the expense of increasingly unproductive investment projects. Investment contributed 43.3% of China's GDP in 2021.[19] At the same time, China's domestic consumption has been growing steadily as its economy has matured. As of December 2021, private consumption accounted for 38.2% of GDP, and public/government consumption accounted for another 15.9%.

China's economic model has largely already shifted toward a domestic consumption–driven economy, with consumption accounting for 54.1% of the nominal 2021 GDP. These figures imply that net exports account for only 2.6% of GDP.[20] Trade has declined from a peak of 64% of GDP in 2006 to only 36% in 2019. In many respects, this is a natural, expected, and normal shift as China matures into the world's second-largest economy. A growing domestic consumer market is expected to increasingly drive growth (rather

---

[17] "Globalization 2.0," 4.

[18] Zhu Fulin, "Gao zhiliang goujian guonei guoji shuang xunhuan xin fazhan geju yanjiu" [Research on Constructing a New Development Pattern of Domestic and International Dual Cycles with High Quality], *Theoretical Horizon* 5 (2023): 56–63.

[19] Data is taken from CEIC, "China Nominal GDP," https://www.ceicdata.com/en/indicator/china/nominal-gdp. CEIC converts quarterly nominal GDP into U.S. dollars. The National Bureau of Statistics press releases provide quarterly data and year-to-date nominal GDP in local currency, while the Federal Reserve Board average market exchange rate is used for currency conversions.

[20] "Dual Circulation: China's Way of Reshoring?" Allianz, October 29, 2020, 6, https://www.allianz-trade.com/en_global/news-insights/economic-insights/Dual-circulation-China-s-way-of-reshoring.html.

than the external global demand that had previously powered rising China's exports). In addition to this developmental transformation, the Chinese economy has begun to grapple with the consequences of inefficient capital allocation, overcapacity, and an aging population in conjunction with low fertility rates. As will be discussed later, this "new normal" slower rate of total GDP growth is likely to have an important continuing geopolitical impact.

China's Foreign Economic Relations: Fostering Dependence

Trade and investment data provides evidence of important links to China's key markets. In particular, China's trade with the United States is emblematic of continued economic links with developed economies. In 2022, U.S. trade in goods with China hit a record $690.6 billion, topping the 2018 record of $658.8 billion.[21] This new mark reflects the strong, post-pandemic recovery of U.S. consumption (which is highly correlated with U.S. imports) and the prominence of the United States' third-largest trading partner, China.

China remains a central hub for many global supply chains. According to the annual threat assessment from the U.S. Office of the Director of National Intelligence, "China is central to global supply chains in a range of technology sectors, including semiconductors, critical minerals, batteries, solar panels, and pharmaceuticals."[22] Firms have long outsourced elements of their manufacturing, assembly, and production to Chinese partners. Over time, these Chinese partner firms have taken costs and inefficiencies out of the production process, even as they have matured and improved their own skills and human capital and solidified their comparative advantages in the global economy. These types of deeply embedded supply chains are unlikely to be carelessly jettisoned by the individual firms that benefit from (and rely on) them.

In addition to its strength in manufacturing, China has become the world's dominant supplier of several important inputs and raw materials, including rare earths and other critical minerals. As stated by the European Commission, this is "a major vulnerability to the United States…that could affect output in civilian and defense manufacturing in the United States and the West."[23] Indeed, these concerns are not merely hypothetical, and the United States has already entered into critical minerals agreements with the

---

[21] U.S. Census Bureau, "Trade in Goods with China," https://www.census.gov/foreign-trade/balance/c5700.html.

[22] U.S. Office of the Director of National Intelligence, *2023 Annual Threat Assessment of the U.S. Intelligence Community* (Washington, D.C., March 2023).

[23] "EU Moves Forward with Critical Minerals Agreement Negotiations with the U.S.," European Commission, Press Release, June 14, 2023, https://ec.europa.eu/commission/presscorner/detail/en/ip_23_3214; and "United States and Japan Sign Critical Minerals Agreement," Office of the U.S. Trade Representative, Press Release, March 28, 2023, https://ustr.gov/about-us/policy-offices/press-office/press-releases/2023/march/united-states-and-japan-sign-critical-minerals-agreement.

EU and Japan. In July 2022, Treasury Secretary Janet Yellen stated that the United States "cannot allow countries like China to use their market positions in key raw materials, technologies, or products to disrupt our economy or exercise unwanted geopolitical leverage."[24] This concern may be well placed, as China has often deliberately sought to cultivate and leverage its economic power. Efforts like the dual circulation strategy and Made in China 2025 prioritize China-centric development in ways that seek to make China less dependent on the rest of the world even as it looks to harness the technology and benefits from international cooperation. According to the Office of the Director of National Intelligence's 2023 threat assessment:

> Beijing uses a variety of tools, from public investment to espionage to try to advance its technological capabilities, protect domestic firms from foreign competition, and facilitate these firms' global expansion. Beijing's willingness to use espionage, subsidies, and trade policy to try to give its firms a competitive advantage represents not just an ongoing challenge for the U.S. economy and its workers, but also advances Beijing's attempts to assume leadership of the world's technological advancement and standards.[25]

Dual circulation, in particular, seeks to make China more economically self-reliant while also fostering foreign nations' dependence on Chinese supplies of high-tech finished goods.

Indeed, the United States is already highly dependent on China for a number of important goods. For example, it is highly dependent on electronics imports, with more than 90% of laptop imports and around 80% of mobile phones coming from China.[26] Although China may be the top source for many U.S. imports, the United States could feasibly diversify at least some of this dependence to Canada and Mexico. Aside from textiles and semiconductors, in most of the other categories in which Beijing is the dominant source of U.S. imports, Canada or Mexico occupies the second or third positions. For basic chemicals, Ireland and Canada are the second- and third-highest exporters to the United States, respectively. This should provide an opportunity to shift supply dependence away from China and toward these alternative countries at a fairly minimal cost, if the need were to arise.

However, for some categories where China's share of imports to the United States is particularly large, including textile mill products, boilers,

---

[24] Christopher Condon, Heejin Kim, and Sam Kim, "Yellen Touts 'Friend-shoring' as Global Supply Chain Fix," Bloomberg, July 18, 2022.

[25] U.S. Office of the Director of National Intelligence, *2023 Annual Threat Assessment of the U.S. Intelligence Community*, 8.

[26] Data on laptop and mobile phone imports is available at Observatory of Economic Complexity (OEC), https://oec.world/en/profile/hs/telephones-for-cellular-networks-or-for-other-wireless-networks; and OEC, https://oec.world/en/profile/hs/automatic-data-processing-machines-portable-weighing-not-more-than-10kg-consisting-of-at-least-a-central-processing-unit-a-keyboard-and-a-display.

shipping containers, computer and communications equipment, household appliances, and electric lighting equipment, diversification will likely be more difficult. In these areas, U.S. firms will be faced with three options. First, they could continue to depend on China for these supplies (which would be the least costly and disruptive in the short term). Second, U.S. firms could decide that they want to make these supplies in the United States at a higher cost. Third, firms could begin the process of seeking other sources, suppliers, and import partners. In most cases, it is useful to note that any shifting of supply chains would be distortionary and thus likely more costly than the status quo. So far, these sorts of costs have been justified on the basis of security concerns and have been concentrated in the semiconductor space. Efforts on a similar scale are not likely to be sustainable across the board.

As is the case with the United States, a significant part of European assembly and manufacturing has been outsourced to China. The resulting finished goods are then imported into the European market. Whether Chinese efforts to become less reliant on key machinery, foreign technology, and equipment will translate into declining European exports to China in the coming decade remains to be seen. The categories of European exports to China that might be most affected by a successful Chinese effort to substitute domestic Chinese products to supplant foreign imports would be machinery and equipment, construction, agrifood, and electronics.

In addition to these dependencies with the United States and Europe, China has significant (often asymmetric) economic links to a range of smaller regional suppliers and other key partners. Frequently these trade flows reflect integrated global value chains that have been built up over decades. **Table 1** provides a condensed overview of China's trade composition.

Those countries that rely heavily on supplying the Chinese market, like intermediate nations in Southeast Asia and the Middle East, unsurprisingly would be the most exposed if China were to make progress in its quest for greater indigenous production. For example, Taiwan, Malaysia, Singapore, Thailand, and Chile seem to be the most vulnerable in a scenario where China moves toward industrial autonomy. These partners' exports of final goods and services rely heavily on Chinese domestic households, government, and Chinese business investment purchases. These exporting nations are at risk of losing market share in China as it moves toward industrial autonomy. Their exports are likely to face increasing substitution pressure from a Chinese economy that has successfully upgraded its industrial capacity. Countries highly reliant on Chinese-bound exports in sectors like construction, machinery and equipment, agrifood, and electronics risk being displaced by competing goods produced domestically by an industrially upgraded Chinese economy. It will be important to keep an eye on how regional

TABLE 1 Trade composition between China and key partners

Country/region	Dependencies on China	China's dependencies
United States	Textile products, basic chemicals, boilers and shipping containers, computer and communications equipment, household appliances, electric lighting equipment, toys	Electrical machinery and electronics; optical, photo, and film equipment; medical instruments; mineral fuels, mineral oils and products of their distillation
Japan, South Korea	Electrical machinery and electronics and machinery, mechanical appliances, and parts (around half of China's exports to them); knitted clothing accessories; iron and steel	Electrical machinery and electronics and machinery, mechanical appliances, and parts (around half of their exports to China); plastics and articles thereof; optical, photo, and film equipment; medical instruments
Europe	Electrical machinery and electronics and machinery, mechanical appliances, and parts (around half of China's exports to them); furniture, bedding, lamps, and prefab buildings	Key machinery, high technology and equipment, construction, agrifood, electronics, cars, tractors, trucks and parts
Taiwan	Electrical machinery and electronics (more than half of China's exports to them); machinery, mechanical appliances, and parts; optical, photo, and film equipment; medical instruments	Electrical machinery and electronics (more than half of their exports to China); machinery, mechanical appliances, and parts; optical, photo, and film equipment; medical instruments
Australia	Computers; broadcasting equipment; furniture; cars; iron structures; plastics	Ores, slag, and ash (more than 70% of their exports to China); mineral fuels, mineral oils, and products of their distillation; precious stones, metals, and pearls
Brazil	Electrical machinery and electronics; machinery, mechanical appliances, and parts; plastics; iron and steel; chemicals; cars	Ores, slag, and ash (one-third of their exports to China); oil seeds, oleaginous fruits, grains, straw, and fodder (one-third); mineral fuels, mineral oils, and products of their distillation
Russia, Saudi Arabia	Electrical machinery and electronics; machinery, mechanical appliances, and parts; iron and steel; furniture, bedding, lamps, and prefab buildings; chemicals; cars; toys; shoes; plastics; clothing	Mineral fuels, mineral oils, and products of their distillation (more than two-thirds of their exports to China)
Vietnam, Singapore, Malaysia	Electrical machinery and electronics; machinery, mechanical appliances, and parts; plastics and articles thereof	Electrical machinery and electronics

middle powers position themselves in light of any potential decoupling. Interestingly, some of the most dynamic growth has been among regional middle powers and raw materials suppliers. As shown in **Figure 1**, these countries have experienced strong growth in their exports to China. Within this group, China's oil and gas partners have recently seen the sharpest rise in their exports to China, as indicated in **Figure 2**. Notably, the data suggests that China has met its growing energy demand by expanding relationships with Russia and the Gulf states.

Beyond the energy picture, China's imports are quite diversified, with almost 87% coming from its top-thirty suppliers (see **Table 2**). That said, many of these suppliers specialize in fairly concentrated niche inputs to China's economy. As indicated in the table of dependencies, for some of these nations, this equates to putting many of their eggs in a single Chinese basket. To the extent that those nations are highly reliant on these concentrated exports for their economic success, China may enjoy some degree of leverage (depending on how badly it requires those imports). Separating out the top-ten suppliers from this data more clearly displays China's largest reliance on Taiwan, South

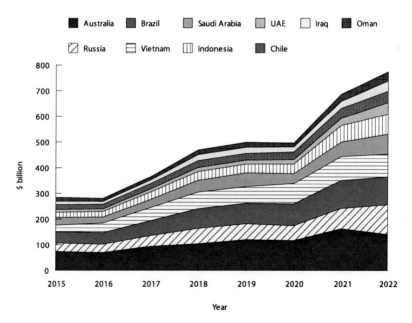

FIGURE 1   China's imports from countries with greatest growth

SOURCE: International Trade Center (ITC) calculations based on General Customs Administration of China statistics since January 2015.

FIGURE 2 China's growing oil and gas partnerships

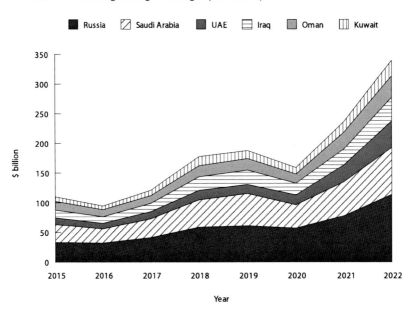

SOURCE: ITC calculations based on General Customs Administration of China statistics since January 2015.

Korea, Japan, the United States, and (more recently) Australia as key partners providing imports to its economy (see **Figure 3**).

China has also sustained a long-term strategy of building stronger economic ties with the global South.[27] Beijing premises its presumptively natural leadership of this group of developing nations on a common experience of colonialism. Often couching its argument in "anti-Western" rhetoric, China frequently seeks to appeal to this segment of nations as it engages both diplomatically and economically across Africa, Central Asia, and Latin America through mechanisms like its Belt and Road Initiative (BRI). The initiative dates back to 2013 and now includes 151 countries around the world as participants. The infrastructure projects that the early iterations of BRI funded were largely designed to enhance Chinese prestige and influence in these countries while facilitating trade with China. BRI projects helped China dominate key markets and often made countries more dependent

---

[27] Wang Yuesheng and Ma Xiangdong, "Quanqiu jingji shuang xunhuan yu xin nan nan hezuo" [Dual Circulation of the World Economy and New South-South Cooperation], *International Economic Review* (2014): 61–80.

TABLE 2 Sources of China's imports (in nominal $ billion)

Exporter	2015	2016	2017	2018	2019	2020	2021	2022
Taiwan	145.0	139.7	154.8	177.3	173.0	200.5	249.9	238.1
South Korea	174.6	159.2	177.5	204.6	173.6	173.1	213.4	199.7
Japan	143.1	145.8	165.5	180.4	171.8	174.7	205.5	184.5
United States	150.5	135.0	154.8	156.0	123.8	136.3	181.0	179.0
Australia	73.9	70.2	94.6	105.1	121.3	117.7	163.7	142.1
Russia	33.2	32.1	41.4	58.9	61.2	57.1	78.1	114.1
Germany	87.7	86.1	96.9	106.3	105.1	105.1	119.9	111.4
Malaysia	53.3	49.1	54.0	63.3	71.9	75.2	98.2	109.9
Brazil	44.3	45.6	58.5	77.1	80.0	85.5	109.9	109.5
Vietnam	25.1	37.2	50.4	64.1	64.1	78.5	92.3	88.0
Saudi Arabia	30.2	23.6	31.8	45.9	54.2	39.1	57.0	78.0
Indonesia	19.8	21.3	28.5	34.2	34.1	37.5	63.9	77.8
Thailand	37.2	38.7	41.8	44.9	46.2	48.1	61.8	56.5
Switzerland	41.2	40.1	33.0	38.7	27.4	17.5	38.1	49.9
UAE	11.5	10.0	12.2	16.3	15.3	17.1	28.6	45.4
Chile	18.7	18.4	20.9	27.0	26.2	29.9	39.5	44.5
Canada	26.3	18.3	20.3	28.4	28.2	22.1	30.5	42.4
Iraq	12.7	10.6	13.8	22.5	23.9	19.3	26.6	39.4
Oman	15.1	12.0	13.2	18.8	19.7	15.7	28.6	36.2
France	25.0	22.6	27.1	32.3	32.6	29.7	39.1	35.6
Singapore	27.6	25.9	34.1	33.6	35.2	31.6	38.8	34.0
South Africa	30.2	22.6	24.8	27.2	25.9	20.8	33.0	32.5
Italy	16.9	16.7	20.4	21.2	21.4	22.3	30.3	27.0
Kuwait	7.5	6.4	8.9	15.4	13.4	10.7	17.8	26.5
Peru	8.2	9.4	13.1	15.2	15.2	14.7	24.2	24.1
Angola	16.0	13.9	20.4	25.7	23.8	14.8	20.9	23.2
Philippines	19.0	17.4	19.1	20.6	20.2	19.3	24.8	23.0
Qatar	4.6	4.0	6.4	9.1	8.7	8.3	13.2	22.6
United Kingdom	18.9	18.7	22.3	23.9	23.9	19.9	25.7	21.8
Rest of world	220.1	209.3	247.8	294.7	295.3	289.7	364.7	376.4

SOURCE: ICT calculations based on General Customs Administration of China statistics since January 2015.

FIGURE 3 China's imports from its top-ten suppliers

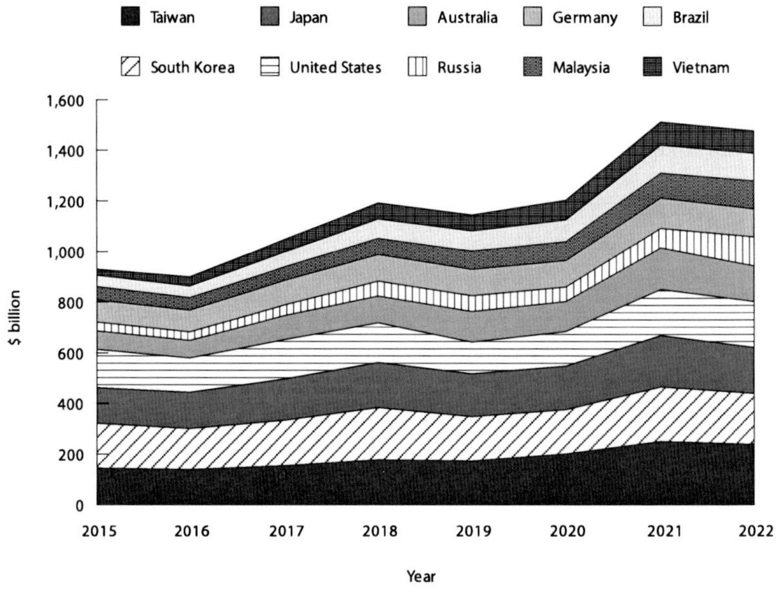

[Legend: Taiwan, Japan, Australia, Germany, Brazil, South Korea, United States, Russia, Malaysia, Vietnam]

SOURCE: ITC calculations based on General Customs Administration of China statistics since January 2015.

on it. These projects are frequently built by Chinese workers rather than providing jobs for locals, helping reduce China's unemployment but fueling resentment in host countries. Countries with important mineral deposits like Congo, Bolivia, Chile, and Papua New Guinea have had a large Chinese presence for years.

A rising interest rate environment is likely to weigh on emerging markets in the near term, but demographic trends and economic catch-up dynamics suggest that the countries in the global South can be an attractive source of potential long-term growth and capacity in the coming decades. A lot will depend on continued social, political, and economic stability to realize this potential. To the extent that Chinese economic engagement is able to help facilitate this stability, it will be a welcome contribution. China seeks to position itself as an important first mover in these markets.

This section covered China's continuing efforts to foster advantageous economic relationships with the outside world. The advanced industrial economies like the United States, the EU, and Japan continue to play a key role for China, especially as final consumers of its exports. China remains an important hub for global supply chains and world-class manufacturing. Much of the data presented in this section illustrates how China's economic relations continue to foster dependence. This is especially poignant for smaller, middle-income economies whose dependence on China represents a disproportionate reliance on concentrated exports. Beijing's engagement with the global South will be an important arena to monitor going forward as these regions hold considerable promise. China is positioning itself to secure a first-mover advantage in many of these emerging economies and is often able to utilize state-backed financing to subsidize otherwise commercially risky investments.

Recent Developments

The Impact of the Covid-19 Pandemic

As has been the case for most economies, Covid-19 has dominated China's most recent developments. After an initially fumbled effort to properly identify and contain the outbreak in Wuhan, China imposed strict lockdown measures for affected regions early in the pandemic in an effort to isolate and limit the spread of the virus. These seemed to serve China comparatively well before the widespread availability of vaccines. China's lackluster vaccination efforts, however, led to prolonged reliance on strict lockdown and quarantine measures that hampered economic growth even as other leading economies began to emerge from the worst of the pandemic. A survey conducted in June 2022 by the US-China Business Council found that 96% of respondents "experienced negative impacts on their China business because of the control measures, with nearly half reporting severe negative impacts." The control measures also affected more than half of companies' future business and investment plans.[28] It remains to be seen whether China will enjoy a post-pandemic recovery boost to its GDP as deferred consumption and pent-up demand are released. In the United States and Europe, this deferred consumption led to supply chain disruptions and shortages as well as inflationary pressures. Lagged fiscal stimulus (designed to offset the drag on economies from the Covid-19 pandemic) also contributed to the current inflationary environment that the U.S. Federal Reserve is seeking to curb.

In 2022, China's GDP growth of 3% fell well short of the targeted rate of 5.5%. The shortfall was mainly attributed to widespread shutdowns in Shanghai and elsewhere that severely curbed economic activity. Lockdown policies were quite strict in response to the continued outbreaks of

---

[28] US-China Business Council, "Member Survey," 2022, https://www.uschina.org/sites/default/files/uscbc_member_survey_2022.pdf.

various strains. By late November and early December 2022, popular protests sprang up around the country as citizens grew increasingly frustrated with draconian lockdown measures. Shortly thereafter, the Chinese leadership reversed course and relaxed many of the restrictions. Perhaps unsurprisingly, this led to a spike in infections even as the population began to return to something closer to normal economic activity. One of the key dynamics to watch is whether this return to normalcy will be accompanied by a post-pandemic bounce driven by deferred consumption or whether the lingering effects of the pandemic (or any of several other possible economic headwinds) will continue to weigh on China's economic performance.[29]

In terms of patterns of trade in goods and services, the most significant recent development has been the diminishing role that trade plays in China's $18.1 trillion economy. Trade as a share of GDP has been falling steadily since its peak of 64% in 2006. By 2019 (the last year of pre-pandemic data), trade had fallen to only 36% of China's total GDP. The growing role of consumption as a key driver of China's economic performance will be one of the most significant structural developments affecting its strategic position in both the region and beyond.[30] Relatedly, China's outsized reliance on investment as a stop-gap engine powering GDP growth is unlikely to be sustainable over the medium to long term. Marginal productivity and returns on investment have been drifting downward. Decreasing total factor productivity combines with a challenging demographic picture to pose serious challenges for China's continued economic growth. Declining productivity and unproductive capital allocations are not the recipe for long-term economic success.

As China's post-pandemic economic position begins to take shape, there are two key dynamics to keep an eye on. The first is the potential challenges that China's economy faces. Slowing economic growth, eroding productivity, rising healthcare costs, continued environmental challenges, mounting local debt, inflationary pressures, income and wealth inequality, ongoing agricultural challenges, energy needs, and a graying population are all likely to generate headwinds going forward. China's demographic trends have been unfavorable for some time, but it now appears that the country is entering a new era with a declining working-age population, even as recent college

---

[29] At the time of writing, the recovery seems to be weaker than might be hoped. See Ella Cao and Kevin Yao, "China to Increase Support for Private Firms to Bolster Recovery," Reuters, July 19, 2023, https://www.reuters.com/markets/asia/china-increase-support-private-companies-bolster-economy-2023-07-19.

[30] A number of Chinese commentators are optimistic that such a shift can successfully occur. See, for example, Li Feng, "Guonei guoji shuang xunhuan: Lilun kuangjia yu Zhongguo shijian" [Dual Circulations of Domestic and International Economy: Theoretical Framework and Chinese Practice], *Journal of Finance and Economics* 47, no. 4 (2021): 4–18.

graduates suffer a record-breaking 20% rate of unemployment.[31] China's population declined in 2022 for the first time since the early 1960s, when the disastrous Great Leap Forward policies and subsequent famine decimated the country. China has long faced the daunting task of having to feed 20% of the world's population on only 7% of the world's arable land. Climate change, water resource mismanagement, and expanding desertification will continue to place additional pressures on China's sustainability.

The second key dynamic is the extent to which China's economy continues to shift toward being driven by domestic consumption.[32] If recent trends hold, trade will likely continue to decline as a percentage of China's overall economy. Such shifts would be exacerbated by the successful implementation of China's efforts to reduce its dependency on foreign sources of technology and other goods. Policies like dual circulation (if fully implemented) would likely accelerate such transformations.[33] But there is some uncertainty surrounding the feasibility of this path forward.[34] Despite the Chinese leadership's stated desire to gain greater autonomy in areas like state-of-the-art semiconductors, jet aircraft engines, precision manufacturing, and a handful of other sectors, China seems to have had a difficult time developing indigenous capabilities. If that pattern were to persist, then trade and investment (at least in these critical areas) would likely continue to be an important dependency. In this scenario, China would need to foster geopolitical and economic conditions conducive to increased access in these areas.

Supply Chains

At the same time that China faces these domestic challenges in the aftermath of the Covid-19 pandemic, growing tensions with the United States have resulted in trade frictions and an increasingly charged regional atmosphere that views China's growing capabilities with alarm. The U.S. Office

---

[31] Clement Tan, "China's Youth Unemployment Hits a Record High, Deepening Its Economic Scars," CNBC, May 29, 2023, https://www.cnbc.com/2023/05/29/record-youth-unemployment-stokes-economic-worries-in-china-.html.

[32] Chen Yanbin, "Xingcheng shuang xunhuan xin fazhan geju guanjian zaiyu tisheng jumin xiaofei yu youxiao touzi" [The Importance of Increasing Residents' Consumption and Effective Investment in the Process of Forming a New Dual Circulation Development Pattern], *Economic Review* (2020): 11–15.

[33] Dong Zhiyong and Li Chengming, "Guonei guoji shuang xunhuan xin fazhan geju: Lishi suyuan, luoji chanshi yu zhengce daoxiang" [China's Double-Circulation New Development Pattern: Source, Implications, and Policy Orientation], *Journal of the Party School of the Central Committee of the CCP* 24, no. 5 (2020): 47–55.

[34] Li Meng, "Xin shiqi goujian guonei guoji shuang xunhuan xianghu cujin xin fazhan geju de zhanlüe yiyi, zhuyao wenti he zhengce jianyi" [Building the New Development Pattern of Domestic and International Double Circulation Mutual Promotion in the New Era: Strategic Significance, Main Problems, and Policy Suggestions], *Contemporary Economic Management* 43, no. 1 (2021): 16–25.

of the Director of National Intelligence's 2023 threat assessment addresses the issue of supply chains directly:

> Beijing is increasingly combining growing military power with its economic, technological, and diplomatic influence to strengthen CCP rule, secure what it views as its sovereign territory and regional preeminence, and pursue global influence. The Government of China is capable of leveraging its dominant positions in key global supply chains in an attempt to accomplish its goals, although probably not without significant cost to itself.[35]

As illustrated by pandemic shutdowns, there continues to be substantial risk to global supply chains.[36] If one looks at the content of global trade flows, more than 50% consists of "computers & telecom, electronics, household equipment, metals, autos & transport equipment, chemicals and machinery & equipment."[37] China features prominently in the global value chains across many of these sectors. For instance, Brazil imports more than 95% of its imported photovoltaic cells from China, and South Korea imports more than 90% of its lithium-ion batteries.[38]

China, too, has several areas in which it continues to be largely reliant on global partners to ensure continued access to key inputs. Much of this reliance is in highly consolidated sectors like mining and agriculture. China is the world's largest importer of iron ore, which makes up almost two-thirds of its mining imports.[39] China is also the world's largest importer of cobalt, nickel, and lithium. Soybeans make up almost half of its agricultural imports, with 95% of the global soybean supply coming from the United States and Brazil. China's exposure to and reliance on this sort of concentrated supply represents an uncomfortable vulnerability.

Even as the political or strategic attractiveness of decoupling may be increasing, there are a number of inertial forces at work. These stubborn facts ought to give prudent pause to analysts suggesting that a radically divided future is imminent. In terms of total worldwide trade, somewhere in the neighborhood of 40% can be considered "concentrated," in the sense that importing economies rely on three or fewer other partners for the imports of a particular good or

---

[35] U.S. Office of the Director of National Intelligence, *2023 Annual Threat Assessment of the U.S. Intelligence Community*.

[36] "U.S. Worries China Will Use Supply Chains as Weapon," *Barron's*, March 8, 2023, https://www.barrons.com/news/us-worries-china-will-use-supply-chains-as-weapon-413d5b2d.

[37] "Globalization 2.0."

[38] Olivia White et al., "The Complication of Concentration in Global Trade," McKinsey Global Institute, January 12, 2023, 10, https://www.mckinsey.com/mgi/our-research/the-complication-of-concentration-in-global-trade.

[39] White et al., "The Complication of Concentration in Global Trade," 11; and Genevieve Donnellon-May and Zhang Hongzhou, "China's Main Food Security Challenge: Feeding Its Pigs," *Diplomat*, July 6, 2022, https://thediplomat.com/2022/07/chinas-main-food-security-challenge-feeding-its-pigs.

commodity.⁴⁰ This suggests that many economies are reliant on a limited number of trading partners for the continued flow of those imports. If there were serious concerns about vulnerability stemming from such concentrated reliance, one would expect to see significantly more diversification to alternative trading partners. However, such diversification would incur additional cost (and presumably some degree of inefficiency). Both of these features would likely result in a microeconomic inertial bias on the part of firms to maintain current arrangements, even in the face of national calls for decoupling. Without legal or financial incentives to change, firms will continue to optimize based on their narrow self-interests. Indeed, the data presented above suggests that continued specialization and integration across supply chains is most likely.

But what about investment patterns? If trade data signals that decoupling may be less likely than headlines suggest, perhaps one could find indications of future relations revealed through investment data. Have China's patterns of investment shifted as a result of the new pressures on economic interdependence? There were large increases in Chinese outward foreign direct investment toward Europe and North America in the pre-pandemic years—often in search of innovation, prestige brands, and technology transfer. Such investments will become harder as these destinations have tightened their screening mechanisms over the past couple of years. According to one Chinese observer, "state-owned capital is especially noticeable in overseas investment and acquisition activities. Because they have strong political attributes, they are easily rejected and scrutinized by overseas companies and host government."⁴¹ Thus, there will likely be a displacement of Chinese investment flows toward the next tier of economies like Indonesia, India, Thailand, Mexico, and Chile. These investment strategies will likely proceed alongside redoubled efforts to develop technology, such as semiconductors, indigenously. According to the U.S. Office of the Director of National Intelligence, "China is leading the world in building new chip factories, with plans to build dozens of semiconductor factories by 2024, most of which will be dedicated to producing older, more mature technologies." The latest threat assessment finds that "because of the difficulties China is facing from export controls by Western nations, it is focusing on lower-capability, commodity chip technology." As a result of these efforts, "China could become a powerhouse in that segment, which could eventually make some buyers more reliant on China."⁴² Indeed, China seems focused on addressing

---

⁴⁰ White et al., "The Complication of Concentration in Global Trade."

⁴¹ Wei Meng, "Fazhan Zhongguo zhudao de xinxing quanqiu bandaoti gongying lian" [Developing a New Global Semiconductor Supply Chain Led by China], *Economic Herald* (2022): 74–77.

⁴² U.S. Office of the Director of National Intelligence, *2023 Annual Threat Assessment of the U.S. Intelligence Community*, 9.

its semiconductor shortcomings with deliberate targeting of Japan, South Korea, Europe, Singapore, and Southeast Asia. Unilateral U.S. efforts toward decoupling will not likely work if other key Chinese trading partners do not follow suit. China seems to be keenly aware of this and intends to do whatever it can to target and peel away potentially vulnerable partners.[43]

China remains a central hub for manufacturing and will presumably foster this strength with deliberate efforts to further indigenize the supply chains of industries that have been explicitly identified as being "strategic emerging industries."[44] For example, firms based in China are on track to control 65% of the lithium-ion battery market by 2025, with China dominant in all parts of the supply chain. Likewise, the country already produces 40% of the world's active pharmaceutical ingredients. Such dominance seems to be designed to both ensure that China will retain autonomous flexibility in key technologies and potentially offer it leverage over others who might become dependent on continued access to Chinese supplies going forward.[45]

Concepts like Made in China 2025 aim to upgrade China's manufacturing base and to indigenize key sectors and technologies. The Standards 2035 effort complementarily seeks to forge state-driven convergence around common industry standards domestically and to promote China-centric standards internationally.[46] Xi Jinping, along with several of the Politburo members who were recently promoted at the 20th Party Congress, has made such ideas the foundation of China's technology and innovation strategy.[47] The current 14th Five-Year Plan (covering 2021–25) strives to operationalize these ambitions into policy, programs, goals, and targets.[48] Generally speaking, this has resulted in a raft of new legislation and measures designed to enhance the ability of the Chinese Communist Party (CCP) to exert control over

---

[43] Wei Meng, "Fazhan Zhongguo zhudao de xinxing quanqiu bandaoti gongying lian."

[44] Zhu Heliang and Wang Chunjuan, "'Shuang xunhuan' xin fazhan geju zhanlüe beijing xia chanye shuzihua zhuanxing: Lilun yu duice" [Industry Digitalization Against the Strategic Background of the New Development Paradigm of "Dual Circulation": Theory and Countermeasures], *Finance and Trade Economics* 42, no. 3 (2021): 14–27; and U.S. Office of the Director of National Intelligence, *2023 Annual Threat Assessment of the U.S. Intelligence Community*, 9–10.

[45] Qian Xuefeng and Pei Ting, "Guonei guoji shuang xunhuan xin fazhan geju: Lilun luoji yu nei sheng dongli" [New Development Pattern of Domestic and International Dual Cycle: Theoretical Logic and Endogenous Power], *Journal of Chongqing University (Social Science Edition)* 27, no. 1 (2021): 14–26.

[46] "Translation: The Chinese Communist Party Central Committee and the State Council Publish the National Standardization Development Outline," Center for Security and Emerging Technology, November 19, 2021, https://cset.georgetown.edu/publication/the-chinese-communist-party-central-committee-and-the-state-council-publish-the-national-standardization-development-outline.

[47] Yang Xiaodong, "2023 Nian Quanguo Lianghui: Ningju gao shuiping keji zili ziqiang de gongshi yu liliang" [The 2023 National Two Sessions: Gathering Consensus and the Strength of High-Level Technological Self-Reliance and Self-Strengthening], *Chinese Talents*, March 2023, 24–26.

[48] Shen Kunrong and Zhao Qian, "Yi shuang xunhuan xin fazhan geju tuidong shisiwu shiqi jingji gao zhiliang fazhan" [Promoting High-Quality Economic Development during the 14th Five-Year Plan Period by Adopting New Development Pattern of Dual Cycle], *Economic Review Journal* (2020): 18–25.

the most dynamic parts of China's economy. Concomitantly, the last few years have seen a public effort to bring the tech industry squarely under the party's control. The power struggle between Jack Ma and the party over Ant Financial's failed IPO is but one example of this very public signal of the CCP's tightening grip.

China's Dual Circulation Strategy

One of the key influences on future Chinese investment is the concept of "dual circulation," a term first proposed by Xi Jinping. This strategy aims to make China less dependent on the outside world as it shifts toward a model of economic growth driven by domestic consumption, even as it also seeks to gain potential leverage by cultivating global or bilateral dependence on China's dominance of strategically targeted sectors.[49] There are two components of dual circulation: "domestic circulation," which prioritizes increasing domestic demand and lowering dependence on foreign inputs to China's economy, and "international circulation," which seeks to maintain export market shares for China and liberalize capital flows.[50] Rebalancing toward domestic demand is not all that innovative. What seems to distinguish dual circulation is the desire to replace the external demand that drove Chinese export-led growth over the previous four decades with domestic consumption met by domestic production.[51] How much of this dual circulation actually ends up driving Chinese patterns of investment remains to be seen; in theory, this strategy is designed to pursue complementary domestic as well as international goals.

The domestic circulation strategy consists of four areas of focus. First, it seeks the expansion of private consumption through expanded social welfare programs, deeper capital markets, and continued urbanization. Second, it looks to arrest the declining productivity discussed above through two lines of effort: one seeks to control, leverage, and deepen capital markets, while the other advocates for market-driven reforms that are designed to improve the

---

[49] Chen Jin, Yang Zhen, and Yin Ximing, "Shuang xunhuan xin fazhan geju xia de Zhongguo keji chuangxin zhanlüe" [China's Science and Technology Innovation Strategy under the New Development Pattern of Dual Circulation], *Modern Economic Science* 43, no. 1 (2021): 1–9.

[50] According to one Chinese observer, since the 2008 global financial crisis, China's economy "has shifted toward focusing on the domestic large circulation as the main body, with domestic demand contributing over 90% to economic growth on average, exceeding 100% in seven of those years." Wang Changlin, "Kexue renshi guonei guoji shuang xunhuan de bianzheng guanxi" [Scientific Understanding of the Dialectical Relationship between Domestic and International Dual Circulation], *People's Daily*, March 10, 2023, http://finance.people.com.cn/n1/2023/0310/c1004-32640789.html. See also Zhu, "Gao zhiliang goujian guonei guoji shuang xunhuan xin fazhan geju yanjiu."

[51] "Outline of the Plan for the Strategy to Expand Domestic Demand (2022–2035)," trans. Center for Security and Emerging Technology, March 23, 2023, https://cset.georgetown.edu/publication/china-domestic-demand-plan.

allocation of resources.[52] Whether the latter makes much headway remains to be seen, since it seems to run contrary to the party's recent actions. The third area is environmental protection. This includes efforts to encourage green technologies and renewable energy sources. The last area of domestic circulation is innovation and upgrading. These include investment programs to move Chinese industry up the value chain through efforts to indigenize technology and processes to capture more lucrative portions of production networks. There seem to be three main lines of effort that promise to influence future investment direction in China: increase and incentivize R&D spending, design reforms that attract FDI into China (with a view toward encouraging technology transfer and spillover effects), and target outward-bound Chinese FDI (e.g., BRI projects) toward specific countries and sectors (e.g., the Digital Silk Road). This last line of effort suggests that one can expect to see future BRI projects disciplined to be more structured and targeted in a way that more directly supports national goals and priorities.

There is also an international circulation dimension to dual circulation.[53] This aspect of the concept seems to involve two key elements. First, there is a desire to maintain China's export market share. As discussed above, this element has been relatively successful thus far, as China's share of global exports has increased even as its exports have become a smaller portion of GDP. The second element is capital account liberalization and the internationalization of China's domestic currency, the renminbi. This monetary dimension is one to continue watching closely. Little progress has been made toward the internationalization of the renminbi, but if the CCP were willing to relinquish greater control over its capital account, there would likely be a global appetite for the currency to play a more significant role as an alternative to the U.S. dollar. However, to date, there has been a marked political unwillingness to tolerate long-term deficits, permit greater market volatility in exchange rates, or facilitate the sorts of macroeconomic policies that would be required for the renminbi to play a greater role in international finance.[54] That said, there are clear indications of a desire to use the renminbi to transact in important commodities like oil. Beijing has also engaged in a number of bilateral swap lines with key trading partners and structured debt arrangements denominated in renminbi.

---

[52] Zhu, "Gao zhiliang goujian guonei guoji shuang xunhuan xin fazhan geju yanjiu."

[53] Jiang Xiaojuan and Meng Lijun, "Nei xunhuan wei zhu, wai xunhuan fu neng yu geng gao shuiping shuang xunhuan: Guoji jingyan yu Zhongguo shijian" [Mainly Inner Circulation, Outer Circulation Empowerment and Higher-Level Dual Circulation: International Experience and Chinese Practice], *Journal of Management World* 37, no. 1 (2021): 1–19.

[54] Chen Weidong and Zhao Xueqing, "Renminbi guoji hua fazhan lujing yanjiu: Jiyu shi nian fazhan de sikao" [Rethinking the Path of RMB: Internationalization in the Past Decade], *International Economic Review* (2020): 28–37.

Related, China has created the Cross-Border Interbank Payment System. This alternative to the global SWIFT (Society for Worldwide Interbank Financial Telecommunication) system to process payments in renminbi has attracted participation from dozens of banks in the aftermath of the financial sanctions related to Russia's invasion of Ukraine. Not surprisingly, Russia is a vociferous supporter of the internationalization of the renminbi and is increasingly using the renminbi in trade and foreign reserves as a lifeline insulated from the brunt of Western sanctions.[55] Also in the monetary realm, China continues to promote a new reserve currency based on a basket of currencies from the BRICS countries (Brazil, Russia, India, China, and South Africa). China sees these sorts of alternative orders that exclude the United States as enhancing its own regional and global leadership position. In areas that are perceived as having been "weaponized" by the United States, China will frequently seek to lead a viable alternative.

As of April 2022, the renminbi accounted for only 3% of global cross-border trade. However, growing U.S. debt and fiscal unreliability—as evidenced by the political brinksmanship over raising the debt ceiling—suggest that the privileged role of the U.S. dollar as the global reserve currency ought not be taken for granted.[56] The prospects of a sovereign default and growing Chinese economic weight in the global system provide some of the necessary precursors for a significant shift in the geopolitical landscape of international monetary relations. That said, most knowledgeable experts on these questions remain quite sanguine about the dollar's relatively unassailable reserve currency status.[57] The United States (along with the entire global economic system) derives considerable benefit and predictability from the hegemonic status of the dollar as the world's reserve currency.[58] Given what is at stake, early indicators of change to that state of affairs deserve to be watched closely, even if the near-term possibility of alteration seems remote from the current vantage point.

---

[55] Chelsey Dulaney and Evan Gershkovich, "Russia Turns to China's Yuan in Effort to Ditch the Dollar," *Wall Street Journal*, February 28, 2023, https://www.wsj.com/articles/russia-turns-to-chinas-yuan-in-effort-to-ditch-the-dollar-a8111457.

[56] Hueling Tan, "China and Russia Are Working on Homegrown Alternatives to the SWIFT Payment System. Here's What They Would Mean for the U.S. Dollar," *Business Insider*, April 28, 2022, https://www.businessinsider.com/china-russia-alternative-swift-payment-cips-spfs-yuan-ruble-dollar-2022-4.

[57] Eric Helleiner and Jonathan Kirshner, *The Great Wall of Money: Power and Politics in China's International Monetary Relations* (Ithaca: Cornell University Press, 2014), chap. 1; Barry Eichengreen et al., "Is Capital Account Convertibility Required for the Renminbi to Acquire Reserve Currency Status?" Centre for Economic Policy Research, July 24, 2022, https://cepr.org/publications/dp17498; and Jonathan Kirshner, "Dollar Primacy and American Power: What's at Stake?" *Review of International Political Economy* 15, no. 3 (2008): 418–38.

[58] Barry Eichengreen, *Exorbitant Privilege: The Rise and Fall of the Dollar and the Future of the International Monetary System* (Oxford: Oxford University Press, 2011).

Given China's dual circulation strategy, what has actually changed? As already mentioned above, the growing role of domestic consumption is clearly a real, structural shift in the composition of China's economic growth model. Most of this evolution is the natural by-product of a nearly $18 trillion economy.[59] In absolute terms, this puts China's economy in a class of its own, second only to the United States in terms of sheer size and scale.[60] Economies of such size enjoy their own internal domestic consumption engines and need not rely as heavily on exports to drive growth. Unfortunately, it is also unrealistic to expect that such large economies can sustainably grow at double-digit rates. This has led to China's overall GDP growth rate slowing to around 4.5% (down from 7.6% in the 2010s).[61]

Strategic Assessment

This section provides an assessment of what U.S. and international efforts at decoupling would mean for China's trajectory, given its economic transition to domestic demand–driven growth and interest in limiting the impact of external pressures. If China successfully transitions away from its export-driven growth model toward a consumption-driven economic engine, it could no longer feel as constrained by economic interdependence. Whether deliberate or not, the export-driven growth model has produced a strong motivation to support international stability. Conflict is generally bad for business. Since so much of its economic success has ridden on international commerce, China has had a strong incentive to maintain peace and ensure that any friction in the system (e.g., territorial conflicts with Japan or in the South China Sea) stays below the point of escalation, beyond which the economic costs prove to be too severe. While past behavior is not necessarily indicative of future strategic calculus, this "economic circuit breaker" logic seems to have held China's most aggressive nationalism below the threshold of war since 1979.

If China were to decouple from the United States or become significantly less reliant on international linkages, global integration might place fewer constraints on a domestically oriented Chinese economic growth engine. China is looking to become more autonomous, more self-sufficient, and less dependent on global linkages. Of course, such debates within China are not monolithic. For example, some voices still advocate for the liberalization

---

[59] CEIC, "China Nominal GDP."

[60] U.S. GDP over the same period was $26.47 trillion. See "Gross Domestic Product, First Quarter 2023 (Advance Estimate)," U.S. Bureau of Economic Analysis, Press Release, April 27, 2023, https://www.bea.gov/news/2023/gross-domestic-product-first-quarter-2023-advance-estimate.

[61] "Dual Circulation: China's Way of Reshoring?" Allianz, October 29, 2020, 2.

and deepening of reforms (e.g., the 2023 government work report of the Two Sessions), but even these tend to look to exploit perceived divisions among European nations and to leverage more "entrepreneurial" interests and political positions that could be more sympathetic to China to avoid decoupling.[62] This self-sufficiency is especially desirable in innovation and emerging technologies.[63] Although China might still have international ties, these ties may no longer be as central to its overall economic growth. For example, luxury goods, consumer products, international brands, and services might not exert much constraining influence since loss of access to them might not be seen as vital. On the other hand, China is likely to continue to be highly dependent on imported sources of oil, even if the economic end to which those energy resources are directed has shifted away from industrial and export production toward domestic consumption. As noted earlier, Russia has considerably increased its energy exports to China (see **Figure 4**).

Russia's pariah status as a result of its invasion of Ukraine has provided China with both a newly desperate strategic partner antagonistic toward the existing international order and a source of oil at fire-sale prices.[64] Just as Russia has long done with natural gas supplies to Europe, China is also likely to continue to seek leverage through control of critical minerals.[65] Close attention ought to be paid to the type and quantity of China's ongoing integration with the global economic system. China's stated desires to leverage its engagement with the global economy for its own narrow benefit provides little consideration for the interests of other nations. China has also demonstrated a willingness to try to leverage partner nations' economic dependence on it to its strategic advantage.

In April 2020, Xi Jinping indicated that China "must tighten international production chains' dependence on China, forming a powerful countermeasure and deterrent capability against foreigners who would artificially cut off

---

[62] See, for example, Wang Yuesheng, "Yingdui guoji jingmao fuza huanjing chongfen fahui waimao he waizi dui jingji fusu de guanjian zuoyong" [Dealing with the Intricate Global Economic and Trade Environment, Fully Leveraging Foreign Trade and Foreign Investment Play a Crucial Role in Economic Recovery], *Review of Economic Research* (2023): 16–18.

[63] Yang Xiaodong, "2023 Nian Quanguo Lianghui: Ningju gao shuiping keji zili ziqiang de gongshi yu liliang"; and Chen, Yang, and Yin, "Shuang xunhuan xin fazhan geju xia de Zhongguo keji chuangxin zhanlüe."

[64] China also sees significant opportunity to grow its ties with Central and Eastern European partners like Hungary. See Li Diao, Ding Yuzhu, and Fan Yunru, "Zhongguo yu Zhong Dong'ou guojia maoyi bianli hua wenti yanjiu" [Research on Trade Facilitation between China and Central and Eastern European Countries], *Russian, East European, and Central Asian Studies* 13 (2023): 23–45.

[65] Andrew L. Gulley, Erin A. McCullough, and Kim B. Shedd, "China's Domestic and Foreign Influence in the Global Cobalt Supply Chain," *Resources Policy* 62 (2019): 317–23; Marc Humphries, "Critical Minerals and U.S. Public Policy," Congressional Research Service, CRS Report for Congress, R45810, June 28, 2019; Steven M. Fortier et al., "USGS Critical Minerals Review," U.S. Geological Survey, June 18, 2019, 35–47, https://www.usgs.gov/publications/usgs-critical-minerals-review; and Dou Shiquan and Xu Deyi, "The Security of Critical Mineral Supply Chains," *Mineral Economics* (2022).

FIGURE 4 China's imports from Russia

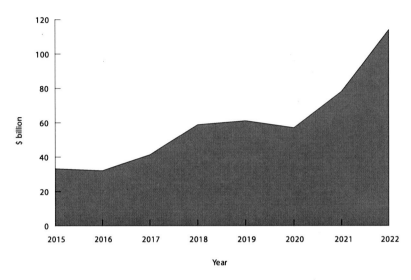

SOURCE: ITC calculations based on General Customs Administration of China statistics since January 2015.

supply [to China]."[66] Pandemic shocks illustrated the risk to global supply chains from links that were unavailable to firms that needed these inputs.[67] Dual circulation seems to encourage Chinese industrial firms to become less reliant on foreign supplies and inputs.[68] In the event that this strategy is successful, Taiwan, Malaysia, Singapore, Thailand, and Chile would be most directly affected by China's ability to indigenize capabilities that it imports today. These are the five economies most at risk of losing market share in China as it moves toward industrial autonomy. Yet there continues to be significant uncertainty around whether such a reorientation would be feasible.[69] Reducing dependence on foreign sources of supply would help make China less dependent on factors that lie largely outside the party's

---

[66] For a translation of this speech, see Xi Jinping, "Certain Major Issues for Our National Medium- to Long-Term Economic and Social Development Strategy," trans. Center for Security and Emerging Technology, November 1, 2020, https://cset.georgetown.edu/wp-content/uploads/t0235_Qiushi_Xi_economy_EN.pdf.

[67] "U.S. Worries China Will Use Supply Chains as Weapon."

[68] "Dual Circulation: China's Way of Reshoring?" 8.

[69] Such uncertainty is also reflected in Chinese discussions about the path ahead. See, for example, Wang Lili, "2023 Quanguo Lianghui: Jianding xinxin zai chufa" [With Firm Confidence, Set Off Once More], *China's Foreign Trade* (2023): 8–15.

control. As such, the dual circulation concept seems likely to appeal to a leadership intensely focused on enhancing its control as a key basis for regime security. The desire to increase the CCP's ability to directly control critical elements of the economy was likely behind the changes from the March 2023 Two Sessions meetings that moved financial regulation directly under the purview of the party (away from state regulatory bodies).[70]

Another important development that will continue to influence China's ability to direct its economic power has been Xi's efforts at party building. These have involved the rejuvenation of many of the CCP's organs that had grown largely irrelevant during the period of rapid growth since Deng Xiaoping's policy of opening and reform. There has been a pattern of increasing the capacity of the Chinese party-state to direct the behavior of commercial actors over the last several years.[71] In some instances, this has involved the creation of new bodies designed to enhance the party's ability to control all key elements of the economy and society. It has also frequently been reflected in an expansion of legal authorities and capabilities. But most often it has focused on breathing new life into what had become largely moribund organs of the party apparatus. These institutional mechanisms have provided the party with the capacity to direct China's commercial actors to behave in ways that are conducive to the party-state's interests.[72]

The threat of China's decoupling is real; however, there are a number of considerations that suggest it may not be as thorough as is sometimes portrayed. Clearly, there has been a pronounced shift away from the heady days of enthusiastic economic integration with China.[73] There is also clear political intentionality on the part of China to deliberately cultivate greater economic and strategic autonomy.[74] But the Chinese economy is so deeply entwined with regional production networks and global value chains that there is good reason to wonder about the extent to which individual firms will adopt the sorts of strategies required for widespread decoupling.[75] At the same time, China's economic ambitions may not fit well with some of its domestic

---

[70] Frank Tang, "China's Financial Overhaul Brings More Power to the Party, with US$58 Trillion in Assets at Stake," *South China Morning Post*, March 18, 2023, https://www.scmp.com/economy/china-economy/article/3213938/chinas-financial-overhaul-brings-more-power-party-us58-trillion-assets-stake.

[71] Simone McCarthy and Nectar Gan, "China Has Widened Its Already Sweeping Counter-Espionage Law. Experts Say Foreign Businesses Should Be Worried," CNN, April 27, 2023, https://www.cnn.com/2023/04/27/china/china-counter-espionage-law-revision-intl-hnk/index.html.

[72] William J. Norris, *Chinese Economic Statecraft: Commercial Actors, Grand Strategy, and State Control* (Ithaca: Cornell University Press, 2016).

[73] US-China Business Council, "Member Survey"; and "Dual Circulation: China's Way of Reshoring?" 5.

[74] Wu, "'Shuang xunhuan' xin fazhan geju de zhanlüe hanyi."

[75] Rigao Liu, Jiakun Jack Zhang, and Samantha A. Vortherms, "In the Middle: American Multinationals in China and Trade War Politics," *Business and Politics* 24, no. 4 (2022): 348–76.

political preferences or party priorities. How those incompatibilities play out remains to be seen. On the U.S. side of the ledger, efforts to broadly decouple from China seem unfeasible. Indeed, current verbiage in Washington seems to have shifted away from decoupling toward the more circumscribed term "de-risking." The United States and Europe are likely to focus their efforts on areas of dependence that have clear national security implications and where substitutability is hard to engineer.

Although the economic dimension is the most dynamic element of China's changing regional engagement, the security, diplomatic, and military components also deserve attention, given that China's growing global presence will manifest in these more traditional forms of hard power as well. For example, regional basing will continue to facilitate Chinese power-projection ambitions. Defense cooperation agreements like the one struck between China and Solomon Islands complement a growing number of dual-use port facilities and dedicated military bases around the Pacific and Indian Oceans. China's more assertive diplomatic and security position is likely to interact with the emerging economic elements discussed in this chapter to produce a potentially dangerous combination of a China that is less constrained by economic linkages. As the country pursues a more risk-acceptant strategy on issues like Taiwan, maritime territorial disputes, and clashes with India, it may be emboldened to believe that its economic fortunes are increasingly insulated from foreign dependencies.

Conversely, if China's economic strategy fails to generate the intended results and its economy stalls, this could give pause to adventurism abroad. Although it is unlikely that the regime would make significant cuts to military expenditures, it is possible that China's stalling economy may not be able to robustly sustain its military modernization (or at least perhaps not at the pace of the last two decades). Unfortunately, the opposite might also be true. If the CCP faces economic headwinds at home, there may be a temptation to generate alternative legitimacy based on nationalism.[76] In the absence of economic success, the regime could resort to aggressive nationalism and a more bellicose posture to generate rally-round-the-flag effects and distract and unite an otherwise discontented domestic population.

---

[76] Domestic political logic has a history of driving China toward harder-line approaches to sensitive issues abroad. See, for example, Jonathan Sullivan and Weixiang Wang, "China's 'Wolf Warrior Diplomacy': The Interaction of Formal Diplomacy and Cyber-Nationalism," *Journal of Current Chinese Affairs* 52, no. 1 (2023): 68–88; and William Norris, "Explaining Recent Senkaku/Diaoyu Tensions: The Domestic Dimension," *Education About Asia* 19, no. 2 (2014): 43–44.

Conclusion

Current turmoil about economic interdependence suggests continued changes in the future direction of China's political economy. This will likely also have implications for the future direction of China's economy. Reduced access to state-of-the-art technology is likely to be a drag on China's economy. According to the International Monetary Fund (IMF), "the historical decomposition shows China's potential growth peaked in 2005–06 and has fallen since in line with weaker productivity growth, less productive capital, and a shrinking workforce."[77] Its "baseline scenario" forecasts that "potential GDP growth rates could drop to about 4 percent on average between 2023–27 and 3 percent on average over 2028–37."[78] A slowing economy could limit China's geopolitical power both directly (by limiting funding for military modernization and weapons development) and indirectly (by making China less attractive to potential regional partners).

Key Uncertainties to Monitor

There are seven key uncertainties to watch going forward. The first uncertainty is the extent to which dual circulation will actually take hold. If all goes according to plan, there is the possibility of a very different Chinese economy emerging, one that is less dependent on the rest of the world.[79] The second is whether China's economy (if the dual circulation strategy succeeds) will be structured such that other nations (especially other Asia-Pacific partners, BRICs nations, and perhaps BRI partners) find that they can meaningfully benefit from it.[80] Such links might strategically incline smaller regional players toward China.

Such an alignment will likely hinge on a third area of uncertainty: China's perceived aggressiveness. If China is seen as increasingly threatening and problematic from a security point of view, the promise of any positive upside

---

[77] Helge Berger et al., "People's Republic of China: Selected Issues," International Monetary Fund, IMF Country Report, no. 23/81, February 10, 2023, 86, https://www.imf.org/en/Publications/CR/Issues/2023/02/09/Peoples-Republic-of-China-Selected-Issues-529473.

[78] Ibid., 87–88.

[79] Xu Feng et al., "Jiyu zuhe yuce moxing dui Zhongguo jingji waimao yicun du de yuce" [Prediction of China's Economic Dependence on Foreign Trade Based on the Combined Forecasting Model], *Journal of Anhui University (Natural Science Edition)* 45, no. 5 (2021): 37–44.

[80] There are indications that China seeks to continue to negotiate international institutional arrangements that it sees as beneficial. Wang Changlin, "Kexue renshi guonei guoji shuang xunhuan de bianzheng guanxi" [Scientific Understanding of the Dialectical Relationship between Domestic and International Dual Circulation], *People's Daily*, March 10, 2023, http://finance.people.com.cn/n1/2023/0310/c1004-32640789.html; and Cao Yujuan, "Jiakuai dazao guonei guoji shuang xunhuan shichang jingying bianli di" [Accelerate the Construction of Convenient Domestic and International Dual-Circulation Market Operations], *Dang Dai Guangxi*, no. 2023 (2023): 7.

that might accrue from its economic success could be overshadowed as concerned communities of shared interests and common values come closer together in oppositional alignment to China's growing power. However, if a more economically successful China requires only easily conceded deference on a limited range of foreign policy preferences, it would be much easier for other nations to bandwagon with China.

The fourth area of uncertainty surrounds the degree of success that China's indigenous innovation efforts will see over the coming decade. According to the U.S. Office of the Director of National Intelligence, "China will persist with efforts to acquire foreign science and technology information and expertise, making extensive use of foreign scientific collaborations and partnerships, investments and acquisitions, talent recruitment, economic espionage, and cyber theft to acquire and transfer technologies and technical knowledge."[81] But there remain questions about China's ability to absorb these kinds of capabilities and the extent to which it will be able to generate its own sources of innovation. China is already dominant in a number of markets important to future innovation, such as green energy. According to the International Energy Agency, the country manufactures over 80% of solar panels and dominates solar photovoltaic global supply chains at all levels. As a result, there may be a need for diversification of both raw materials and finished products in this key area of the energy transition.[82] Also in the green energy space, China is the second-largest producer of electric batteries and "controls 92% of processed materials, 71% of cell assembly, and 65% of battery components used in electric vehicles."[83]

The fifth trend to watch is the continued performance of China's economy. According to the IMF, "without reform efforts, aging and declining productivity would likely continue to suppress growth over the long term, beyond our forecast horizon," suggesting "the need to rebalance away from the investment-led, carbon-intensive, growth model towards more sustainable growth drivers, in particular consumption."[84]

An obvious sixth area of uncertainty is whether there will be an acute crisis involving Taiwan in the next few years. This development would have the potential to radically alter the strategic landscape and conditions under

---

[81] U.S. Office of the Director of National Intelligence, *2023 Annual Threat Assessment of the U.S. Intelligence Community*, 8.

[82] Naoko Eto, "How Xi Jinping Is Fortifying China's Economic Security," *Japan Times*, March 2, 2023, https://www.japantimes.co.jp/opinion/2023/03/02/commentary/world-commentary/china-economic-security.

[83] Bryce Baschuk, "U.S. Electric-Vehicle Tax Breaks Draw Ire from Allies EU, Korea," Bloomberg, September 15, 2022, https://www.bloomberg.com/news/newsletters/2022-09-15/supply-chain-latest-us-ev-tax-breaks-draw-ire-from-allies-eu-korea.

[84] Berger et al., "People's Republic of China," 90.

which China operates. Finally, the issue of Xi Jinping's succession and any associated potential instability continues to hang over Beijing's future. Even barring any health challenges before then, this will become an increasingly pressing source of uncertainty over the next decade.

The Significance of Firms: De-risking Rather Than Decoupling

An important finding from this chapter is that most firms outside the national security space prefer to continue business as usual (despite U.S.-China diplomatic and political tensions) with some limited hedging and de-risking. Thus, de-risking rather than decoupling may be a more realistic path forward (indeed, de-risking is now a goal of the Biden administration). The reality of many of China's economic linkages with the region and the rest of the world is that they are fundamentally a product of firm-level optimization. As a result, it will be firms that ultimately need to systematically re-examine their risk exposure.[85] That risk comes in at least two forms: operational risk and revenue risk.

Operational risk might involve considerations of inputs and over-reliance on China for critical goods or other types of sole-source suppliers in firms' value chains. It would also behoove firms to deliberately re-examine their value chains to identify China-related risk exposure in their manufacturing, assembly, and distribution channels. Finally, there is an important emerging operational risk associated with technology and research and development exposure to China. Firms might not be able to depend on access to technology from China and could also be concerned about the security of their own technology because of their exposure to China going forward.

Many firms also have an important China component to their revenue models that could involve increased risk. This risk can be current revenue that depends on access to the Chinese market, but it could also be related to future revenue risk based on planned growth or future opportunities in the expanding Chinese consumer market. Ultimately, de-risking will come down to an aggregated firm-level evaluation of costs and benefits. Corporate executives and boards of directors need to engage in a deliberate and systematic effort to periodically examine their firms' risk exposure to China. For some firms, the benefits will be so large that they will outweigh potential risks of such continued exposure. For others, simple moves to diversify

---

[85] My use of the term "de-risking" is more firm-centric than European Commission president Ursula von der Leyen's use. In a speech in April 2023, she mainly focused on government-driven measures and instruments. I am suggesting that individual firms need to assess the risks they are exposed to and de-risk where appropriate. See "Speech by President von der Leyen at the European Parliament Plenary on the Need for a Coherent Strategy for EU-China Relations," European Commission, April 18, 2023, https://ec.europa.eu/commission/presscorner/detail/en/speech_23_2333.

production and markets, build in contingency planning, stockpile some level of reserves, and adopt other types of proactive preparatory measures will enable them to weather future shocks more gracefully than their competitors. For those well-prepared firms, such shocks could provide an opportunity to take market share. Thoughtfully designed hypothetical tabletop exercises can productively engage the private sector to more deliberately weigh the risks and make informed decisions.

Firms that do not engage in such clear-eyed optimization will be treated more harshly by the market, while firms that have prepared for possible disruptions will be well-positioned to take market share from their competitors. Such de-risking preparation will likely entail additional costs that will need to be carefully weighed against the potential benefits. Assessing the costs and benefits will be best done at the firm level, but industry associations can play a valuable role by raising awareness, providing the appropriate data, and tailoring recommendations for some of the idiosyncratic challenges facing particular sectors. Because of the continued upside for many firms, such microeconomic de-risking is unlikely to degenerate into total decoupling at the national level.

Looking Ahead

For the region, a Chinese shift toward domestic consumption could produce at least two effects. First, it could present an opportunity for other countries in the region to supply their own exports to help meet this new source of demand. Second, if China determines that its international economic links are less indispensable than they once were, its commitment to regional stability might be more easily trumped by crisis-driven dynamics or assertive nationalism.

The most disquieting implication from this analysis is found in the context of the U.S.-China relationship. China's rise has been largely predicated on its successful integration into what was effectively a U.S.-dominated global economic order. To the extent that the economic benefits of international cooperation become less strategically significant to China, this may have the effect of lessening China's motivation to find common ground and integrate into that global community. Since 2017, the U.S.-China trade war has accelerated this dynamic. A disillusionment with dependence might "free" China to pursue its own narrow interests more aggressively without fear of what such a course of action might mean for its economic growth. Once liberal mechanisms of international peace are no longer operative, the U.S.-China relationship might be more prone to conflict and friction.

China's consumption-driven growth model would make it less reliant on the global economy. This reduced reliance promises to remove some of the external limitations that may currently be constraining China's strategic options regarding the pursuit of Chinese interests in its region and vis-à-vis the United States.

EXECUTIVE SUMMARY

This chapter examines the systematic efforts by the Japanese government to minimize security vulnerabilities from economic dependence on China and finds scarce evidence for broad decoupling.

MAIN ARGUMENT

Japanese international business has two simultaneous trends: an increased diversification of trade and investment and a deepening reliance on China in key sectors. State policy reflects this bifurcation. The state-led liberal strategy promotes regional economic integration (including with China) while maintaining policies focused on supply chain resilience, critical technologies, and diversification away from China. There is no evidence suggesting that full-scale decoupling is currently occurring or likely to occur in the near future, but there is private-sector diversification in the region. Japanese business strongly supports globalization, and it is unlikely that the Japanese government will broadly implement policies that harshly restrict business opportunities with China. However, evidence indicates that industries under threat of economic coercion or severe disruption respond to government incentives and are actively diversifying. At the same time, Japan is engaged in international efforts to improve supply chain resilience. Japan is also participating in some multilateral export controls and sanctions regimes.

POLICY IMPLICATIONS

- Japan is eager to engage in multilateral initiatives to improve supply chain resilience. The U.S. should include Japan in relevant policies to benefit from Japanese expertise and technical skill in critical technologies.

- Japan has a track record of diversification in critical minerals and their downstream products and continues to pursue more opportunities. Multilateral cooperation in these industries should be welcomed.

- Broad demands to decouple or de-risk from China will not be treated seriously by key Japanese business actors and could hinder cooperation on more targeted, though still costly, economic security measures.

Japan

Japan's Approach to Economic Security and Regional Integration

Kristin Vekasi

When a long-standing territorial dispute between Japan and China flared up in 2010, Beijing imposed an informal ban on rare earth exports to Japan. The risks of economic coercion from high levels of trade dependence were vividly revealed through this incident, and Japanese state and private actors vigorously began to diversify their supply chains. In many ways, their efforts have been successful. By 2014, Japan had gone from near 90% dependence on Chinese rare earths to less than 50% and was part of a regional critical rare earth supply chain independent of China. Shares of Chinese trade in downstream products, such as magnets, also seemed to have peaked at around 45% dependence and then held steady at around a third, with most remaining imports coming from other countries in the region. But the rare earth diversification story did not end there, demonstrating the complexity of Japan's place in the global economy and the tall barriers standing in the way of the country disentangling itself from the Chinese economy. In 2021, in the face of rising demand and limited supply, Japanese trade dependence on rare earths from China began to once again increase. In 2022, it stood at nearly 70%. Over the same time period, dependence on China for another critical mineral (lithium) had deepened, increasing from 13% in 2014 to over 60% by 2022.[1]

This dichotomous economic trend of increased diversification and deepening reliance is more broadly reflected in the Japanese

---

Kristin Vekasi is an Associate Professor in the Department of Political Science and the School of Policy and International Affairs at the University of Maine. She can be reached at <kristin.vekasi@maine.edu>.

[1] UN Comtrade, "UN Comtrade International Trade Statistics Database," available at https://comtrade.un.org.

government's policies. In recent years, Japanese foreign policy has promoted regional economic integration (including with China), a state-led approach that complements the technological and manufacturing strengths of the private sector. Policies have included negotiating bilateral and multilateral free trade or economic partnership agreements that facilitate integrated regional supply chains or distribution networks. For the private sector, in addition to "Japan branded" products such as automobiles or home electronics, the new business approach focuses on small, high value–added components that are inside non–Japanese branded products, such as smartphones. These "Japan inside" businesses require deep regional integration and complex supply chains for continued profitability and success.

However, geopolitical and epidemiological developments, particularly the U.S.-China trade conflict, the Covid-19 pandemic, China's saber-rattling toward Taiwan, and Russia's invasion of Ukraine, also threaten the ability of business actors to successfully follow a regional strategy without disruption. Concerns over high levels of economic dependence on China—either for specific raw materials and products or more generally—have led to a separate set of policies focused on resilience, diversification, and in some cases securitization of the economy. While some of the first policies were directed at rare earths, they have expanded since the onset of the Covid-19 pandemic to include other critical minerals and their downstream products, as well as pharmaceuticals, personal protective equipment, semiconductors, and other goods. In late 2021, these concerns were codified into law with the Economic Security Promotion Act (ESPA).

This chapter discusses how the Japanese economy is responding to these different sets of incentives: increased regional globalization and fragmentation of supply chains (including with China) versus increased diversification and a shift away from reliance on the Chinese market. In Japan, there is deep and broad business support for globalization. Its high value–added position in global supply chains makes a full-scale shift away from the Chinese economy unlikely, and the data and analysis presented in this chapter show that full-scale decoupling is neither occurring nor likely to occur in the near future. However, an approach of targeted economic security could position Japan to withstand (and perhaps utilize) economic coercion. There is limited evidence of Japanese firms pursuing diversification that could make the country's economy resilient to economic coercion in certain strategic sectors. Further, there is no evidence of broad decoupling; limited evidence of de-risking in strategic sectors such as critical minerals, batteries, magnets, and semiconductors; and some evidence of diversification in nonstrategic sectors such as footwear, textiles, and home electronics.

The chapter proceeds as follows. The first section describes Japan's contemporary economy and changing trade and investment patterns over the last two decades. This is followed by a comparison of the forces pushing for greater economic integration and regionalization with those pushing to economically distance from China, including a discussion of how the business community and state assess these differing perspectives. While there remains broad enthusiasm for the market opportunities found within China, there is growing concern among companies and their associations about security risks. The Japanese state is also pursuing a menu of policies, some of which continue to integrate the Japanese and Chinese economies, while others seek more separation. The chapter concludes with an analysis of trade in key sectors and firm entrants and exits to empirically assess current trends in Japan's decoupling.

Japan's Economic Position in the World

Despite years of low GDP growth and what many call "lost decades," Japan is the world's third-largest economy and is still a leader in technology and manufacturing. The Japanese economy is trade- and export-oriented, with a private sector that is deeply committed to cross-border integrated supply chains. Approximately one-third of Japan's economy is trade-based, more than in the high growth of the 1970s and twice as much as during the stagnation of the 1990s.[2] In the heyday of Japan's rapid economic growth and bubble economy, Japan-branded products were the core of the highly profitable economy. These included products such as automobiles and consumer electronics like the Sony Walkman and Panasonic televisions. At the same time, Japan was a major global player in high-tech precision components like integrated circuits. Today, Japan's economy has evolved from that model. Japanese companies still focus on high value–added precision parts, machinery, and components, but it is no longer the final Japan-branded products that are highly profitable. Instead, "Japan inside" products are what bring the highest margins to Japanese companies, with the exception of the automobile sector.[3] These products still include things like high-end chips, manufacturing equipment or materials, chemicals, and other components that require high levels of precision.[4]

---

[2] World Bank, World Bank Open Data, https://data.worldbank.org. See merchandise trade as a percent of GDP.

[3] Ministry of Economy, Trade and Industry (Japan), *2019-nenban monozukuri hakusho* [2019 Monozukuri White Paper] (Tokyo, June 2019), 22–48.

[4] Ulrike Schaede, *The Business Reinvention of Japan: How to Make Sense of the New Japan and Why It Matters* (Stanford: Stanford University Press, 2020).

This business landscape is embedded within regionalizing trade and investment patterns and supported by a growing architecture of trade and economic partnership agreements. Both of these trends—the private sector's move into niche sectors requiring cross-border integration and the state's pursuit of agreements that deepen regional trade ties, including with China—should give pause to any decoupling predictions. **Figure 1** shows Japanese imports and exports from 2000 to 2022. Before China joined the World Trade Organization (WTO) in 2001, the United States was Japan's single-largest trade partner. In the first decade after China's accession, Chinese and U.S. trade flows with Japan followed a symmetric pattern: as Chinese inflows or outflows increased, trade share with the United States decreased. Following this first reconfiguration, a similar pattern appeared between China and the rest of Asia: as trade with China decreased, trade with the rest of the region correspondingly increased. This data shows a definitive shift away from the centrality of European and U.S. trade for Japan to a pattern that is much more focused on its regional neighborhood. In 2000, 43% of Japan's trade was with other Asian countries, and 48% was with Europe and the United

FIGURE 1 Japanese exports and imports, 2000–2022

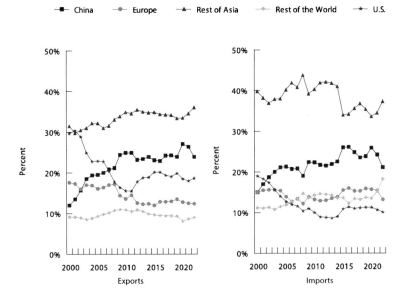

SOURCE: UN Comtrade, https://comtradeplus.un.org.

States. By 2014, Japan was exporting almost 60% of its goods to Asia and importing 64% from the region. By contrast, exports to and imports from Europe and the United States had declined to 31% and 23%, respectively. According to the most recent 2022 data, Japan now exports 60% of its goods to Asia and imports 58% of its goods from the region. These numbers, particularly those from China, are almost certainly depressed due to the Covid-19 pandemic. From 2020 to 2022, Chinese trade with Japan was markedly down. Whether this decline is evidence that Japanese companies are pursuing diversification or even exit strategies, or it is simply a temporary by-product of China's zero-Covid lockdowns, is explored later in the chapter.

Figure 2 shows Japan's stock of foreign direct investment flows from 2000 to 2021. Similar to trade, investment patterns show a shift over the last two decades toward Asia. However, China does not hold nearly as commanding a share of investment compared to trade as measured by net flows. In 2000, 67% of all Japanese FDI was in the United States and Europe, 5.5% in China or Hong Kong, and 12% in the rest of Asia. By 2014, China and Hong Kong had increased to 11% and the rest of Asia to 18%, while the United States

FIGURE 2   Percentage of Japanese FDI stock by region, 2000–2021

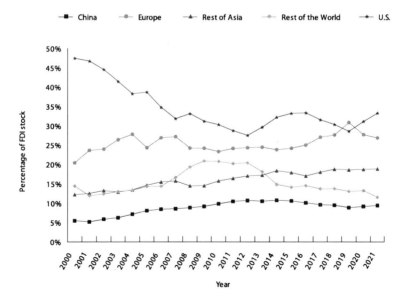

SOURCE: Japan External Trade Organization, "FDI Stock (Based on International Investment Position, Net)," 2022, https://www.jetro.go.jp/en/reports/statistics.html.

and Europe had declined to 56%. In the most recent data, 9% of Japanese FDI is in China, the rest of Asia accounts for 19%, and the United States and Europe hold 60%. More Japanese FDI is still in the United States and Europe, which remain the first and second most preferred destinations for overseas Japanese capital. That said, there are over ten thousand Japanese subsidiaries doing business in China, and 23% of Japanese overseas subsidiaries were located in China in 2022.[5] Japanese FDI in China has been a core part of the global Japanese business approach, including the "Japan inside" position, which takes advantage of the unique niche strengths of Japanese firms in global supply chains.

The Japanese state is pursuing a regional architecture friendly to a liberal trade regime and the strengths of the Japanese private sector. The Ministry of Economy, Trade and Industry (METI) has focused on products that are both highly profitable and where Japan has a major global value share by identifying them as "niche sectors."[6] These are things like materials or machinery to make advanced chips, components in smartphones, and medical equipment. As Ulrike Schaede explains, these shifts are responses to fierce market competition, largely from China:

> Companies have begun to augment the existing industrial structure… in particular in product categories where they can own or can build core competencies that Chinese companies, in particular, either do not have yet or do not want. These industry segments involve high-tech, very difficult-to-imitate and difficult-to-make manufacturing products, such as advanced materials based on specialty chemicals, and they are often in small niches.… Thus, Japan's new strategy to compete with China is to dominate through an aggregate niche strategy: an approach in which Japan competes against, and coexists with, its giant neighbor as an agile, technically sophisticated leader in a set of advanced products and industries critical to the global supply chain.[7]

Such niche products are often invisible to consumers—hence, the "Japan inside" label. These products and, more importantly, their manufacturing models require integration into cross-border supply chains, particularly those that include China, in order to retain profitability. Japan neither holds nor is pursuing end-to-end domestic supply chains for most of its most profitable products. The country does not hold a comparative advantage in many of the production stages and would have large efficiency costs. Rather, Japanese manufacturing is located at the high value–added downstream of

---

[5] *Kaigai shinshutsu kigyou souran 2023* [Overseas Japanese Companies Data 2023] (Tokyo: Toyo Keizai, 2023).

[6] Ministry of Economy, Trade and Industry (Japan), *2019-nenban monozukuri hakusho*, 22–48.

[7] Schaede, *The Business Reinvention of Japan*, 4.

the production process and relies on other countries (typically in Asia) for raw materials, some intermediate components, and final assembly.[8]

Japan's economic diplomacy over the past two decades has also reflected the shift from Japan-branded to Japan-inside products. The Japanese government has supported partnerships and free trade agreements that not only lower trade barriers and increase market access but also push for shared production standards, as well as shared labor and environmental standards to some extent.[9] These agreements facilitate deeply integrated regional supply chains by lowering costs and increasing confidence that components and processes in different countries will seamlessly work together in the assembly of final products. This diplomatic approach, the "state-led liberal strategy," has been led by the government, not the private sector.[10]

One example of such an agreement was the Trans-Pacific Partnership (TPP), rebranded as the Comprehensive and Progressive Agreement for Trans-Pacific Partnership (CPTPP) after the United States withdrew in 2017. The CPTPP facilitates supply chain integration by establishing "rules in a wide range of areas, such as intellectual property, electronic commerce, state-owned enterprises, and the environment while creating the foundation for further expanding a free and fair economic order in the region."[11] More recently, the Regional Comprehensive Economic Partnership (RCEP), which has fifteen regional members and came into force in 2022, encourages regional production networks by lowering costs via the new cumulative Rules of Origin agreement.[12] Since the agreement went into effect, companies have followed these rules to lower costs for supply chains based in Northeast and Southeast Asia.[13] While these trade initiatives are state-led, the Japanese business community, particularly large businesses represented by organizations such as Keidanren (the Japanese Business Federation) or Keizai Doyukai (the Japan

---

[8] According to the "smile curve" model of supply chains, the most profitable elements are at the initial upstream research and design stages and the final downstream stages. Midstream production stages, particularly those not involving technical expertise, add lower value. See Gary Gereffi, *Global Value Chains and Development: Redefining the Contours of 21st Century Capitalism* (Cambridge: Cambridge University Press, 2018).

[9] Ministry of Foreign Affairs (Japan), "Free Trade Agreement (FTA) / Economic Partnership Agreement (EPA) and Related Initiatives," https://www.mofa.go.jp/policy/economy/fta/index.html.

[10] Saori N. Katada, *Japan's New Regional Reality: Geoeconomic Strategy in the Asia-Pacific* (New York: Columbia University Press, 2020).

[11] "Signing of the Comprehensive and Progressive Agreement for Trans-Pacific Partnership," Ministry of Foreign Affairs (Japan), Press Release, March 9, 2018, https://www.mofa.go.jp/press/release/press4e_001944.html.

[12] Asian Development Bank, *An Analysis of the Product-Specific Rules of Origin of the Regional Comprehensive Economic Partnership* (Mandaluyong City: Asian Development Bank, 2022), https://www.adb.org/publications/product-specific-rules-origin-rcep.

[13] Ministry of Economy, Trade and Industry (Japan), "Nihonshokokaigisho de no gensanchi shomeisho hakkyu" [Certificate of Origin Issues by the Japanese Chamber of Commerce and Industry], https://www.meti.go.jp/policy/external_economy/trade_control/boekikanri/gensanchi/coo.html.

Association of Corporate Executives), has broadly supported them. However, these agreements were also politically costly, particularly the CPTPP, which asked for significant and long-resisted market access concessions for Japanese agriculture. Thus, the government has made trade integration a political priority, despite domestic contestation.[14]

The configurations of Japan's trade agreements show that regional integration—including with China—is not just due to the private sector seeking higher profits. It is also part of the Japanese government's institutional response to the changing balance of economic power. China is a major player in the RCEP, which is led by the Association of Southeast Asian Nations (ASEAN), and the Japanese government has not excluded China as an economic partner. Japanese participation in the U.S.-led Indo-Pacific Economic Framework (IPEF) is not solely about economic security but also about continuing to pursue a state-led liberal strategy with the United States after it withdrew from the TPP. The high utilization rates of the agreement similarly show Japanese companies' enthusiasm for integrating into these regional supply chains, which include China as a key player in both midstream and downstream production.[15] Against these economic and political trends of further integration, the next section considers an alternative perspective focused on economic security.

The Case for Decoupling: The Economic Security Perspective

Concurrent with the economic opportunities that have emerged, Japan has also been exposed to geopolitical business risks and has become warier of globalization without more national security guardrails. The government is particularly sensitive to these concerns. At the same time, the private sector is simultaneously embracing a securitized approach to economic relations with China, even as it still enthusiastically pursues market opportunities there.

The contemporary situation to some extent resembles the "cold politics, hot economics" situation of the 2000s and 2010s, where the economic relationship between Japan and China flourished even as political relations soured, sometimes severely. In that context, political frictions largely unrelated to state-level strategic economic competition or market concerns of the business sector periodically severely disrupted diplomacy. Amid the political

---

[14] Mireya Solís, *Dilemmas of a Trading Nation: Japan and the United States in the Evolving Asia-Pacific Order* (Washington, D.C.: Brookings Institution Press, 2017).

[15] Ministry of Economy, Trade and Industry (Japan), "Nihonshokokaigisho de no gensanchi shomei-sho hakkyu."

crises of the 2000s, economic relations were not only robust in the face of political challenges but in fact skyrocketed upward (see Figure 1), defying expectations that popular nationalist protests, boycotts, or a diplomatic freeze would chill the Japanese private sector's appetite for business in China.[16] In the 2010s, however, a series of political crises both confirmed and challenged the "cold politics, hot economics" formulation in ways that inform predictions about how the private sector will respond to increased political and security risks today. Nonetheless, a crucial difference is that the current securitization of the economy arises from state-level security concerns directly related to economic relations in all the key stakeholder countries.

The crises of the 2010s revealed political risks for Japanese companies doing business or trade with China. First, in 2010 the collision of a Chinese fishing trawler with Japanese coast guard boats near the disputed Senkaku/Diaoyu Islands resulted (in part) in the informal ban of rare earth exports to Japan.[17] In 2012, Japan's de facto nationalization of the same islands led to a two-year diplomatic freeze, popular protests and calls for boycotts, and isolated incidents of violence against Japanese businesses and properties in China.[18] High-visibility Japanese companies found themselves targeted by nationalist activists and locked out of business opportunities. Both of these crises presented business risks but were actively managed by Japanese companies in order to maintain an economic relationship with China.[19] With respect to trade, while imports from China were unaffected, Japanese exports declined until Prime Minister Shinzo Abe and President Xi Jinping shook hands at the 2014 Asia-Pacific Economic Cooperation (APEC) summit.[20]

Japanese companies reacted and adjusted to these challenges in a variety of ways.[21] For the most part, companies (especially smaller ones focused on manufacturing and export rather than direct-to-consumer sales) took heart from reassurances of safety and business continuity from local Chinese officials and Japanese business organizations based in China, kept their heads

---

[16] Christina L. Davis and Sophie Meunier, "Business as Usual? Economic Responses to Political Tensions," *American Journal of Political Science* 55, no. 3 (2011): 628–46.

[17] Sophia Kalantzakos, *China and the Geopolitics of Rare Earths* (Oxford: Oxford University Press, 2017); and Kristin Vekasi, "Politics, Markets, and Rare Commodities: Responses to Chinese Rare Earth Policy," *Japanese Journal of Political Science* 20, no. 1 (2019): 2–20.

[18] Yanming Li, *Nicchuu kankei to nihon keizaikai: kokkou seijouka kara "seirei keinetsu" made* [Japan-China Relations and the Japanese Business Community: From Normalization to "Cold Politics, Hot Economics"] (Tokyo: Seiso Shobo, 2015); and Keisuke Iida, *Japan's Security and Economic Dependence on China and the United States: Cool Politics, Lukewarm Economics* (Abingdon: Routledge, 2018).

[19] Kristin Vekasi, *Risk Management Strategies of Japanese Companies in China: Political Crisis and Multinational Firms* (Abingdon: Routledge, 2019).

[20] Xiaojun Li and Adam Y. Liu, "Business as Usual? Economic Responses to Political Tensions between China and Japan," *International Relations of the Asia-Pacific* 19, no. 2 (2019): 213–36.

[21] For more detail, see Vekasi, *Risk Management Strategies of Japanese Companies in China*.

down, and mostly calmly stayed the course. Some companies, particularly those that had been directly targeted, invested in public diplomacy, largely under the moniker of corporate social responsibility.[22] At the same time, companies in some sectors began to diversify out of China, following the logic of the "China Plus One" strategy.[23] While they largely did not exit or retreat from trade with China, a significant proportion of their new economic activity shifted from China to Southeast Asia, particularly in sectors that had been affected by the political crises. However, the shift in trade and investment is only observed as a share of new activity. Even though the share of new cumulative trade and investment in Southeast Asia increased, while China's share of trade decreased, it should be noted that overall trade and investment in both countries increased. While Japanese companies were beginning to actively seek new regional opportunities to lower geopolitical risk and production costs, China remained attractive as an investment destination. Part of the attraction is "structurally locked in place."[24] Japanese production networks depend on manufacturers in regional production ecologies in China that make it impossible for a firm to exit or even relocate.

Throughout this period, the policies of the Japanese government vis-à-vis private sector diversification from China were relatively muted, except in one notable case: rare earths. Although the Japanese state apparatus (particularly acting through the government-funded Japan External Trade Organization, or JETRO) had encouraged Japanese companies to avoid overdependence on China as far back as the early 2000s, this encouragement was relatively mild. However, in the case of rare earths, a variety of state agencies, including METI, the Ministry of Foreign Affairs, and the publicly owned Japan Oil, Gas and Metals Corporation (JOGMEC), cooperated with the private sector to diversify with some success.[25] With the assistance of public funding, Japanese companies have worked with Australian and Malaysian partners to establish a rare earth supply chain without China.

The three major shocks—the U.S.-China trade war, the Covid-19 pandemic, and the full-scale Russian invasion of Ukraine—occurred in this context. In particular, the effects of the latter two shocks on supply chain resiliency were broadly visible even to the general public and led to an

---

[22] Kristin Vekasi, "Transforming Geopolitical Risk: Public Diplomacy of Multinational Firms for Foreign Audiences," *Chinese Journal of International Politics* 10, no. 1 (2017): 95–129.

[23] "China Plus One" is a business strategy that aims to diversify business away from China and into other growing economies, many of which are in Southeast Asia.

[24] Vekasi, *Risk Management Strategies of Japanese Companies in China*, 92.

[25] Vekasi, "Politics, Markets, and Rare Commodities"; and Eugene Gholz and Llewelyn Hughes, "Market Structure and Economic Sanctions: The 2010 Rare Earth Elements Episode as a Pathway Case of Market Adjustment," *Review of International Political Economy* 28, no. 3 (2021): 611–34.

acceleration of the shift toward economic security in Japan. This approach is clearly articulated in the 2022 National Security Strategy:

> Economic security is to ensure Japan's national interests, such as peace, security, and economic prosperity, by carrying out economic measures…Japan will coordinate ideas on necessary economic measures and execute these measures… to enhance Japan's self-reliance and to secure the advantage and indispensability concerning our technologies and others. Specifically, Japan will reinforce its mechanisms for promoting economic security policies, and work with its ally and like-minded countries, as well as in cooperation with the private sector, to take measures…in a whole-of-government manner.[26]

In particular, the strategy document points to curbing "excessive dependence on specific countries" and identifies semiconductors, rare earths, and other "critical goods" as central to the policy. Although China is not named as the "specific country," economic security and supply chain resiliency policies in Japan are highly focused on China's perceived economic threats.[27]

The economic security approach has three major components. First, the Japanese government supports private-sector economic security efforts through industrial policy, which includes subsidies and incentives to diversify critical or strategic sectors as well as financial support for the development of emerging technologies. The second element is ESPA. Planning for this piece of legislation began in 2019, largely due to concerns about the deteriorating U.S.-China relationship and pressure from the United States to deepen security cooperation on all fronts. It passed into law in May 2022 and implementation is ongoing. The final element is multilateralism and the new approaches Japan is taking to increase its economic security through international cooperation.

With respect to industrial policy, the first major case in this era was government support offered to the private sector following the crisis over rare earth exports. The next, and broader, wave of industrial policy did not occur until the pandemic. METI, in conjunction with JETRO, offered financial support to Japanese companies to either return production of critical materials to Japan (reshoring) or diversify production to Southeast Asia, particularly Vietnam, Thailand, and Indonesia.[28] The primary sectors that were targeted by these industrial policies, for which there have been

---

[26] Ministry of Foreign Affairs (Japan), *National Security Strategy* (Tokyo, December 2022), https://www.mofa.go.jp/fp/nsp/page1we_000081.html.

[27] Akira Igata and Brad Glosserman, "Japan's New Economic Statecraft," *Washington Quarterly* 44, no. 3 (2021): 25–42.

[28] Mireya Solís, "The Big Squeeze: Japanese Supply Chains and Great Power Competition," in *Joint U.S.-Korea Academic Studies 2021*, ed. Gilbert Rozman (Washington, D.C.: Korea Economic Institute, 2021); and Japan External Trade Organization, "Kaigai sapuraichen tagen-ka-to shien jigyo no sabisu" [Overseas Supply Chain Diversification Support Project], https://www.jetro.go.jp/services/supplychain.

eight rounds of awards, included medical supplies and personal protective equipment, semiconductors, batteries, magnets, and critical minerals.

ESPA was developed by an interagency process via the Cabinet Office in close consultation with members of the business community and other experts.[29] The Cabinet Office convened the Expert Panel on Economic Security Legislation comprising eighteen representatives: nine academics, three representatives from business consulting firms, and six representatives of business, including Keidanren, Keizai Doyukai, the Japan Chamber of Commerce and Industry (JCCI), ANA Holdings, Canon, and Sumitomo.[30] The members of the business community represented large and multinational firms, with the exception of the JCCI, which has more small and medium-sized enterprises (SMEs) in its ranks.

There are four primary elements in ESPA. First, it outlines new protections on sensitive intellectual property by keeping patents for technologies deemed potentially detrimental to national security secret for a time and compensating firms that are unable to publish them. The second element promotes public-private partnerships in the research and development of critical technologies. This section focuses on emerging technologies, particularly in areas that might give the Japan Self-Defense Forces new capacity and increase Japan's deterrence and military readiness. Third, ESPA aims to enhance the security of core infrastructure, including energy, water, telecommunications, finance, transportation, postal services, and of course cybersecurity. The last element is supply chain security. ESPA has targeted industries that the Cabinet Office has identified as core to Japan's national security. In December 2022 the Cabinet Office specified eleven critical products: antibiotics, fertilizers, permanent magnets, machine tools and industrial robotics, specific aircraft parts, semiconductors, batteries, computer programs used for cloud services, conventional combustible natural gas, critical minerals, and specific marine equipment.[31] These products are still broadly defined, and officials must narrow the scope of possible targets for subsidies and support. When companies in the targeted sectors wish to receive subsidies, they apply to the Cabinet Office section on economic security, or alternatively the Cabinet Office identifies promising companies. If decoupling from China happens, it will most likely be in these targeted sectors.

---

[29] Izumi Koyu et al., "Japan's Economic Security Promotion Act: Background and Overview," *Asia-Pacific Review* 29, no. 3 (2022): 28–55.

[30] Cabinet of Japan, "Keizai anzen hosho hosei ni kansuru yushikisha kaigi no kaisai ni tsuite" [On Convening the Expert Panel on Economic Security Legislation], July 25, 2020, https://www.cas.go.jp/jp/seisaku/keizai_anzen_hosyohousei/r4_dai1/siryou1.pdf.

[31] Cabinet of Japan, "Outline of the Economic Security Promotion Act," December 2022, available at https://www.japaneselawtranslation.go.jp/outline/75/905R403.pdf.

Japan has also pursued multiple international efforts on economic security and supply chain resilience. Japan and the United States, in particular, have deepened cooperation in sensitive and strategic sectors. Before the passage of ESPA, the two countries had pledged cooperation in critical technologies through initiatives like the U.S.-Japan Competitiveness and Resilience Partnership, as well as supply chain resiliency efforts that can defend against attempts at economic coercion or disruptions from other risks.[32] For technology cooperation, one of the goals of ESPA is to facilitate private-sector cooperation in the U.S.-Japan defense relationship by tightening patent secrecy and establishing a clearance system that is acceptable to the U.S. government.[33] The two allies have also materially cooperated on an offensive economic security approach in conjunction with the Netherlands: export controls on advanced semiconductor equipment to China.[34]

In addition to bilateral efforts, Japan has been developing supply chain resilience through forums like the G-7 and the IPEF. The G-7 explicitly adopted a coordinated economic security approach, culminating thus far in a 2023 joint statement that aligns with Japan's ESPA goals of resilient supply chains, the protection of critical infrastructure, and defense against economic coercion.[35] Within the IPEF, there are efforts to coordinate efforts across the region and create more geographically diversified production capacity. Thus far, many of these efforts have focused on critical minerals and semiconductor cooperation with Taiwan. In the future, there could be a broader approach to building supply chain resilience with like-minded or friendly countries.[36]

One such country is India. The Japanese government, as well as the Japanese private sector, has long wanted India to be an alternative to China for Japanese investment, production, and supply chain diversification. However, economic statistics do not yet bear out this enthusiasm.[37] While Japanese trade and investment in India have tripled and trade volume has

---

[32] White House, "U.S.-Japan Competitiveness and Resilience (CoRe) Partnership," Fact Sheet, April 16, 2021, https://www.whitehouse.gov/briefing-room/statements-releases/2021/04/16/fact-sheet-u-s-japan-competitiveness-and-resilience-core-partnership.

[33] Erika Kobayashi, "Japan Plans Security Clearances Similar to U.S. and Europe," *Nikkei Asia*, June 7, 2023, https://asia.nikkei.com/Politics/Defense/Japan-plans-security-clearances-similar-to-U.S.-and-Europe.

[34] Tim Kelly and Miho Uranaka, "Japan Restricts Chipmaking Equipment Exports as It Aligns with U.S. China Curbs," Reuters, March 31, 2023, https://www.reuters.com/technology/japan-restrict-chipmaking-equipment-exports-aligning-it-with-us-china-curbs-2023-03-31.

[35] "G7 Leaders' Statement on Economic Resilience and Economic Security," White House, May 20, 2023, https://www.whitehouse.gov/briefing-room/statements-releases/2023/05/20/g7-leaders-statement-on-economic-resilience-and-economic-security.

[36] "Indo-Pacific Nations Vow to Fortify Supply Chains for Critical Items," *Japan Times*, May 28, 2023, https://www.japantimes.co.jp/news/2023/05/28/business/us-indo-pacific-deal.

[37] UN Comtrade, "UN Comtrade International Trade Statistics Database"; and Deloitte, "India-Japan Trade Relations: Catalysing Mutually Beneficial Ties," December 2022, https://www2.deloitte.com/content/dam/Deloitte/in/Documents/finance/in-India-Japan-Trade-Relations-report-noexp.pdf.

increased by seven times over the past two decades, there has not been a corresponding increase in economic share, as has been observed in Southeast Asia. The enthusiasm was evident early in Shinzo Abe's conceptualization of the region as the "Indo-Pacific" and has continued with Japan's key role in the creation of the Quad (comprising Australia, India, Japan, and the United States). As early as 2006, Abe saw India as key to "Japan's national interest" and to countering Chinese regional hegemony,[38] and in 2015 he commented that the country was "blessed with the largest potential for development of any bilateral relationship anywhere in the world."[39] In the early years of the crisis over rare earths, some Japanese state money went to India, although those investments have yet to come to fruition.

In summary, Japan has at least two decades of experience balancing political uncertainties with profitable economic enterprise. The contemporary landscape differs from the "cold politics, hot economics" era in that the Japanese government is taking a more active role in promoting diversification and the explicit securitization of specific sectors by introducing new incentives. However, Japanese companies have extensive experience dealing with the uncertainties and risks of doing business with China, even when political relations get tense.

Corporate Perspectives

Business with China

From a business perspective, China's rise generally incentivizes deeper economic cooperation. Japanese companies initially invested in China to take advantage of the "world's factory" to cheaply manufacture goods for export. But China is no longer the country with the lowest wages or most attractive investment incentives, and Japanese companies' goals have shifted accordingly. In 2023, less than 9.2% of Japanese firms invested in China for its low labor costs, compared with 12.2% in 2010. Notably, 23.0% of firms reported activity in a global production network and 29.2% reported local market access as their investment goals in 2010, compared with 31.5% and 26.3%, respectively, in 2010, showing a decrease in firms embedded in production networks and an increase in those seeking access to Chinese customers.[40] These numbers

---

[38] Tobias Harris, *The Iconoclast: Shinzo Abe and the New Japan* (London: Hurst, 2020), 237.

[39] Ministry of Foreign Affairs (Japan), *Diplomatic Bluebook 2016* (Tokyo, July 2016), chap. 1, https://www.mofa.go.jp/policy/other/bluebook/index.html.

[40] *Kaigai shinshutsu kigyou souran 2010* [Overseas Japanese Companies Data 2010] (Tokyo: Toyo Keizai, 2010); and *Kaigai shinshutsu kigyou souran 2023*. Note that in the 2023 survey, Toyo Keizai specified "international production networks" and "international distribution networks" as possible goals, whereas in the 2010 survey it combined these categories and used different terminology.

alone provide sobering skepticism on both the willingness and ease for Japanese business activity or trade to shift from China.

Annual surveys conducted by the Japan Bank for International Cooperation on the attitudes of Japanese companies are in line with the data reported by Toyo Keizai. From 2007 to 2021, there has been remarkable stability in both the benefits that companies seek when doing business in China and the risks they cite. The top draw is the current size and future potential of China's domestic consumer market, with the number of firms citing its appeal more than doubling from 30% to 66%. Risks include rising labor costs (68%) and fierce market competition (64%), as well as a lack of transparency in the system, intellectual property rights issues, and government investment restrictions (all 40% or less). Risk assessments have not changed significantly over the past fifteen years. In short, the market appeal of China for the Japanese business community is seemingly as compelling today as in the past, and market risk assessments are unchanged. Given this data, the possibility of finding evidence of decoupling remains dubious.

Corporate Responses to the Economic Security Approach

If decoupling is to happen between Japan and China, the most likely place to find it is under the auspices of ESPA and the sectors or products it targets. Looking at the business community's reactions to this legislation gives insight into how it may respond to the new incentives and environment. Surveys of Japanese companies directly asking about economic security show awareness and concern on the part of businesspeople, particularly those in large firms. A 2021 survey by the Asia-Pacific Initiative (API) of mostly large companies and research institutes showed that 98% of respondents were somewhat or very aware of economic security and that 87% of those same firms were making specific efforts to address the issue, with half attempting to either shift or diversify their suppliers.[41] In contrast, a 2022 survey that included SMEs found that 30.2% of respondents did not know or understand whether the economic security law would affect their business and an additional 24.6% believed it would have no effect.[42] While the API survey showed 50.6% of respondents taking action to diversify, the Teikoku Databank survey found that only 20.5% of large firms and 17.5% of SMEs were doing the same.

The surveys contain common themes: companies want more political certainty from their own government and from the United States and fewer

---

[41] "Main Survey Results (Key Findings): 100 Companies' Responses to the Economic Security Survey," Asia Pacific Initiative, December 24, 2021, https://apinitiative.org/GaIeyudaTuFo/wp-content/uploads/2021/12/API-Economic-Security-Survey-Key-Findings_Dec2021.pdf.

[42] "Keizai anzen hosho ni taisuru kigyo no ishiki chosa" [Survey on Corporate Awareness of Economic Security], Teikoku Databank, July 7, 2022, https://www.tdb.co.jp/report/watching/press/pdf/p220702.pdf.

national security–related regulations, but they also acknowledge the risks arising from the geographic concentration of supply chains. The biggest challenge for addressing economic security issues was uncertainty in U.S.-China relations (75%), followed by reasons related to uncertainty and information in the political environment, including risk assessment (62%), gathering information on international affairs (57%), and uncertainty in Japanese government policy (44%). One respondent in the Teikoku survey remarked that the biggest challenge was "difficulty securing raw materials or other necessary resources from alternative sources, especially for materials concentrated in one area/country." Companies also cited the challenge of future economic security regulations shrinking their business in China or increasing the uncertainty of the business environment. While many Japanese companies were concerned about long-term business success in China due to uncertainty and changes in Chinese government policy (76%), many companies also cited uncertainty in the U.S. political environment as a possible business risk.

Companies want the government to take profitability and the corporate perspective seriously in the policymaking and implementation process, as well as more clarification on Japan's economic security policy. While the API survey was conducted prior to the bill's implementation, the Teikoku Databank survey was conducted afterward, and the calls for clarity had not decreased. A key takeaway of the surveys is that economic security risks are largely perceived through the lens of U.S.-China competition, with the possible exception of raw materials and energy resources. There, high levels of dependence on single geographic sources came to the forefront and were more aligned with the government's national security mindset.

Representative industry and corporate associations, in addition to companies, show a similar dual approach to economic relations with China as the Japanese government. They recognize concerns about dependence on a single supplier, and some acknowledge the security risks, but China is still key to their current and future business plans. Business associations consistently express concerns about uncertainties arising from new policies from their own government. Finally, some industry associations and companies highlight the opportunities to receive more support from the state or gain new domestic markets under the economic security approach. This is particularly evident for batteries and pharmaceuticals, but also for SMEs that are more domestically focused. Information technology firms, including those involved with cloud computing, are more reluctant to incur the high costs that might be needed for compliance with the new legislation or economic security approach.

With some exceptions, business groups and associations are cautiously supportive of ESPA. The largest and arguably most influential group—Keidanren—has acknowledged that there are geopolitical risks while emphasizing the importance of economic relations with China. In March 2022 a Keidanren press release called for the early passage of ESPA:

> As the international situation becomes increasingly severe, it is no longer possible to separate the economy and security, and ensuring security on the economic front is also an urgent issue...[B]ased on the recommendations compiled through intensive discussions by the Expert Panel on Economic Security Legislation, the bill takes into account freedom of economic activity and consistency with international rules as a whole.... On the other hand...the targets should be narrowed down as much as possible so as not to place an excessive burden on business operators.[43]

This quote highlights the ambivalence in the business community, which emphasizes that "full consideration should be given to compatibility with free economic activities" while "implementing economic measures to ensure security."[44] Both Keizai Doyukai and the JCCI expressed similar concerns about the balance between efficiency, business opportunity, and national security.[45] While generally demonstrating support, Keizai Doyukai emphasized concerns about the possible discretionary expansion of the law's coverage. Member companies expressed concern that as emerging technologies develop, they will be constrained by regulations made before the nature of the technologies and their development are truly understood.[46] A JCCI member company summarized this perspective: "I understand the importance of economic security, but I feel that the enforcement of the law may become an excessive burden."[47]

In addition to regulatory burdens, company representatives also expressed concerns about capacity. The JCCI emphasized that an "international division of labor" and "Japanese overseas economic activities" are key to Japan's

---

[43] "Keizai anzen hosho suishin hoan no soki seiritsu o motomeru" [Call for the Early Passage of the Economic Security Promotion Bill], Keidanren, March 3, 2022, https://www.keidanren.or.jp/policy/2022/025.html.

[44] "Toward the Reconstruction of the Free and Open International Economic Order," Keidanren, September 13, 2022, https://www.keidanren.or.jp/en/policy/2022/081_proposal.html.

[45] Kengo Sakurada, "Statement by Kengo Sakurada, Chairman of Keizai Doyukai on Enactment of Law for Promotion of Economic Security," Keizai Doyukai, May 11, 2022, https://www.doyukai.or.jp/en/chairmansmsg/articles/ksakurada/220511a.html; and Japan Chamber of Commerce and Industry (JCCI), "Chiseigaku risuku, u~izu korona jidai ni okeru chushokigo no kaigai bijinesu sokushin ni mukete o kohyo 'teigen'" [Announcement of Proposal to the Government Geopolitical Risk, Toward Promoting Overseas Business of SMEs in the Era of Corona], October 10, 2022, https://www.tokyo-cci.or.jp/file.jsp?id=1032126.

[46] Sakurada, "Statement by Kengo Sakurada, Chairman of Keizai Doyukai on Enactment of Law for Promotion of Economic Security."

[47] JCCI, "Chiseigaku risuku, u~izu korona jidai ni okeru chushokigo no kaigai bijinesu sokushin ni mukete o kohyo 'teigen.'"

economic prosperity and that Japan's economic partnership agreements are critical for making those overseas relationships work. However, it also expressed concern about the capacity of SMEs to build resilient supply chains or diversify due to a lack of financial and human resources. While large companies may have subsidiaries in multiple countries, there are many Japanese SMEs that have only a single subsidiary in China and do not have the capital to diversify.[48] Other companies are "locked in place" in production networks, although their number is on the decline.

At the same time, others see opportunities stemming from economic security. The JCCI emphasized that support for domestic reshoring of critical and strategic industries could be a meaningful business opportunity for SMEs that are unable to compete with the complex multi-country supply chains of large manufacturers.[49] Similarly, in the Teikoku Databank survey, one respondent commented that "if overseas supply chains are returned [reshored], I hope that will increase sales opportunities for my company."[50] The Japan Pharmaceutical Manufacturers Association recognized the increasingly insecure international situation and how pharmaceuticals could be a strategic asset, saying that the time has come to discuss pharmaceutical industry policy from "the perspective of national security policy."[51] Similarly, the Battery Association for Supply Chain specifically mentioned the difficulty of competing with China and states optimistically that cutting-edge technologies could propel Japanese companies forward in the industry, commenting that "the U.S. and China are decoupling their supply chains, and cheapness won't be the only way to measure value in the self-driving age."[52] These sectors or companies may find new competitive advantages when economic security is taken into consideration.

Finally, some groups were more adamant in their reluctance to consider national security concerns. Citing the unpredictability arising from U.S.-China frictions and pandemic-related issues, the JCCI in China specifically emphasized the importance of China for Japanese firms:

---

[48] Vekasi, *Risk Management Strategies of Japanese Companies in China*, chap. 4.

[49] JCCI, "Chiseigaku risuku, u~izu korona jidai ni okeru chushokigo no kaigai bijinesu sokushin ni muketo o kohyo 'teigen.'"

[50] "'Keizai anzen hosho ni taisuru kigyo no ishiki chosa.'"

[51] "'Seiyakukyo kaicho kisha kaiken' o kaisai okada yasushi shin kaicho ga shoshin hyomei" [Press Conference by the Heads of the Pharmaceutical Manufacturers of Japan: New Chairman Yasushi Okada Announces His Views], Japan Pharmaceutical Manufacturers Association, May 20, 2021, https://www.jpma.or.jp/news_room/newsletter/204/04tn-01.html.

[52] Shoya Okinaga, "Japan Battery Material Producers Lose Spark as China Races Ahead," *Nikkei Asia*, April 4, 2022, https://asia.nikkei.com/Business/Materials/Japan-battery-material-producers-lose-spark-as-China-races-ahead.

> Japanese companies are striving to develop with China in the future as the economy becomes globalized and supply chains become complicatedly intertwined.... Japanese companies hope to further expand their businesses in China and continue contributing to the development of China's economy and society in the future, and for this reason, it is expected that the business environment in China will improve, and the predictability will increase.[53]

The Japan Electronics and Information Technology Industries Association, while acknowledging the government's dictates to develop domestic cloud-based storage and data sovereignty capacity, commented that "companies have *no choice* but to deal with regulations in relation to economic security" (emphasis added).[54] For sectors like information technology where compliance with economic security legislation is difficult, or where companies are already deeply invested in China, any form of decoupling or additional security procedures are costly and unwelcome.

Large Japanese companies and business associations had a seat at the table in the formulation of ESPA. To some extent, the concerns that businesses expressed about the final version were reflected in the bargaining process, resulting in the final legislation having lighter regulatory burdens and penalties. The penalties for noncompliance with the patent protections in ESPA are up to one year's imprisonment or a fine of up to 500,000 yen (approximately $5,000), far more lenient than what some of the national security bureaucrats had initially proposed. There are concerns within the Ministry of Defense, for example, that the law is not strong enough to truly protect critical technologies or to deter the private sector from simply going its own way. Similarly, although the drafters of the legislation considered an outward foreign investment screening process for sensitive sectors, the provision was opposed by businesses and did not survive the negotiations.

In summary, while there are compelling reasons to continue business as usual with China, Japanese companies also have concerns about economic security. In particular, some companies specifically discuss supply chain dependency and suggest decoupling to manage risk. The next section presents a framework to analyze these two divergent approaches and assess how the private sector has responded to these mixed incentives.

---

[53] Japanese Chamber of Commerce and Industry in China, "Chuugoku keizai to Nihon kigyoo 2022 nen hakusho" [Chinese Economy and Japanese Enterprises 2022 White Paper] (Beijing, 2022), https://www.cjcci.org/detail/576/576/4210.html.

[54] Kazuaki Nagata, "Amid Geopolitical Tensions, Japan Firms Put Focus on Economic Security," *Japan Times*, June 13, 2022, https://www.japantimes.co.jp/news/2022/06/13/business/japan-firms-economic-security-divisions.

Evidence For and Against Decoupling

Expectations and Analytical Approach

If Japanese companies are retreating from China, the following can be expected in the data, depending on the strategy they choose. Firms can either follow the most extreme version of exit—decoupling—or pursue some other form of soft diversification, or "de-risking." It is important to measure these strategies using multiple forms of data to the extent possible. Trade flows can miss important dependencies in supply chains that can be more clearly seen in the movements of individual firms. **Table 1** summarizes the expectations based on the potential approach.

TABLE 1 Varieties of market retreat

Level of diversification activity	Definition	Observable implications	Test cases
Extreme	Decoupling: Japanese business activities and trade are shifting away from China to other regions of the world or returning to Japan.	Trade and investment with China decrease overall, with more firm exits and fewer new entrants to the market.	Aggregate trade, investment, firm entrants and exits.
Middle ground	De-risking: economic activity in China decreases for certain strategic or risky sectors, but stays steady otherwise.	Trade and investment with China decrease in sectors deemed strategic by the Japanese government.	Strategic products such as critical minerals (e.g., lithium, rare earths, and cobalt), semiconductors, batteries, and magnets; nonstrategic products such as home electronics, textiles, and shoes; aggregate cross-time analysis of firm entrants and exits, investment activity.
	China Plus One: economic activity in China stays relatively steady, but activity in other regions grows disproportionally.	The share of trade, investment, and corporate activity from China to China Plus One countries shifts.	
Status quo	Staying the course: economic activity in China does not change, nor do regional patterns shift.	No change is observed in economic activity.	The status quo is indicated by the failure to find evidence in other cases.

If full decoupling is occurring, the data will show broad movement away from China at the trade, investment, and firm levels. We should see exits from China increase and new entrants decrease. Given the macro-level data shown earlier in this chapter, we already know that full-scale decoupling has not occurred, although there have been shifts away from China to other parts of Asia in recent years. Firm- and sector-level data will help confirm whether any moves toward decoupling in the near future are expected.[55]

The middle-ground strategies are not necessarily mutually exclusive. De-risking and China Plus One could be happening simultaneously, with the difference revealed at the sectoral level. For de-risking, the data should show a retreat from the Chinese market for strategic or critical industries and a shift toward domestic production or trade and investment in allied countries.[56] These sectors could include but are not limited to the following: critical minerals, batteries, magnets, pharmaceuticals, and integrated circuits (chips). These sectors are the most likely to find evidence of de-risking, and are the sectors that have been targeted by ESPA and prior state subsidies. This chapter analyzes the following "most likely" cases for de-risking: rare earths, lithium, cobalt, batteries, magnets, and semiconductors.

Private sector–driven China Plus One diversification is most likely in areas where manufacturing is no longer as competitive in China given the increasing costs of doing business. These include labor-intensive industries that are not focused on the Chinese consumer market but rather re-export back to Japan or third countries. These are not strategic or critical industries that have been targeted by the Japanese government and are therefore ripe for de-risking, but are places where evidence for diversification may potentially be found. This chapter analyzes footwear and textiles for possible China Plus One strategies. There are also parts of the economy that are most likely to stay the course, namely those that are not strategic and rely on domestic market access in China. Economic activities that rely on consumer sales in China and are not restricted by security concerns are the least likely candidates for any decoupling strategy. For example, home electronics are likely to maintain the status quo.

---

[55] FDI data is not granular enough at the sectoral level to perform relevant analysis, so the sector-level analysis relies on trade data.

[56] Note that this chapter does not systematically assess reshoring or the return of industries to domestic production.

Results and Discussion

Figure 3 shows the change in Japanese imports in selected sectors from 2011 to 2021. A decrease in dependence on a single source for a critical product, particularly from China, would be evidence of de-risking. Looking at critical minerals, there is strong evidence of de-risking for rare earths from 2013 to 2020, when Japanese companies were diligently seeking alternative sources. However, over the last few years, dependence on China has once again increased and almost returned to 2012 levels. This result demonstrates the strong pull of efficiency, especially when demand rapidly surges.[57] China has high competence and low prices in the rare earth sector, which is a particularly strong draw when global prices and demand surge.[58]

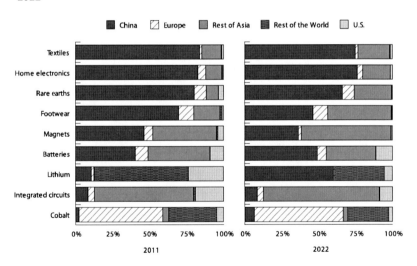

FIGURE 3 Products as percetages of Japanese imports by country, 2011 and 2022

SOURCE: UN Comtrade database.

---

[57] "Post-2030: Unfathomable Rare Earth Demand Growth Awaits," Adamas Intelligence, September 28, 2020, https://www.adamasintel.com/unfathomable-rare-earth-demand-growth.

[58] Kristin Vekasi, "The Geoeconomics of Critical Rare Earth Minerals," *Georgetown Journal of International Affairs* 22, no. 2 (2021): 271–79; and "The 2020 Super Recovery: EVs, Battery Metals, and Rare Earths," Adamas Intelligence, March 2021, 15.

Lithium shows increased dependence on China, increasing from 10% to over 60% over the past decade. While lithium has long been identified as a critical mineral by the Japanese government, it has not had the same sort of focused industrial policy as rare earths. If such a focus emerges, it is reasonable to anticipate a similar pattern for rare earths in 2014–20. The tools of public-private partnership, particularly through assistance from METI and JOGMEC, are already in place. By contrast, cobalt trade patterns have remained static over the past decade. Japanese imports of cobalt largely come through Europe, although most are mined in the Democratic Republic of the Congo. In the most likely case of de-risking—rare earths—there is confirmatory evidence, but it is not clear that diversification has proved robust to demand shocks. For other critical minerals, there is either no change or an increase in dependence on China. In short, evidence in favor of the de-risking hypothesis is mixed at best.

There is evidence of a more diverse market for batteries and magnets. For these key products, Japanese trade is almost completely in the region, but the trade data does not indicate potential chokepoints at the macro-sectoral level. Japan imports the vast majority of its batteries and magnets from Asia, which is unsurprising given the supply chain production networks for electronics in the region. Over the past decade, there has been a shift in magnet imports, with more coming from non-Chinese Asian countries and China's share declining. Batteries, on the other hand, show a modest increase in the Chinese share and a decrease for the rest of Asia.

Finally, Japanese trade behavior in integrated circuits has not shifted in recent years. If anything, Japan has become more dependent on Asia. In this case, the country is less worried about import dependence on China and more worried about the security risks of overdependence on Taiwan in the case of an armed cross-strait conflict. With respect to Japanese trade with the rest of Asia, almost 80% of Japanese chips originate from South Korea and Taiwan. Trade is not the only de-risking factor in semiconductors, particularly in Japan, which used to be a global leader in the industry. Japan, like the United States, has been pursuing a domestic reshoring policy. The Japanese government has provided subsidies to global giant Taiwan Semiconductor Manufacturing Company (TSMC) to build a fabrication plant in Kumamoto Prefecture.[59] This project is still in its early stages, but it would increase the sector's resiliency in the face of geopolitical or other risks. While Japan's semiconductor policy does not pursue a strategy of de-risking or decoupling

---

[59] "Sony Eyes Building New Semiconductor Plant in Kumamoto," *Japan Times*, December 16, 2022, https://www.japantimes.co.jp/news/2022/12/16/business/corporate-business/sony-new-semiconductor-plant.

from China per se, it is still driven by concerns about the uncertainty of China's international posture.

Footwear and textiles are likely sectors for the China Plus One strategy. These are labor-intensive industries where China is no longer as competitive as Central and Southeast Asia. The same symmetric pattern is found in the aggregate trade data in both of these industries. Even as shares of trade with China have decreased, trade volume has been steady or increased, indicating expansion to new markets, not exits from the Chinese market. With footwear, the pattern of gradually retreating from China and moving to other parts of Asia is quite clear. Over the past decade, Japanese imports have gone from around 70% from China to 50% and from 20% in the rest of Asia to approximately 50%. Textiles show a similar but less dramatic pattern. China has lost about 10% of its share of Japanese imports, and the rest of Asia has gained that same 10%.

Home electronics is the sector most likely to stay the course, and the evidence confirms this expectation. Here, Japanese trade is once again dominated by Asia, but China has not lost any market share. Home electronics is a sector where Japanese companies are manufacturing in China not only to re-import back to Japan but also to target the domestic Chinese market. As such, they have little incentive to change their manufacturing patterns since the industry is oriented toward the Chinese consumer market.

In summary, the trade data for the most likely and unlikely culprits for decoupling, de-risking, or China Plus One shows limited to mixed evidence of a retreat from the Chinese market. While there is some indication of a shift from China to Southeast Asia in labor-intensive and nonstrategic products like footwear, even in products like rare earths that have long been deemed critical and for which alternative supply chains have been developed, China's market strength is compelling. As of 2022, it is difficult to conclude that Japan is decoupling from China, whatever the definition.

Adjusting to new trade patterns and building new production networks take time. Decoupling may not be evident because of the time delay between companies' decisions to exit the Chinese market and evidence of their new economic activity in available trade data. New market entrants and exits in China and the rest of Asia are an early indicator. **Figure 4** shows the percentage of new firms in China and the rest of Asia and the movement of new firm activity from China to the rest of Asia from 2000 to 2022. The surge of new investments in China following its accession to the WTO is astounding, reaching 50% of all new overseas subsidiaries in the early 2000s. However, over the last decade, far more new subsidiaries have opened throughout Asia that are not based in China. Similar to the pattern seen in footwear and textiles, the overall number of new subsidiaries has continued

FIGURE 4 Percentage of new subsidiaries in China and the rest of Asia

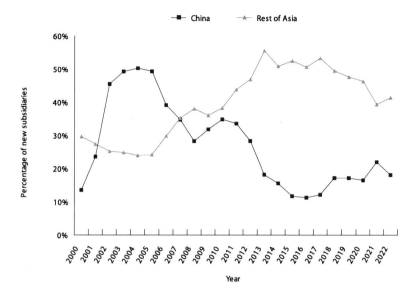

SOURCE: Author's calculations based on Toyo Keizai, *Kaigai shinshutsu kigyou souran* [General Survey of Overseas Firms] (Tokyo: Toyo Keizai, various years).

to increase in China as well as in other countries, even as the percentage has declined in favor of the rest of the region. While the new subsidiaries do not necessarily translate into decreased dependence on China, and certainly are not a guarantee of imminent full-scale decoupling, they do show that there are broadening investment patterns and the possibility of Japanese companies diversifying into the region and not always utilizing their Chinese subsidiaries.

Finally, **Figure 5** shows the percentage of firms exiting China, the rest of Asia, North America, and Europe from 2014 to 2022. China consistently tops the list for the most exits. As the most popular destination for overseas subsidiaries, this is unsurprising. An increase in the percentage of Chinese firms exiting and a decrease in other regions would be evidence of a broad exit from China and movement to other regions. But this pattern is not evident. While not shown here, the total number of exits follows a similar pattern, with exits from China as well as the rest of Asia actually declining over the past five years. Taken together, Figures 4 and 5 show evidence of private-sector diversification in a China Plus One pattern but not of companies pursuing a decoupling strategy by actually exiting China.

FIGURE 5 Exits of overseas Japanese firms

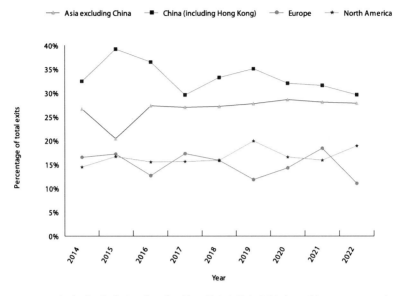

SOURCE: Author's calculations based on Toyo Keizai, *Kaigai shinshutsu kigyou souran*, various years.

Given the cumulative data on firm-level entrants and exits and the trade data on strategic sectors, there is no evidence of decoupling and limited evidence of de-risking. While some regional trade patterns are shifting, Japanese companies, at least thus far, seem committed to the Chinese market.

Conclusion

At this point, it is too early to definitively assess if Japan's economic security approach has fundamentally altered the trajectory of the Japanese economy, or if the private sector would have followed the same course regardless. Some recent research concludes that Japanese industrial policy and government inducements have been ineffective in reshoring industry.[60] The results in this chapter also suggest the limited efficacy of state efforts to build more resilience in critical supply chains. That said, in some sectors, the argument for policy efficacy is quite strong, particularly for rare earths. After

---

[60] Saori N. Katada, Ji Hye Lim, and Ming Wan, "Reshoring from China: Comparing the Economic Statecraft of Japan and South Korea," *Pacific Review* 36, no. 5 (2023).

the 2010 crisis, when China imposed an informal ban on rare earth exports to Japan, those private companies that diversified did so with the assistance of state intervention. The public-private partnership model in the case of critical minerals has not always led to new supply chains, but the non-Chinese supply chains that exist between Japan, Australia, and Malaysia succeeded because of state support. Despite the return to high levels of trade dependence on China, Japan's rare earths situation is fundamentally different because of state policy. Similarly, the private sector is pursuing production facilities and reshoring efforts for semiconductors that would not have occurred without government inducement. It is too soon to say whether those efforts will successfully diversify the supply chain, but the new joint venture with TSMC in Kumamoto would not exist without some level of state intervention.

Available data and the perspectives of the Japanese business community help trace potential futures. Businesses are accustomed to dealing with uncertainty in the policy environment and a lack of transparency from the Chinese government. These are, to a certain extent, already part of their risk assessments. Japan's experience during the "cold politics, hot economics" era suggests that Japanese firms, particularly large firms, have experience maintaining business as usual in many different political environments. We should expect them to keep their heads down and wait out this period of uncertainty, as they have in previous periods. If any of the worst-case scenarios do come to pass, such as an armed cross-strait conflict or a war between the United States and China, business behavior will certainly change, at a minimum to protect personnel and for political solidarity.

The gravitational pull of China's enormous economy and reluctance to change course are also key. The example of India provides an important cautionary tale. Despite long-held enthusiasm from both political elites and businesspeople, Japanese businesses have not flocked from China to India. Underlying business fundamentals such as costs and location have proved stronger than diplomatic efforts and appeals to shared democratic values. If large firms follow through on their stated intentions to diversify due to economic security concerns and shift their production networks out of China, then the SMEs in their supplier networks will follow, and there could be rapid diversification. However, given the centrality of the Chinese consumer market to Japanese business goals, a China Plus One pattern is more likely, except in certain strategic sectors.

Given the large number of sectors targeted by the state, the lack of product specificity in those sectors, and the reluctance of companies to suffer additional economic security regulations, it is impossible to make highly specific predictions about which areas will see more diversification. However, the evidence indicates that industries with previous experience of disruption or the threat of economic coercion are more amenable to government intervention and quicker to respond.

The case of rare earths shows that diversification is possible, even in an industry where China has a strong competitive advantage. Projecting forward five years, it is likely that Japan will have more diverse supply chains in at least a portion of the sectors it has identified in the National Security Strategy and ESPA, including other critical minerals, downstream batteries and magnets, and some machine parts critical to defense readiness such as aircraft and marine equipment. Diversification will likely be actualized through targeted subsidies, public-private cooperation, and the acceptance of higher costs and efficiency losses in the name of national security. Though economically costly, this approach could be rewarded with less disruption and greater resilience when the next crisis arises. Other targeted sectors, such as cloud services, will be more challenging to diversify. Japanese companies are nearly completely dependent on U.S.-based companies such as Amazon, Google, and Microsoft for cloud services and will need to develop enormous capacity without the motivation of an external security threat.

It is also unlikely that the Japanese government will implement policies that harshly restrict business opportunities with China. The voices of large manufacturing firms in the formulation of ESPA show that the interests of globalized manufacturing powerhouses are well represented within the Japanese government. Harsh policies that demand systematic reshoring or decoupling would damage the interests of a key constituency as well as the overall economic prosperity of the country.

Japan is eager to engage in multilateral initiatives for supply chain resilience, particularly those that involve expanding trade and investment opportunities rather than imposing restrictions. The state strategy for economic resilience is not to turn toward autarky or economic nationalism. Japan has been involved in at least seven different international efforts over the past fifteen years to build more resilient and diversified supply chains for critical minerals. At the same time, it is cooperating with the United States on national security issues such as export controls against China (e.g., on semiconductor manufacturing equipment) and participating in the multilateral sanctions against Russia. However, in the case of export controls, Japan is cooperating because its ally asked, not because it necessarily thought this policy was in its best national security interest.

Japan is proactively facing the simultaneous challenges of economic dependence on China, the intersection of national security and globalization, and the emergence of new technologies. It was a harbinger of supply chain resiliency policies with its response to the 2010 rare earths crisis and is an early adopter of a comprehensive and formal approach to economic security through ESPA. Japan has joined or initiated international supply chain resiliency efforts with like-minded countries and is pursuing diversified trading networks through its trade agreements and regional economic diplomacy. Although these policies have not yet resulted in broad decoupling or de-risking from China—a mark of the scope of economic integration and strong business incentives for maintaining the status quo—they have established tools and methods for promoting diversification. Whether those efforts will succeed in making the Japanese economy resilient to future coercion or disruption remains to be seen, but the capacity Japan is developing is a model the world should take seriously.

EXECUTIVE SUMMARY

This chapter examines how weaponized interdependence and pressures to decouple have affected South Korea's foreign policy.

MAIN ARGUMENT

Given its asymmetric economic interdependence with China, on the one hand, and Washington's demand for decoupling from Beijing, on the other, South Korea faces three key challenges: ensuring supply chain resilience, reducing heavy reliance on China for critical materials, and sustaining an adequate level of economic interdependence under decoupling pressure. Two areas where these challenges will be especially acute are the semiconductor industry and the supply chain for critical raw materials. In both cases, the South Korean government's policies have focused on reducing the vulnerabilities entailed by economic interdependence and finding ways to navigate great-power rivalry. More broadly, South Korea's search for strategic autonomy and economic prosperity requires a proactive and holistic approach that includes both individual and collective efforts for managing economic interdependence responsibly.

POLICY IMPLICATIONS

- While South Korea is concerned with reducing vulnerabilities arising from its interdependence with China, its economic statecraft is more preoccupied with U.S. pressures to decouple.

- South Korea seeks to define the scope of technologies sensitive to national security. There is a need for multilateral forums that set norms and rules that strike a balance between national security and economic interdependence.

- South Korea needs internationally coordinated strategies that constantly monitor risks to its supply chains, discourage the abuse of economic interdependence, and establish a new regional architecture that renovates value chains, resists overt protectionism, and promotes inclusive and resilient globalization.

South Korea

South Korea's Economic Statecraft: Between Interdependence and National Security

Yul Sohn and Hyo-young Lee

The Republic of Korea (ROK, or South Korea) has immensely benefited from the expanded cross-border networks of economic interdependence that have developed under an open multilateral trading system. The country has also thrived through a web of free trade agreements (FTAs) cultivated with a number of important economies, including the Association of Southeast Asian Nations (ASEAN), the United States, the European Union, China, Canada, and India. Fundamentally, its export-oriented growth strategies elevated South Korea to the status of a major economic power with highly sophisticated and technologically advanced markets.

During the past decade, however, South Korea has faced unprecedented challenges at a time when it has sought deeper trading relationships with its two major partners: the United States as a critical security ally and China as its largest export market. The United States shifted its status from a champion of globalization to a principal source of deglobalization as the Trump administration withdrew from the Trans-Pacific Partnership (TPP) agreement and applied various protectionist measures under the banner of "America first." Meanwhile, China ostensibly upholds the values of globalization, but it

---

Yul Sohn is a Professor in the Graduate School of International Studies and the Underwood International College at Yonsei University and President of the East Asia Institute in Seoul. He can be reached at <yulsohn@yonsei.ac.kr>.

Hyo-young Lee is an Associate Professor at the Korea National Diplomatic Academy. She can be reached at <hylee17@mofa.go.kr>.

sustains state capitalism with a wide range of unfair economic practices that impose numerous barriers to market access.[1]

Another challenge has come from weaponized interdependence, whereby one state exploits its position in an interdependent network to coerce vulnerable partners.[2] Given its deep yet asymmetrical economic interdependence with China, South Korea is more vulnerable to the costs associated with weakening or severing economic ties and thus more likely to consider strategic concessions to China. The dynamics of weaponized interdependence compel South Korea to either sacrifice its economic benefits in favor of strategic interests or vice versa. The same is true in the case of U.S.-ROK relations, especially when U.S.-China strategic competition intensifies and spills over to affect trade and technology policy. As heated strategic competition between the two great powers leads toward selective decoupling in strategic sectors, South Korea is left with a considerable strategic dilemma. There is pressure from Washington to align with U.S.-led decoupling efforts, while at the same time Beijing warns that the already fraught relationship between China and South Korea will only further deteriorate if Seoul insists on leaning toward the United States.[3]

In this regard, South Korea's economic statecraft needs to focus on reducing vulnerabilities brought on by asymmetric economic interdependence. It also needs to find ways to navigate the great-power rivalry and alleviate U.S. pressures to decouple from China. If the recent shift in language from "decoupling" to "de-risking" reflects Washington's attempt to take a more moderate and realistic stance for its European and Asian allies concerned about severing economic ties with China,[4] it is likely that South Korea will find room for maneuvering with a practical approach to strike a

---

[1] Elizabeth C. Economy, *The World According to China* (Cambridge: Polity, 2021).

[2] Daniel W. Drezner, "Introduction: The Uses and Abuses of Weaponized Interdependence," in *The Uses and Abuses of Weaponized Interdependence*, ed. Daniel W. Drezner, Henry Farrell, and Abraham L. Newman (Washington, D.C.: Brookings Institution Press, 2021), 1.

[3] Zhang Huizhi, "South Korean Economy under Thickening Cloud," *Global Times*, May 11, 2023, https://www.globaltimes.cn/page/202305/1290566.shtml.

[4] "Joint Statement by President Biden and President von der Leyen," White House, Press Release, March 10, 2023, https://www.whitehouse.gov/briefing-room/statements-releases/2023/03/10/joint-statement-by-president-biden-and-president-von-der-leyen-2; Janet L. Yellen, "Remarks by Secretary of the Treasury Janet L. Yellen on the U.S.-China Economic Relationship at Johns Hopkins School of Advanced International Studies," U.S. Secretary of the Treasury, April 20, 2023, https://home.treasury.gov/news/press-releases/jy1425; Jake Sullivan, "Remarks by National Security Advisor Jake Sullivan on Renewing American Economic Leadership at the Brookings Institution," U.S. National Security Adviser, April 27, 2023, https://www.whitehouse.gov/briefing-room/speeches-remarks/2023/04/27/remarks-by-national-security-advisor-jake-sullivan-on-renewing-american-economic-leadership-at-the-brookings-institution; and "G-7 Hiroshima Leaders' Communiqué," White House, Press Release, May 20, 2023, https://www.whitehouse.gov/briefing-room/statements-releases/2023/05/20/g7-hiroshima-leaders-communique.

proper balance between economic interdependence and national security, thus accommodating China while increasing U.S. engagement.

This chapter is divided into five main sections. The first section overviews South Korea's trade patterns and their changes vis-à-vis China, with a focus on changes in global value chains. The next section highlights the structural vulnerabilities that affect South Korea's foreign policy and presents key challenges and tasks for its economic statecraft. In the following two sections, South Korea's strategic approach to economic interdependence is presented through an examination of the supply chains for semiconductors and critical minerals. This chapter concludes by suggesting that South Korea pursue a collective and multilateral approach to establish norms and rules defining the scope of technologies sensitive to national security and to restore an international economic order that ensures inclusive and resilient globalization.

Changing Trends in South Korea's Foreign Trade

South Korea is a highly trade-dependent country, with trade accounting for more than 70% of its GDP and a continuous trade surplus since the late 1990s. The country's trade growth rates have surpassed those of the rest of the world since the 1960s, and its share of world trade has accounted for more than 2% since 1990. Since 2010, South Korea has ranked ninth in world trade volumes.[5] Its major exports are semiconductors, automobiles, telecommunications equipment, computers, ships, and petroleum products. These industries are supported by an industrial base that began to be established in the 1980s through the strategic alignment of government resources and assets and the expansion of private sector R&D investment. Until the late 1990s, the United States and Japan accounted for almost 70% of South Korea's total trade, but more diverse trade relationships with Europe and other Asian markets have since been established.[6]

China, however, became South Korea's top export destination in 2004, accounting for nearly 22% of its total exports. Following the establishment of bilateral trade and investment agreements in 1992, exports to China increased rapidly, especially in equipment and intermediate goods, as South Korean companies expanded their direct investment in China.[7] Furthermore, the complementary industrial structures and natural resources in both countries, with South Korea's stage of economic development preceding that of China

---

[5] Ministry of Trade, Industry and Energy (ROK), *2019-2020 Saneup Tongsang Jawon Baekseo* [2019-2020 Trade, Industry, and Energy White Paper] (Seoul, 2020).

[6] Korea International Trade Association (KITA), "Hanguk muyeoksa" [History of Korean Trade], 2006.

[7] Ibid.

at a sufficient level to enable technology transfer, contributed to expanding bilateral trade. Most of the bilateral trade took the form of processing trade. Direct investments by South Korean companies into labor-intensive sectors in China led to increased exports of South Korean components and intermediate capital goods to these sectors, which in turn led to increased bilateral trade through re-export to South Korea or other foreign markets.

South Korea's Trade Patterns in 2021–22

Despite the dire conditions caused by the prolonged effects of Covid-19, China's economic slowdown, escalating U.S.-China tensions, and the Russia-Ukraine war, South Korea has seen continuous growth in foreign trade, recording increases in both export and import volumes in 2021–22.

In 2021, South Korea's exports and imports grew by 24.1% and 29.5%, respectively, during the global economic recovery from the Covid-19 pandemic. Exports were mainly led by growth in major items, such as semiconductors, petrochemicals, steel, automobiles, and car components. The country's foreign trade volumes rose faster than in most other major trading countries, recording a 27.9% trade growth rate, which trailed only China (34.2%) and Italy (32.5%). South Korea's exports of semiconductors, which used to be the main contributor to growth, have declined in recent years. The proportion of semiconductor exports to total growth in exports peaked in 2018 (92.3%) but sharply dropped in 2019 (52.3%) and 2020 (17.6%), before recovering only slightly in 2021 (20.2%).[8] In fact, by 2021, South Korea's growth in exports had been driven by a more diversified portfolio of export products, such as semiconductors (20.2%), petrochemicals (15.2%), petroleum products (9.3%), automobiles (7.7%), steel (7.0%), and machinery (4.1%). In comparison, its exports growth was far more concentrated among a few items in 2018, namely semiconductors (94.2%), petroleum products (35.5%), petrochemicals (18.1%), and machinery (16.5%).[9]

In 2022, despite the negative economic impacts of Covid-19 lockdowns, China's sluggish economy, and geopolitical tensions involving China and Russia, South Korea's exports grew by 7.1% ($690 billion) and imports by 19.5% ($735 billion). In particular, rising oil prices in the aftermath of the Russia-Ukraine war led to increased imports of energy products and a drastic

---

[8] The proportion of a product's exports growth to South Korea's total exports growth is calculated by dividing the product's year-on-year increase or decrease in exports volume by South Korea's total increase or decrease in exports volume of the corresponding year.

[9] "2021 suchulip pyunga mit 2022 junmang" [Export and Import Trends in 2021 and Prospects for 2022], KITA, Trade Focus, no. 35, 2021, 14. The total of percentages exceeds 100% because the percentages represent the proportion (or contribution rate) of the product's export growth to South Korea's total exports growth.

surge in total import volumes. As a result, South Korea recorded a trade deficit for the first time in fourteen years. Export growth rates of several major items continued to show upward trends, with petroleum products increasing by 75.6%, automobiles by 13.6%, and steel by 10.9%. On the other hand, exports of semiconductors and LCD displays initially showed high growth rates of 8.3% and 5.1%, respectively, but started to level off after the third quarter of 2022.[10]

A notable change in South Korea's export structure is the drastic rise in the export growth rates of electric vehicles (EVs) (41.8%), aerospace products (40.7%), next-generation semiconductors (12.1%), and LCD displays (12.1%). The proportion of next-generation products in South Korea's total exports has been growing continuously since 2018, increasing from 14% to 19% from 2018 to 2022. The main items contributing to this trend are next-generation semiconductors (10.6%), bio-health products (2.4%), next-generation displays (2.2%), renewable energy–related products (1.4%), and EVs (1.3%).[11]

South Korea's Trade Patterns with China

During the past 30 years, bilateral trade between South Korea and China has grown exponentially, recording a 38-fold increase in volume from $6.4 billion in 1992 to $241.5 billion in 2020. Due to complementary industry structures, bilateral trade patterns became highly dependent, especially for South Korea, to the point that China accounted for 24.6% of its total trade in 2020 (up from 4.0% in 1992). China has been South Korea's top export destination since 2004 for products such as semiconductors, LCD displays, synthetic resins, mobile telecommunications equipment, computers, and petroleum. On the other hand, South Korea only accounted for 6.0% of China's total trade in 2020 (up from 4.2% in 1992).[12]

As shown in **Figure 1**, South Korea's trade with China during the past twelve years exhibits an overall increasing trend in terms of both exports and imports. Since 2010, South Korea has been exporting to China more than it imports, leading to a consistent trade surplus during the past decade. However, since 2019, South Korea's exports have dropped significantly, while imports have remained the same. In 2021, despite a rebound in exports, imports from China also grew significantly, resulting in a decreased trade surplus. In terms of trade ratio, China has accounted for an average of

---

[10] KITA, "2022 suchulip pyunga mit 2023 junmang" [Export and Import Trends in 2022 and Prospects for 2023], Trade Focus, no. 31, 2022, 11.

[11] Ibid., 23.

[12] KITA, "Hanjung sukyo 30 junyun muyeokgujo byunhwawa shisajeom" [30 Years of Korea-China Diplomatic Relations: Change in Trade Structure and Implications], Trade Focus, no. 38, 2021, 6–7.

FIGURE 1 South Korea's trade volume and trade ratio with China (2010–21)

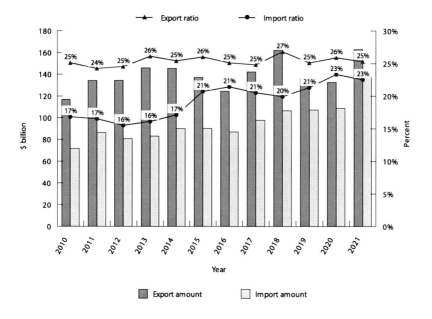

SOURCE: Compiled by authors from UN Comtrade database.

25.3% of South Korea's exports during the past twelve years. China's share in South Korea's exports peaked in 2019 at 26.8%, but has dropped since 2020. However, China's share of South Korea's imports exhibited a consistent upward trend during the 2010–21 period, growing from 16.8% in 2010 to 22.5% in 2021. The implication is that South Korea has become increasingly reliant on imports from China.

In 2021, large percentages of South Korean exports were destined for China, in particular semiconductors (38.6%), LCD displays (37.9%), synthetic resins (33.6%), telecommunications equipment (27.2%), and computers (26.7%). In 2020 and 2021, China was South Korea's top export destination, accounting for 25.9% and 25.3% of its total exports, respectively.[13] In 2022, however, China's share in South Korea's total exports dropped to 23.1%, mainly due to China's restrictive zero-Covid policy and sluggish economy. The structure of ROK-China trade has become more characteristic of intra-industry trade. Intermediate products account for the highest share of

---

[13] KITA, "Hanjung sukyo 30 junyun muyeokgujo byunhwawa shisajeom," 7.

bilateral trade items, in terms of not only exports (80.1% in 2021) but also imports (64.5% in 2021).[14] Although China is still South Korea's top exporting partner as of 2022, its share of ROK exports has recorded its sharpest drop (-2.2%), while the export shares of ASEAN countries (1.6%), Australia (1.2%), and the United States (1.0%) have all increased (see **Figure 2**).

The ASEAN region has emerged as South Korea's second-largest export destination, particularly in intermediate goods such as semiconductors (22.5%) and LCD displays (33.2%). Exports of petroleum products also increased significantly (53.2%), mainly due to international oil price hikes and increased demand for fuel. South Korea has expanded its exports to Vietnam as the country has become a global production hub. Exports to Vietnam

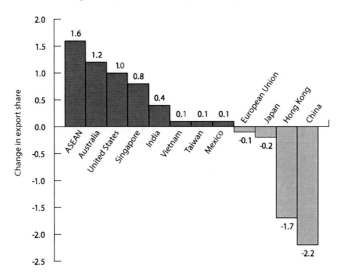

FIGURE 2 Change in export share of top-ten export destinations (2022)

SOURCE: KITA, "2022 suchulip pyunga mit 2023 junmang" [Export and Import Trends in 2022 and Prospects for 2023], Trade Focus, no. 31, 2022.

---

[14] KITA, "Hanjung sukyo 30 junyun muyeokgujo byunhwawa shisajeom," 8–9.

of semiconductors (20.4%) and LCD displays (12.7%) have shown steady growth trends but are expected to slow as South Korean companies diversify and build production facilities in other ASEAN countries, such as Indonesia, in order to lower the risk of concentration and supply chain vulnerabilities.

More recently, the trade relationship between South Korea and China has become highly competitive, particularly in the mid-tech (e.g., chemical products, machinery, and automobiles) and high-tech (e.g., pharmaceuticals, medical and precision machinery, computers and office machines, electronics, and telecommunications equipment) sectors (see **Figures 3** and **4**). Since U.S.-China tensions began to escalate in 2018, South Korean mid-tech exports have been competing more with Chinese products in ASEAN markets. This is mainly due to China reorienting its exports to ASEAN countries since the U.S. market has been stifled by various trade-restrictive measures. Average export growth rates of South Korean high-tech goods to ASEAN markets dropped sharply from 14.0% (2011–18) to 3.8% (2018–20), while China's increased from 10.1% (2011–18) to 15.2% (2018–20).[15]

On the other hand, South Korean exports of mid-tech products to the U.S. market grew faster than Chinese products during 2018–20. This compares favorably to 2011–18, when Chinese mid-tech exports grew at 7.6% and South Korean exports grew at 5.3%. In the high-tech sector, however, exports of both South Korean and Chinese products dropped, although China recorded a more modest decrease (-4.6%) than South Korea (-7.9%).

South Korea is also highly dependent on China for imports of the raw materials used in various manufactured products. Among the 3,941 imports that are more than 80% reliant on a single source, almost half (1,850 items) are from China. In particular, 100% of South Korea's magnesium ingots (an essential input for producing the aluminum alloy used in automobile bodies, vehicle seat frames, and lightweight aircraft), 94.7% of its tungsten oxide (used in medical devices and semiconductors), and 83.5% of its lithium hydroxide (used in EV batteries) rely on China as the dominant import source.[16]

Amid intensifying U.S.-China tensions, China has been strengthening its manufacturing capacity to become more self-sufficient in key strategic technology sectors, including semiconductors and LCD displays, which are South Korea's main export items. As a result, ROK-China competition has been intensifying in many third-country markets, especially in ASEAN countries. Although China is still South Korea's top export destination, the changing structure of China's domestic economy and its participation in global value chain activities are causing changes to bilateral trade patterns.

---

[15] KITA, "Hanjung sukyo 30 junyun muyeokgujo byunhwawa shisajeom," 36–39.
[16] Ibid., 40.

FIGURE 3   Annual average export growth rates in mid-tech sectors in the ASEAN market

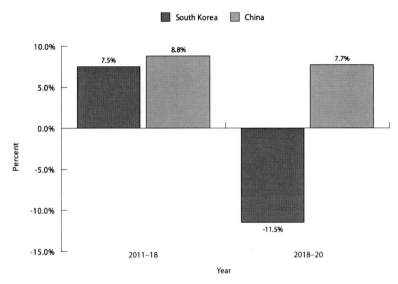

SOURCE: KITA, "Hanjung sukyo 30 junyun muyeokgujo byunhwawa shisajeom" [30 Years of Korea-China Diplomatic Relations: Change in Trade Structure and Implications], Trade Focus, no. 38, 2021.

FIGURE 4   Annual average export growth rates in high-tech sectors in the ASEAN market

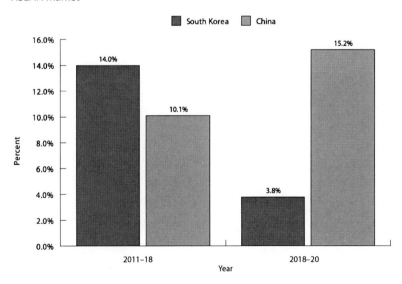

SOURCE: KITA, "Hanjung sukyo 30 junyun muyeokgujo byunhwawa shisajeom."

South Korean exports of manufactured products to China have been dropping even though China's consumer goods and services markets have been growing. South Korea's export volumes in the mid- and high-tech sectors have also been deteriorating in world markets as a result of heightened competition with Chinese technology products. These changes warrant a serious review and drastic change of trade strategy to focus attention on the strategic aspects of key technology sectors as part of South Korea's foreign trade policy.

Principal Challenges to South Korea's Economic Statecraft

As the asymmetric economic interdependence between China and South Korea deepens, South Korea increasingly worries about which structural vulnerabilities could be exploited politically. To understand the ways in which structural vulnerabilities affect South Korea's foreign policy, this section reviews three cases of the dynamics at play among China, the United States, and South Korea during the past decade.

The first case concerns the TPP. In late 2010, the United States requested that South Korea join TPP negotiations. Because the TPP not only served business interests but also strategic interests to counteract China's economic sway in the region, China responded by engaging in FTA negotiations with South Korea as a means to counterbalance U.S. influence and pressure it to not join the TPP.[17] Seoul pursued these negotiations, believing that its best interests are in capitalizing on bilateral FTAs with three major markets (the United States, the EU, and China) to become a global trading hub. Washington, however, pressured Seoul to reconsider placing FTA negotiations with China ahead of the TPP.[18]

Second, the China-led Asian Infrastructure Investment Bank (AIIB) created another strategic dilemma. When the AIIB, which enhances infrastructural investment in Asia, was proposed by China in 2013, South Korea was reluctant to support it because of U.S. opposition to an initiative that might dilute the influence of postwar Bretton Woods institutions like the World Bank and the Asian Development Bank.[19] Even though South Korean businesses would stand to gain from infrastructure projects built through AIIB funding, Seoul stayed silent for almost two years until the deadline

---

[17] Ann Capling and John Ravenhill, "Multilateralising Regionalism: What Role for the Trans-Pacific Partnership Agreement?" *Pacific Review* 24, no. 5 (2011): 553–75.

[18] Doug Palmer, "U.S. Encourages South Korea to Join Trans-Pacific Trade Talks," Reuters, April 3, 2013, https://www.reuters.com/article/us-usa-trade-asiapacific-idUSBRE93210D20130403.

[19] Saori N. Katada and Jessica Liao, "China and Japan in Pursuit of Infrastructure Investment Leadership in Asia," *Global Governance* 26, no. 3 (2020): 449–72.

to become a prospective founding member of the new bank approached. Weighing economic values against security concerns, South Korea finally jumped on the bandwagon and signed on as a founding member in 2015 with 56 other countries.

The third case is China's economic coercion of South Korea after it decided to deploy the Terminal High Altitude Area Defense (THAAD) system. While South Korea allowed the United States to install the system to protect against potential strikes from an increasingly erratic North Korea, China claimed that the powerful radar that THAAD uses to detect missiles would undermine its conventional and nuclear deterrence and viewed the deployment as proof of U.S. plans to encircle China and contain its rise.[20] Accordingly, China exerted full-fledged pressure on South Korea by applying economic tools that included the cancellation of popular cultural exchanges, the suspension of Chinese tourism to South Korea, and various non-tariff measures against South Korean goods and services.[21] Faced with China's economic coercion, South Korea did not back down on the deployment of THAAD. Instead, the Moon Jae-in government sought diplomatic compromises, known as the "three no's": no additional THAAD deployment, no integration into a U.S.-led regional missile defense system, and no participation in a trilateral military alliance with the United States and Japan.[22] South Korea reportedly even pledged to restrict the operation of the THAAD system.[23]

In these cases, South Korea's concerns are twofold. First, the country is highly vulnerable to geoeconomic pressure because, as discussed in the previous section, the pattern of economic interdependence with China is highly asymmetric. Second, escalating U.S.-China rivalry forces South Korea to devise a complex approach to economic interdependence that does not irk China and at the same time guarantees U.S. security protection.

By the late 2010s, when U.S.-China competition moved from trade to advanced technology, South Korea's dilemmas had magnified. National security concerns have soared, and technological competition has been recognized as crucial to strategic competition because advanced technologies such as semiconductors and artificial intelligence are dual-use and can benefit society but also pose threats to national security. The United States' call to

---

[20] Michael D. Swaine, "Chinese Views on South Korea's Deployment of THAAD," *China Leadership Monitor*, February 14, 2017.

[21] For additional context, see "China Opposes Possible U.S. THAAD Deployment in ROK," *China Daily*, February 13, 2016, http://www.chinadaily.com.cn/world/2016-02/13/content_23465685.htm.

[22] Bonnie S. Glaser and Lisa Collins, "China's Rapprochement with South Korea: Who Won the THAAD Dispute?" *Foreign Affairs*, November 7, 2017, https://www.foreignaffairs.com/articles/china/2017-11-07/chinas-rapprochement-south-korea.

[23] Kang Seung-woo, "Seoul Reiterates That '3 Nos' Policy Is Not Commitment to China," *Korea Times*, August 10, 2022, https://koreatimes.co.kr/www/nation/2023/03/120_334199.html.

its allies and partners to join its efforts to lessen imports in critical sectors and mitigate China's weaponized interdependence is difficult to answer for third parties like South Korea that develop key technologies exported to the Chinese market.[24] Likewise, through retaliatory measures, including tariffs, export controls, and regulatory mechanisms, and its "dual circulation" strategy to achieve market self-sufficiency and technological self-reliance in critical sectors, China has fostered closer economic ties with South Korea as a significant supplier of capital and advanced technologies.

Viewed in this way, several key challenges to South Korea's economic statecraft emerge. First, South Korea's structural vulnerabilities critically concern supply chain disruptions. Because global supply chains for South Korean tech companies are heavily concentrated in China, when disruptions occur, the entire supply chain can be severely damaged. For example, due to the Covid-19 outbreak in early 2020, which caused the closure of auto parts factories in China, South Korean automakers found it difficult to import parts and thus temporarily stopped production at their domestic factories. As China becomes a global manufacturing hub, South Korean industries rely more on Chinese imports and the local production of intermediary goods, which enables them to increase their competitiveness. As in the case of semiconductor manufacturing, South Korean companies need to manage the risks associated with reshaping the supply chain to account for possible disruptions.

The second challenge is single-source dependencies. Reliance on a single supplier or a small group of suppliers from a single country for critical components or raw materials creates vulnerabilities. As a dominant supplier of rare earths, China banned their export to coerce Japan following the 2010 territorial dispute over the Senkaku/Diaoyu Islands. China is the primary producer and supplier of various mineral resources essential to key South Korean industries like electronics, steel, EVs, and renewable energy. Therefore, decreasing vulnerability to disruptions in the supply of raw materials is crucial for South Korea to ensure not only the resilience and stability of its companies' global supply chains but also its strategic autonomy.

Third, the presence of structural vulnerabilities means that South Korea is susceptible to economic coercion. As seen in Beijing's retaliations over the deployment of THAAD, China can easily weaponize interdependence by exploiting multiple chokepoints in supply chains, especially for critical minerals, to affect South Korea's foreign policy. To mitigate this threat, South Korea should consider strategies that diversify trade and investment and strengthen domestic industries. It could also work together with like-

---

[24] Adam Segal, "Huawei, 5G, and Weaponized Interdependence," in Drezner, Farrell, and Newman, *The Uses and Abuses of Weaponized Interdependence*, 149–66.

minded countries to address challenges posed by China's coercive behavior and take collective action by sharing information, coordinating policies, and imposing sanctions.

A fourth set of challenges come from the U.S. decoupling strategy. As seen above, South Korea has its own reasons to reduce overdependence on China, but it also has much to lose from decoupling, both economically and strategically. While Seoul is well aware of China's growing military expansion in East Asia, China poses no immediate security threat to South Korea. Rather, Seoul is mindful of Beijing's relationship with Pyongyang, believing that only China can influence and change North Korean behavior. Thus, South Korea needs a pragmatic approach to the structural dilemma—one that is capable of accommodating U.S. demands while at the same time courting China by sending a signal that it does not exclude the country.

South Korea's Strategic Approach to Economic Interdependence in Semiconductors

The semiconductor industry has become a critical sector for maintaining leadership in the global competition in advanced technologies. As a critical component that is used as an input in producing almost all technical devices, ranging from electronic home appliances to military weapons, the semiconductor sector and its supply chains increasingly rival oil and gas in terms of strategic importance in international relations. Several major economies in the Asia-Pacific region, such as China, Japan, South Korea, Taiwan, and the United States, play pivotal roles in the global semiconductor industry. Such concentration in the supply of semiconductors among several major players enables the "weaponization of the supply chain." As a result, the ROK government has placed strengthening the resilience and stability of the sector's supply chains high on the agenda of its economic security policy.

South Korea's Position in the Global Semiconductor Supply Chain

South Korea is an active player in the global semiconductor supply chain, as both a major exporter and importer of various products, components, materials, and equipment. Its top export destination is China, which accounts for 43.2% ($41.2 billion) of South Korea's total exports of semiconductor components and equipment (see **Figure 5** for an overview of South Korea's major export partners). Combined with exports to Hong Kong, the share of Korean semiconductor exports to China is an overwhelming 61.5%. After China and Hong Kong, Vietnam is South Korea's third-largest export partner (9.6%), followed by the United States (7.9%) and Taiwan

FIGURE 5 Share of South Korean semiconductor exports and imports per major country (2020)

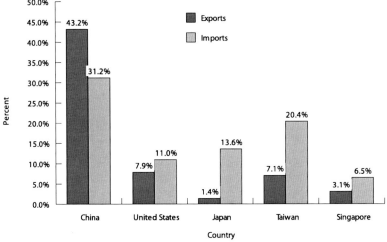

SOURCE: Korea Institute for International Economic Policy (KIEP), "Mijung bandoche pegwon gyungjenggwa global gongeubmang jepyun" [U.S.-China Competition in Semiconductors and Global Supply Chain Restructuring], Research Report, no. 21–28, 2021.

(7.1%). As such, the top-five export partners account for 86.1% of South Korea's semiconductor exports.[25]

The largest share of South Korean semiconductor exports is in memory semiconductors, 71.3% of which are exported to China.[26] The second-largest export item is system semiconductors, for which the highest share of exports goes to China with 46.6%. Vietnam is the second-largest importer (17.4%), followed by Taiwan (12.5%), the United States (2.6%), and Japan (0.9%). China also accounts for the largest share of South Korean semiconductor manufacturing equipment exports, at nearly 70%.

For semiconductor materials, such as silicon wafers, die-bonding film, and lead frames for manufacturing integrated circuits, China also accounts for the largest share of South Korean exports (33.4%), followed by Vietnam (16.6%) (see **Figure 6**). The two countries are major importers of Korean-

---

[25] Korea Institute for International Economic Policy (KIEP), "Mijung bandoche pegwon gyungjenggwa global gongeubmang jepyun" [U.S.-China Competition in Semiconductors and Global Supply Chain Restructuring], Research Report, no. 21–28, 2021, 160–61.

[26] Ibid., 162.

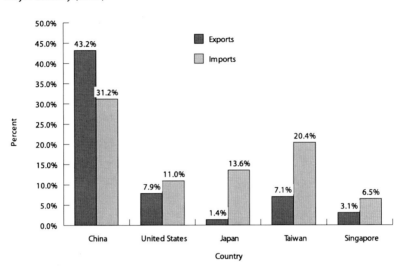

produced materials for semiconductor manufacturing due to the fact that South Korean companies that invested in China and Vietnam are importing those products as inputs for their local production facilities.

In terms of imports, South Korea is dependent on China (31.2%), Taiwan (20.4%), Japan (13.6%), the United States (11.0%), and Singapore (6.5%). The top-five importers of South Korean semiconductor products also account for 82.7% of the country's total semiconductor imports. System semiconductors contribute the largest share of import items, accounting for 39.1% of South Korea's total semiconductor imports. This is mainly due to the fact that South Korean companies that do not produce system semiconductors import them from abroad instead of buying them from domestic competitors. Its top import partner for system semiconductors is Taiwan, which accounts for 44.6%. The second-largest exporter of system semiconductors to South Korea is the United States (13.6%), followed by China (10.6%) and Japan (7.6%).

FIGURE 6 Share of South Korean exports per semiconductor item (2020)

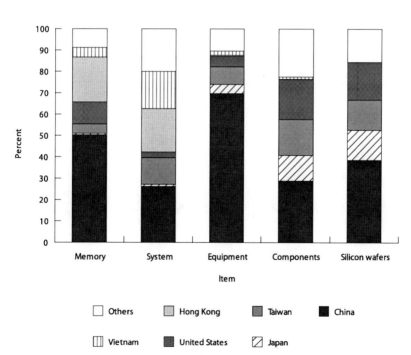

SOURCE: KIEP, "Mijung bandoche pegwon gyungjenggwa global gongeubmang jepyun."

In total, these four countries account for 76.4% of South Korea's total imports of system semiconductors.[27]

The second-largest share of semiconductor imports is memory semiconductors, which account for 31.7% ($18.1 billion) of total imports. Memory semiconductors are mostly imported from China (76.7%) (see **Figure 7**). When combined with imports from Hong Kong, the total share amounts to an overwhelming 78.3%. In total, the combined imports of system semiconductors and memory semiconductors from China account for a significant percentage of South Korea's total semiconductor imports. The reason behind this highly dependent import structure is that South Korea's major semiconductor industries and their manufacturing processes are strongly connected to the semiconductor production processes in China.

FIGURE 7   Share of South Korean imports per semiconductor item (2020)

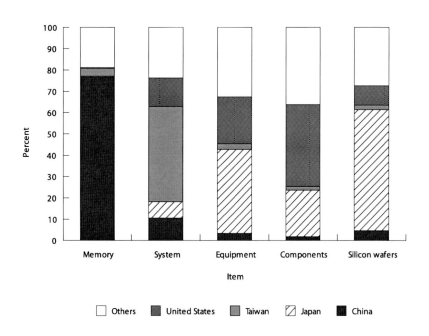

SOURCE: KIEP, "Mijung bandoche pegwon gyungjenggwa global gongeubmang jepyun."

---

[27] KIEP, "Mijung bandoche pegwon gyungjenggwa global gongeubmang jepyun," 151–52.

Companies such as Samsung and SK Hynix have factories located in China that process the semiconductor components, materials, and equipment that are made in South Korea and then re-import them back to the country.

In the case of semiconductor manufacturing equipment, South Korea imports most of these products from Japan (39.3%), the United States (21.9%), and Singapore (19.9%). As for components for semiconductor manufacturing equipment, it imports 38.4% from the United States and 21.8% from Japan. Unlike the previous cases, imports of semiconductor manufacturing equipment and their components, which require high-tech manufacturing capabilities and better quality control, are mostly imported from Japan and the United States. On the other hand, semiconductor products that are more price-competitive tend to be imported overwhelmingly from China.

Supply Chain Risks Faced by South Korea's Semiconductor Industry

The reason behind South Korea's strong dependence on the Chinese market as a trading partner for semiconductor exports and imports is that semiconductors are an intermediate product that takes the form of intra-industry trade. Export and import volumes and destinations are determined based on where companies decide to invest and build their semiconductor production facilities. South Korea has been importing semiconductor products that are processed in South Korean semiconductor manufacturing facilities located in China that use the semiconductor components and equipment that were originally exported from South Korea.

More recently, however, trade volumes of semiconductors between South Korea and China have been showing signs of decreasing due to the establishment of integrated production systems in Korean-invested Chinese manufacturing facilities. Several South Korean semiconductor companies have built local manufacturing facilities in China in order to maintain closer proximity to local customers of their products. For example, China accounts for more than 50% of the global demand for NAND flash products.[28] As a result of demand-induced foreign direct investment by South Korean semiconductor firms, intra-industry trade volumes have actually dropped. However, at the same time, these companies have also expanded domestic production facilities within South Korea, while striving to diversify export and import sources of semiconductor products. Such efforts have enabled South Korea to enjoy continuous growth in trade volumes with various foreign partners. Furthermore, FDI by South Korean semiconductor firms in foreign markets has also led to increased exports of semiconductor materials, components, and equipment. This trend coincides with recent efforts by the

---

[28] KIEP, "Mijung bandoche pegwon gyungjenggwa global gongeubmang jepyun," 170.

ROK government to promote its domestic semiconductor industry, which began in earnest after the semiconductor product shortage in the aftermath of Japan's export restrictions on key materials. In June 2022 the Japanese government removed South Korea from the white list for imposing export controls on dual-use goods, resulting in strengthened export controls on three types of intermediate items needed for manufacturing semiconductors in South Korea.

As a consequence, South Korea's high reliance on China for its semiconductor trade can be a major supply chain risk if there is ever any disturbance in the continuous flow of semiconductor products between the two countries. Any form of export control that restricts the exports of South Korean semiconductor products to the Korean-invested semiconductor facilities in China would upset the supply chain, with negative impacts on South Korean firms in terms of not only sales revenue but also their R&D and investment performance. At the same time, South Korea should also consider how quickly the Chinese semiconductor industry is becoming competitive, backed by the Chinese government's will to strengthen its global presence in semiconductors and other high-tech sectors. While China still lags one generation behind in the advanced stages of the semiconductor manufacturing process (i.e., silicon wafers), it currently holds an overwhelming share of the semiconductor packaging process, on which South Korea is highly reliant. Furthermore, as shown above, South Korea's strong dependence on China for exports and imports of memory semiconductors is also a potential supply chain risk in the event of any geopolitical incidents in the Asia-Pacific region.

Notably, the semiconductor industry itself features a monopolistic structure which is inherent in most high-technology areas. Currently, there are more than 50 semiconductor products and technologies for which the global market share of a single import source exceeds 65%.[29] Advanced technology areas tend to be dominated by certain global firms and countries that form a global supply chain among themselves. Such dominance is further strengthened by global demand for the products and technology, which is expected to further grow in the era of the digital economy. In the global semiconductor market, semiconductor companies from advanced economies are currently dominating the advanced stages in the manufacturing process. For example, Japan, the United States, and the Netherlands are the dominant sources of imports for semiconductor manufacturing equipment. Therefore, South Korea is highly reliant not only on China at the lower levels in the semiconductor manufacturing process but also on Japan and the United States at the higher levels.

---

[29] KIEP, "Mijung bandoche pegwon gyungjenggwa global gongeubmang jepyun," 175.

Most of the dominant major sources and players in the global semiconductor supply chain are located in Northeast Asia. Semiconductor supply chains are thus highly vulnerable to any disruptions caused by natural disasters or geopolitical tensions in the region. More worrisome is the fact that the escalating U.S.-China tensions over leadership in the global semiconductor market are increasingly being influenced by geopolitical tensions in the Asia-Pacific. Such tensions, which often take the form of export controls, foreign investment restrictions, and other disruptions to the stable supply of key inputs in the semiconductor supply chain, are likely to have a largely negative effect on semiconductor firms and the trade performance of countries.

Prospects for Global Semiconductor Supply Chains

The Covid-19 pandemic had a major impact on global supply chains, raising concerns about efficiency and low-cost production lines while increasing awareness of the need for stable and resilient supply chains. As a result, the diversification of supply sources and stockpiling of critical resource materials have become important strategies for achieving this goal. Technological advancements that enable automation of production processes have improved domestic investment conditions for companies while also enabling governments to provide more incentives for reshoring businesses that have made investments abroad. As trade protectionism and economic nationalism spread, existing supply chains will inevitably change.

Chinese industries have also been undergoing structural changes, resulting in higher labor and production costs, thereby weakening China's current position in global and regional supply chains. Current tensions with the United States are also working against China. Foreign companies that are contemplating making further investments in China recognize the increased non-economic costs and are moving their production facilities to other Asian countries. Such is the case with Vietnam, which has concluded FTAs with many countries, contributing to more competitive trade and investment conditions and increasing its attractiveness as a new production hub in the region.

The implications of these developments for South Korea are that its high dependence on and concentration in certain foreign import sources and export destinations may have to be reshuffled in the medium to long term to address future unexpected shocks. While decoupling or even de-risking from China using highly restrictive measures such as export controls might be unfeasible, it may be a more practical option for South Korea to begin reducing the share of its semiconductor trade. At least while U.S.-China tensions continue, South Korea will need to seek more viable options through diversifying its semiconductor trade partners and reconsidering its existing strategy of expanding manufacturing capabilities in the Chinese market.

Besides China, the policies of other major countries in the semiconductor industry also have severe implications for their trading partners that are linked through the supply chains. Since these countries can dominate certain technologies with their high-tech prowess, their policies tend to have the greatest impact on the global supply chain. Examples include U.S. policies related to the semiconductor industry, such as the passage of the 2022 CHIPS and Science Act, which strengthens export controls against China, and efforts to establish the "Fab 4" chip alliance among the four major semiconductor manufacturing countries excluding China. Depending on how these policies are implemented, there is a high probability that the existing global supply chain for semiconductors could be reconfigured with the United States at its new center. The Biden administration is committed to reshoring semiconductor capabilities by aggressively using industrial subsidies to strengthen the domestic manufacturing capacity. Due to the broad applications of semiconductors, which include military uses, leadership in the global semiconductor market is not only an economic issue but also one of national security.

As part of its efforts to navigate the conditions attached to subsidies offered by the CHIPS and Science Act, the ROK government has requested that the United States provide more leeway for Korean-invested production facilities operating in China. While the guardrail provisions in the act prohibit any material expansion that increases production capacity by 10% in existing facilities, the ROK government has requested that these limits be expanded to avoid creating any circumstances that illegitimately burden foreign companies looking to invest in the United States. In a coordinated move, South Korean semiconductor companies have also petitioned the U.S. Commerce Department for clarification of the conditions attached to receiving subsidies.[30]

Prioritizing economic security, the United States is including its allies and partners in measures to strengthen its semiconductor supply chain. The semiconductor supply chain is currently fragmented among the countries and technology firms that have dominated its respective sectors, and the existing structure cannot be easily transformed. The U.S. government's efforts to become self-sufficient by strengthening the domestic semiconductors supply chain will take time; in the meantime, it will need to cooperate with its partners and allies to reform the current structure. It is also becoming evident that the new rules and standards used to demarcate the line between

---

[30] "Korean Government Steps Up to Help Semiconductor Businesses amid U.S.-China Tensions," *Korea JoongAng Daily*, May 25, 2023.

partners and non-partners for configuring new supply chains include stricter environmental and labor provisions, protection of proprietary technology through strengthened intellectual property rights, and fair competition. As a consequence, countries that are not able to meet the new criteria for entering the supply chains may risk being alienated from global semiconductor commercial activity. The burden for commercial businesses to use environmentally friendly technology and labor-friendly production methods will increase, also contributing to further concentration of the semiconductor industry in players that can afford the social costs in the manufacturing process.

Strategic Approach to the Semiconductor Industry

Considering South Korea's current position in the global semiconductor market, its most important task should be increasing its strengths by upgrading its technological capabilities to remain an attractive partner for advanced countries in the supply chain (such as the United States and Japan) and to maintain the technology development gap with fast-growing developing countries (i.e., China). To this end, the ROK government should pursue an active strategy to support its domestic semiconductor businesses with various fiscal incentives so that companies will engage in more R&D to develop foundational and applied technologies and support the development of skilled personnel to work in the industry. As part of these efforts to strengthen the country's competitiveness, the government announced the K-Semiconductor Strategy to help promote its domestic semiconductor industry in May 2021. The strategy comprises five major strategies and seventeen tasks (see **Table 1**).

As shown above, South Korea's national strategy for the semiconductor industry aims to provide for its overall growth through various support measures, with renewed interest in fostering growth in advanced technology areas. The basic approach appears to be the promotion of domestic competitiveness in order to engage more actively in the global semiconductor supply chain and maintain interdependence with major semiconductor countries. There is notable emphasis on the importance of developing skilled experts and human resources. Due to the features of technology that are mostly transferred or leaked through personnel or joint R&D projects, there is also renewed emphasis on the need for strengthened management of these human resources as part of a strategy for technology protection. This has instigated a number of efforts to realign South Korea's strategy for protecting key strategic technologies through the combined efforts of various administrative offices. The strategy covers government-wide initiatives to

TABLE 1 South Korea's K-Semiconductor Strategy

Strategy	Tasks
1. Establish the K-Semiconductor Belt to stabilize supply chains	1. Manufacturing base
	2. Components, materials, equipment
	3. Advanced equipment
	4. Packaging
	5. Fabless
2. Expand infrastructure investment for becoming a hub in semiconductor manufacturing	6. Tax credits
	7. Financial support
	8. Improvement of regulations
	9. Infrastructure
3. Invest in developing skilled personnel, markets, and technology for the semiconductor industry's growth	10. Personnel development
	11. Coalition and cooperation
	12. Technology development
4. Strengthen crisis response mechanisms for promoting domestic semiconductor ecosystem	13. Legislation of a special act for semiconductors
	14. Semiconductors for vehicles
	15. Technology protection
	16. Carbon neutrality
5. Create domestic technology for industrial water	17. High purity industrial water technology

establish a preemptive system for protecting critical technologies, prevent leakage of human resources, establish a domestic system for maintaining strategic resources, protect small and medium-sized enterprises, promote technology capabilities, prevent cyber theft of technology, and strengthen government-wide efforts to promote international cooperation and trade. As such, the South Korean government's efforts to maintain economic interdependence with the global community can be viewed as being focused on strengthening and fostering domestic capacities, resources, and skills. This is not very different from how other countries are addressing the risks and vulnerabilities caused by the current geopolitical tensions in the region.

South Korea should also take part in international efforts to establish rules to prevent countries from resorting to unilateral sanctions against the semiconductor trade. Rules to ensure that technology is protected from illegal attempts to obtain proprietary knowledge and technology skills may also need to be strengthened. South Korea is a victim of these attempts due to its position as a major semiconductor manufacturing country with high levels of technology.

Against this backdrop, while it is important to maintain cooperation with China, it is also necessary to reconsider whether South Korea needs export controls and foreign investment restrictions to protect any leakage of key national technologies. To this end, the government should (1) constantly monitor risks to its semiconductor supply chain, (2) prevent leakage of skilled personnel and promote the recruitment of new personnel, and (3) maintain the technology gap in areas where it has a comparative advantage through strategic R&D investment in innovative technology areas.

Strategic Approach to the Critical Minerals Supply Chain

The stable supply of critical minerals that are used as inputs for manufacturing batteries for EVs has gained increasing importance amid the global efforts to address climate change issues. Currently, due to various economic and environmental reasons, the supply of critical minerals inputs is dominated by not only a limited number of countries with abundant resources but also those with sufficient levels of processing technologies and lax environmental regulations. This has also enabled the weaponization of critical minerals supplies, pushing industrialized countries to beef up their own supplies of critical minerals and to form global partnerships to collaborate on access to the clean energy inputs. South Korea, which owns several key large firms that produce EVs and batteries as well, has a high stake in securing and strengthening its supplies of critical minerals. This section examines the importance of the critical minerals supply chain in the context of economic security and introduces South Korea's approach to address the issues and challenges arising from economic interdependence.

The Global Critical Minerals Supply Chain

Critical minerals are essential raw materials that are used in a variety of industries, including renewable energy equipment, EVs, high-capacity batteries, and defense articles. Global demand for critical minerals has been on the rise during the transition to clean energy in major economies and the growth of related green industries. Demand is expected to rise fourfold by 2040 due to the zero-carbon policies pursued by major economies and the global transition to clean energy–based infrastructure.[31]

---

[31] Ministry of Trade, Industry and Energy (ROK), *Haekshim gwangmul hwakbo junryak* [Critical Minerals Security Strategy] (Seoul, February 2023).

Despite this high level of demand, the supply of critical minerals is concentrated in only a few countries, including China and several countries in Africa and Latin America. For various reasons, these resource-abundant countries are resorting to export-restrictive measures that pose a severe risk to the stable supply of critical minerals for resource-importing countries. Due to the concentrated supply and production, there is increased competition among major importers for what resources are available. The Covid-19 pandemic, U.S.-China tensions, and the Russia-Ukraine war have also exacerbated the situation by raising concerns about China's possible imposition of export controls on raw materials. With these risks, prices have surged: the price of lithium has increased by 13.3 times and nickel by 2.1 times. Relatedly, there are also environmental issues during the refining process of these critical raw materials that serve as another barrier for efforts to export them to resource-importing countries.

By 2030, the global EV market is expected to grow tenfold and the battery market thirteenfold. EV production requires six times the amount of critical minerals as the production of diesel motor vehicles. Every stage of the global EV and battery market is largely controlled by China.[32] While the mining stage is distributed among various countries, China dominates the processing and production stages and has a commanding share of the supply chain in key critical materials for manufacturing EV batteries, such as lithium, nickel, cobalt, and graphite.

While global sales of automobiles were weak during the pandemic, EV sales rose by nearly 100% year-on-year, resulting in 6 million vehicles sold in 2021 compared with 3.3 million in 2020. The growth in global sales is expected to continue for quite some time, mainly due to aggressive subsidization policies by major economies promoting the EV industry and restrictions on selling diesel motor vehicles. The high demand for EVs and their batteries will also affect the demand for critical minerals, which will increase up to 42-fold by 2040.[33]

Supply Chain Risks for Critical Minerals

Global demand for critical minerals is expected to grow exponentially due to economic development and industrial upgrades in both developing and advanced countries. In particular, China's desire to become a leading nation in advanced technologies is reportedly one of the major reasons behind the surge

---

[32] For an illustration of China's dominance, see the chart showing the concentration of materials for major countries along the EV and batteries supply chain in International Energy Agency (IEA), "Global EV Outlook," May 2022, https://iea.blob.core.windows.net/assets/ad8fb04c-4f75-42fc-973a-6e54c8a4449a/GlobalElectricVehicleOutlook2022.pdf.

[33] Ibid.

in demand for critical minerals. More generally, the recent series of global shocks have contributed to the rise in prices of resources and raw materials, compounding the problem of supply chain vulnerability. Furthermore, while the mining of certain critical minerals is concentrated in several countries, such as 69% of cobalt in Congo, 64% of graphite in China, and 52% of lithium in Australia, the refining process is mainly concentrated in China—87.1% of raw earths, 57.8% of lithium, 64.7% of cobalt, and 40.0% of copper.[34]

The development of new mines is not an easy task, mainly due to potential conflict with a local community over environmental problems caused by the mining process and the long time required (fifteen to twenty years) for a mine to become operational. Governments can also attempt to nationalize the ownership of critical minerals or impose export controls to leverage their dominance in raw materials. For example, Mexico passed legislation to nationalize its lithium industry, established a state-owned lithium corporation in 2022, and inaugurated a coalition with other countries that own lithium reserves that account for 58% of global lithium production.[35] Similarly, in 2022 and 2023, Indonesia announced plans to impose export restrictions on bauxite and copper ore as part of measures to increase the value of its mineral reserves by inducing foreign investment in domestic production facilities that process them.[36] Export controls are also used to secure domestic supplies, expand government revenues, and influence international prices.

South Korea's Strategic Approach to Critical Minerals

In February 2023 the ROK government announced a strategy to stabilize supply chains for critical minerals to mitigate import reliance on certain countries and use domestic mineral resources to the extent possible (see **Table 2**).[37] To this end, 33 critical minerals were selected, and among them 10 were identified as "strategic critical minerals" needed for supply chain resilience in advanced technology industries such as semiconductors and EVs. The ten strategic critical minerals are lithium, nickel, cobalt, graphite, manganese, cerium, lanthanum, neodymium, dysprosium, and terbium. The criteria for selection considered each mineral's overall impact on the economy and possible supply chain risks. These included the volume of and increase in imports, importance to industry (i.e., value added), role in achieving net-zero carbon levels, concentration of resources, instability in supply chains, risk response capabilities, and environmental, social, and corporate

---

[34] IEA, "The Role of Critical Minerals in Clean Energy Transitions," May 2021.

[35] KITA, "Critical Minerals for Batteries Supply Chain: Lithium," *Trade Focus*, no. 21, 35.

[36] Ibid.

[37] Ministry of Trade, Industry and Energy (ROK), *Haekshim gwangmul hwakbo junryak*.

TABLE 2   South Korea's critical minerals strategy

Vision	Sustainable advanced industry through a stable critical minerals supply chain	
Objectives (by 2030)	Ten strategic critical minerals: Reduce dependence on certain countries to 50% level; increase recycling ratio to 20%	
	Strategies	Tasks
1.	Strengthening crisis response capacity	1. Global map for critical minerals
		2. Early-warning system
2.	Diversifying sources of critical minerals	3. Strengthening of bilateral and multilateral cooperation
		4. Development of foreign and domestic reserves
		5. Recycling infrastructure
		6. Increased stockpiling
3.	Establishing infrastructure for systemic management of critical minerals	7. Realignment of rules and regulations
		8. Training and technology development

SOURCE: Ministry of Trade, Industry and Energy (ROK), *Haekshim gwangmul hwakbo junryak* [Critical Minerals Security Strategy] (Seoul, February 2023).

governance (ESG) aspects. As part of its strategy to secure critical minerals, the government has created a global map that provides information on mines overseas that are needed for obtaining them, including information on reserves and production capacity per country and the type of minerals mined. In order to establish an early-warning system for supply chain risks, indexes for assessing the stability of the supply of minerals were also developed.[38]

In terms of measures to strengthen cooperation in critical minerals supply chains, the government has selected 30 countries as "strategic cooperation countries" based on an analysis of each country's mineral reserves capacity, attractiveness for development, and accessibility. These countries could be subject to long-term supply contracts and financial support for mine development through memoranda of understanding on private-public cooperation projects and FTAs with renewed provisions on joint research, information exchange, and trade facilitation. On the multilateral level, South Korea has become a member of the Minerals

[38] Ministry of Trade, Industry and Energy (ROK), *Haekshim gwangmul hwakbo junryak.*

Security Partnership, in which members share information on related projects, engage in investment networks, establish ESG-related rules, and encourage recycling of critical minerals.

As part of its efforts to induce private investment in the critical minerals industry, the ROK government has expanded financial support and tax incentives through the Export-Import Bank of Korea and the Korea Trade Insurance Corporation. It has also reintroduced tax credits for overseas investment projects developing foreign resources (previously terminated in 2013), while expanding the scope of compensation for losses and alleviating tax burdens for foreign-affiliated companies. In order to secure domestic resource development capacity, the government also plans to establish a circulation system under which critical minerals can be recycled as well as an industrial cluster for reclaiming waste materials, recycling, distributing, and stockpiling.

Conclusion

This chapter has explored how weaponized interdependence and decoupling pressures have affected South Korea's foreign policy. Given its asymmetric economic interdependence with China, on the one hand, and Washington's demand for decoupling from Beijing, on the other, South Korea faces three key challenges: ensuring supply chain resilience, reducing its heavy reliance on China for critical materials, and sustaining an adequate level of economic interdependence under decoupling pressure. Focusing on the ROK semiconductor industry and the supply chain for critical raw materials, this chapter examined the country's efforts to address the structural dilemmas that it faces in managing supply chain disruptions, decreasing vulnerabilities vis-à-vis China through diversification, and building capacity in domestic manufacturing.

In addressing these challenges, South Korea's central concern is exploring a pragmatic approach to reducing structural vulnerabilities to China while at the same time maintaining economic interdependence. In other words, the task is to strike a balance between national security and economic interdependence. This concern is widely shared. For instance, the EU perceives fewer national security risks in its relations with China than the United States, which has pressured its allies to take harder decoupling stances through its CHIPS and Science Act. Although EU-U.S. China policy on trade and technology has been aligned, the 27 EU member states remain split over how far they will follow it. The shift from decoupling to de-risking indicates that the United States is willing to accommodate its allies' demands for softening its efforts to deter China's high-tech drive. These efforts have thus far seemed quite successful. For example, the leaders at the 2023 G-7 summit declared that they will coordinate their "approach to economic resilience and economic security that is based on diversifying and deepening partnerships and de-risking, not decoupling."[39]

According to the United States, de-risking involves restricting the trade of "a narrow set of advanced technologies" that are critical for national security, "technologies that could tilt the limitary balance."[40] This means that technologies that pose risks to national security are subject to decoupling from China. However, because modern high-tech products are dual-use in nature, this could include vast sectors of U.S. manufacturing. If risks to national security are broadly framed, a de-risking policy toward China could become closer to decoupling. What is needed, then, is a collective and coordinated effort to delimit the scope of technologies and industries that are critical for national security.

South Korea's economic statecraft needs to follow a collective and multilateral approach to establishing rules and norms to define the scope of "national security" as invoked in a de-risking effort. Further, it should work to ultimately restore an international economic order that strikes a balance between economic interdependence and national security and ensures the re-globalization of the post-pandemic world order. The government must combine this effort with other strategies that (1) constantly monitor risks to South Korea's supply chains, (2) prevent leakage of skilled personnel and promote the recruitment of new personnel, and (3) maintain the technology gap in areas where South Korea has a comparative advantage through strategic R&D investment in innovative technology.

---

[39] "G7 Hiroshima Leaders' Communiqué."

[40] Paul Gewirtz, "Words and Policies: 'De-risking' and China Policy," Brookings Institution, May 30, 2023, https://www.brookings.edu/articles/words-and-policies-de-risking-and-china-policy.

EXECUTIVE SUMMARY

This chapter examines the implications of U.S.-China decoupling for Taiwan's integration with the Chinese and world economies and explores how this economic fragmentation is shaping the context in which the Taiwanese are determining their island's future.

MAIN ARGUMENT

As the U.S. and Chinese economies decouple, Taiwan is navigating challenges posed by strategic competition between two great powers. In an increasingly fragmented global economy, Taiwan shares democratic values and strategic goals with the U.S. However, U.S. policies aiming to retain technological supremacy over China, especially in the semiconductor sector, lack coordination with Taiwanese and international stakeholders and are hurting Taiwan, whose growth depends on global economic integration, particularly with the Chinese market. This has raised doubts about U.S. leadership within Taiwanese society, which is grappling with domestic challenges to economic resilience amid deepening political polarization. How the U.S. engages with Taiwan will not only shape perceptions of the U.S. but also influence Taiwan's ability to support U.S. strategic goals in competing with China.

POLICY IMPLICATIONS

- The U.S. must reassess semiconductor reshoring policies, analyze the impact of its export controls and investment restrictions on Taiwan and other partners in Europe and Asia, and offer concrete incentives to ensure ongoing compliance.
- The U.S. must engage Taiwan's business community, government, and civil society when considering new rules for regional and international economic collaboration to maintain trust and support from Taiwanese society.
- The U.S. must continue supporting Taiwan's pursuit of deeper regional economic integration and greater international involvement, which remain vital for enhancing Taiwan's resilience and capacity to contribute to the U.S.-led liberal order.

EXECUTIVE SUMMARY

This chapter examines the implications of U.S.-China decoupling for Taiwan's integration with the Chinese and world economies and explores how this economic fragmentation is shaping the context in which the Taiwanese are determining their island's future.

MAIN ARGUMENT

As the U.S. and Chinese economies decouple, Taiwan is navigating challenges posed by strategic competition between two great powers. In an increasingly fragmented global economy, Taiwan shares democratic values and strategic goals with the U.S. However, U.S. policies aiming to retain technological supremacy over China, especially in the semiconductor sector, lack coordination with Taiwanese and international stakeholders and are hurting Taiwan, whose growth depends on global economic integration, particularly with the Chinese market. This has raised doubts about U.S. leadership within Taiwanese society, which is grappling with domestic challenges to economic resilience amid deepening political polarization. How the U.S. engages with Taiwan will not only shape perceptions of the U.S. but also influence Taiwan's ability to support U.S. strategic goals in competing with China.

POLICY IMPLICATIONS

- The U.S. must reassess semiconductor reshoring policies, analyze the impact of its export controls and investment restrictions on Taiwan and other partners in Europe and Asia, and offer concrete incentives to ensure ongoing compliance.
- The U.S. must engage Taiwan's business community, government, and civil society when considering new rules for regional and international economic collaboration to maintain trust and support from Taiwanese society.
- The U.S. must continue supporting Taiwan's pursuit of deeper regional economic integration and greater international involvement, which remain vital for enhancing Taiwan's resilience and capacity to contribute to the U.S.-led liberal order.

Taiwan: Walking the Tightrope between the United States and China

Syaru Shirley Lin

As the global economy moves away from globalization to regionalization, Taiwan's previous model of economic development through technological and policy innovation and integration with global supply chains is becoming less resilient and competitive. The island faces supply chain fragmentation, decoupling, and reshoring of critical industries, in part because of protectionist policies by the United States, China, and other actors.[1] This chapter describes these changes and examines what they mean for Taiwan's integration with the Chinese market and world economy, for Taiwan's future as a global technology hub, and for the Taiwanese people. Intended to make democratic societies, especially the United States, more resilient, the policies driving "decoupling" have made economic and societal resilience even more difficult for Taiwan to enhance and may be producing a backlash on the island against the global liberal order and the commercial networks of which Taiwan is a part.

Taiwan's economic success has relied on deep integration with the global economy and especially China through export-oriented manufacturing.

Syaru Shirley Lin is Founder and Chair of the Center for Asia-Pacific Resilience and Innovation, Research Professor at the Miller Center of Public Affairs at the University of Virginia, and a Nonresident Senior Fellow in the Foreign Policy Program at the Brookings Institution. She can be reached at <shirley@virginia.edu>.

The author thanks Caroline Fried and Siwei Huang at the Center for Asia-Pacific Resilience and Innovation for their research, writing, and editorial support.

[1] "Decoupling" is a contested term in policy discussions on U.S.-China relations. In this chapter, it refers to the steady reduction of economic and technological interdependence with China, with broader strategic implications. Recently, "de-risking" has become more accepted in policy discussions in Europe and focuses primarily on economic diversification away from China. See Paul Gewirtz, "Words and Policies: 'De-risking' and China Policy," Brookings Institution, May 30, 2023, https://www.brookings.edu/articles/words-and-policies-de-risking-and-china-policy.

Taiwanese businesses had the capital, expertise, cultural proximity, and operational capabilities to enhance Taiwan's international competitiveness by investing in China—despite restrictions by the Taiwanese government and little legal protection from China. As globalization reverses, Taiwanese firms, especially in technology, have been among the first affected by tariffs, export controls, and investment restrictions on China as well as disruptions caused by the ongoing Covid-19 pandemic. In addition, lagging domestic consumption, rising labor costs, and tightening social controls in the Chinese market make it less lucrative and riskier. However, Taiwanese businesses have found few alternatives, even with mounting U.S. pressure to move away from China. Many Taiwanese agree with diversification in principle but disagree on how it should be conducted and at what speed.

The global semiconductor ecosystem, in which Taiwan is a leader, is the most important example of how fragmentation threatens global resilience. Public-private partnership in Taiwan pioneered the contract manufacturing model, enabling a globally interdependent value chain in which technology firms worldwide depend on Taiwan's foundries to manufacture integrated circuit chips, especially through severe shortages during the Covid-19 pandemic. However, the United States, the European Union, and China now view this interdependence as a source of instability rather than resilience, investing in reshoring the supply chain within their own borders, enacting protectionist policies on intellectual property (IP), and approaching the technology industry—from human capital to chip manufacturing—from a national security perspective. Broad export controls, which have affected many sectors globally, have forced the semiconductor supply chain to reconfigure at immense costs for all parties, especially Taiwanese firms, which are also losing investor confidence as tensions rise in the Taiwan Strait. If the objective of U.S. policymakers is to slow Chinese development in dual-use technology (with both civilian and military applications), Taiwanese—in both the public and private sectors—must be treated as partners to build a more resilient global economy.

While proud of their country's economic and technological development, Taiwanese voters are keenly aware that the Taiwanese economy's dependence on the information and communications technology (ICT) industry means walking a tightrope between Washington and Beijing. And some Taiwanese believe that decoupling will reduce Taiwan's economic resilience and exacerbate Taiwan's domestic structural problems. Voters are reassessing the reliability of the United States as a strategic partner and the suitability of Washington's advice on weapons acquisition and defense strategy. Furthermore, continued exclusion from global trade and health regimes leaves Taiwan vulnerable to future economic and health crises. Both major political parties—the Democratic Progressive Party (DPP) and the Kuomintang (KMT)—as well as third parties all reject China's "one country, two systems" formulation for Taiwan, but they offer few alternatives for cross-strait relations.

A successful and resilient Taiwan can be a stronger partner to the United States technologically and economically while remaining an example of a Chinese society espousing democratic values. Taiwan has relied on innovation to navigate changing geopolitical and economic landscapes by closely integrating with the global economy, encouraging talent circulation, and promoting public-private collaboration. Economic fragmentation, deteriorating trust in international society, and domestic political polarization are eroding the foundations of Taiwan's success, even as China poses a growing threat to the island. To counter increasing marginalization in the global political economy, Taiwan needs more integration with the United States and the Asia-Pacific to design and implement effective policy that promotes freedom and democracy. This requires civic engagement in policymaking as well as independent and innovative thinking on how to navigate a changing geopolitical landscape, enabling all of Taiwanese society to contribute to making U.S. policy successful.

This chapter begins with a review of structural trends in Taiwan's foreign economic relationships and the evolving patterns of economic interdependence with China. It then focuses on the evolution of Taiwan's semiconductor industry within the context of U.S.-China strategic competition and the pressure the industry faces to decouple from China. Subsequently, the chapter discusses the implications of Beijing's and Washington's policies toward Taiwan and the dynamics of its domestic socioeconomic and political landscape leading up to the 2024 election. The chapter concludes with a discussion of the future of the Taiwan-U.S. partnership, assessing the prospects for Taiwan as it faces decoupling and considering policy options for the United States.

Taiwan Reconsiders Cross-Strait Interdependence

Taiwan's Economic Development

Taiwan's economic success relied on deep integration with the international economy during the Cold War and especially with China since the late 1980s. Over the last three decades, Taiwan's economy took off, with its export-oriented manufacturing sectors helping further expand its international trade. Taiwan's export-to-GDP ratio increased from approximately 40% in the 1990s to over 60% in 2022.² Exports in the past three decades have predominantly been in the industrial sector, compared with only 1% in agricultural products. The composition of industrial exports has also changed substantially, with textiles dwindling from over 20% in 1980 to only 2% currently. In the same period, machinery and electrical equipment have grown from around 20% to over 60% of Taiwan's total exports, consisting primarily of ICT products and electronic components, which are also the majority of Taiwan's total imports. Mineral fuels, including coal, petroleum, and natural gas, constituted 20% of Taiwan's imported goods in 2022, rising from approximately 10% in 2001, reflecting a growing demand for and dependence on imported energy to fuel Taiwan's rapid industrial development.

With the establishment of its first science-based industrial park in 1979 in Hsinchu, Taiwan began developing capital- and technology-intensive industries, particularly in electronics and ICT. The ICT sector now constitutes 40% of the country's GDP, led by a highly competitive semiconductor industry, which now supplies over 60% of the world's integrated circuit chips and over 90% of the most advanced ones.³

The evolving pattern in exports aligns with trends in Taiwan's overseas investments. Starting in the 1990s, outward foreign direct investment gradually shifted from mining and light industries toward capital-intensive electronics and ICT manufacturing. This sector now accounts for one-fifth of Taiwan's cumulative outbound FDI.⁴ The top destination of outward FDI had been Southeast Asia until the 1970s, when it was replaced by the United States. After China's reform and opening, Taiwan began to invest heavily in China, which soon eclipsed the United States as its top investment destination.

Growing Interdependence with China through the Taishang

Early in China's reform and opening in the 1980s, the growth of the country's cheap and educated labor force, known as the "demographic dividend," offered Taiwanese businesses an immense opportunity to drive down manufacturing costs by making China the world's factory.⁵ Beijing

---

² Trade data is from the Ministry of Finance (Taiwan), and GDP data is from the Executive Yuan (Taiwan), Directorate General of Budget, Accounting and Statistics.

³ "Taiwan's Dominance of the Chip Industry Makes It More Important," *Economist*, March 6, 2023, https://www.economist.com/special-report/2023/03/06/taiwans-dominance-of-the-chip-industry-makes-it-more-important.

⁴ Ministry of Economic Affairs (Taiwan), Investment Commission.

⁵ Cai Fang, "How Has the Chinese Economy Capitalised on the Demographic Dividend during the Reform Period?" in *China's 40 Years of Reform and Development: 1978–2018*, ed. Ross Garnaut, Ligang Song, and Cai Fang (Acton: Australian National University Press, 2018), 235–56.

further encouraged cross-strait interdependence through incentives and subsidies such as tax deductions and reduced land rental fees for foreign investors and especially Taiwanese entrepreneurs.[6] Known as Taishang, these Taiwanese businesspeople found China extremely friendly, given the cultural and linguistic familiarity and geographic proximity. Along with overseas Chinese from Southeast Asia and Hong Kong, the Taishang applied their financial capital, technical expertise, and operational know-how to build economies of scale by producing in China. Establishing industrial clusters throughout the coastal cities, they set up local supply chains and became deeply embedded in the Chinese economy as exporters who could respond to shifting global demands with agility and efficiency, serving primarily multinational corporations.

More recently, as the Chinese middle class grew and its spending power increased, Taiwanese firms began investing in retail for the Chinese consumer market. Many Taishang who had originally focused on export markets began to build capacity to manufacture and promote their own brands for the Chinese market. They also began entering the service and hospitality industries by opening restaurants and hotels. Taiwanese technology firms invested heavily in China, starting with laptop manufacturers and later the semiconductor industry.[7]

Business expansion into China has continued to grow since 1991, with cumulative investments in China exceeding two-thirds of Taiwan's total outward FDI at its height in 2011 (see **Figure 1**). Although investment flows have slowed substantially during the Covid-19 pandemic, over $200 billion of the cumulative $380 billion in Taiwanese FDI remained in China as of 2022, with over 30% in the ICT sector.[8] Despite constant tension in the Taiwan Strait, the market attraction of China—first as a low-cost manufacturing base with high productivity and later as the world's largest consumer market—outweighed the risks for Taiwanese businesses. Furthermore, with the launch of Xi Jinping's Made in China 2025 initiative in 2015 to encourage indigenous competition, remaining in China became even more crucial for multinational corporations and Taishang alike, who must ensure their products are "made in China" to continue selling to Chinese consumers. With competition

---

[6] Syaru Shirley Lin, *Taiwan's China Dilemma: Contested Identities and Multiple Interests in Taiwan's Cross-Strait Economic Policy* (Stanford: Stanford University Press, 2016), 61.

[7] The Taiwanese personal computer industry started investing in China in the 1990s, but semiconductor companies were not allowed to invest in China until the early 2000s. See Chyan Yang and Hung Shiu-Wan, "Taiwan's Dilemma Across the Strait: Lifting the Ban on Semiconductor Investment in China," *Asian Survey* 43, no. 4 (2003): 681–96.

[8] Chad P. Bown and Yilin Wang, "Taiwan's Outbound Foreign Investment, Particularly in Tech, Continues to Go to Mainland China Despite Strict Controls," Peterson Institute for International Economics, February 27, 2023, https://www.piie.com/research/piie-charts/taiwans-outbound-foreign-investment-particularly-tech-continues-go-mainland.

FIGURE 1 Taiwan's outbound FDI to the world and to China, 1990–2022

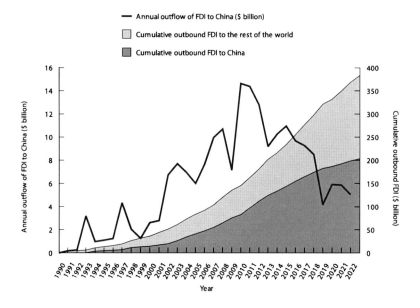

SOURCE: Ministry of Economic Affairs (Taiwan), Investment Commission.

increasing from domestic businesses (often with Beijing's support) to form a "red supply chain," Taishang have been losing market share, but few other markets are as attractive as China's.[9]

As Taiwan's investments in China have increased, the share of its bilateral trade with China has increased to approximately 25% (over 40% if trade with Hong Kong is included) of total trade. Total trade with China surpassed that with the United States in 2004, making China Taiwan's largest trading partner. Despite declining investments in China over the last seven years due to Taiwanese government pressure and rising costs in China's coastal cities, Taiwan's trade surplus with China reached an all-time high of $43 billion in 2021 (see **Figure 2**). That same year, its trade surplus with the United States was only $26 billion.[10]

---

[9] Hannah Chang, "Taiwan Businesses: Exiting China Not an Option amid Struggle for Survival," *CommonWealth Magazine*, July 8, 2021, https://english.cw.com.tw/article/article.action?id=3030.

[10] Ministry of Finance (Taiwan), Trade Statistics Database.

FIGURE 2 Taiwan's trade with China, 1990–2022

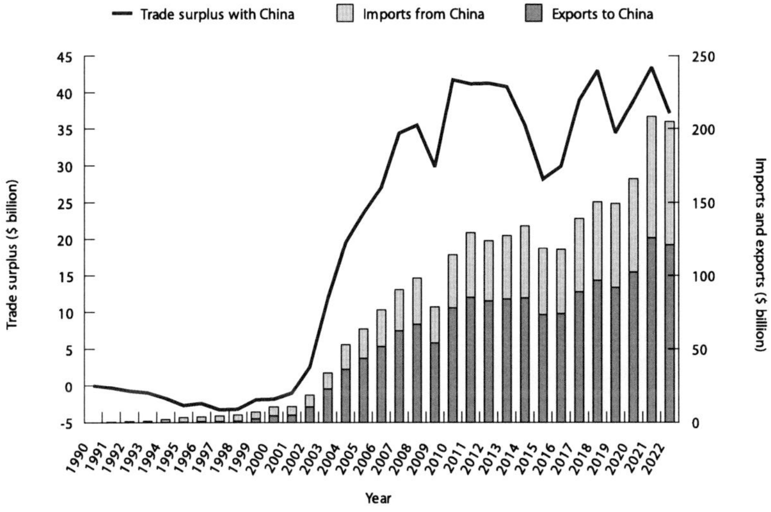

SOURCE: Ministry of Finance (Taiwan), Trade Statistics Database.

Despite growing cross-strait economic interdependence, in 2014 young Taiwanese people led a wave of protests against further liberalization of trade and services with China through the Cross-Strait Service Trade Agreement, which was a follow-up agreement under the Economic Cooperation Framework Agreement (ECFA) developed and signed under KMT president Ma Ying-jeou.[11] In the aftermath of these protests, dubbed the Sunflower Movement, Taiwanese voters in 2016 elected President Tsai Ing-wen, whose DPP administration vowed to uphold Taiwan's sovereignty and counter infiltration by Beijing. To diversify away from China, President Tsai began to promote investments in Southeast Asia under the New Southbound Policy (NSP) and attract Taishang to reinvest in Taiwan through incentives and subsidies. In President Tsai's second term (2020–24), the policy has resulted in more frequent people-to-people exchanges and increased investments in Southeast Asia, with total investments in NSP countries now a quarter of

---

[11] JoAnn Fan, "The Economics of the Cross-Strait Services Agreement," *Diplomat*, April 18, 2014, https://thediplomat.com/2014/04/the-economics-of-the-cross-strait-services-agreement.

Taiwan's cumulative outward FDI at $50 billion.¹² In 2022, new Taiwanese investments in NSP countries exceeded $5 billion, surpassing investments in China for the first time.¹³ Taiwanese investments in the United States and Europe are also increasing, although not as quickly as in NSP countries. Since 2019, the Tsai administration's three major programs to help Taishang reinvest in Taiwan have attracted over $60 billion from overseas Taiwanese.¹⁴ Overall, the recent decline in Taiwanese investment flow to China mirrors a general decrease in global investments in China, which in 2022 declined to their lowest level in eighteen years.¹⁵

For Taiwanese firms, expansion into China now involves risks and restrictions far greater than those facing other foreign competitors. In the 1980s the Chinese government offered incentives to foreign investors through preferential land use and tax policies in special economic zones along China's coast. However, despite the regulations offering nominal legal protection to foreign firms, Taiwanese firms in reality faced great legal risk because they were deemed "Chinese," and the Taiwanese government could not protect Taishang legally.¹⁶ Furthermore, Taiwanese investment in China has always been subject to scrutiny by the Taiwanese government, especially in sectors considered to have national strategic importance. Investments in strategic industries—namely petrochemicals and semiconductors—and any investment over $50 million in China still require approval. Semiconductor investments in China were essentially banned by Taipei until 2002. Both the United States and Taiwan have long-standing restrictions on leading-edge semiconductor technology entering China, and Taiwan has effectively stopped the most advanced technologies from moving to China.¹⁷

Taiwan Caught in U.S.-China Decoupling

Even when facing these regulatory constraints, Taishang have been flexible and resilient, seizing opportunities in China faster than their competitors. However, as the Trump administration began to view China

---

¹² Satu Limaye, Robert Wang, and Russell Hsiao, "Assessing Trends and Demand Signals for Taiwan's New Southbound Policy and Building a U.S.-Taiwan Coordination Mechanism," Taiwan-Asia Exchange Foundation, January 30, 2023, https://www.taef.org/doc/1082.

¹³ Ministry of Economic Affairs (Taiwan), Investment Commission.

¹⁴ "Three Major Programs for Investing in Taiwan," Ministry of Economic Affairs (Taiwan), InvesTaiwan, https://investtaiwan.nat.gov.tw/showPagecht1135?lang=eng&search=1135.

¹⁵ Iori Kawate, "Foreign Investment in China Slumps to 18-Year Low," *Nikkei Asia*, February 28, 2023, https://asia.nikkei.com/Economy/Foreign-investment-in-China-slumps-to-18-year-low.

¹⁶ Shelley Rigger, *The Tiger Leading the Dragon: How Taiwan Propelled China's Economic Rise* (Lanham: Rowman and Littlefield, 2021), 38.

¹⁷ Lin, *Taiwan's China Dilemma*, 72, 156.

as a strategic competitor, the United States increasingly enacted restrictive measures to contain Chinese economic development. Taiwanese and other foreign firms were hurt immediately, initially by global tariffs on steel and textiles and subsequently by export controls, sanctions, and investment restrictions. Technology companies were also hard hit. In the name of national security and resilience, the United States is leading the global economy toward regionalization and segregation, viewing its R&D, production, and human capital as assets that must reside in a "small yard with a high fence."[18] This strategy necessitates supply chain duplication in every region. The Covid-19 pandemic, which severely disrupted global supply chains, further exacerbated this trend.

The U.S. restrictions mirror China's long-held strategy even after China joined the World Trade Organization in 2001—welcoming trade and investments but implementing top-down regulation to keep economies segregated to benefit China's "catching up" and economic sovereignty. Despite these challenges, for Taiwanese manufacturers who serve large multinational clients, there seems to be no readily available alternative to China. Foxconn, the leading Taishang in China, is a case in point. Foxconn supplies 95% of Apple's iPhones and computers and is deeply embedded in the Chinese economy, which constitutes nearly a quarter of Apple's global sales.[19] Pursuing just-in-time manufacturing efficiency and flexibility at an immense scale, the company has recently doubled down by setting up a new global business center in Zhengzhou in central China, where it runs the world's biggest iPhone factory.[20] Although Foxconn tried to diversify away from China, surveying Europe, Vietnam, and India and agreeing to invest in Wisconsin in 2017, little has come of these investment plans.[21]

Furthermore, China remains a gateway for Taiwan to participate in cost-efficient regional trade, especially given that Taiwan does not have access to regional free trade agreements (FTAs) such as the Regional Comprehensive Economic Partnership (RCEP). Signed in 2020, the RCEP is the world's

---

[18] "Remarks by National Security Advisor Jake Sullivan on the Biden-Harris Administration's National Security Strategy," White House, October 12, 2022, https://www.whitehouse.gov/briefing-room/speeches-remarks/2022/10/13/remarks-by-national-security-advisor-jake-sullivan-on-the-biden-harris-administrations-national-security-strategy.

[19] Patrick McGee, "How Apple Tied Its Fortunes to China," *Financial Times*, January 17, 2023, https://www.ft.com/content/d5a80891-b27d-4110-90c9-561b7836f11b.

[20] Ben Jiang, "Apple Supplier Foxconn Sets Up Global Business Base in iPhone City in Show of Commitment to China," *South China Morning Post*, April 25, 2023, https://www.scmp.com/tech/policy/article/3218313/apple-supplier-foxconn-sets-global-business-base-iphone-city-show-commitment-china.

[21] Lauly Li, "Foxconn Aims to Build EV Factories in Europe and India by 2024," *Nikkei Asia*, October 20, 2021, https://asia.nikkei.com/Business/Technology/Foxconn-aims-to-build-EV-factories-in-Europe-and-India-by-2024.

largest FTA and includes all ten members of the Association of Southeast Asian Nations (ASEAN) plus Australia, New Zealand, Japan, South Korea, and China. Taiwan's exclusion means that its exports from China to ASEAN countries benefit from more preferential tariffs than those from Taiwan do. This grants Taishang investments in China easier access to the ASEAN market through China's trade advantages with those countries.[22] Taiwan applied to join the Comprehensive and Progressive Agreement for Trans-Pacific Partnership (CPTPP) in September 2021, just after China's bid; yet whether Taiwan can join remains uncertain because of China's objection.[23]

Despite the advantages the Chinese economy still offers Taishang, it is increasingly difficult to navigate. As China confronts a range of domestic socioeconomic challenges, including rising inequality, high public and private debt, and youth unemployment, Xi Jinping has sought to restructure the economy in ways that exact a large toll on the private sector. As a result of the Covid-19 pandemic and increasing restrictions by the United States, foreign and domestic firms alike in China are operating under severe political stress while facing lagging domestic consumption, rising labor costs, and tightening social and political control.

Navigating Changes in the Global Semiconductor Industry

Taiwanese businesses have excelled at precision and low-cost manufacturing in the ICT sector, which has led Taiwan's economic growth. Central to this sector is the semiconductor industry, which has become the foundation for all new technologies. The global semiconductor ecosystem, in which Taiwan plays a vital role, is the most important example of the current trend of fragmentation threatening global resilience, especially as U.S.-China strategic competition intensifies. With lower-cost engineers, a precision hardware manufacturing culture, trust from U.S. and European customers, and a just-in-time delivery mindset, Taiwanese firms that manufacture for global brands became a leader and soon extended its highly successful business model to China. Taiwanese semiconductor companies' footprint in the Chinese market has always been closely scrutinized by the Taiwanese people and government and is now under pressure from the United States, China, and other major economies that have moved from

---

[22] Lotta Danielsson, "The Importance of a U.S.-Taiwan Bilateral Trade Agreement," National Bureau of Asian Research (NBR), December 21, 2020, https://www.nbr.org/publication/the-importance-of-a-u-s-taiwan-bilateral-trade-agreement.

[23] Kathrin Hille and Edward White, "Taiwan Follows China with Bid to Join Transpacific Trade Pact," *Financial Times*, September 23, 2021, https://www.ft.com/content/cc1e4e0a-803d-43be-9f4d-ba9980a5c203.

engagement to strategic competition, threatening the sustainability of the entire semiconductor industry. The decoupling threat comes on multiple fronts. Lower-end ICT and semiconductor manufacturers are increasingly squeezed by indigenous Chinese firms, which are catching up technologically. For the most advanced technologies, the indispensability of Taiwan's leading foundries and chip design houses has suddenly become a national security issue for economies concerned about China's ability and will to unify with Taiwan and seize control over its semiconductor industry.

Semiconductors are critical components of nearly all modern electronic systems and devices, and their military applications make them key to national security. For four decades, China has been able to force technology transfer, attract direct investment, and hire international talent, including approximately three thousand Taiwanese engineers as of 2019, to become a technological powerhouse.[24] Although U.S.-imposed controls limit the Chinese semiconductor industry's technological advancement in processing, which remains two generations behind that of the United States, Chinese capabilities have continued to grow.

Taiwanese companies in China have always been highly regulated. Since 2002, the Taiwanese government has allowed semiconductor firms to invest in China but regulated their production scale and limited the process technologies that could be transferred. As demonstrated by the intense debate during Taiwan's elections on permitting semiconductor investments in China, Taiwanese voters have always viewed such strategic investments with skepticism, favoring high barriers to ensure that semiconductor companies were delayed in entering China, even as U.S. companies such as Intel and domestic players emerged in the Chinese market. Only a handful of investments have ever been approved; leading foundries, including Taiwan Semiconductor Manufacturing Company (TSMC) and United Microelectronics Corporation (UMC), entered first, followed by many other Taiwanese firms in the semiconductor supply chain.[25] Today, China is the largest producer of older-generation or legacy chips, but it still imports the most advanced chips from TSMC, which manufactures 92% of its chips in Taiwan.[26] China has become the largest end market for semiconductors, which fuel the country's industries in telecommunications, electric vehicles, and solar panels, as well as artificial intelligence (AI) and the military.

---

[24] Kensaku Ihara, "Taiwan Loses 3,000 Chip Engineers to 'Made in China 2025,'" *Nikkei Asia*, December 3, 2019, https://asia.nikkei.com/Business/China-tech/Taiwan-loses-3-000-chip-engineers-to-Made-in-China-2025.

[25] Lin, *Taiwan's China Dilemma*, 156.

[26] Katie Tarasov, "Inside TSMC, the Taiwanese Chipmaking Giant That's Building a New Plant in Phoenix," CNBC, November 8, 2022, https://www.cnbc.com/2021/10/16/tsmc-taiwanese-chipmaker-ramping-production-to-end-chip-shortage.html.

Creating Foundries by Leveraging the Global Semiconductor Supply Chain

The semiconductor industry is a successful example of public-private collaboration in the United States. Such partnerships have driven U.S. technological leadership and fueled an entire innovation ecosystem of academic research, venture capital, and talent attraction concentrated in Silicon Valley.[27] As Japan, South Korea, and Taiwan entered the industry starting in the 1970s as contract manufacturers, the technologies and related IP were retained by the manufacturers' U.S. customers, who invested heavily in R&D.

Taiwan then pioneered the contract manufacturing model that has enabled rapid innovation and the cost-effective, at-scale production of integrated circuit chips. As Taiwan invested further in its export-oriented sector and selected "ten major industries" for investment across basic and heavy industry in the 1960s and 1970s, the government also established the Industrial Technology Research Institute (ITRI) to upgrade Taiwan's industries through technological innovation. ITRI's work with partners in the United States transferred technology and know-how in integrated circuit design, manufacturing, and assembly, testing, and packaging (ATP) to Taiwan. In 1987, TSMC was founded with ITRI's support to manufacture chips under contract with other companies. This business model revolutionized an industry that until then comprised only integrated device manufacturers such as Intel, which managed the entire process of producing devices and their integrated circuit chips in-house, from planning and design to manufacturing and testing. As semiconductors became integral parts of consumer goods, the pure-play foundry model pioneered by TSMC and supported by industrial clustering through ITRI's investments and projects enabled fabrication plants ("fabs") to specialize in the capital-intensive and highly precise fabrication step of chip production. In turn, companies worldwide could save costs by going "fabless," specializing in innovative R&D and chip design. Global brands and design firms such as Qualcomm and Apple have flourished because they could trust Taiwanese foundries to produce their products' chips cost-effectively.

This business model and industrial clustering created an ecosystem of firms of all sizes driving innovation and growth in the industry worldwide and especially in Taiwan, resulting in a globally segmented but highly interdependent value chain. The United States and Europe, as well as a group of Taiwanese firms, lead the world in R&D and fabless chip design, outsourcing fabrication to the Asia-Pacific, where Taiwan leads in producing logic chips

---

[27] Sebastian Mallaby, *The Power Law: Venture Capital and the Making of the New Future* (New York: Penguin Press, 2022), 1–39.

(i.e., processors) and South Korea leads in memory chips. Reserves of silicon, wafers of which form the base of an integrated circuit, and gallium, which is increasingly used as a more efficient alternative to silicon, are mainly based in China. Europe plays a large role in supplying the chemical components of semiconductor production. TSMC and UMC retain most of their production in Taiwan, especially for TSMC's most advanced chips. Yet they also have fabs in Singapore, Japan, and China. Fabs use highly specialized semiconductor manufacturing equipment produced and serviced by a handful of companies, including ASML in the Netherlands, Applied Materials and Lam Research in the United States, and Tokyo Electron in Japan. ATP also occurs largely in Taiwan, China, and Southeast Asia, where labor costs are low.

Taiwan's semiconductor prominence extends beyond manufacturing, with strengths in R&D, design, and ATP. Over the last 40 years, the government, private sector, and higher education system have invested the capital, time, and expertise to support the ICT ecosystem, making the sector Taiwan's primary driver of economic growth and Taiwan the world's primary chip supplier.[28] Taiwanese firms also account for over half of the world's ATP market share.[29] R&D and design houses such as MediaTek, a competitor to U.S. mobile chip designer Qualcomm, plus the small and medium-sized enterprises that supply fabs with wafers and other inputs, also established themselves in the island's industrial and science parks. The ICT sector employs most of Taiwan's engineering graduates, who earn much higher salaries than their peers in other industries but work longer hours, even by East Asian standards. TSMC alone must hire thousands of new master's and PhD graduates each year. Taiwan now faces a shortage of local semiconductor talent, with declining interest in STEM fields and a shrinking population that threatens the long-term expansion of the industry.[30]

Concentrated growth in the ICT sector continued through the Covid-19 pandemic. As lockdowns and economic slowdowns disrupted supply chains worldwide, Taiwan used proactive border controls and effective quarantining and contact-tracing protocols that prevented the virus from spreading during the first eighteen months of the pandemic. Consequently, the foundries continued to supply the world with chips, and Taiwan's economy enjoyed

---

[28] Kharis Templeman and Oriana Skylar Mastro, "Deepening U.S.-Taiwan Cooperation through Semiconductors," in *Silicon Triangle: The United States, Taiwan, China, and Global Semiconductor Security*, ed. Larry Diamond, James O. Ellis Jr., and Orville Schell (Stanford: Hoover Institution Press, 2023).

[29] "Overview on Taiwan Semiconductor Industry (2023 Edition)," Taiwan Semiconductor Industry Association, June 14, 2023, https://www.tsia.org.tw/api/DownloadOverview?ID=33.

[30] Lee Chee Yang, "Taiwan Lacks Young Passionate Workers in Semiconductor Industry," ThinkChina, November 7, 2022, https://www.thinkchina.sg/taiwan-lacks-young-passionate-workers-semiconductor-industry.

decade-high economic growth of 3% and 6.57% in 2020 and 2021, respectively, whereas the Japan, Singapore, and Hong Kong economies all shrank.[31]

Despite Taiwan's ability to keep its population healthy and its fabs operating during the pandemic, the sudden increase in global demand for automobiles and consumer electronics in 2020 and 2021 caused bottlenecks in the supply chain and global shortages of semiconductors. Against the backdrop of deteriorating U.S.-China relations and supply chain fragility exposed by the pandemic, the United States, the EU, and China started to view the concentration of manufacturing in Taiwan for processing logic chips and South Korea for memory chips, as well as the global dispersion of the supply chain, as sources of instability. Moreover, the United States and its Western allies view Taiwan as a security risk because of the threat that China could use force to achieve unification.

For many in the U.S. government and private sector, this presents an opportunity to return the semiconductor industry to the United States, which has had few successful foundries. Intel, the United States' semiconductor leader and an integrated device manufacturer, announced in 2021 a new business arm, Intel Foundry Services, that will compete with TSMC, Samsung, and UMC for clients. While rising tension across the Taiwan Strait is perceived to be a risk to TSMC, it also enables U.S. firms such as Intel to argue for a geographically balanced semiconductor supply chain.[32]

Changing Semiconductor Policies: National Security through Economic Resilience

The United States, the EU, and Japan are all targeting economic resilience in semiconductors by encouraging onshoring through subsidies and other incentives, enhanced by policies to protect trade secrets and IP. China is also investing heavily in its own technology sector to become a world economic leader and escape the middle-income trap while responding to Western trade controls with both incentivizing and protective policies of its own. The new policy environment is challenging for Taiwan's government and private sector to navigate, and whether U.S. policies can successfully establish a robust supply chain in the United States remains unclear.

Since 2016, the United States has aimed to slow China's rise as a technological power and retain leadership with its allies and partners in the global economy by staying on the leading edge of innovation. Reaching this

---

[31] International Monetary Fund, World Economic Outlook Database, April 2023 edition, https://www.imf.org/en/Publications/WEO/weo-database/2023/April.

[32] Yifan Yu and Ting-Fang Cheng, "How Intel Plans to Rival TSMC and Samsung as a Chip Supplier," *Nikkei Asia*, December 3, 2019, https://asia.nikkei.com/Business/Business-Spotlight/How-Intel-plans-to-rival-TSMC-and-Samsung-as-a-chip-supplier.

goal has involved substantial investment in domestic manufacturing and R&D capacity, as well as preventing advanced technology from reaching China by working with Western partners to ensure compliance. Since 2017, these policies have targeted Chinese technology companies, such as telecommunications firms Huawei and ZTE, because of concerns that they could engage in espionage, steal IP, and violate trade rules. In May 2020, a further ban on foreign semiconductor manufacturers from shipping products that use American technology to Huawei implicated TSMC, which was a major supplier to Huawei. That same month, TSMC made twin announcements that it would build a fab in the U.S. state of Arizona and stop supplying Huawei to comply with U.S. sanctions. In 2023, TSMC made further commitments to build fabs in Kumamoto, Japan, and Dresden, Germany.[33]

The cancellation of Huawei orders and similar restrictions halved TSMC's revenue from China, its second-largest market after the United States, from 20% to 10% of its total revenue in 2021.[34] Although TSMC was able to quickly recover from lost Huawei sales due to high demand for chips from competitors such as Apple to reach $74 billion, its withdrawal still comes at the cost of rebuilding a semiconductor supply chain in the United States. TSMC's Arizona fab is already experiencing construction delays due to a shortage of workers with the specific expertise to build a foundry and high costs in the United States.[35] Replicating Taiwan's foundry success is highly complex and requires a supply chain of many small and medium-sized firms, multiple sources of talent, workers beyond engineers with PhDs, and reliable sources of utilities and raw materials. Subsidies and incentives cannot create this industrial clustering overnight.[36]

China has been trying to replicate Taiwan's success in semiconductors for 30 years with little progress. Even with heavy investments in integrated chip production and STEM education, China has been unable to develop its own technology to compete effectively with the West. China realizes that the industry depends highly on talent. Even with the right equipment, insufficient talent to develop advanced processes with a precision manufacturing mindset has hampered the profitability and efficiency of

---

[33] Cheng Ting-Fang and Lauly Li, "TSMC Reveals $11 Billion Deal to Build First European Chip Plant," *Nikkei Asia*, August 8, 2023, https://asia.nikkei.com/Business/Tech/Semiconductors/TSMC-reveals-11-billion-deal-to-build-first-European-chip-plant.

[34] TSMC, "TSMC Annual Report 2022," March 12, 2023, https://investor.tsmc.com/sites/ir/annual-report/2022/2022%20Annual%20Report-E.pdf.

[35] Nicholas Gordon, "TSMC Complains It Can't Find Enough Skilled Workers to Get Its Arizona Chip Plants Ready in Time, Delaying Mass Production to 2025," *Fortune*, July 21, 2023, https://fortune.com/2023/07/21/tsmc-complains-cant-find-enough-skilled-workers-arizona-chip-plants-ready-delay-mass-production-2025.

[36] Jordan McGillis and Clay Robinson, "Why the CHIPS Act Will Fail," *National Review*, May 11, 2023, https://www.nationalreview.com/magazine/2023/05/29/why-the-chips-act-will-fail.

legacy chip production in China. In 2000, China enticed Richard Chang, a U.S.-trained Taiwanese engineer, to establish Semiconductor Manufacturing International Corporation in Shanghai. He was later joined by other former TSMC engineers, including co-executive Liang Mong Song and former vice chair Chiang Shang-yi. This aggressive recruitment of Taiwanese engineers has raised concerns in Taipei about the potential transfer of proprietary knowledge to China.[37] Meanwhile, intensifying tensions across the Taiwan Strait and an increasingly repressive domestic environment are making China less appealing to Taiwanese workers.[38]

Given China's goals of innovation leadership and self-sufficiency, U.S. policy has prioritized investing in the United States' own technological edge and blocking China from benefiting from it. The CHIPS (Creating Helpful Incentives to Produce Semiconductors) and Science Act, signed into law in August 2022, broadly allocates $280 billion to upgrade U.S. competitiveness in semiconductors, with $52.7 billion designated to increasing manufacturing capability on U.S. soil as well as funding R&D, education, workforce development, defense, and international security activities to maintain U.S. leadership in semiconductor innovation. Notably, the act has guardrails to ensure that firms receiving U.S. federal subsidies are restricted for ten years from further expansion in China for leading-edge and advanced facilities. A separate set of export controls announced by the Department of Commerce in October 2022 further restricted the export of advanced logic, dynamic random-access memory (DRAM), and NAND flash chips to China and the licensing of certain U.S. technologies used for semiconductor and supercomputer development to China-owned technology companies.[39]

By December 2022, 36 Chinese companies had been added to the Department of Commerce's entity list, which restricts exports to foreign companies that pose a risk to U.S. national security. Additionally, the Biden administration signed an executive order initiating a "reverse–Committee on Foreign Investment in the United States" process to review U.S. outbound investments to China in sensitive technologies with critical military,

---

[37] Yimou Lee, "Taiwan Raids Chinese Firms in Latest Crackdown on Chip Engineer-Poaching," *Reuters*, May 26, 2022, https://www.reuters.com/technology/taiwan-raids-chinese-firms-latest-crackdown-chip-engineer-poaching-2022-05-26.

[38] Jane Perlez, Amy Chang Chien, and John Liu, "Engineers from Taiwan Bolstered China's Chip Industry. Now They're Leaving," *New York Times*, November 16, 2022, https://www.nytimes.com/2022/11/16/business/taiwan-china-semiconductors.html.

[39] Gregory C. Allen, "Choking Off China's Access to the Future of AI," Center for Strategic and International Studies, October 11, 2022, https://www.csis.org/analysis/choking-chinas-access-future-ai.

intelligence, surveillance, and cyber-enabled capabilities.[40] The United States has negotiated with European and Japanese semiconductor manufacturing equipment firms to similarly block the sale and servicing of certain equipment in China, with Japan and the Netherlands enacting restrictions to comply with U.S. regulations in 2023. These restrictions have effects across the supply chain because a handful of companies in the West have the proprietary technology that all manufacturers need.

With global fragmentation and protectionist U.S. policies accelerating, Taiwan's chip firms now face pressure on both the contracting and sales sides of their businesses. Because Taiwanese policy has limited chipmakers' ability to offshore high-tech capabilities to China, the most advanced chip manufacturing remains in Taiwan. TSMC and UMC operate fabs in China only for older, mature-node chips. U.S. export controls place Taiwanese manufacturers in a bind because the policies limit the sale of chips based on American IP to China, and foundries are restricted from selling to Chinese companies even through intermediaries. Moreover, Taiwanese firms are under closer scrutiny than their U.S. peers because U.S. officials have long viewed Taiwan as a loophole through which China can access technology and talent. For example, in 2018, UMC was indicted by the Department of Justice for not properly monitoring employees who stole DRAM technology from U.S. memory chip designer Micron and transferred it to UMC's partner in China. UMC eventually reached a settlement in late 2021, paying a fee to Micron. More recently, Chinese firm Phytium Technology reportedly acquired chips from TSMC to conduct research on hypersonic missiles for the Chinese military.[41] Phytium was later placed on the U.S. entity list, and Taipei has banned Taiwanese firms from exporting chips to the company.[42] Taiwanese companies are thus finding themselves caught between the United States and China because neither side is sympathetic to these firms, and the Taiwanese government cannot advocate for them either.

---

[40] "Executive Order on Addressing United States Investments in Certain National Security Technologies and Products in Countries of Concern," White House, August 9, 2023, https://www.whitehouse.gov/briefing-room/presidential-actions/2023/08/09/executive-order-on-addressing-united-states-investments-in-certain-national-security-technologies-and-products-in-countries-of-concern.

[41] Ellen Nakashima and Gerry Shih, "China Builds Advanced Weapons Systems Using American Chip Technology," *Washington Post*, April 9, 2021, https://www.washingtonpost.com/national-security/china-hypersonic-missiles-american-technology/2021/04/07/37a6b9be-96fd-11eb-b28d-bfa7bb5cb2a5_story.html.

[42] Debby Wu, "Taiwan Pledges to Keep Advanced Chips from Chinese Military," Bloomberg, October 5, 2022, https://www.bloomberg.com/news/articles/2022-10-05/taiwan-pledges-to-keep-advanced-chips-from-chinese-military.

Policy Implications for Taiwan and the United States

U.S. Policy Needs More Consultation with Partners and Allies

Many of the policies discussed in the preceding section were designed and implemented by the United States without consultation with industry leaders—either domestically or abroad—or an understanding of the elements of success and the time frame needed to produce results.[43] Among the gravest concerns is that U.S. technology policies will accelerate Beijing's investments in competitive indigenous technology through more subsidies. Along with the United States, Taiwan dominates the integrated circuit design industry, with three of the world's ten largest design companies owning 18% of the global market share.[44] These companies are only slightly ahead of China, which has 15% of the market share. Even if China cannot produce the most advanced technologies, China may overtake Taiwan and the United States in a large segment of the value chain, starting with integrated circuit design, where it has sufficient talent and can create domestic demand with state support. This view is common among industry associations and leading players who believe that U.S. policy fueling decoupling will only propel China to subsidize the industry even further.[45]

These experiences so far show that duplicating the global semiconductor supply chain at the national level in the United States, China, and Europe is highly questionable. Goldman Sachs Research estimated in October 2022 that the CHIPS Act's incentives could not "fully" support even a 1% increase in U.S. market share of global chip capacity due to higher production costs in the United States compared with Asia. These higher costs result from higher capital expenditures and operational costs as well as lower production efficiency in the United States due to differences in culture and management styles, which have been exposed in the construction delays at TSMC's Arizona fab. While the Goldman Sachs analysts viewed the CHIPS Act as a hedging strategy against future disruptions and geopolitical risk, it may be extremely costly and might not replace Asia's crucial position in the global semiconductor supply chain.[46] Stopping technology theft and unfair

---

[43] Jane Rickards, "Storm Clouds Ahead for Semiconductor Sector," *Taiwan Business TOPICS*, December 28, 2022, https://topics.amcham.com.tw/2022/12/storm-clouds-ahead-for-semiconductor-sector.

[44] Jack Wu, "IC Design White Paper (2): Global Market Share and Competitive Advantages of Taiwan's IC Design Sector," DIGITIMES Asia, March 17, 2023, https://www.digitimes.com/news/a20230315PD204/ic-design-white-paper-ic-design-mediatek-taiwan.html.

[45] See Jenny Leonard and Ian King, "Chip CEOs to Meet Brainard, Sullivan Over China Restrictions," Bloomberg, July 18, 2023, https://www.bloomberg.com/news/articles/2023-07-17/chip-ceos-to-meet-with-biden-officials-over-china-export-rules.

[46] "Why the CHIPS Act Is Unlikely to Reduce U.S. Reliance on Asia," Goldman Sachs Research, October 26, 2022, https://www.goldmansachs.com/intelligence/pages/why-the-chips-act-is-unlikely-to-reduce-the-us-reliance-on-asia.html.

competition against the West by Chinese companies is a desirable U.S. strategy that should have been implemented decades ago. The right policy may finally start to achieve this aim, but it comes at a cost to U.S. and Taiwanese players who are complying with restrictions, with no certainty that results will be time-effective.

As stated earlier, Taiwanese firms are receiving little support from either the United States or their own government. Current U.S. policy seeks to preserve the United States' technological supremacy by demanding that Taiwanese firms reverse their achievements of the last 40 years, transferring their technology and know-how to American soil and stopping sales of chips containing U.S. technologies to Chinese customers. Public-private collaboration brought policy and practice together to drive semiconductor innovation under the KMT's authoritarian rule; however, little collaboration is occurring among different stakeholders in Taiwan, South Korea, Japan, Europe, and the United States to advise U.S. policymakers on how to effectively protect their technology and industry. Joint efforts by Taiwan and the United States are needed to narrow gaps in understanding among U.S. policymakers regarding their expectations and the operational reality of the complex semiconductor ecosystem. The first wave of regulations during the Trump administration mainly created compliance costs, with few benefits for the United States or Taiwan in strategic competition.[47] The October 2022 policies targeting semiconductors reflect a somewhat more strategic approach by simultaneously leveraging U.S. dominance across different chokepoints of the semiconductor value chain.[48]

If well-designed, export controls and sanctions might give the United States and its allies the advantage they deserve in cutting-edge and especially dual-use technology while allowing the world's consumers to benefit from AI and 5G applications developed globally. Unless policies are undertaken thoughtfully, supply chain duplication will cost taxpayers and consumers and will not stop China's technological theft, resulting in a less secure world and less resilient global economy. The success of U.S. policy initiatives such as the "Chip 4" alliance with South Korea, Japan, and Taiwan will depend on the willingness and ability of those countries to comply. Yet China remains these three countries' largest trading partner and an important production

---

[47] Chad P. Bown, "How Trump's Export Curbs on Semiconductors and Equipment Hurt the U.S. Technology Sector," Peterson Institute for International Economics, September 28, 2020, https://www.piie.com/blogs/trade-and-investment-policy-watch/how-trumps-export-curbs-semiconductors-and-equipment-hurt.

[48] Allen, "Choking Off China's Access to the Future of AI."

site for the memory chip industry led by South Korea and the United States.[49] For Taiwan, common values of democracy and a commitment to the liberal world order are the foundation for the partnership with the United States, but not an excuse for extracting economic benefits. Compliance with U.S. policy must be feasible and beneficial to democratic partners in Asia and Europe, who need to convince their voters that such compliance is in their interest.[50] This could be achieved through additional intelligence sharing as well as closer economic cooperation through trade and investment agreements including Taiwan to explore markets beyond China, thereby offsetting negative economic impacts.[51]

Beijing Policies toward Taiwan: More Sticks and Fewer Carrots

Under Xi Jinping, China has been doubling down on its carrot-and-stick strategy toward Taiwanese businesses. On the one hand, in early 2018, Beijing issued "31 Preferential Policies for Taiwan" to attract and retain Taiwanese investments and businesses in China, followed by another set of "26 Measures for Taiwan" that included R&D in 5G technology and investment in the service sector, intending to utilize the capital and know-how of Taiwanese businesses to fuel the Chinese economy.[52] On the other hand, Beijing has exerted more political control over the private sector, its own citizens, and the Taishang. For example, a Chinese court imposed fines in 2021 on the Far Eastern Group, which was accused of having links to the DPP.[53] Over the last two decades, other Taiwanese companies, such as Chi Mei Corporation,

---

[49] Kim Jaewon and Cheng Ting-Fang, "Samsung and SK Hynix Face China Dilemma from U.S. Export Controls," *Nikkei Asia*, October 25, 2022, https://asia.nikkei.com/Business/Tech/Semiconductors/Samsung-and-SK-Hynix-face-China-dilemma-from-U.S.-export-controls; and Molly Schuetz, "Micron Says Half of Sales Tied to China-HQ Clients at Risk," Bloomberg, June 16, 2023, https://www.bloomberg.com/news/articles/2023-06-16/micron-says-about-half-of-china-hq-customer-data-revenue-at-risk.

[50] Syaru Shirley Lin, "Great Power Competition, Economic Fragmentation and the International Global Order," Bruegel Annual Meetings, Session 5a, September 6, 2023, https://www.bruegel.org/annual-meetings/bruegel-annual-meetings-6-7-september-2023.

[51] Chad P. Bown, "The Return of Export Controls: A Risky Tactic That Requires Cooperation from Allies," *Foreign Affairs*, January 24, 2023, https://www.foreignaffairs.com/united-states/return-export-controls.

[52] Sarah Zheng, "Beijing Extends Sweeteners for Taiwanese Weeks before Taipei Election," *South China Morning Post*, November 4, 2019, https://www.scmp.com/news/china/politics/article/3036194/beijing-extends-sweeteners-taiwanese-weeks-taipei-election.

[53] Feng Ziwei, "Taiwan's Far Eastern Group Bows to China after Hefty Fines," *Taiwan News*, November 30, 2021, https://www.taiwannews.com.tw/en/news/4360495.

HTC Corporation, and the Hai Pa Wang restaurant chain, have faced pressure from Beijing and were forced to make statements in support of unification.[54]

On the Chinese Communist Party's overall Taiwan policy, Xi has stated that he intends to achieve unification in his lifetime.[55] China's strategy includes military incursions, gray-zone warfare, and disinformation campaigns, as well as public statements condemning perceived "provocation" by the United States and Taiwan, such as President Tsai's and Vice President William Lai Ching-te's 2023 transit stops in the United States as well as then U.S. House Speaker Nancy Pelosi's visit to Taiwan in August 2022. The frequency of incursions by the People's Liberation Army (PLA) around Taiwan, with expanded operations and combinations of military aircraft and vessels, has increased to an unprecedented level over the past three years. Beijing sent 1,727 planes into Taiwan's air defense identification zone in 2022, compared with 960 in 2021 and 380 in 2020. Equally important are Beijing's gray-zone tactics to test Taiwan's capabilities and gradually change the status quo, wearing down its defense capability.[56] In addition, Beijing has increasingly sanctioned politicians and think tanks in both Taiwan and the United States to deter closer ties between Taipei and Washington.[57] China also suspended official dialogues with the United States on climate change and military relations in retaliation for the Pelosi visit.

U.S. Policies toward Taiwan: Mixed Messages from Washington

Although U.S. economic policies, as noted above, have added tremendous pressure to Taiwan's economy and semiconductor sector, the United States has been enhancing its relationship with Taiwan politically. The 2018 Taiwan Travel Act and the 2020 Taiwan Allies International Protection and Enhancement Initiative Act are examples of friendly U.S. legislation to allow

---

[54] Founder Wen-Long Shi of Chi Mei Corporation released a statement supporting the "one-China principle" and Beijing's Anti-Secession Law in 2004. Chairperson Cher Wang of HTC Corporation claimed in a speech that the company was Chinese in 2010. Hai Pa Wang published a statement endorsing Beijing's "one-China principle" in 2016. See Lin, *Taiwan's China Dilemma*; and Liang-Sheng Lin and Jonathan Chin, "Hai Pa Wang Move Might Trigger 'One China' Domino Effect," *Taipei Times*, December 10, 2016, https://www.taipeitimes.com/News/taiwan/archives/2016/12/10/2003660927.

[55] Syaru Shirley Lin, "Xi Jinping's Taiwan Policy and Its Impact on Cross-Strait Relations," *China Leadership Monitor*, June 1, 2019, https://www.prcleader.org/_files/ugd/10535f_ce0fbf8d3dd54c60a6fe4cd1f0755d21.pdf.

[56] "China's Warplane Incursions into Taiwan Air Defence Zone Doubled in 2022," Agence France-Presse, January 2, 2023, available at https://www.theguardian.com/world/2023/jan/02/chinas-warplane-incursions-into-taiwan-air-defence-zone-doubled-in-2022; and Kathrin Hille and Demetri Sevastopulo, "How China's Military Is Slowly Squeezing Taiwan," *Financial Times*, July 24, 2023, https://www.ft.com/content/f7922fdb-01bf-4ffd-9c5c-79f15468aa71.

[57] Liz Lee and Ben Blanchard, "China Imposes Sanctions on Taiwan's U.S. Envoy, Institutions," Reuters, April 7, 2023, https://www.reuters.com/world/asia-pacific/china-imposes-further-sanctions-taiwans-us-representative-2023-04-07.

more high-level visits and exchanges with Taipei. Furthermore, President Joe Biden has verbally promised to help defend Taiwan on four different occasions, angering Beijing.[58] As China continues its aggressive posturing, the Biden administration has approved $3.9 billion in arms sales, mostly missiles, artillery, and spare aircraft parts, to Taiwan. Although the DPP government has increased spending on defense to 2.4% of GDP, the United States is deeply concerned that this spending is insufficient and leaves Taiwan unprepared to defend itself.

Within Taiwan, concern is growing that the United States is treating Taiwan as an "asset," or what Beijing calls a "card" to be played for the United States' benefit, rather than as a strusted partner with whom the United States will collaborate on more equal terms.[59] As Washington enhances the political and security relationship, it imposes economic costs on Taiwan without clearly aligned interests. These misgivings are further enhanced by widespread Chinese-language disinformation and misinformation on social media.[60]

Taiwan has FTAs with only eight countries, which contribute less than 5% to Taiwan's aggregate trade volume.[61] Under the ECFA it signed with China in 2010, Taiwan will continue to rely more on the Chinese market than on other trade partners because it has few other bilateral agreements. Taiwan's exclusion from the RCEP and potentially the CPTPP means that U.S.-led trade initiatives such as the Indo-Pacific Economic Framework for Prosperity would be a welcome move to demonstrate U.S. leadership and commitment to the region.[62] Progress on the U.S.-Taiwan Initiative on 21st Century Trade is also a breakthrough in deepening bilateral economic relations. This initiative, for which negotiations began in August 2022, aims to facilitate trade and investment between the two countries. It covers customs and border procedures, regulatory practices, and small businesses. The first agreement was signed on June 1, 2023, and passed in Taiwan's legislature on July 26, 2023.

---

[58] Charles Hutzler, Joyu Wang, and James T. Areddy, "Biden's Pledge to Defend Taiwan Chips Away at Longstanding U.S. Policy," *Wall Street Journal*, September 23, 2022, https://www.wsj.com/articles/bidens-pledge-to-defend-taiwan-chips-away-at-longstanding-u-s-policy-11663962151.

[59] Ryan Hass, "Taiwan Is a Partner with the United States, Not an Asset," *Taipei Times*, July 24, 2023, https://www.taipeitimes.com/News/editorials/archives/2023/07/24/2003803639; and Zhu Songling, "Taiwan a Risky Card for U.S.-Led West to Play," *China Daily*, July 13, 2023, https://www.chinadaily.com.cn/a/202307/13/WS64afb0ada31035260b81643c.html.

[60] Brian Hioe, "U.S. Bioweapons Story Reignites Concerns about Disinformation in Taiwan," *Diplomat*, July 14, 2023, https://thediplomat.com/2023/07/us-bioweapons-story-reignites-concerns-about-disinformation-in-taiwan.

[61] The eight countries Taiwan has signed FTAs or economic cooperation agreements with are New Zealand, Singapore, Eswatini, Paraguay, Guatemala, Panama, Belize, and the Republic of the Marshall Islands.

[62] Roy Chun Lee, "CPTPP Membership for Taiwan: Rationales, Challenges, and Outlook," in *China, Taiwan, the UK and the CPTPP: Global Partnership or Regional Stand-off?* ed. Chun-yi Lee and Michael Reilly (Singapore: Palgrave Macmillan, 2023), 19–45.

Implications for Domestic Politics in Taiwan

As Beijing sows fear and Washington creates uncertainty on the island, a divisive debate is occurring in Taiwan on how to address China's rise. Debate centers on whether Taiwan should accommodate Beijing, given the asymmetric military power that is increasing the inevitability of unification, or stand up for its democratic way of life by working closely with like-minded international partners and resisting China at all costs. This has important implications for the prospects of different presidential candidates and political parties in Taiwan.

Analysts have attributed Taiwan's DPP landslide victory in the 2020 presidential and legislative elections to Beijing's heavy-handed control of Hong Kong after a wave of anti-China protests in 2019. Originally designed for Taiwan, Beijing's "one country, two systems" is now unacceptable to Taiwanese voters, and with PLA incursions in the Taiwan Strait reaching unprecedented levels, the three major political parties represented in Taiwan's parliament, known as the Legislative Yuan, have toed the same basic line of maintaining peace and stability.[63] However, they have not yet defined clear positions on China. Furthermore, voters are eager to evaluate proposed policy solutions to Taiwan's domestic socioeconomic problems, which can be characterized as challenges of the "high-income trap" shared by other developed economies, especially Japan and South Korea. Having escaped the middle-income trap through export-oriented growth in the 1980s and 1990s, these economies now have a high standard of living and large middle class. Yet they face prolonged socioeconomic challenges of slow growth, wage stagnation, increasing inequality, demographic decline, unsustainable entitlements, inflated asset markets, and political polarization. Taiwan's ability to escape the trap requires consensus on difficult policy issues, such as energy, housing, and defense, which are all closely linked to Taiwan's cross-strait and technology policies.[64]

In Taiwan's domestic politics, governance remains the focal point for voters in local elections, but the China issue is the most salient issue in national and presidential elections. After eight years of leadership under Tsai Ing-wen with majority representation in the Legislative Yuan, the DPP seeks to defend the party's performance after major losses to the KMT in the 2018 and 2022 local elections.[65] The DPP must demonstrate that its strong position against

---

[63] Chen Yu-fu and Jake Chung, "Less than 20% Back China on Taiwan Related Affairs," *Taipei Times*, March 24, 2023, https://www.taipeitimes.com/News/taiwan/archives/2023/03/24/2003796647.

[64] Syaru Shirley Lin, "Taiwan in the High-Income Trap and Its Implications for Cross-Strait Relations," in *Taiwan's Economic and Diplomatic Challenges and Opportunities*, ed. Mariah Thornton, Robert Ash, and Dafydd Fell (London: Routledge, 2021), 49–77.

[65] Brian Hioe, "Once Again, KMT Scores Big in Taiwan's Local Elections," *Diplomat*, November 28, 2022, https://thediplomat.com/2022/11/once-again-kmt-scores-big-in-taiwans-local-elections.

Chinese coercion and for alignment with the United States will not ignore—or at least not exacerbate—Taiwan's socioeconomic problems. Conversely, the KMT has traditionally advocated for more rapprochement with China. The party believes that its leadership would pacify Beijing, thereby benefiting Taiwan's overall interests, and accuses the DPP of promoting the U.S. agenda and fueling cross-strait tensions.[66] The impacts of the 2024 election are being carefully watched by Beijing, Washington, and the rest of the world as Taiwanese decide how to navigate the U.S.-China competition.

Given the distinct pro-U.S. position of the DPP versus the KMT's growing skepticism of the United States, voters supporting either party will indirectly endorse either the U.S. or China position. Full support of U.S. policy toward China would mean gradually reducing exposure to China in trade, investments, and human capital. Many believe such reductions would weaken Taiwan's economic and societal resilience. Furthermore, a recent poll showed that 38% of Taiwanese believe that supporting and complying with U.S. demands for decoupling from China and purchasing more arms may provoke Beijing, threatening Taiwan's national security and overall investment climate.[67] Others perceive mixed intentions in U.S. actions, have sympathy toward the Chinese for being cornered by U.S. policy, and hope that Taiwan can continue to economically benefit from China.[68] These voters emphasize the U.S. withdrawal from Afghanistan and the high costs of compliance with U.S. policy for Taiwanese firms. Another poll shows that a majority of Taiwanese have worried about national security since Russia's invasion of Ukraine, yet nearly half of respondents did not believe that the United States would come to Taiwan's aid if conflict with China were to occur.[69] Some voters argue that the United States is penalizing or exploiting Taiwan to "make America great again" rather than rewarding Taiwan for being a trusted technological leader in chip fabrication.

---

[66] Gerrit van der Wees, "Taiwan's Mid-Term Elections: Most Politics Is Local, the KMT Remains a Force to Be Reckoned with, and the DPP Needs to Regroup," *Taiwan Insight*, November 30, 2022, https://taiwaninsight.org/2022/11/30/taiwans-mid-term-elections-most-politics-is-local-the-kmt-remains-a-force-to-be-reckoned-with-and-the-dpp-needs-to-regroup.

[67] "January 2023 Public Opinion Poll—English Excerpt," Taiwan Public Opinion Foundation, January 17, 2023, https://www.tpof.org/wp-content/uploads/2023/01/andrej-lisakov-3A4XZUopCJA-unsplash.pdf.

[68] A recent poll showed that nearly 60% of Taiwanese agree that the United States supports Taiwan for its own national interest, while 76% of Taiwanese favor reducing tension across the Taiwan Strait and the resumption of cross-strait exchanges. See "March 2023 Public Opinion Poll—English Excerpt," Taiwan Public Opinion Foundation, March 21, 2023, https://www.tpof.org/wp-content/uploads/2023/03/20230321-TPOF-March-2023-Public-Opinion-Poll-%E2%80%93-English-Excerpt.pdf.

[69] See "February 2023 Public Opinion Poll—English Excerpt," Taiwan Public Opinion Foundation, February 21, 2023, https://www.tpof.org/wp-content/uploads/2023/02/20230221-TPOF-February-2023-Public-Opinion-Poll-%E2%80%93-English-Excerpt.pdf.

Taiwan's Structural Challenges in the High-Income Trap and Alternative Solutions

Taiwan's domestic challenges have intensified under the DPP's leadership, exacerbated by severe disruptions in the global economy. Structurally, Taiwan's policymakers need to make painful policy trade-offs as the population shrinks and the economy experiences a downward trajectory over the past two decades, despite performing well during the Covid-19 pandemic. The ICT sector has outperformed the rest of the economy but has also produced disenfranchisement among workers and especially young people outside the sector.[70] Although some voters focus on China as the source of political polarization and Taiwan's largest threat, others see China as the best solution for providing continued economic growth. Furthermore, some are convinced that continued DPP leadership beyond 2024 will increase the military threat from Beijing, leading to more defense spending and economic uncertainty.[71] Although the DPP platform captures most voters' sense of national identity and desire to support democracy and the U.S.-led liberal order, many voters are waiting for the tangible results of the party's reforms to address Taiwan's critical socioeconomic challenges.

When the DPP won control of both the Executive and Legislative Yuans in 2020, voters had enormous expectations that the party would reverse inequality, provide affordable housing, and focus on sustainability and energy security. Achieving these goals was challenging from the start. The Covid-19 pandemic worsened unequal growth. While Taiwan's ICT exports grew because of surging global demand, the service and hospitality sectors suffered from reduced domestic consumption and foreign tourism. Although Taiwan's per capita GDP has grown 53% over the last decade, the increase was only 24% for workers not in the electronics manufacturing sector, where wages grew 65%.[72]

The DPP has had limited success in demonstrating that it has reversed inequality or tackled the long-term issue of affordable housing, which affects young people in large cities. After a decade of financialization and low-interest environments fueling property markets, the house price-to-income ratio in Taipei has exceeded 15.2, higher than that of New York (7.1)

---

[70] Syaru Shirley Lin, "Taiwan's Continued Success Requires Economic Diversification of Products and Markets," Brookings Institution, March 15, 2021, https://www.brookings.edu/articles/taiwans-continued-success-requires-economic-diversification-of-products-and-markets.

[71] A recent poll reveals that nearly half of Taiwanese who work in the private sector disapprove of Tsai's leadership. See Li Weixuan, "Disidu zhizheng kunjing: Jinban guoren buzantong Tsai Ing-wen guojia lingdao fangshi" [The Fourth Predicament: Near Half of Citizens Disagree with the Way Tsai Ing-wen Leads the Country], Storm Media, July 22, 2023, https://www.storm.mg/article/4838952.

[72] Executive Yuan (Taiwan), Directorate General of Budget, Accounting and Statistics.

and London (8.7), making it one of the most expensive cities to live in.[73] Housing prices are rising not only in Taipei but also in cities experiencing chip-driven property booms as technology companies expand. Homes in Hsinchu, where TSMC and several other technology companies are based, have doubled in price since 2019, growing three times as fast as Taiwan's average as demand for housing by high-earning engineers and investors rises. Slim prospects of upward social mobility and rising costs of living are driving disappointment and anger, especially among young voters who must support Taiwan's aging society.

In the long term, Taiwan's most difficult challenge is sustainability and energy resilience, on which the DPP has made little progress.[74] Despite being historically focused on sustainability, the DPP government did not pass the Climate Change Response Act until January 2023, which finally committed Taiwan to net-zero carbon emissions by 2050. As of 2022, renewable energy accounted for only 8% of Taiwan's electricity supply, and the government has already revised its target of achieving 20% renewable energy by 2025 down to 15%. Approximately 97% of Taiwan's energy supply is imported, the majority being fossil fuels that contribute to over 80% of the country's total electricity generation.[75] Occasional brownouts during the pandemic have shown that the lack of a long-term sustainable energy solution threatens the future of the economy. Taiwan's primary sources of growth—the petrochemical and electronics manufacturing industries, including advanced semiconductor manufacturing—are the main sources of carbon emissions as well as large consumers of energy and water. Although TSMC has sought to achieve 100% renewable energy in its international operations, Taiwanese companies are struggling to develop renewable energy plans within Taiwan due to limited green energy supply.[76] Because Taiwan is a mountainous island with high population density in urban areas, large-scale solar and wind farms are difficult to develop domestically. Partly due to Asia's fragmented market, renewable energy is unlikely to grow quickly, and nuclear energy has again

---

[73] "Fangjia fudan nengli tongji" [Housing Affordability Statistics], Ministry of the Interior (Taiwan), https://pip.moi.gov.tw/v3/e/scre0105.aspx; and "Demographia International Housing Affordability, 2023 Edition," Urban Reform Institute and Frontier Centre for Public Policy, March 2023.

[74] Syaru Shirley Lin, "Population, Power Generation, Political Polarization, and Parochialism Are Also Long-Term Threats to Taiwan's Success and Survival," *China Leadership Monitor*, June 1, 2021, https://www.prcleader.org/lin-1.

[75] Sha Hua, "Taiwan Has a Big National-Security Risk: It Imports 97% of Its Energy," *Wall Street Journal*, July 7, 2023, https://www.wsj.com/articles/taiwan-has-a-big-national-security-risk-it-imports-97-of-its-energy-f1faced.

[76] Cheng Ting-Fang, Lauly Li, and Kim Jaewon, "From TSMC to Samsung, Asia's Chipmakers Struggle to Go Green," *Nikkei Asia*, June 30, 2023, https://asia.nikkei.com/Business/Business-Spotlight/From-TSMC-to-Samsung-Asia-s-chipmakers-struggle-to-go-green.

become a contentious policy issue.⁷⁷ The DPP has opposed nuclear energy since its founding and maintained a "nuclear-free homeland 2025" policy. Only one of Taiwan's four nuclear power plants is currently in operation, and it is scheduled to shut down by 2025.

The DPP has launched several initiatives to rebalance the economy, address inequality, and enter FTAs, including the 5+2 Industrial Innovation Plan and the NSP to divert trade and investment to Southeast Asia. However, polls suggest that most Taiwanese have been consistently dissatisfied with the administration's economic policy, with 60% of Taiwanese feeling that their well-being has not improved under the party.⁷⁸ The main opposition parties are highly critical of the DPP's compliance with the United States' decoupling strategy and advocate for rapprochement with China. The KMT also claims that it will be more successful at joining the CPTPP and signing FTAs. The rising Taiwan People's Party has been even more provocative, with its 2024 presidential candidate, former Taipei mayor Ko Wen-je, proposing to revive the controversial Cross-Strait Service Trade Agreement under the ECFA in order to revitalize Taiwan's economy through further integration with China. For an export-dependent island, discussion of how to effectively govern always involves the question of whether Taiwan should rely more on China or the United States, both economically and politically.

Managing Rising Geopolitical Tension

The 2024 election will focus on Taiwan's economic and societal security in the shadow of deteriorating U.S.-China relations. Although the DPP has been viewed as a pro-independence party hostile to Beijing, President Tsai has demonstrated restraint in managing cross-strait relations by not pandering to her base, which may otherwise support independence.⁷⁹ Instead, the Tsai administration's policies have focused on reducing economic dependence on China.⁸⁰ The DPP government has made progress since 2016 in deepening the relationship with the United States by attracting high-profile visits to Taipei

---

[77] Joy Tseng and Teng Pei-ju, "Taiwan's Energy Transition Efforts 'Far Behind Schedule': AmCham," *Focus Taiwan*, June 7, 2023, https://focustaiwan.tw/business/202306070015.

[78] "January 2023 Public Opinion Poll—English Excerpt."

[79] According to a poll result in August 2022, over 80% of DPP supporters prefer "Taiwan independence" over "cross-strait unification." See "Zhonggong junyan chongji tongdu rentong? You Ying-lung bao zuixin mindiao: 'Guoren pan yongyuan weichi xianzhuang' shi huangyan" [Is Chinese Military Exercise Affecting Taiwanese Public Opinion on Unification-Independence Stance? The Latest Survey Shows That It Is a Lie to State "Taiwanese Want to Maintain Status Quo Indefinitely"], *Storm Media*, August 18, 2022, https://www.storm.mg/article/4477924.

[80] Syaru Shirley Lin, "How Taiwan's High-Income Trap Shapes Its Options in the U.S.-China Competition," in *Strategic Asia 2020: U.S.-China Competition for Global Influence*, ed. Ashley J. Tellis, Alison Szalwinski, and Michael Wills (Seattle: NBR, 2020), 133–60.

by U.S. politicians and several congressional delegations. The NSP and the launch of the U.S.-Taiwan Initiative on 21st Century Trade show promise in reducing investments in China and increasing investments in the United States, Europe, and Southeast Asia.

The more urgent issue regarding deterring Beijing is conscription, which has been extended from four to twelve months for Taiwanese men. Although all three parties appear to endorse the extension, doubts remain over whether the training provided is sufficient to strengthen the combat readiness of the military. As Taiwan's birth rate declines and many families have only one child, lengthening the compulsory military service period has caused anxiety. The policy also includes a monthly salary increase (from $207 to $648), which requires growing the defense budget. Despite recent increases, the defense budget has reached only 2.6% of Taiwan's GDP. Countries facing similar external security threats, such as Israel, have defense budgets of approximately 5% of GDP. Drawing lessons from Ukraine and in consultation with the U.S. military, the Tsai administration recently shifted arms purchases from traditional warfare assets to equipment suitable for asymmetrical warfare.

The KMT argues that such defense spending and conscription policies would be unnecessary if cross-strait tensions were eased.[81] The KMT has consistently used the U.S. withdrawal from Afghanistan and uncertainty surrounding continued U.S. support for Ukraine to warn Taiwanese voters of the United States' unreliability.[82] Both the KMT and Taiwan People's Party fuel skepticism of the United States, which they view as destabilizing a difficult situation and imposing costs on the Taiwanese through increased arms sales and longer conscription.

Competing Policy Stances Leading Up to 2024: Reflection of a Divided Taiwanese Society

Public satisfaction with the DPP government was considerably undermined by its management of the Covid-19 pandemic. Although early pandemic policies were successful, the slow purchase of vaccines led to a delayed rollout and public discontent.[83] As voters experience "DPP fatigue" after eight years of heightened tension in the Taiwan Strait and see little sign

---

[81] Yimou Lee, "Taiwan Opposition Presidential Candidate Vows to Shorten Military Service," *Reuters*, July 4, 2023, https://www.reuters.com/world/asia-pacific/taiwan-opposition-presidential-candidate-vows-shorten-military-service-2023-07-04.

[82] Ogasawara Yoshiyuki, "Skepticism about the U.S. Spreading in Taiwan," *Discuss Japan—Japan Foreign Policy Forum*, March 14, 2023, https://www.japanpolicyforum.jp/diplomacy/pt20230314200052012992.html.

[83] Anneke Schmider, Siwei Huang, and Caroline Fried, "Resilience in the Asia Pacific: Vaccines and the 'Triple Challenge,'" Center for Asia-Pacific Resilience and Innovation (CAPRI), October 26, 2021, https://caprifoundation.org/resilience-in-the-asia-pacific-vaccines-and-the-triple-challenge.

that its reform policies have been effective, the DPP may have fewer seats in the legislature. Polls show voter opposition to the DPP controlling both the executive and legislative branches of government.[84] If the DPP does not control both the presidency and the legislature, then it will not be able to enact long-needed structural reforms.

The backlash against the DPP's President Tsai, widely regarded as a moderate internationalist, is evident in the campaigns of the three leading presidential candidates, who are former mayors with little experience in foreign or cross-strait policy. Their campaigns largely focus on addressing domestic structural challenges of inequality, living and housing costs, and energy security rather than foreign policy. The DPP presidential candidate, current vice president and former mayor of Tainan William Lai, seeks to defend the party's policy agenda by continuing President Tsai's strategy and improving Taiwan's economic resilience. The opposition parties have vowed to prioritize areas where DPP policies have not met expectations in the last eight years, such as providing affordable housing and achieving security and sustainability by other means. Whereas Lai vehemently opposes restarting any of Taiwan's nuclear power plants, the KMT advocates restarting them to guarantee a steady supply of electricity. Its candidate, Hou Yu-ih, former mayor of New Taipei City, has focused on "stability, safety, and decarbonization."[85] The Taiwan People's Party's Ko Wen-je has also criticized the DPP's anti-nuclear policy and advocated the recommissioning of Taiwan's nuclear power plants to meet energy demands during the transition to alternative energy sources.[86]

On cross-strait policy, Lai promotes upholding Taiwanese identity and autonomy, consistent with the DPP's party platform. However, Beijing has clearly indicated that Lai becoming president would be unacceptable not only because of the DPP's historical commitment to eventual independence but also because of his 2015 statement that he is a "pragmatic Taiwan independence worker" and his opinion that Taiwan's presidents should visit the White House.[87] People in Washington also have concerns that Lai may

---

[84] "May 2023 Public Opinion Poll—English Excerpt," Taiwan Public Opinion Foundation, May 16, 2023, https://www.tpof.org/wp-content/uploads/2023/05/20230516-TPOF-May-2023-Public-Opinion-Poll-%E2%80%93-English-Excerpt.pdf.

[85] Su Szu-yun and Evelyn Kao, "Hou Supports Restarting No. 1 Nuclear Plant If No Safety Concerns," Focus Taiwan, July 3, 2023, https://focustaiwan.tw/politics/202307030017.

[86] Wu Hai-ruei, "Ko Charges into Energy Debate, but Lacks Vision," *Taipei Times*, June 12, 2023, https://www.taipeitimes.com/News/editorials/archives/2023/06/12/2003801378.

[87] Thompson Chau, "Taiwan's Ruling DPP Names William Lai as Presidential Candidate," *Nikkei Asia*, April 12, 2023, https://asia.nikkei.com/Politics/Taiwan-s-ruling-DPP-names-William-Lai-as-presidential-candidate; and Cindy Wang, "Taiwan Candidate Says Its Presidents Should Visit White House," Bloomberg, July 11, 2023, https://www.bloomberg.com/news/articles/2023-07-11/taiwan-candidate-says-its-presidents-should-visit-white-house.

change the status quo. Lai has sought to reassure the United States of his commitment to Tsai's moderate line of not seeking Taiwan's independence and upholding the constitution.[88] By contrast, Hou hopes to return to a Taipei-defined 1992 consensus—by which Taipei and Beijing agree that there is one "China" but respect that each side interprets "China" differently—as the basis for re-engagement with Beijing. The KMT has portrayed its campaign against the DPP as a choice between "peace and war." Meanwhile, the Taiwan People's Party brands itself as a pragmatic force in cross-strait affairs and would like to encourage more dialogue. Ko has argued that Taiwan should be more strategic and independent from the United States in its military strategy and defense spending.[89] Overall, attacks on the DPP are founded on Beijing's refusal to enter official exchanges with the party. Both opposition parties advocate more economic and people-to-people exchanges with China and are confident that they would outperform the DPP in this realm.

The Way Forward

Future of the Taiwan-U.S. Partnership and U.S. Policy Options

The resilience of Taiwan's democracy is under more pressure than ever as the country navigates an uncertain world. As reflected in Europe, South America, and elsewhere, an incapable government can easily turn a progressive society into a populist one that distances itself from the liberal democratic camp. If Taiwan's future leadership turns to Beijing for solutions and peace across the Taiwan Strait, the U.S.-Taiwan partnership could break down, dealing a deep blow to the United States in its strategic competition with China.

To compete with an alternative model of governance, the U.S.-led coalition of partners and allies, especially technological leaders and those under pressure by Russia and China, must work together. Southeast Asia, South America, and even Europe have seen populists, on both the right and left, cast doubt on the liberal world order after observing political chaos and polarization in the United States since 2016. Taiwan's voters continued to support progressive and democratic values in re-electing President Tsai in 2020, despite heavy pressure from China, but the 2024 election shows declining support for the ruling party.

---

[88] Sean Scanlan, "Vice President Lai Says He Will Not Declare Taiwan Independence," *Taiwan News*, May 17, 2023, https://www.taiwannews.com.tw/en/news/4894155; and Lai Ching-Te, "My Plan to Preserve Peace in the Taiwan Strait," *Wall Street Journal*, July 7, 2023, https://www.wsj.com/articles/my-plan-to-preserve-peace-between-china-and-taiwan-candidate-election-race-war-7046ee00.

[89] Teng Pei-ju, "Taiwan Must 'Prepare for War' but Seek Dialogue with China: TPP Chairman," Focus Taiwan, April 21, 2023, https://focustaiwan.tw/cross-strait/202304210018.

With a resilient and innovative Taiwan, Washington will be better prepared to preserve its technological advantage over Beijing, especially in cutting-edge fields like quantum computing and supercomputing. This goal is shared by U.S. partners and allies in the Asia-Pacific that are focused on the crucial semiconductor industry to power these innovations. On the policy level, however, the effectiveness of the current U.S. approach to strengthen domestic innovation and contain Beijing's development of advanced technologies is unclear. As analyzed in this chapter, the forced reshoring of semiconductor production will be more time- and cost-intensive than expected, with no clear projected returns on investments. The long-term success of the latest set of export controls and investment restrictions by the Biden administration—though much more sophisticated than the trade war launched by the Trump administration—depends on whether other partners holding key technologies in the global value chain, such as South Korea, Japan, and the Netherlands, are willing to continue coordinating fully with the United States on its technology and China policies.

As the United States attempts to revive its semiconductor industry to create jobs and ensure technological leadership, it must help Taiwan and other Asia-Pacific partners find alternatives to China to build economic resilience. Consultations with the Taiwanese business community, government, and civil society are needed as U.S. policymakers consider new trade rules to ensure buy-in and trust in the United States as a credible partner that understands Taiwan's interests. The United States cannot expect seamless compliance with changing rules if foreign companies view them as too disruptive, difficult to implement, or unaligned with circumstances on the ground. Biden's proposed Chip 4 alliance could be a step in the right direction to coordinate regional policy if the group can be consolidated on a platform for productive dialogue.[90] Unilateral export controls contribute to skepticism toward the United States among Taiwan's voters, creating the dilemma of a dichotomous choice between a democratic United States and an authoritarian China. The Taishang have shown for decades that operating in both is possible, and U.S. policies should consider the nuanced interests of Taiwanese businesses in China. Taiwanese partners need practical and material benefits for cooperating with the United States; they will not comply with a strategy to enhance the United States' competitiveness if it actually diminishes the economic resilience of the United States' partners.

Furthermore, the United States and Europe, as well as partners such as Japan and Australia, can support Taiwan's efforts at deeper economic

---

[90] Erik M. Jacobs, "Challenges and Opportunities for the 'Chip 4' Group," Global Taiwan Institute, November 2, 2022, https://globaltaiwan.org/2022/11/challenges-and-opportunities-for-the-chip-4-group.

linkages and policy dialogue. Alternatives to China should include Taiwan's further integration into regional economic and trade architecture so that the country can more easily diversify away from Chinese markets. This regional integration is key to building economic resilience, especially outside Taiwan's high-technology sector. Bilateral trade agreements with the United States are a good start but should extend to U.S. allies. Broader economic engagement can reduce the influence of skeptics who warn that the United States is leveraging Taiwan only to benefit itself. A sound economy is a prerequisite to building Taiwan's defense capability and countering China's coercion. Otherwise, the Taiwanese will be vulnerable to pressure.

Finally, Taiwan cannot continue to be excluded from the international community. As long as China systematically excludes Taiwan from international organizations and even limits its ability to sign bilateral trade agreements, it will perceive the need to remain embedded in China's political economy to stay competitive. The Covid-19 pandemic, for example, has highlighted how Taiwan can navigate the most difficult economic challenges to achieve resilience while finding new growth opportunities without international recognition. Taiwan could continue manufacturing because of its early and successful management of the public health crisis. However, due to the absence of a regional framework for multilateral collaboration in the realm of public health and the lack of access to the World Health Organization, Taiwan cannot coordinate with international partners on information sharing or policy responses in health emergencies. Taiwan remains vulnerable to the next pandemic, which may emerge from Asia again. The United States and its allies must view Taiwan not as a U.S.-China issue but as a global issue for critical interests, including supply chain security, military security, and pandemic preparedness, all of which could center on Taiwan. However, no strategic interest is more important than what Taiwan represents: an innovative society whose citizens stand for freedom and democracy.

Prospects and Solutions for Taiwan Walking the Tightrope

Taiwan was one of the first countries to connect with China economically because of its geographic and cultural proximity, and Taiwan's economy has become highly integrated with China's. Decoupling is much more difficult for Taiwan than for other countries because cross-strait interdependence extends from trade and investment to human capital, technology, and societal and interpersonal relations. As the United States and Europe began shifting from globalization to top-down industrial policy to promote economic security, export controls and sanctions had an adverse impact on Taiwanese firms. While they are increasing their investments back in Taiwan, Taiwanese firms are not leaving China entirely. Moreover, bilateral trade remains strong because of supply chains built up over decades without the emergence of meaningful alternatives. Much of Taiwan's exports to China are components tied to supply chains organized by multinational corporations that still view China as an important market.

Taiwan must determine how to diversify its sources of economic growth, which may involve aligning itself with more cost-intensive and distant manufacturing centers. Bilateral trade talks between Taiwan and the United States show promise for accelerating talent circulation, especially through Silicon Valley. However, successfully upgrading Taiwan's economy to address inequality, sustainability, health, and innovation requires thoughtful solutions developed by an active civil society working closely with others in the region. More investments are needed in future-oriented sectors, including AI and biotechnology. Creating new engines of growth will require an overhaul of education, with a focus on foundational research, interdisciplinary training, and application as well as theory. Taiwan's population decline and rigid education system also mean that cultivating domestic talent is insufficient. Attracting international talent in all fields must be prioritized to upgrade the economy, which will require changes in immigration and education policies.[91]

Taiwan's democracy is increasingly polarized because the country's China dilemma is at the heart of domestic political competition. The challenges associated with Taiwan's high-income trap that divide society, with some people seeing China as a solution and others viewing it as a problem, are similar to many of Taiwan's neighbors. Effective solutions within the Asia-Pacific are needed to address the issues raised by different groups and enhance economic resilience while managing the China threat. Taiwan is not alone in facing this threat. As former Australian prime minister Malcolm Turnbull noted at the 2023 annual forum of Taiwan's first international think tank, "problem-solving must happen across borders and sectors.... As authoritarian, populist, and protectionist regimes gain traction worldwide, democratic leaders in Asia and the Pacific should work together to build a collaborative ecosystem for solving the world's toughest challenges." In essence, Taipei needs an ecosystem focused on policy research and civic education to help political leaders become more strategic and focused on the long term. Think tanks, universities, and platforms for competing ideas within Taiwan and across the region are needed to bridge the gap between policymakers and

---

[91] Lin, "Population, Power Generation, Political Polarization, and Parochialism."

experts and develop policy alternatives.[92] Furthermore, consultation with different stakeholders on policy initiatives must improve to create a less polarized Taiwan. Taiwan finds itself at the center of not only Beijing's and Washington's attention but the world's, and it must be equipped to create innovative policy solutions for itself and others.

Conclusions

Since my chapter "How Taiwan's High-Income Trap Shapes Its Options in the U.S.-China Competition" was published in *Strategic Asia 2020*, Taiwan's China dilemma has intensified because of several external factors. China's tightened control over Hong Kong has completely removed "one country, two systems" as an acceptable option for Taiwan as part of a unified China. Another factor is the fear that the United States will abandon Taiwan as it did in 1979, when diplomatic relations and the defense treaty with Taiwan were terminated, although the Taiwan Relations Act moderated the impact. While being touted as a leading emerging democracy with a high-technology foundation, Taiwan is a model for developing countries that the West admires but cannot fully support because of China's opposition. The perceived hypocrisy of the international order has produced skeptics in Taiwan who believe that the United States and Europe are weak and self-interested and argue that Taiwan should accommodate China because it has no choice. Others simply believe that China is a better choice than relying on a declining and increasingly self-serving Western alliance. The United States' decoupling policy toward China, especially semiconductor policies that have damaged Taiwan's economic future, only bolsters claims that Taiwan is a pawn rather than a partner in a geopolitical rivalry between superpowers.

The world and Taiwan have much at stake. Taiwan's 2024 presidential and legislative elections have intensified ongoing debates over the issues examined in this chapter. The lack of cross-strait and international experience among the leading candidates is indicative of the parochial nature of politics from Latin America to Southeast Asia. The major parties' platforms demonstrate societal polarization, offering different views on the implications of decoupling and great-power rivalry for Taiwan. Although younger voters are focused on democracy and freedom, they are less wedded

---

[92] This was a major idea discussed during the annual forum of the Taipei-based Center for Asia-Pacific Resilience and Innovation at which Turnbull spoke. Sunjoy Joshi, Alicia Garcia Herrero, and Harry Harding also spoke about the role of think tanks in today's uncertain world, especially in the Asia-Pacific. See "Center for Asia-Pacific Resilience and Innovation (CAPRI) Convenes International Advisory Council Members Led by Malcolm Turnbull in Taipei Annual Forum," CAPRI, Press Release, May 29, 2023, https://caprifoundation.org/capri2023annualforum-pressrelease.

to any political party than in the past. As a result, the long-term prospect for Taiwan to build a resilient democracy is more uncertain than ever.

Taiwan's challenge of prioritizing and fulfilling competing demands from society is shared by many other countries, but especially the most competitive countries in Asia. The Taiwanese have navigated challenges by relying on innovation, which emerges from international mindsets, close public-private collaboration, and free-flowing talent. More entrepreneurial organizations, including think tanks, can provide platforms for civic engagement in policy and innovative thinking on navigating an increasingly fraught geopolitical landscape.

The United States must lead efforts to include Taiwan in the global political economy and bring it out from the shadow of China, whether in public health, advanced education, or economic partnerships. The stakes are even higher for Xi Jinping, whose tight grip on power must be bolstered by a strong economy and international presence, both of which he believes require reining in Taiwan. China has become economically indispensable to the world, and whether such power extends to become an appealing model elsewhere depends on winning over Taiwan through economic or even military coercion, as well as through rhetoric against the U.S.-led liberal order. Taiwan's ability to walk the tightrope will be a testament to whether the new order in the global economy enhances democratic resilience around the world or simply serves the interests of those who set the ever-changing rules.

EXECUTIVE SUMMARY

This chapter examines how India, contrary to its ambition to be an important strategic player in the Indo-Pacific, has been a reluctant participant in the region's emerging economic architecture and argues that decoupling from China could be harmful for the Indian economy.

MAIN ARGUMENT

The Indian economy has expanded significantly in the last 25 years and become more integrated with other Asian economies. Although trade links between India and China have also multiplied, investment and connectivity links are still limited. To improve their global value chains, most Asian economies are integrating with China and participating in mega trade deals like the Regional Comprehensive Economic Partnership and Comprehensive and Progressive Agreement for Trans-Pacific Partnership. These agreements will affect India even if it is not participating in them. Therefore, India must either join this emerging economic architecture or help create an entirely new one. Thus far, New Delhi's quest for greater strategic influence is not matched by confident foreign economic policies. Instead of framing its economic ties with China in terms of "decoupling" or "de-risking," India needs to develop an independent economic strategy to strengthen its linkages within the Indo-Pacific region, including with the Chinese economy. Reluctant participation in the emerging economic architecture and decoupling from China will likely be a self-defeating strategy.

POLICY IMPLICATIONS
- India's strategic importance in the Indo-Pacific depends on its ability to integrate itself economically within the region, in terms of both trade and connectivity.
- The improvement of India's manufacturing capacity and exports is crucial for the success of its external economic policy initiatives.
- Serious decoupling from China could be counterproductive for India in terms of both domestic manufacturing and exports.

India

India's Reluctant Participation in the Evolving Indo-Pacific Economic Architecture

Gulshan Sachdeva

Over the last 25 years, India's external economic engagement has undergone serious transformation. As a result of comprehensive reforms initiated in 1991, which have been further accelerated by all successive governments, the Indian economy has expanded, further integrated with the global economy, and emerged as one of the fastest-growing economies in the world. Between 1900 and 1950, the Indian economy grew on average by 0.8% a year. As the population grew at the same pace, per capita income was almost stagnant.[1] After India gained independence from Britain in 1947, from 1950 to 1980 economic growth averaged around 3.6% per year. With limited liberalization, economic growth accelerated to around 5.6% per year in the 1980s. Since the early 1990s, the average economic growth in India has been above 6% per year.

A 2018 study by the World Bank classified India's economic growth since 1991 into three phases: 1991–2003, when growth was around 5.5% a year; 2004–8, when growth accelerated to 9% a year; and 2009–17, when growth declined to around 7% a year. Although the upward trend is continuing, the average growth since 2014 under the Modi administration has declined

---

Gulshan Sachdeva is a Professor and Jean Monnet Chair at the Centre for European Studies in the School of International Studies at Jawaharlal Nehru University in New Delhi. He can be reached at <gulshanjnu@gmail.com>.

[1] Gurcharan Das, "India: How a Rich Nation Became Poor and Will Be Rich Again," in *Developing Cultures: Case Studies*, ed. Lawrence E. Harrison and Peter L. Berger (London: Routledge, 2006).

slightly to around 5.4% per year.[2] The impacts of the Covid-19 pandemic and the Russia-Ukraine war are the primary drivers of this trend. The latest International Monetary Fund projections, however, indicate that among the major economies, only India will grow by as much as 6% in 2023 and 2024.[3] Despite serious challenges like global geopolitical tensions, energy security, poverty, an infrastructure deficit, regional disparities, and internal security, there are indications that strong Indian growth will continue. The main drivers of growth are likely to be favorable demographics, a relatively large middle class, a strong information technology (IT) sector, and investment in infrastructure. Global geopolitical tensions may also favor India, as many Western firms could relocate some of their business away from China.

India has already surpassed China's population and has become the largest country in terms of population. Whereas India was the thirteenth-largest economy in the world in 2000 (at current exchange rates), it is now the fifth-largest economy and is likely to become the third-largest by 2029, behind only the United States and China. If there is no major disruption, the Indian economy is likely to be one of the fastest-growing major economies in the medium run and achieve developed-economy status by 2047. According to some scenarios, it will cross the milestones of $5, $10, and $20 trillion in market exchange rate terms by 2028, 2036, and 2045, respectively.[4]

Although the Bharatiya Janata Party (BJP) was expected to be more market-friendly than the socialist Indian National Congress, constraints on the domestic political economy have forced the BJP to follow the existing economic policy framework with limited changes. Some officials in the government have tried to define the new framework as a "*Bharatiya* (Indian) model of inclusive development."[5] Major policy reforms initiated by the Modi administration include FDI liberalization, deregulation of energy prices, the creation of digital public goods, production-linked incentives, a masterplan for multimodal connectivity, ambitious targets for renewables, a new national education policy, and a large number of welfare schemes.

---

[2] Between 1992–93 and 2022–23, the average growth in gross national income at constant prices was around 6% a year. The growth rate continued at around 6% per year for the period between 2001–2 and 2022–23, though for the period between 2014–15 and 2022–23 the average growth was around 5.4% per year. These figures are the author's calculations based on data released by the Ministry of Finance (India), "Economic Survey 2022–23: Statistical Appendix Table 1.2: Annual Growth Rates of Gross National Income and Net National Income," January 2023, 5–6, https://www.indiabudget.gov.in/economicsurvey/doc/stat/tab12.pdf.

[3] International Monetary Fund (IMF), *World Economic Outlook Update: Near-Term Resilience, Persistent Challenges* (Washington, D.C.: IMF, 2023), https://www.imf.org/en/Publications/WEO/Issues/2023/07/10/world-economic-outlook-update-july-2023.

[4] "India@100: Realizing the Potential of a US$26 Trillion Economy," Ernst & Young, 2023, https://www.ey.com/en_in/india-at-100.

[5] Arvind Virmani, "Sabka Sath, Sabka Vikas, Sabka Vishwas, Sabka Prayas: Bharatiya Model of Inclusive Development," NITI Aayog, Policy Paper, June 2023.

This chapter first looks at the dynamics of India's external economic engagement, particularly through bilateral and multilateral trade or other economic agreements. Second, it explains Chinese linkages with the Indian economy in terms of trade and investment. The third section then describes the decoupling measures initiated by India in the last three years. Next, the chapter analyzes the options for India's economy to integrate with the evolving economic architecture in the Indo-Pacific. The chapter concludes by assessing possible trajectories for India's economy and emphasizing the need for an independent Indian policy toward the Indo-Pacific economic architecture.

The Dynamics of India's External Economic Engagement

High economic growth in the last 25 years has had an impact on India's external economic engagement as well as strategic thinking in New Delhi. India's evolving external economic policy framework has developed within the context of domestic political economy compulsions, evolving global and Asian geopolitics, and, more recently, heightened India-China tension and the Indo-Pacific narrative.

The significance of trade in the Indian economy has seen a steady increase over the years. The proportion of trade in goods and services relative to GDP has displayed a notable upward trajectory, climbing from 17% in 1991 to 49% in 2022. This proportion has consistently remained above 40% since 2005. To put this into perspective, during the 1980s, trade accounted for an average of 14% of GDP, which increased to 22% in the 1990s. Between 2001 and 2012, trade contributed to 43% of the GDP, and from 2013 to 2022 it maintained an average share at 37%. The highest point in this trend was witnessed in 2011 and 2012 when trade peaked at 56% of GDP.[6] The merchandise trade is the predominant component of global trade. In contrast to the global average of around 50%, India's merchandise trade as a share of GDP stood at 35% in 2022. After hitting its highest point at 43% in 2012, merchandise trade consistently declined before experiencing a resurgence in 2021. Notably, over the last decade, the average remained at approximately 32%.[7]

Today, global trade dynamics have undergone substantial transformations, with a significant portion of global trade now characterized by the movement of commodities within production networks. Indian trade policy seems to be at variance with these developments. In the 1990s the focus was on reducing tariffs and quotas as well as moving toward a market-based

---

[6] Author's calculations based on World Bank data, https://data.worldbank.org/indicator/NE.TRD.GNFS.ZS?locations=IN.

[7] Author's calculations based on World Bank data, https://data.worldbank.org/indicator/TG.VAL.TOTL.GD.ZS?locations=1W-IN.

exchange rate system. The focus has shifted toward export enhancement in the last two decades, but there is no concrete policy toward participation in global value chains. A lower share in intermediate goods in India's exports also indicates limited participation in value chain–related trade.[8] Domestic economic as well as geopolitical factors in the last few years have resulted in a cautious approach toward imports. The average applied most-favored-nation tariff increased from 13% in 2014–15 to 14.3% in 2020–21.[9] On the whole, India is still a marginal player in global trade participation. Its share in global merchandise exports is only 1.8%, and its share in services is around 4%.[10] In comparison, China's share in global exports of goods was around 15% in 2020.[11] In recent years, composition of trading items remained largely unchanged. Petroleum and mineral products, precious stones and metals, organic and inorganic chemicals, drugs and pharmaceuticals, and textiles have been among the leading Indian exports. Similarly, petroleum products, precious stones and metals, chemicals, machinery, and electrical equipment are the country's main imports.

In 1990 the Indian economy was mainly dependent on the markets in Europe, the Soviet Union, and the United States. As a result of economic diversification, however, more of India's trade is now with countries in Asia, and a resurgent Africa has also become crucial for natural resources and developing new markets (see **Figure 1**).[12] As the share of goods and services trade in the GDP is likely to increase further in the coming years, export performance will be crucial for economic growth and job creation. In 2022–23, Indian trade reached $1,164 billion ($450 billion in exports and $714 billion in imports), out of which around $640 billion, or 55%, was with Asia. In 2000–2001, by contrast, India's trade with Asia was only around 32% of total trade. In comparison, trade with North America and Europe in 2022–23 was around $334 billion, or 29% of total Indian trade, down from around 40% in 2000–2001.[13] India-Africa trade has reached around

---

[8] Amita Batra, *India's Trade Policy in the 21st Century* (New York: Routledge, 2022).

[9] World Trade Organization (WTO), "Trade Policy Review: India," November 2020, 9, https://www.wto.org/english/tratop_e/tpr_e/s403_e.pdf.

[10] Rajeev Jayaswal, "India's Merchandise Exports to Seven Top Trading Partners Contract," *Hindustan Times*, November 17, 2022, https://www.hindustantimes.com/india-news/indias-merchandise-exports-to-seven-top-trading-partners-contract-101668627916014.html.

[11] UN Conference on Trade and Development, "Evolution of the World's 25 Top Trading Nations," 2021, https://unctad.org/topic/trade-analysis/chart-10-may-2021.

[12] Gulshan Sachdeva, "India-Africa Development Partnership Dynamics," Forum for Indian Development Cooperation, FIDC Discussion Paper, no. 3, December 2020, https://fidc.ris.org.in/sites/fidc.ris.org.in/files/Publication/FIDC_DP-Gulshan-Sachdeva.pdf.

[13] Author's calculation based on Ministry of Commerce and Industry (India), "Export Import Data Bank," https://tradestat.commerce.gov.in/eidb/default.asp.

FIGURE 1 India's trade with major regions of the world, 2022–23 ($ billion)

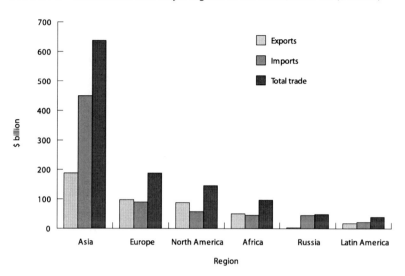

SOURCE: Ministry of Commerce and Industry (India), "Export Import Data Bank," https://tradestat.commerce.gov.in/eidb/default.asp.

$100 billion.[14] As a result of discounted oil purchases, India-Russia trade has increased to $50 billion after hovering around $10 billion for many years. Although Asian countries are major trading partners, Europe, North America, and Africa are still important export markets for India.

Trade Agreements

India has signed bilateral trade agreements (including preferential or partial trade agreements) with Sri Lanka (1998), Afghanistan (2003), Thailand (2003), Singapore (2005), Bhutan (2006), Chile (2006), Nepal (2009), South Korea (2009), Japan (2011), Malaysia (2011), Mauritius (2021), the United Arab Emirates (UAE) (2022), and Australia (2022). At the multilateral level, it is a member of the Asia-Pacific Trade Agreement (1975) and the South Asian Free Trade Agreement (2004). Due to difficult India-Pakistan relations, however, the latter agreement has not been fully implemented. India also signed a partial trade agreement with the Southern

---

[14] "India and Africa Are Natural Partners with Historical and Cultural Ties: Union Commerce and Industry Minister Shri Piyush Goyal," Ministry of Commerce and Industry (India), Press Release, June 15, 2023, https://pib.gov.in/PressReleaseIframePage.aspx?PRID=1932726.

Common Market in 2004. The most important multilateral trade initiative has been the India–Association of Southeast Asian Nations (ASEAN) trade agreement, which was signed in 2010 and extended to services in 2014. Trade agreements with ASEAN and its member states, as well as with South Korea and Japan, clearly illustrate the focus of India's Look East (now Act East) policy on Southeast and East Asia. **Table 1** provides a summary of India's engagements with trade deals.

India's active pursuit of trade agreements, however, ended when its exports began to stagnate in 2012.[15] For many years, the Modi government did not sign any major trade agreements, and exports remained stagnant at $300 billion per year.[16] Only in the last two years, when exports crossed $400 billion, has this approach changed.[17] In 2021 the Modi government signed a trade agreement with Mauritius, and in 2022 it signed two very important agreements with the UAE and Australia. India's approach to these free trade agreements (FTAs) is different. They allow deep access into the partner country's market, safeguards in case of import surges, commitments on government procurement, and better rules of origin.[18] Rules on foreign investment protection, however, are not clearly defined. There are indicators that New Delhi is also eager to forge trade agreements with European countries. This has become important as Indian exports of textiles, footwear, and other goods have been affected by increasing exports to Europe from Bangladesh, Cambodia, and Vietnam.

In 1993, during initial economic liberalization, India formulated text for a model bilateral investment treaty (BIT). The first BIT was signed with the United Kingdom in 1994, and by 2015 83 countries had signed BITs, 74 of which were enforced. In 2015, new model BIT text was adopted, and New Delhi terminated its agreements with 77 countries. BITs were still enforced with only Bangladesh, Colombia, Libya, Senegal, Lithuania, and the UAE. Only Belarus, Brazil, Kyrgyzstan, and Taiwan have signed agreements based on the new template.[19] Therefore, unless new agreements are signed, either as stand-alone treaties or as part of a larger FTA, new investments from

---

[15] V.S. Seshadri, *Free Trade Agreements: India and the World* (Kolkata: Oxford University Press, 2023).

[16] See WTO, Regional Trade Agreements Database, http://rtais.wto.org/UI/charts.aspx.

[17] See, for example, Reserve Bank of India, *Handbook of Statistics on the Indian Economy, 2022–23* (Mumbai, September 2023), 185, https://rbidocs.rbi.org.in/rdocs/Publications/PDFs/HBS20222023FULLDOCUMENT2FB950EDD2A34FE2BAE3308256EAE587.PDF.

[18] V.S. Seshadri, "Fresh Approaches Seen in India's Two New FTAs," Delhi Policy Group, May 25, 2022, https://www.delhipolicygroup.org/publication/policy-briefs/fresh-approaches-seen-in-indias-two-new-ftas.html.

[19] Parliamentary Standing Committee on External Affairs (2020–21) (India), "India and Bilateral Investment Treaties," September 2021, https://eparlib.nic.in/bitstream/123456789/811585/1/17_External_Affairs_10.pdf.

TABLE 1 India's engagement with trade agreements

Agreement name	Type	Coverage	Year of signature	Year of entry into force	Current signatories
Asia-Pacific Trade Agreement (earlier Bangkok Agreement)	PSA and EIA	Goods and services	1975 (goods), 2011 (services)	1976	Bangladesh, China, India, South Korea, Laos, Sri Lanka
India–Sri Lanka	FTA	Goods	1998	2000	India, Sri Lanka
India-Afghanistan	PSA	Goods	2003	2003	Afghanistan, India
India-Thailand	PSA	Goods	2003	2004	India, Thailand
South Asian Free Trade Area	FTA	Goods	2004	2006	Afghanistan, Bangladesh, Bhutan, India, Maldives, Nepal, Pakistan, Sri Lanka
Southern Common Market–India	PSA	Goods	2004	2009	Argentina, Brazil, Paraguay, Uruguay, India
India-Singapore	FTA, EIA	Goods and services	2005	2005	India, Singapore
India-Bhutan	PSA	Goods	2006	2006	Bhutan, India
India-Chile	PSA	Goods	2006	2007	Chile, India
India-Nepal	PSA	Goods	2009	2009	India, Nepal
India-ASEAN	FTA and EIA	Goods and services	Goods (2009), services (2014)	Goods (2010), services (2015)	All ten ASEAN countries, India
India–South Korea	FTA and EIA	Goods and services	2009	2010	India, South Korea
India-Japan	FTA and EIA	Goods and services	2011	2011	India, Japan
India-Malaysia	FTA and EIA	Goods and services	2011	2011	India, Malaysia
India-Mauritius	FTA and EIA	Goods and services	2021	2021	India, Mauritius
India-UAE	FTA and EIA	Goods and services	2022	2022	India, UAE
India-Australia	FTA and EIA	Goods and services	2022	2023	India, Australia

Table 1 continued.

Under negotiation (selected)		
Agreement parties	**Type**	**Notes**
India-EU	FTA and EIA	After 13 rounds between 2007 and 2013, negotiations were frozen in 2013; since 2021 negotiations on three separate deals on trade, investment, and geographic indicators have begun; FTA covers 23 policy areas; 5 new rounds completed.
India-UK	FTA and EIA	Negotiations started in 2022 and cover 26 policy areas; twelve rounds have been completed; 14 out of 26 chapters have been closed.
India–European Free Trade Association	FTA	Negotiations are at advanced stage.
India–Canada Early Progress Trade Agreement	FTA	7 rounds of negotiations have been completed; negotiations were paused in September 2023.
India-Israel	FTA and EIA	10 rounds of negotiations have been completed since 2010.
India–Gulf Cooperation Council	FTA	Negotiations occurred between 2006 and 2008 and were restarted in 2022.
Bay of Bengal Initiative for Multi-Sectoral Technical and Economic Cooperation (BIMSTEC)	FTA and EIA	A framework agreement was signed in 2004; an FTA still being negotiated.
India–Eurasian Economic Union	FTA and EIA	Many positive statements have been issued in the last few years, but no concrete development has been made.
India–Southern African Customs Union	PSA	Initial talks held between 2007 and 2010; were restarted in 2020, with five rounds held.
India and Central American Integration System	FTA	Talks are at an advanced stage.

SOURCE: Compiled by the author.

NOTE: PSA stands for partial scope agreement, FTA stands for free trade agreement, and EIA stands for economic integration agreement.

other countries are not fully protected in India. Given that none of the major investment partners has signed a new BIT with India so far, the Modi government finally might be changing its approach and tweaking the new model BIT with some key strategic partners.[20] Still, India would like foreign investors to not invoke arbitration until all local remedies are fully exhausted.

Some important new trade deals are being negotiated. Negotiations on a comprehensive FTA with the European Union started in 2007. The initial agenda included goods and services trade, investment, public procurement, intellectual property, and competition. However, after sixteen rounds and widening gaps in ambitions from both sides, the negotiations were frozen in 2013. In 2021, Prime Minister Narendra Modi met with all 27 EU leaders, and they decided to restart parallel negotiations on three separate agreements related to trade, investment, and geographic indicators, respectively. Thus far, five rounds of negotiations have been completed. India-UK FTA negotiations are also at an advanced stage, with twelve rounds having been completed. Talks between India and the European Free Trade Association (EFTA), a four-nation bloc, are moving fast as well. As a result of the deterioration in India-Canada relations stemming from the murder of a Sikh separatist leader, bilateral trade negotiations, which had recently resumed after a decade, have been halted again.[21] Between 2006 and 2008, India and the six-nation Gulf Cooperation Council negotiated a trade deal, and these negotiations resumed in 2022. India has also initiated action to review existing FTAs with Singapore, South Korea, and ASEAN, and in August 2023 it finally agreed with ASEAN to start the review and complete the process by 2025.

At the moment, India is not a member of the Regional Comprehensive Economic Partnership (RCEP) or the Comprehensive and Progressive Agreement for Trans-Pacific Partnership (CPTPP). It had been a founding member of the RCEP negotiations but dropped out at the last minute in 2019, mainly due to China's dominance in the grouping. In the parliament, the government explained that the RCEP's structure "did not adequately address the ambitions and concerns of India's stakeholders."[22] By contrast, New Delhi has decided to join three pillars of the Indo-Pacific Economic Framework (IPEF) related to supply chains, tax and anticorruption, and clean energy.

---

[20] "India UK Bilateral Investment Treaty Likely to Be Finalised Soon, to Differ from 2016 Model," *Indian Express*, August 28, 2023, https://indianexpress.com/article/business/india-uk-bilateral-investment-treaty-free-trade-agreement-2016-model-bit-european-union-8912276.

[21] "India-Canada FTA Talks Paused Due to Political Reasons," *Mint*, September 15, 2023, https://www.livemint.com/news/india/indiacanada-free-trade-agreement-negotiations-halted-over-political-concerns-khalistan-issue-remains-unresolved-11694800223521.html.

[22] Ministry of Commerce and Industry (India), "Lok Sabha Unstarred Question No. 1079: RCEP," February 8, 2023, https://commerce.gov.in/wp-content/uploads/2023/02/1141_merged.pdf.

Still, due to possible binding commitments on labor, the environment, and digital trade, New Delhi has opted out of the trade pillar.

In addition to India's recent activity in signing and negotiating trade deals, it aspires to play an important role in the G-20, BRICS (Brazil, Russia, India, China, South Africa), the India–Brazil–South Africa grouping, the South Asian Association for Regional Cooperation (SAARC), the Indian Ocean Rim Association (IORA), and the Shanghai Cooperation Organisation.

Overall, the government has adopted a new foreign trade policy to boost India's goods and services exports to $2 trillion by 2030.[23] High economic growth has also forced India to synchronize its energy security issues with its external engagement. In the past, external energy policy meant securing reliable supplies from the Persian Gulf. Later, it focused on multiple strategies of diversification by acquiring assets abroad and navigating pipeline politics. Now the Modi government's pledge to achieve net-zero emissions by 2070 (with a target of increasing renewables capacity to 500 gigawatts and reducing emissions intensity by 45% by 2030) has also become an important factor. India's actions and commitments in all these energy areas will shape its relations with the Middle East, Europe, Russia, and the United States.

Connectivity Initiatives

India has not announced any connectivity strategy, but it is trying to build a narrative based on the many strategic partnerships and FTAs the country has signed over the last twenty years. India is also weaving its connectivity initiatives through the Act East policy, the Connect Central Asia policy, SAARC, IORA, and the India-Africa Dialogues, as well as engagements in Afghanistan and the Middle East, into the narrative. These are linked with the International North-South Transport Corridor, the Asia-Africa Growth Corridor, the Security and Growth for All in the Region framework, the India–Middle East–Europe Economic Corridor (IMEC), Project Mausam, Make in India, and Digital India, among other initiatives. India is also trying to improve its connectivity with the ASEAN region via two main routes: the Mekong-India Economic Corridor and the India–Myanmar–Thailand Trilateral Highway. The economic corridor enhances connectivity between Ho Chi Minh City, Phnom Penh, Bangkok, and Dawei by road and further to Chennai by sea route, while the trilateral highway improves connectivity between northeast India and ASEAN. These routes will be connected to India's Golden Quadrangle national highway network as well as the Delhi-Mumbai Industrial Corridor.

---

[23] "Foreign Trade Policy 2023 Announced," Ministry of Commerce and Industry (India), Press Release, March 31, 2023, https://pib.gov.in/PressReleaseIframePage.aspx?PRID=1912572.

Building connectivity has thus become an important part of India's development cooperation activities abroad, which include lines of credit, capacity-building programs, and grant assistance projects. By March 2023, the Export-Import Bank of India had signed 303 lines of credit covering 68 countries in Africa, Asia, the Commonwealth of Independent States, and Latin America, with credit commitments of around $32 billion.[24] Apart from lines of credit, infrastructure support is also extended under grant assistance projects, mainly in the neighborhood and Africa. **Table 2** summarizes India's connectivity projects.

To a significant extent, connectivity narratives in the Indo-Pacific region are influenced by China's Belt and Road Initiative (BRI).[25] Of late, many of India's Western partners have framed BRI in terms of global norms, financial responsibility, transparency, debt burdens, environmental sustainability, and respect for sovereignty and territorial integrity. India has taken an independent view on the initiative from the very beginning. Apart from sovereignty-related issues concerning the China-Pakistan Economic Corridor, its focus has been on the geopolitical impact of infrastructure projects in its neighborhood and the wider Indian Ocean region. As a result, Indian perceptions are mainly shaped by the geopolitical dimensions of BRI rather than broader developmental aspects.[26] The increasing profile of BRI has forced some of its critics to pursue initiatives of their own based on transparent behavior, sustainable financing, and quality infrastructure. India is now partnering with Japan on the Asia-Africa Growth Corridor and has also established a connectivity partnership with the EU.

The announcement of the IMEC in September 2023 on the sidelines of the G-20 summit in New Delhi has added a new dimension to India's connectivity designs. This transnational shipping and rail corridor will link India and Europe via the UAE, Saudi Arabia, Jordan, and Israel through two separate corridors: the eastern corridor will connect India to the Persian Gulf region, and the northern corridor will connect this region to Europe.[27] Besides shipping and rail corridors, IMEC may also include electric cables, hydrogen pipelines, and high-speed data cables. All of this is part of the Partnership for Global Infrastructure and Investment, launched in 2022 at

---

[24] Export-Import Bank of India, *Annual Report 2022–23* (Mumbai, August 2023), 9, https://www.eximbankindia.in/Assets/Dynamic/PDF/Publication-Resources/AnnualReports/32file.pdf.

[25] Gulshan Sachdeva, "Connectivity Strategies in the Indo-Pacific and Its Geopolitical Implications," in *Handbook of Indo-Pacific Studies*, ed. Barbara Kratiuk et al. (London: Routledge, 2023).

[26] Gulshan Sachdeva, "Indian Perceptions of the Chinese Belt and Road Initiative," *International Studies* 55, no. 4 (2018): 285–96.

[27] "Partnership for Global Infrastructure and Investment (PGII) & India-Middle East-Europe Economic Corridor (IMEC)," Prime Minister's Office (India), Press Release, September 9, 2023, https://pib.gov.in/PressReleaseIframePage.aspx?PRID=1955921.

TABLE 2   India's connectivity engagements

Name of the project	Countries involved	Details
International North South Transport Corridor	Founding members: India, Iran, and Russia; others: Armenia, Azerbaijan, Belarus, Kazakhstan, Oman, Syria, Tajikistan, Ukraine, and Kyrgyzstan	7,200-km long multi-modal (ship-rail-road) transport network; mainly links India with Europe (Russia) via Iran/Caspian Sea or Azerbaijan; New Delhi is keen to add India-built Chahbahar port in Iran into network.
Bangladesh, China, India, and Myanmar Economic Corridor	Bangladesh, China, India, and Myanmar	Started from a second-track dialogue as part of Kunming Initiative in 1999; in 2015, China included it as one of the main BRI corridors; at the second BRI meeting it was not mentioned as a BRI project.
India-Myanmar-Thailand Trilateral Highway	India, Myanmar, and Thailand	Connecting Moreh (India) to Bagan (Myanmar) and Mae Sot (Thailand).
Mekong-India Economic Corridor	Vietnam, Myanmar, Thailand, and Cambodia	Connecting Ho Chi Minh City, Dawai, Bangkok, Phnom Penn, and Chennai.
Kaladan Multimodal Transport Project	India and Myanmar	Connecting Kolkata (India) to Sittwe and Paletwa (Myanmar).
Asia-Africa Growth Corridor	India, Japan (plus countries across Asia, Africa)	Promotes development cooperation projects, quality infrastructure, and institutional connectivity; enhances capacities and skills; builds people-to-people partnerships.
India-EU Connectivity Partnership	India, EU (plus countries across Africa, Central Asia, and the Indo-Pacific)	Promotes digital, energy, transport, and people-to-people connectivity.
Chennai-Vladivostok Maritime Corridor	India and Russia	Announced in 2019; covers the Sea of Japan, East China Sea, and South China Sea through the Malacca Strait to reach the Bay of Bengal.
India–Middle East–Europe Economic Corridor	India, UAE, Saudi Arabia, EU, France, Germany, Italy, and the United States	Announced on the sidelines of the G-20 summit in New Delhi in September 2023; this rail and shipping project will link India to Europe via UAE, Saudi Arabia, Jordan, and Israel.

SOURCE: Compiled by the author.

the G-7 summit in Germany. The IMEC aspires to make trade between India and Europe 40% faster.[28] The Indian Adani Group has already acquired Haifa Port in Israel and also plans to buy ports in Greece, though at present, Greece's largest port, Piraeus, is controlled by the Chinese shipping firm COSCO.[29] If the IMEC is backed by appropriate funding, it will likely increase India's trade with the Middle East and Europe by 10%–20% due to cost advantages, further integrating the regions.

Before the IMEC, the International North-South Transport Corridor was India's answer to BRI. Founding members Russia, Iran, and India have been joined by many other countries that use the corridor to facilitate the movement of goods via Iran, the Caspian Sea, and Astrakhan to Russia and adjoining countries in the Commonwealth of Independent States. With increasing energy trade between India and Russia, the corridor may become even more viable.

Chinese Linkages to the Indian Economy

A large number of studies are available to describe India-China relations in strategic affairs. Only recently has attention been paid to the importance of increasing Chinese economic linkages to India's modernization. Traditionally, China's strategy in South Asia has been focused on maintaining a strategic balance. In practical terms, this has meant checking India's rise by supporting Pakistan in the context of difficult India-Pakistan relations. However, over the last two decades, China's economic rise and economic liberalization in India and other South Asian countries have provided many new opportunities for Beijing to expand its profile and influence. As Chinese objectives have become more diverse, simple balance-of-power calculations are not enough to capture current India-China dynamics. There are clear signs that China has shifted its priorities from geostrategic calculations to wider economic interests.

Earlier China operated mainly within the regional security complex. Its economic relations with all countries in the region, including India and Pakistan, were modest. This change has affected not only China-India

---

[28] Ursula von der Leyen, "Statement by President von der Leyen at the Partnership for Global Infrastructure and Investment Event in the Framework of the G20 Summit," President of the European Commission, September 9, 2023, https://ec.europa.eu/commission/presscorner/detail/en/statement_23_4420.

[29] "Adani Group Acquires Israeli Port of Haifa for $1.2 Billion, Netanyahu Lauds Deal as 'Enormous Milestone,'" *Outlook* (India), January 31, 2023, https://www.outlookindia.com/business/adani-group-acquires-israeli-port-of-haifa-for-1-2-billion-netanyahu-lauds-deal-as-enormous-milestone--news-258396; Paran Balakrishnan, "Adani Eyeing Greek Ports to Serve as Gateway for Indian Exports Bound for Europe: Greek Media," *Telegraph* (India), August 27, 2023, https://www.telegraphindia.com/business/adani-group-eyeing-greek-ports-to-serve-as-gateway-for-indian-exports-bound-for-europe-greek-media/cid/1961916; and Kaki Bali, "In Greece's Largest Port of Piraeus, China Is the Boss," Deutsche Welle, October 30, 2022, https://www.dw.com/en/greece-in-the-port-of-piraeus-china-is-the-boss/a-63581221.

trade but also Chinese investments in various BRI projects (e.g., the China-Pakistan Economic Corridor). China's long-term plans are to integrate all countries in the region, including India, with Chinese economic and strategic calculations. Due to sustained high economic growth since 1978, the Chinese economic base has become large, and the gap between the Chinese and Indian economies has widened. Beijing now feels that it will be difficult for India to continue to be a security challenge to China. Meanwhile, all regional economies, including India, will be increasingly pulled into China's economic orbit.[30] The main challenge for India is not only how to respond strategically to an assertive China but also how to respond to the economic strategies of a neighboring economy that is five times as large as the Indian economy.

A Timeline of India-China Trade

After the Sino-Indian War in 1962, trade between the two countries did not resume until 1978. In 1978, bilateral trade was only around $25 million. Although India and China signed a trade agreement in 1984, trade remained insignificant until the mid-1990s. In 1997–98, bilateral trade reached $2 billion, and by 2000, it rose to $3 billion. Trade figures since the early 2000s clearly indicate that China has emerged as a major trading partner for India in the last fifteen years. Improvement in diplomatic ties, China's accession to the World Trade Organization, and high economic growth in India helped stimulate commercial ties. By 2006–7, China had become India's second-largest trading partner, with around $28 billion in annual trade. Since then, China has remained India's top or second-largest trading partner. By 2013–14, bilateral trade crossed $65 billion. Although political relations have soured in the last three years, bilateral trade has grown from $82 billion in 2019–20 to $114 billion in 2022–23. This trend, however, has been one-sided. Imports from China have increased from $60 billion in 2014–15 to $100 billion in 2022–23, while Indian exports have remained at around $15 billion. As a result, the trade deficit with China has increased from $48 billion in 2014–15 to more than $83 billion in 2022–23—one-third of the total Indian trade deficit (see **Figures 2**, **3**, and **4**).

To fully capture India-China trade, trade with Hong Kong also needs to be taken into account. Many products from China are re-exported to other destinations via Hong Kong. India's combined trade with China and Hong Kong reached $146 billion in 2021–22, and the combined deficit in 2022–23 was more than $90 billion. In 2021–22, when there was a slight decline in

---

[30] Gulshan Sachdeva, "China's Current South Asia Strategy," in *China's Grand Strategy: A Roadmap to Global Power?* ed. David B.H. Denoon (New York: NYU Press, 2021), 146–73.

FIGURE 2   India-China trade from 2000–2001 to 2013–14 ($ billion)

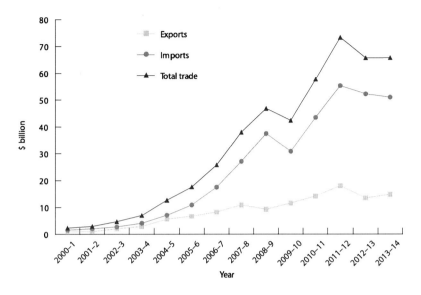

SOURCE: Ministry of Commerce and Industry (India), "Export Import Data Bank."

FIGURE 3   India-China trade from 2014–15 to 2022–23 ($ billion)

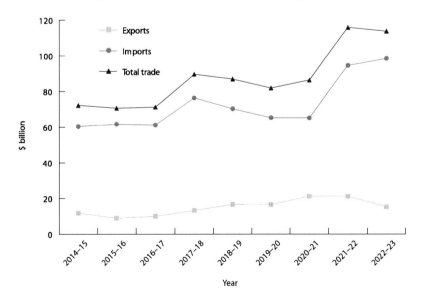

SOURCE: Ministry of Commerce and Industry (India), "Export Import Data Bank."

FIGURE 4 India's goods trade balance with China, 1997–98 to 2022–23 ($ billion)

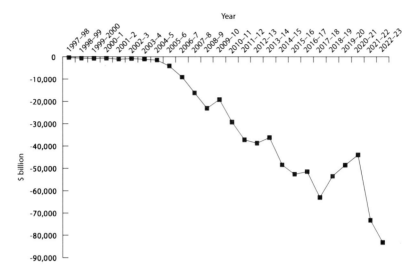

SOURCE: Author's calculations based on Ministry of Commerce and Industry (India), "Export Import Data Bank."

imports from China, imports from Hong Kong were on the upswing (see **Table 3**).

Figures 2 and 3 show that India-China trade has continued to increase in absolute terms as a result of the Indian economy's expansion as well as growth in bilateral trade. However, viewed as a percentage of total Indian trade, trade between India and China has actually declined in the last two years (see **Figure 5**). It is still too early to confirm a definite trend, but this could be the result of decoupling measures, which will be discussed in detail in the next section.

A few Indian manufacturing sectors are highly dependent on Chinese imports. This includes active pharmaceutical ingredients (APIs), electronics, motor vehicle spare parts, photovoltaic (PV) cells, telecommunications and electronics, and household products. Some studies have shown that India's claim to be the "pharmacy of the world" has weak foundations.[31] For a large number of APIs—from common antipyretics to anti-inflammatory medicines and antibiotics—Indian companies rely almost exclusively on China. In some

---

[31] Biswajit Dhar and K.S. Chalapati Rao, "India's Economic Dependence on China," *India Forum*, July 23, 2020, https://www.theindiaforum.in/article/india-s-dependence-china.

TABLE 3   India's trade with China plus Hong Kong, 2014–15 to 2022–23 ($ million)

Year	India-China trade		India–Hong Kong trade		Exports to China plus Hong Kong	Imports from China plus Hong Kong	Trade with China plus Hong Kong	Trade balance with China plus Hong Kong
	Exports	Imports	Exports	Imports				
2014–15	11,934	60,413	13,599	5,572	25,533	65,985	91,518	-40,452
2015–16	9,011	61,708	12,092	6,001	21,103	69,912	91,015	-48,809
2016–17	10,172	61,283	14,047	8,204	24,219	69,487	93,706	-45268
2017–18	13,334	76,380	14,690	10,676	28,024	87,056	115,080	-59,032
2018–19	16,752	70,320	13,002	17,887	29,754	88,207	117,961	-58,453
2019–20	16,613	65,261	10,967	16,935	27,580	82,196	109,776	-54,616
2020–21	21,187	65,212	10,984	19,096	32,171	84,308	116,479	-81,137
2021–22	21,260	94,571	10,984	19,096	32,244	113,667	145,911	-81,423
2022–23	15,306	98,506	9,892	18,274	25,198	116,780	141,978	-91,582

SOURCE: Ministry of Commerce and Industry (India), "Export Import Data Bank."

FIGURE 5 India-China trade as a percentage of total Indian trade from 2014–15 to 2022–23

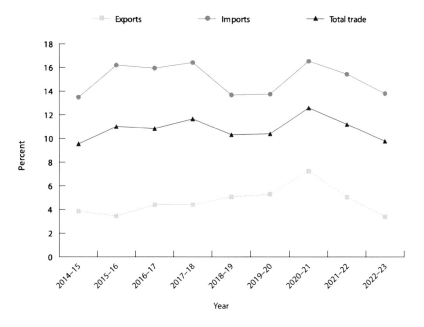

SOURCE: Author's calculations based on Ministry of Commerce and Industry (India), "Export Import Data Bank."

cases, they rely on China for almost 100% of APIs. Imports of motorcycle parts and PV cells are also significant. Imports of telecom and electronic products have also increased significantly over the years. India's imports are increasingly moving toward intermediate goods and capital goods, which include consumer durables. In exports, raw materials and intermediates dominate, while capital and consumer goods are insignificant. Overall, "India [is] supplying raw material and intermediates to China, while importing capital goods and critical intermediates for its pharmaceutical industry, the two-wheeler industry, and for synthetic yarn, among other goods."[32]

Another worrying factor for India is China's increasing economic linkage with other South Asian countries. Traditionally, India considered South Asia as its exclusive sphere of influence, especially in the economic domain. Chinese economic linkages with most countries in the region were minimal.

---

[32] Dhar and Rao, "India's Economic Dependence on China."

This has changed dramatically in the last two decades. Overall, in 2022 China had close to $200 billion in trade with South Asia, out of which $175 billion was exports. It exported products worth $27 billion to Bangladesh, $23 billion to Pakistan, and $4 billion to Sri Lanka. Since South Asian exports were only around $22 billion, China had a surplus of more than $150 billion with the region. Excluding India, China's trade with other South Asian countries was $61 billion ($56 billion in exports); by contrast, in 2022, India exported only $32 billion worth of goods to seven South Asian countries. Still, for countries like Bhutan, Nepal, and Sri Lanka, the Indian export market is still larger than China's.[33]

The Changing Nature of Chinese Investment in India

Despite growing trade with China, Indian authorities have always been somewhat cautious about Chinese investments in India. Exact information about FDI into India is difficult to find because close to 50% of inflows are routed through Mauritius and Singapore. Not only do a large number of foreign companies invest through this route, but many Indian companies also reroute their investments through these countries to gain certain benefits. According to official Indian statistics, Chinese companies invested only around $2.5 billion into the Indian market between 2000 and 2023. This amounts to only 0.4% of total equity inflows into the Indian market during this period.[34] Most of this investment was made through state-owned companies.

However, according to estimates based on Chinese statistics, some independent studies have concluded that by the end of 2019 the total current and planned Chinese investment in India was around $26 billion, of which $15 billion was pledged for various unapproved infrastructure projects.[35] This is the sum of investment coming both directly from China and through third parties like Singapore or Hong Kong. For example, mobile and telecom firm Xiaomi invested more than $500 million through its Singapore subsidiary. Chinese companies have already started investing, with big expansion plans, in industrial parks, coal-based power plants, renewables, automobiles, mobile

---

[33] These figures have been calculated by the author from the IMF, Direction of Trade Statistics, https://data.imf.org/?sk=9d6028d4-f14a-464c-a2f2-59b2cd424b85.

[34] Department for Promotion of Industry and Internal Trade (India), "Fact Sheet on Foreign Direct Investment (FDI) Inflow, from April, 2000 to March, 2023," March 2023, https://dpiit.gov.in/sites/default/files/FDI_Factsheet_March_23.pdf.

[35] Ananth Krishnan, "Following the Money: China Inc's Growing Stake in India-China Relations," Brookings India, March 30, 2020, https://www.brookings.edu/wp-content/uploads/2020/03/China-Inc's-growing-stake-in-India-China-relations_F.pdf.

phones, consumer goods, and real estate.[36] Some reports indicate that between 2010 and 2020, 28 Chinese corporations, led by Tencent, Xiaomi, and Alibaba, invested in Indian start-ups. Similarly, 41 Chinese venture capital firms, including Shunwei Capital, Hillhouse Capital, Axis Capital, NGP Capital, and Morningside, among others, have invested in Indian start-ups.[37] Other studies have also highlighted this phenomenon. A 2020 Gateway House report showed that Chinese funding agencies in Singapore, Mauritius, and Hong Kong have routed their investments with a special focus on Indian start-ups.[38] These companies have also penetrated the Indian online space through mobile apps. Compared with other parts of Asia, where Chinese firms have made major investments in the infrastructure sector, their focus in India has been on new businesses. By 2020, Chinese companies and funding agencies had significantly invested in 18 out of 30 Indian "unicorns" (see **Table 4**).

Despite Indian concerns about the widening trade deficit, before 2020, both countries were trying to build synergies between their economies. The India-China Strategic Economic Dialogue, which was established in 2010, convened for its sixth meeting in September 2019. The dialogue included six working groups on infrastructure, energy, high-tech, resource conservation, and policy coordination. Significant progress was made on the project to upgrade the Chennai-Mysuru high-speed rail corridor and the training of senior Indian railway management staff in China. The two sides also explored the possibility of working on the Delhi-Kolkata high-speed rail corridor and made progress on digital partnership and data governance; environmental protection, renewables, e-mobility, and energy storage; and complementary advantages in the pharmaceutical industry.[39] Later, when Prime Minister Modi and President Xi Jinping met for an informal summit in Chennai in October 2019, they agreed to establish a high-level economic and trade dialogue mechanism and to encourage mutual investments.[40]

---

[36] Krishnan, "Following the Money."

[37] "Despite Hype about Billion-Dollar Deals, China Is a Minor Investor in India," *Mint*, June 26, 2020, https://www.livemint.com/news/india/despite-hype-about-billion-dollar-deals-china-is-a-minor-investor-in-india-11593135238246.html.

[38] Amit Bhandari, Blaise Fernandes, and Aashna Agarwal, "Chinese Investments in India," Gateway House, February 2020, https://www.gatewayhouse.in/wp-content/uploads/2020/07/Chinese-Investments_2020-Final.pdf.

[39] "Sixth India-China Strategic Economic Dialogue Concludes," NITI Aayog, Press Release, September 9, 2019, https://pib.gov.in/PressReleseDetail.aspx?PRID=1584574.

[40] "2nd India-China Informal Summit," Prime Minister's Office (India), Press Release, October 12, 2019, https://pib.gov.in/PressReleseDetailm.aspx?PRID=1587918.

TABLE 4 Chinese funding in Indian start-ups

Indian brand name	Main Chinese investor	Investment ($ million)
Snapdeal (e-commerce)	Alibaba Group, FIH Mobile (subsidiary of Foxconn Technology Group)	>700
Ola Cabs (ridesharing)	Tencent Holdings, Steadview Capital, Sailing Capital and China, Eternal Yield International, China-Eurasia Economic Cooperation Fund	>500
Swiggy (food ordering and delivery)	Meituan Dianping, Hillhouse Capital, Tencent Holdings, SAIF Partners	>500
Paytm (digital payment)	Alibaba Group (Alipay Singapore Holding), SAIF Partners	>400
Flipkart (e-commerce)	Steadview Capital, Tencent Holdings	>300
Zomato	Alibaba Group (Alipay Singapore and Ant Financial Services Group), Shunwei Capital	>200
Big Basket (online grocery)	Alibaba Group, TR Capital	>250
Policy Bazaar (insurance)	Tencent Holdings	130–150
Hike (messenger)	Tencent Holdings, Foxconn	>150
Paytm Mall (shopping app)	Alibaba Group	>100
Udaan (B2B portal)	Tencent Holdings	>100
Oyo (online hotel booking)	Di Chuxing, China Lodging Group	>100
Byju's (online learning)	Tencent Holdings	>50
Delhivery (logistics and supply chain)	Fosun	>25
Rivigo	SAIF Partners	>25
Main Chinese company	**Investment in Indian start-ups**	
Alibaba Group	Big Basket, Snapdeal, Zomato, Dailyhunt, Healofy, Paytm, Paytm Mall, Ticketnew, Vidooly, Xpressbees, Rapido	
Tencent	Ola Cabs, Byju's, Dream11, Flipkart, Hike, Swiggy, Udaan, Doubtnut, Niyo, Gaana, Khatabook, Mx Player, My Gate, Pine Labs, Pocket FM, Practo, Policy Bazaar, Ibibo	
Xiaomi (Shunwei Capital)	CityMall, Hungama Digital Media Entertainment, Marsplay Internet, Oye Rickshaw, Rapido, ShareChat, ZestMoney, Vokal	
Fosun	MakeMyTrip, Delhivery, LetsTransport	

SOURCE Bhandari et al., *Chinese Investments in India* (Mumbai: Gateway House, 2020); and various media reports.

Decoupling Measures

In June 2020, expanding India-China economic ties were suddenly disrupted by the fatal clash between the two countries' armies in the Galwan Valley. Even though various de-escalation measures have been taken by both sides, the situation is still tense. While speaking in 2021, Minister of External Affairs Subrahmanyam Jaishankar asserted that even before 2020 the "relationship witnessed decisions and events that reflected the duality of cooperation and competition," but now India and China are "truly at a crossroads."[41] After three years, relations are still described as "not normal" by Indian policymakers.[42] The border dispute has definitely affected economic ties. In the last three years, India has broadly taken four kinds of measures to decouple the Indian economy from China: (1) reducing Chinese imports, (2) banning Chinese mobile apps to safeguard Indian users, (3) tightening the screening of Chinese investments, and (4) encouraging domestic manufacturing capacities to make the country self-reliant in key industries.

Long before the recent downturn in political relations, Indian policymakers were already worried about the impact of Chinese goods on Indian industry. Between 1994 and 2017, the Directorate General of Anti-Dumping and Allied Duties initiated 214 anti-dumping investigations against China. In comparison, there were only 86 cases against the EU and 41 each against Japan and the United States.[43] Between 2018 and July 2023, another 80 anti-dumping cases against China were added.[44] By the middle of 2018, definite anti-dumping duties were already in place against 102 Chinese products. In July 2018, the Parliamentary Standing Committee on Commerce presented a report on the impact of Chinese goods on Indian industry that looked at a few specific industries such as pharmaceuticals, solar, textiles, toys, bicycles, and firecrackers. After finding that most APIs are imported from China, the committee asserted that "such a strategic product cannot be left at the mercy of China as it impacts the nation's health security."[45]

---

[41] Subrahmanyam Jaishankar, "Keynote Address by External Affairs Minister at the 13th All India Conference of China Studies," Minister of External Affairs (India), January 28, 2021, https://mea.gov.in/Speeches-Statements.htm?dtl/33419.

[42] Singh Rahul Sunilkumar, "'India-China Relations Not Normal': Jaishankar on Meet with Chinese Counterpart Qin Gang," *Hindustan Times*, May 5, 2023, https://www.hindustantimes.com/india-news/india-china-standoff-s-jaishankar-sco-meet-qin-gang-lac-disengagement-101683296819401.html.

[43] Parliamentary Standing Committee on Commerce (India), "Impact of Chinese Goods on Indian Industry," July 2018, https://prsindia.org/policy/report-summaries/impact-of-chinese-goods-on-indian-industry.

[44] "Anti-Dumping Cases," Directorate General of Trade Remedies (India), https://www.dgtr.gov.in/anti-dumping-cases.

[45] Parliamentary Standing Committee on Commerce (India), "Impact of Chinese Goods on Indian Industry."

Similarly, 84% of the equipment for the ambitious National Solar Mission came from China. All the Indian companies that used to export solar products to European markets had disappeared. Many textile firms in Bhiwadi and Surat were facing serious challenges due to either direct imports of human-made fibers from China or imports of garments using Chinese fabric from less developed countries like Bangladesh. Similar situations were found in the toy, bicycle, and firecracker industries.

The committee found that most anti-dumping measures were largely ineffective due to various loopholes. For example, almost 75%–80% of Chinese steel products were covered by anti-dumping duties, yet imports of such products were increasing. Despite government measures, Chinese products were still being imported as a result of under-invoicing or being routed through third countries. Since this policy to reduce Chinese imports and the overall trade deficit has not worked, the government is now focusing on reducing dependence on China for certain critical inputs. According to the vice chair of NITI Aayog, the public policy think tank of the Indian government, "the right response is to diversify to other sources of supply for critical inputs including active pharmaceutical ingredients (APIs) and supply chain for renewables."[46]

Ban on Mobile Apps

On June 29, 2020, the Indian government banned 59 Chinese mobile apps. This included the video-sharing app TikTok, which had been downloaded an estimated 600 million times in India; UC Browser, a web browser widely used by low-cost smartphone users; and other popular apps like SHAREit, Baidu, Weibo, and WeChat. The official reason for the ban was "concerns on aspects relating to data security and safeguarding the privacy" of Indian citizens and that these apps "pose a threat to [the] sovereignty and integrity of [India]."[47] Allegations contend that data was being sent to Chinese servers through the apps. After the first ban, the government issued bans on four subsequent occasions of 47, 118, 43, and 54 apps, respectively.[48] Altogether, 321 Chinese

---

[46] "India's Focus Should Be on Reducing Dependence on China for Certain Critical Inputs: NITI Aayog's Suman Bery," *Economic Times*, February 5, 2023, https://economictimes.indiatimes.com/news/india/indias-focus-should-be-on-reducing-dependence-on-china-for-certain-critical-inputs-niti-aayogs-suman-bery/articleshow/97621539.cms.

[47] "Government Bans 59 Mobile Apps Which Are Prejudicial to Sovereignty and Integrity of India, Defence of India, Security of State and Public Order," Ministry of Electronics and Information Technology (India), Press Release, June 29, 2020, https://pib.gov.in/PressReleseDetailm.aspx?PRID=1635206.

[48] A list of banned mobile apps is available at Karan Chhabra, "Full List of 321 Chinese Apps Banned in India," Sarkari Yojana, April 5, 2023, https://sarkariyojana.com/digital-strike-list-chinese-apps-banned/#digital-strike-5-54-apps-banned-update-on-14-february-2022.

mobile apps have been banned in India. Without providing evidence, some Chinese sources claimed that TikTok parent company ByteDance could lose up to $6 billion after investing $1 billion in the Indian market.[49] Some Indian reports, however, have indicated that the estimated revenue loss for Chinese firms would be around $200 million, with PUBG Mobile incurring $100 million in losses a year. Overall revenue generation from Indian users was still estimated to be around $200 million.[50]

Investment Screening

To tighten the screening of Chinese investments, the Indian government tweaked its FDI policy in April 2020. It introduced a "governmental route" for all investments originating from countries that share land borders with India.[51] In theory, this amendment applies to all foreign investments coming from Afghanistan, Bangladesh, Bhutan, China, Nepal, and Pakistan, but in practical terms it is intended to target China. Prior to the amendment, approval from the Ministry of Home Affairs was required only for investments in critical sectors such as defense, telecommunications, and private security, in addition to any investments originating from Pakistan and Bangladesh. In June 2022 the government further announced that any national from a country that shares a land border with India must seek security clearance from the Ministry of Home Affairs to be appointed as director in any Indian company.[52]

After around nine months of initial freezes, however, the government started clearing noncontroversial FDI proposals on a case-by-case basis in early 2021.[53] Since then, this has been done through a special committee comprising officers from the Ministries of Home Affairs, External Affairs, and Commerce and Industry and NITI Aayog. During the first nine months, around 45 Chinese proposals worth $2.4 billion from China,

---

[49] "ByteDance Loss May Hit $6B after India Bans Chinese Apps," *Global Times*, July 1, 2020, https://www.globaltimes.cn/content/1193243.shtml.

[50] Nidhi Singal, "Apps Ban to Cost Chinese Firms $200 Million a Year—and a Future; PUBG to Lose $100 Million," *Business Today* (India), September 3, 2020, https://www.businesstoday.in/technology/news/story/apps-ban-to-cost-chinese-200-million-a-year-and-a-future-pubg-to-lose-100-million-272008-2020-09-03.

[51] Department for Promotion of Industry and Internal Trade (India), "Review of Foreign Direct Investment (FDI) Policy for Curbing Opportunistic Takeovers/Acquisitions of Indian Companies Due to the Current Covid-19 Pandemic," July 17, 2020, https://dpiit.gov.in/sites/default/files/pn3_2020.pdf.

[52] Ministry of Corporate Affairs (India), "Notification," June 1, 2022, https://www.mca.gov.in/bin/dms/getdocument?mds=U4Pl6Cz4l3T9YHrD1ZOq2g%253D%253D&type=open.

[53] Surojit Gupta and Sidhartha, "After 9-Month Freeze, Centre Starts Clearing China FDI Plans," *Times of India*, February 22, 2021, https://timesofindia.indiatimes.com/business/india-business/after-9-month-freeze-centre-starts-clearing-china-fdi-plans/articleshow/81143248.cms.

Singapore, and Hong Kong had piled up.[54] Even if the government started selecting Chinese proposals, limited information was available publicly. Since imposing restrictions, the government reportedly had received 382 proposals as of April 2022. Out of these, 80 proposals involving Chinese entities were cleared. Though it is unconfirmed how many were rejected, reports indicate that proposals involving a minority stake, capital-intensive sectors, and manufacturing were preferred to those involving e-commerce and financial services.[55]

In addition to restrictions, the government has been monitoring companies and professionals who might be circumventing the FDI rules. To enable greater transparency, accountability, and sharing of information, the government passed a new law that brings chartered accountants, cost accountants, and company secretaries onto a single platform.[56] Under the law, the government has recommended action against 400 chartered accountants and company secretaries for allegedly helping Chinese shell companies that do not comply with Indian laws.[57] Subsequently, the Institute of Chartered Accountants of India issued disciplinary notices to more than 200 accountants for their alleged role.[58] The Ministry of Corporate Affairs has also registered around 700 cases against companies that have Chinese nationals on their boards, and many were using their positions for illicit purposes.[59] One product that has come under greater scrutiny is smartphones. Despite crackdowns on Chinese firms, there was a steady increase of China's 5G smartphone shipments to India. During the second quarter of 2022, Chinese smartphones were still in four out of five top spots in the Indian smartphone market. The Indian Directorate of Revenue Intelligence in August of that year declared that it had detected significant evasion of customs duties by Chinese phone

---

[54] "As Border Cools, Chinese FDI Set to Flow In Again," *New Indian Express*, February 23, 2021, https://www.newindianexpress.com/nation/2021/feb/23/as-border-cools-chinese-fdi-set-to-flow-in-again-2267668.html.

[55] Pavan Burugula, "India Approved 80 FDI Proposals Involving Chinese Entities: Data," *Economic Times*, July 6, 2022, https://economictimes.indiatimes.com/tech/technology/india-approved-80-fdi-proposals-involving-chinese-entities-data/articleshow/92684499.cms.

[56] "RS Passes Bill to Amend Chartered Accountancy, Cost Accountancy, Company Secretary Laws," *Print*, April 5, 2022, https://theprint.in/politics/rs-passes-bill-to-amend-chartered-accountancy-cost-accountancy-company-secretary-laws/903732.

[57] "Govt Calls for Action Against 400 CAs for Allegedly Incorporating Chinese Shell Companies," Wire (India), June 20, 2022, https://thewire.in/government/govt-calls-for-action-against-400-cas-for-allegedly-incorporating-chinese-shell-companies.

[58] K.R. Srivats, "Company Law Breaches by Chinese Firms: ICAI Disciplinary Notices to Over 200 CAs," *Business Line*, August 17, 2022, https://www.thehindubusinessline.com/companies/chinese-firms-violations-icai-sends-disciplinary-notices-to-over-200-cas/article65779416.ece.

[59] Rashmi Rajput, "Govt Mulls Winding Up Companies with Chinese Links," *Economic Times*, May 6, 2022, https://economictimes.indiatimes.com/news/company/corporate-trends/govt-mulls-winding-up-companies-with-chinese-links/articleshow/91355239.cms.

companies and issued customs demand notices.[60] By the fourth quarter, Samsung had increased its market share to become number one in India's smartphone market.[61]

In March 2023, Finance Minister Nirmala Sitharaman told the Indian parliament that there is no proposal under consideration to ease restrictions on Chinese companies. As of March 2023, 54 FDI proposals received in the last year from China and Hong Kong were still waiting for approval by the government.[62] As a result of all these measures, China has not emerged as a significant investor in India. Increasing wariness of Chinese investment, particularly in the technology sector, will further reduce its relevance to the Indian economy. Select investments are still being approved, mainly in the manufacturing sector or in cases when Chinese companies are collaborating with major Indian firms.[63] Yet, even as India may lose out on some Chinese investments, it could benefit from Western firms trying to move away from China.

Building Domestic Manufacturing Capacities

As tensions between India and China were building, Prime Minister Modi launched the Self-Reliant India Mission (Atmanirbhar Bharat Abhiyan) in May 2020 to promote Indian goods in global supply chains and reduce outside dependence. The genesis of the program was a pandemic-related stimulus package of around $270 billion to help domestic manufacturing and make India a hub of the global supply chain. Later, the situation at the border with China further accelerated the process.[64] Some studies indicate that around 40 subsectors, such as chemicals, automotive components, cosmetics, and consumer electronics, have the potential to reduce dependence on imports from China without any major

---

[60] "India Sees Spurt in 5G Smartphone Shipments from China Despite Recent Crackdowns on Alleged Tax Evasion," *Economic Times*, August 4, 2022, https://economictimes.indiatimes.com/industry/cons-products/electronics/india-sees-spurt-in-5g-smartphone-shipments-from-china-despite-recent-crackdowns-on-tax-evasion/articleshow/93338843.cms.

[61] Danish Khan, "Samsung Pips Xiaomi to Become India's Top Smartphone Brand in Q4: Market Trackers," *Economic Times*, January 19, 2023, https://telecom.economictimes.indiatimes.com/news/samsung-becomes-indias-top-smartphone-brand-in-q4-in-india-vivo-ranked-second-canalys/97117190.

[62] Ministry of Finance (India), "Lok Sabha Starred Question No. 362: Foreign Investments from Neighbouring Countries," March 27, 2023, https://pqals.nic.in/annex/1711/AS362.pdf.

[63] Ananth Krishnan, "Chinese Investments Returning to India with Greater Opacity," *Hindu*, July 5, 2023, https://www.thehindu.com/news/national/chinese-investments-returning-to-india-with-greater-opacity/article67046854.ece.

[64] "Self-Reliant India (Atmanirbhar Bharat Abhiyaan)," India Brand Equity Foundation, https://www.ibef.org/government-schemes/self-reliant-india-aatm-nirbhar-bharat-abhiyan.

new investment. With an appropriate policy framework, India could significantly reduce its trade deficit within a year.[65]

In March 2020 the Indian government announced its Production Linked Incentive (PLI) scheme for various sectors. Although this first round only included three sectors, in November 2020 another ten sectors were added, and in September 2021 drones and drone components were also included. Specific ministries or departments are identified to implement each scheme. To reduce dependence on imports, the PLI schemes intend to promote domestic manufacturing capacities and also attract foreign investment. The total incentive outlay for all schemes is around $26 billion.[66] At the time of writing, the following fourteen sectors are covered under PLI schemes:[67]

1. Key starting materials, drug intermediates, and APIs
2. Large-scale electronics manufacturing
3. Manufacturing of medical devices
4. Electronic and technology products
5. Pharmaceutical drugs
6. Telecommunications and networking products
7. Food products
8. Air conditioners and LED lights
9. High-efficiency solar PV modules
10. Automobiles and auto components
11. Advanced chemistry cell batteries
12. Textile products
13. Specialty steel
14. Drones and drone components

By June 2023, the government had approved 733 applications in all sectors. Apart from large companies, more than 176 micro, small, and medium-sized enterprises were also selected for bulk drugs, medical devices, telecommunications, white goods, food processing, and drones. Some sectors

---

[65] For details, see "Scope to Reduce Trade Deficit with China by $8 Billion in FY21–22," Acuité Ratings and Research, https://www.acuite.in/India-China-Trade-Deficit.htm.

[66] "PLI Schemes Contribute to Increase in Production, Employment Generation, and Economic Growth," Ministry of Commerce and Industry (India), Press Release, June 13, 2023, https://pib.gov.in/PressReleaseIframePage.aspx?PRID=1932051.

[67] "Production Linked Incentive (PLI) Schemes in India," Invest India, https://www.investindia.gov.in/production-linked-incentives-schemes-india.

covered by PLI schemes, such as pharmaceuticals, food products, and medical appliances, have seen significant FDI inflows and added high-value products to the export basket.

In 2022–23, incentives worth around $350 million were given to eight sectors: large-scale electronics manufacturing, IT hardware, bulk drugs, medical devices, pharmaceuticals, telecommunications and networking products, food products, and drones and drone components. Reportedly, major smartphone companies are shifting to India, and the value added to mobile manufacturing in the country has gone up by 20%. Out of the total $101 billion in electronics production in 2022–23, smartphones constituted $44 billion, including $11 billion in exports. The government further asserts that 60% import substitution has been achieved in the telecommunications sector and that there is a significant reduction in imports of raw materials in the pharmaceutical sector.[68]

However, results from the PLI schemes have been mixed at best. Many economists including the former governor of the Reserve Bank of India, Raghuram Rajan, have raised questions about the scheme. Even in mobile phone manufacturing, which has been projected as one of the success stories, the subsidy is paid only for finishing phones in India and not on the value added. Most of the components of mobile phones are still imported.[69] Similarly, it has been argued that leading sectors like pharmaceuticals may not need support through PLI because much of the investment would have been made anyway, even without the incentive of a PLI subsidy.

Integrating the Indian Economy into the Indo-Pacific Economic Architecture

Over the last few years, foreign policy discourse in India has been dominated by the Indo-Pacific narrative. The narrative emphasizes building coalitions, forums, and platforms to balance the impact of a rising and assertive China. India's border standoff with China and stronger ties with the United States have reinforced this narrative, sharpening the argument for the Quad (Australia, India, Japan, and the United States).

India faces a serious dilemma. As discussed in the first section, the Indian economy has become more integrated with other Asian economies, and this trend will continue. Yet nearly all the important Asian economies are also

---

[68] "PLI Schemes Contribute to Increase."

[69] "Former RBI Governor Raghuram Rajan Asks If Modi Govt's PLI Scheme Is a Failure," *Economic Times*, May 30, 2023, https://economictimes.indiatimes.com/news/economy/policy/former-rbi-governor-raghuram-rajan-asks-if-modi-govts-pli-scheme-is-a-failure/articleshow/100615521.cms.

deeply integrated with the Chinese economy through trade, investment, and supply chains. Developing Asia is also being courted by China through BRI projects. Therefore, India must either become part of this emerging economic architecture or create an entirely new economic architecture with its Quad partners. If none of this happens, India might have no choice but to isolate itself and settle for a relatively low level of economic equilibrium. Though the Indian economy will continue to be an attractive destination due to its size and growth potential, the current economic policy framework might not produce an integrated Indo-Pacific economy capable of challenging Chinese dominance. A large country like India has the capacity to change the architecture of supply chains in the Indo-Pacific. Despite its rhetoric, however, the last ten years have shown that New Delhi is still a reluctant participant in the process that could make it an important player in global value chains.

Amitendu Palit has examined the dichotomy between India's quest for greater strategic influence and its restrictive trade policies.[70] He has attributed India's approach to a lack of competitiveness in Indian industry, a lack of pro-trade domestic constituencies, and discomfort in negotiating new-generation trade issues. Priya Chacko demonstrates that India's "new mercantilist" economic nationalism seeks to protect domestic industries while trying to attract foreign investment and integrate India into global value chains. This, she argues, is the result of a "changing geopolitical environment—including a broader global impetus toward neo-mercantilist policies and conflict with China."[71] Aseema Sinha has further argued that India's slowing economy and deglobalization trends have created an incongruence between its domestic economic policies and global ambitions. She further argues that "if the domestic-global economic links are not strengthened towards a more open economy, India's relevance to emerging Western alliances may be thrown in doubt."[72] There are others who continue to believe that sustained economic growth has increased India's economic heft and that geoeconomics is now playing an important role in foreign policy.[73]

More than half of global trade is through value chains. China has long been at the center of supply chains, but over time rising labor costs have prompted many companies to diversify their manufacturing away from China—known as a China-plus-one strategy. Many Southeast Asian countries

---

[70] Amitendu Palit, "Will India's Disengaging Trade Policy Restrict It from Playing a Greater Global Role?" *World Trade Review* 20, no. 2 (2021): 203–19.

[71] Priya Chacko, "A New Quest for Self-Reliance: East Asia and Indian Economic Nationalism," *Journal of Indian and Asian Studies* 2, no. 2 (2021).

[72] Aseema Sinha, "India in a Changing Global World: Understanding India's Changing Statecraft and Delhi's International Relations," *Round Table: The Commonwealth Journal of International Relations* 111, no. 3 (2022): 398–411.

[73] Amit Ahuja and Devesh Kapur, "India's Geoeconomic Strategy," *India Review* 17, no. 1 (2018): 76–99.

have taken advantage of this trend and become suppliers to production networks linked with China. In the last few years, changing geopolitics and the U.S.-China trade war pushed many companies to further diversify their operations. The Covid-19 pandemic reinforced this trend. It is not that companies are abandoning China altogether. Instead, while utilizing their base in China, they are linking some of their operations to neighboring countries. This helps diversify production, expand markets, and reduce political risks. In this way, firms can continue production and exports even when the main site in China faces disruptions and uncertainties. The strategy has been beneficial to all parties involved—the diversifying firms, the plus-one host economies, and China itself. Firms benefit through diversifying risk and reducing costs, the plus-one host economies benefit from investment and technology inflows, and China benefits by moving resources higher up the value chain.

When decoupling from China became a buzzword in the United States and Europe, many analysts in India also started using the concept in an Indian context.[74] Now both Europe and the United States are shifting from decoupling to "de-risking." As a result, nations are returning to a China-plus strategy (minus linkages in critical technology areas). Instead of framing future economic ties with China in terms of decoupling or de-risking, India must work out an independent economic strategy to strengthen its economic linkages with the evolving economic frameworks within the Indo-Pacific region, including with the Chinese economy. Some have even argued that decoupling with China could be detrimental to the Indian economy in the medium term.[75]

Many in India hope that the country can also become a hub of global manufacturing by decoupling or using a China-plus-one strategy. In sectors like pharmaceuticals and mobile phones, Chinese imports are critical for Indian exports, but most other imports are largely for the domestic market and not linked with Chinese supply chains. Therefore, instead of imports, the challenge is to link more Indian industries with large Chinese bases for production and create new arrangements with other Asian markets for export.

India (like the United States) is not a member of the RCEP or the CPTPP. These agreements, however, will affect India even if it does not belong to them,

---

[74] Atul Singh, Manu Sharma, and Vikram Sood, "Why Are the Indian and Chinese Economies Decoupling?" Fair Observer, September 3, 2020, https://www.fairobserver.com/region/central_south_asia/atul-singh-vikram-sood-manu-sharma-india-china-decoupling-economy-border-dispute-latest-world-news-78914.

[75] Raj Verma, "India's Economic Decoupling from China: A Critical Analysis," *Asia Policy* 18, no. 1 (2023): 143–66.

as both encourage deep supply chain integration among their members.[76] To be economically relevant in the region, the United States launched the IPEF in May 2022.[77] Currently, it consists of fourteen nations. Many view the IPEF as a move to counter China's growing economic influence in the Indo-Pacific. It thus has the potential to provide a solid platform for both India and the United States to frame economic rules in an economically dynamic Indo-Pacific region. Countries that are members of all three groupings—the CPTPP, the RCEP, and the IPEF—might have close strategic ties with the United States but are still integrated with China-centered value chains. For them, the IPEF is an additional layer of integration in the Indo-Pacific under U.S. patronage and balances increasing Chinese economic dominance.

Through the IPEF, the United States and its allies and partners thus want to enhance their economic engagement in Asia and the broader Indo-Pacific. As trade and supply chains are deeply integrated with each other, all the members except India have agreed to take part in negotiations on all four pillars of the IPEF. As noted earlier, India has joined the three pillars related to supply chains, tax and anticorruption, and clean energy, but it opted out of the trade pillar due to possible binding commitments on labor, the environment, and digital trade.[78] Though labor standards have been cited as a major concern for not joining the trade pillar, even the supply chain pillar clearly mentions that partner countries "will seek to ensure that the work promotes the labor standards that underpin fair, sustainable, and resilient supply chains."[79]

India's reluctance to participate in the IPEF's trade pillar indicates a lack of confidence in the competitiveness of Indian industry. The manufacturing sector accounted for 15.5% of the Indian economy in 2003–4. To increase this share to 25% within a decade, the National Manufacturing Policy was announced in 2011.[80] The share increased to 17.2% in 2012–13 and 18.2% in 2017–18. During the pandemic, it declined to 17.1% in 2019–20, but it

---

[76] Jeffrey J. Schott, "Which Countries Are in the CPTPP and RCEP Trade Agreements and Which Want In?" Peterson Institute for International Economics, July 27, 2023, https://www.piie.com/research/piie-charts/which-countries-are-cptpp-and-rcep-trade-agreements-and-which-want.

[77] "Statement on Indo-Pacific Economic Framework for Prosperity," White House, Press Release, May 23, 2022, https://www.whitehouse.gov/briefing-room/statements-releases/2022/05/23/statement-on-indo-pacific-economic-framework-for-prosperity.

[78] "India Opts Out of IPEF's Trade Pillar; to Wait for Final Contours," Moneycontrol, September 10, 2022, https://www.moneycontrol.com/news/india/india-opts-out-of-ipefs-trade-pillar-to-wait-for-final-contours-9157851.html.

[79] "United States and Indo-Pacific Economic Framework Partners Announce Negotiation Objectives," Office of the U.S. Trade Representative, Press Release, September 9, 2022, https://ustr.gov/about-us/policy-offices/press-office/press-releases/2022/september/united-states-and-indo-pacific-economic-framework-partners-announce-negotiation-objectives.

[80] "Steps Taken to Boost Manufacturing Growth," Ministry of Commerce and Industry (India), Press Release, April 29, 2013, https://pib.gov.in/newsite/PrintRelease.aspx?relid=95197.

recovered to 17.7% in 2022–23.[81] Besides Make in India, the government has launched other initiatives to boost the manufacturing sector.[82] Despite these measures, the manufacturing sector has not really taken off, and its share in the national economy has remained roughly the same over the last decade. Apart from a few sectors (e.g., mobile phones), India is not emerging as an attractive alternative, even as some companies are in the process of relocating units from China. World Bank data on Indian manufacturing between 1991 and 2022 shows a similar trend of declining value added as a percentage of GDP (see **Figure 6**). Some argue that during the economic liberalization of the 1990s a few sectors such as IT, pharmaceuticals, and automobiles produced world-class Indian multinationals. In comparison, new emerging

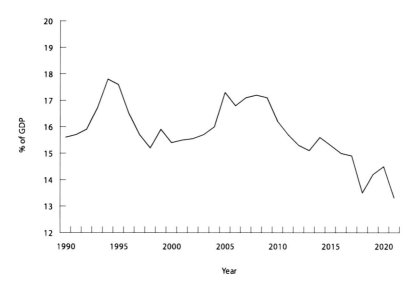

FIGURE 6 India's manufacturing, value added (% of GDP) for 1991–2022

SOURCE: World Bank, DataBank, https://data.worldbank.org/indicator/NV.IND.MANF.ZS?locations=IN.

---

[81] "India's Slow but Sure De-industrialisation Is Worrying," *Mint*, June 15, 2023, https://www.livemint.com/opinion/columns/indias-manufacturing-sector-faces-worsening-decline-implications-for-growth-employment-and-income-11686851477882.html.

[82] For a list of initiatives, see "Initiatives Taken by the Government to Boost Manufacturing," Ministry of Commerce and Industry (India), Press Release, December 9, 2022, https://pib.gov.in/PressReleaseIframePage.aspx?PRID=1882145.

have multiplied over the last two decades, and despite decoupling measures, China continues to be one of India's leading trade partners. Beyond imports, linkages in investment and connectivity are limited. Although Chinese imports threaten some domestic industries, they are useful in domestic manufacturing and exports and are critical for some sectors. However, economic ties are being adjusted to the realities of a contentious border and antagonistic political relations. As a result, the government has taken measures to reduce imports and the trade deficit, ban mobile apps, and screen investments, among other initiatives. Still, some crucial minority shareholding investment proposals are being cleared quietly. A serious effort is also being made to strengthen domestic manufacturing by easing rules and incentives. So far, the impact of these measures has been limited.

Most Asian economies are deeply engaged with the Chinese economy through trade, investment, supply chains, trading arrangements, and BRI projects. Despite apprehensions, they are still integrating with China. These supply chains are being strengthened through the participation of many countries in the RCEP and CPTPP and balanced by the U.S.-led IPEF. India will have to either become part of this emerging economic architecture or help create an entirely new economic architecture along with its Quad partners. Although India is reluctant to fully participate in any of these frameworks, its manufacturing troubles and stagnating exports underscore its economic vulnerabilities. The Indian economy will continue to be an attractive destination for foreign companies due to its size and growth potential. However, the current economic policy framework may not lead India to become an economic heavyweight in an integrated Indo-Pacific. Therefore, instead of framing future economic ties with China in terms of decoupling or de-risking, India should work to create an independent economic strategy to strengthen its linkages with the existing economic frameworks within the Indo-Pacific region, including with the Chinese economy. This strategy, however, will likely not be viable without de-escalation at the border with China.

In the meantime, a number of measures have been initiated to strengthen domestic manufacturing. Growing exports in the last two years seem to have given policymakers the confidence needed to push for new trade deals with countries such as Australia and the UAE. To improve connectivity with major trading partners, the IMEC was also announced in September 2023. Despite developing a global partnership with the United States, India's importance within the evolving Indo-Pacific economic architecture will depend on its own economic expansion and its linkages with neighboring regions. Even if reducing economic ties with China and not joining multilateral trade deals could make it "self-reliant," India must aim to be at the center of Indo-Pacific economic dynamism rather than outside it.

companies like Ola Cabs and Flipkart are just cloning Western techniques and lack technological innovation.[83]

India's cautious approach toward the RCEP indicates that the country is not yet ready to participate in Asia's economic rise. Influential opposition to this and other trade agreements from the Swadeshi Jagran Manch and Bharatiya Kisan Sangh, the two affiliates of Rashtriya Swayamsevak Sangh (RSS) has been an important factor in India's refusal to join the grouping. The RSS, which forms the backbone of the ruling BJP, is the foremost advocate of Swadeshi, emphasizing economic self-reliance. With such opposition to trade negotiations and investment treaties, it is difficult for India to play an important role in global value chains. Even in the global apparel trade, its share has stagnated at around 4%, despite India having the advantage of a large domestic market for scaling, a large domestic supply of cotton and other raw materials, and a large labor pool. Bangladesh and Vietnam are already bigger players than India on this front. Due to distortions in land and labor markets, as well as weaknesses in infrastructure and the banking sector, Indian companies continue to struggle in traditional areas.

Likewise, with a protectionist mindset, increasing income inequality, and a lack of resources available for public higher education and research, it is not easy for India to emerge as an important player in areas of high technology. Though a few centralized teaching and research institutions may be able to compete internationally, a large-scale technological transformation of the industry and society may not happen easily. A recent study by Sunitha Raju shows that "imports from China have a positive association with manufacturing output and exports."[84] China is a low-cost supplier in 30% of products, and in many sectors Chinese components are not easily substitutable. Raju concludes that a decoupling or self-reliance policy "will not be effective unless the domestic manufacturing is propelled to high technology products." Therefore, reforms in the public higher education sector are crucial for any new high-tech sector to take off.

Conclusion

The Indian economy is expanding and integrating with other Asian economies. Foreign trade in goods and services is becoming more important for the economy. These trends are likely to continue. India-China trading links

---

[83] S.A. Aiyar, "2010s: The Decade Is Ending on a Sour Note for Indian Economy," *Times of India*, September 7, 2019, https://timesofindia.indiatimes.com/blogs/Swaminomics/2010s-the-decade-is-ending-on-a-sour-note-for-indian-economy.

[84] Sunitha Raju, "Impact of Imports from China on Indian Manufacturing Performance: An Analysis of Trade Competitiveness," *International Journal of Emerging Markets* (2023).

EXECUTIVE SUMMARY

This chapter examines how Southeast Asian economies have been affected by U.S.-China rivalry, how the region's economic policies have responded, and how the U.S. should reconsider its economic policies toward the region.

MAIN ARGUMENT

Southeast Asia has experienced transformative economic growth, driven by its embrace of globalization. Although the U.S. is the region's largest source of FDI, China has become the region's preeminent economic power by becoming its largest trading partner and external official creditor. So far, U.S.-China economic rivalry appears to have benefited Southeast Asia. Both countries have increased their trade with the region, compete to provide development finance, and permit broad access to new technologies. Southeast Asian countries have hedged their economic relations between the U.S. and China. While they look to China to further economic interests, they look to the U.S. for security against China's aggressive posture in the South China Sea and possible use of economic coercion. The U.S. needs to overhaul its agenda of economic engagement in Southeast Asia if it is to shape the region's rules and norms of international economic relations for the 21st century. Urgently needed are greater strategic coherence in its economic assistance programs and improved program effectiveness through more, and more sustained, government funding.

POLICY IMPLICATIONS

- For greater strategic coherence, the U.S. could make the Indo-Pacific Economic Framework (IPEF) its central vehicle for economic engagement with the region, use the IPEF's trade pillar as a stepping stone to reach a 21st-century trade agreement with Southeast Asia, and make human capital, climate change, and infrastructure signature elements within the IPEF.

- For greater program effectiveness, the U.S. needs to provide increased multiyear fiscal support for bilateral assistance, leverage its bilateral support through multilateral initiatives, and reconsider its position on membership in the Asian Infrastructure Investment Bank.

Southeast Asia

U.S.-China Economic Rivalry in Southeast Asia and Its Implications

Vikram Nehru

Unlike other chapters in this volume, this chapter covers an entire region. Southeast Asia comprises ten countries that differ vastly in size, per capita income, resource endowments, political systems, religions, colonial histories, and, most importantly, development strategies.[1] The largest (Indonesia) is 700 times as populous as the smallest (Brunei); the per capita income of the most economically developed (Singapore) is almost 80 times that of the poorest (Myanmar). Political systems in Southeast Asia range from Communism to military rule to thriving democracies, with virtually everything in between. Different parts of the region were colonized by Britain, the Netherlands, and France at different times in their histories, with Thailand as the sole exception.

Notwithstanding this remarkable diversity, Southeast Asia's successful economic performance points to four common forces at work. The first is the region's strategic location. It sits astride the Malacca Strait, which is the world's second-busiest shipping channel and the second most traversed oil tanker route. The waterway gives the region access to the Pacific and Indian Oceans and makes it a strategic chokepoint of great interest to regional and global powers. The second is its proximity to China, Asia's rapidly growing, resource-hungry giant. China has dramatically increased demand for

---

Vikram Nehru is a Senior Fellow at the Foreign Policy Institute, Johns Hopkins University School of Advanced International Studies. He can be reached at <vnehru1@jhu.edu>.

[1] For ease of analysis, the ten countries considered part of Southeast Asia for this chapter are Brunei, Cambodia, Indonesia, Laos, Malaysia, Myanmar, the Philippines, Singapore, Thailand, and Vietnam, which are also the ten members of the Association of Southeast Asian Nations (ASEAN). Timor-Leste is physically located in Southeast Asia but is excluded from this analysis for three reasons: first, it is not a member of ASEAN; second, its GDP (in current dollars) is a quarter the size of Brunei's, ASEAN's smallest economy; and third, economic data on Timor-Leste is scarce compared with the other countries in the region.

commodities from Southeast Asian economies, helping transform them from "dominoes to dynamos."[2] The third is Southeast Asia's abundance of natural resources, which have over the centuries attracted traders, colonists, and, more recently, foreign investors. The region is blessed with timber, rice, palm oil, cocoa, coffee, a variety of minerals, and a range of energy sources (hydro, oil, natural gas, and geothermal). Finally, a shared institutional and trade architecture has facilitated regional economic integration, promoted dialogue on economic and security issues, and created avenues for peaceful resolution of disagreements among Southeast Asian states and between Southeast Asia and its immediate neighbors. As a result, over the last half century, cross-border conflicts have been few, short, and contained; and with one exception (Myanmar), domestic political insurgencies have gradually been resolved.

Taken as a whole, Southeast Asia's population of 662 million is twice the size of the United States' and smaller than that of only two countries, China and India. Likewise, just four countries in the world—the United States, China, Japan, and Germany—exceed the region's GDP of $3.2 trillion. Southeast Asia's trade-to-GDP ratio of over 100% makes it the world's most trade-dependent region, which has helped propel its growth over decades while simultaneously linking its economy tightly to the rest of the world.[3] Therefore, the policies and performance of China and the United States—the world's two largest economies—have profound implications for Southeast Asia.

This chapter points to three important conclusions. First, Southeast Asia has not been hurt by U.S.-China economic rivalry so far and may even have been a beneficiary. Second, while the United States remains the preeminent strategic power in the region, China has gained ascendancy in relative economic power. Beijing is understandably using that power to shape the rules and norms governing international economic relations and propel its own strategic interests, which may be at variance with those of Southeast Asia and the United States. Third, to ensure a peaceful and prosperous Indo-Pacific that serves Southeast Asian as well as U.S. interests, Washington would be well advised to rethink the strategic coherence of its economic policies toward Southeast Asia and make them more effective by backing them with adequate multiyear funding.

The rest of this chapter elaborates on these key themes. The first main section examines how and why Southeast Asia's embrace of globalization has driven its remarkable economic performance. The subsequent

---

[2] John Bresnan, *From Dominoes to Dynamos: The Transformation of Southeast Asia* (New York: Council on Foreign Relations, 1994).

[3] See Vikram Nehru, "Southeast Asia: Thriving in the Shadow of Giants," in *China, the United States, and the Future of Southeast Asia: U.S.-China Relations*, vol. 2, ed. David B.H. Denoon (New York: New York University Press, 2017), 33.

section examines the forces that have shaped—and are still shaping—the region's economic relations with the world. The third section analyzes the consequences of U.S.-China competition on different aspects of Southeast Asia's economic trajectory, how Southeast Asians view the two global superpowers, and how this is shaping the region's international economic policies. The final section assesses the implications of these developments for U.S. policy.

Globalization: The Lifeblood of Southeast Asian Economies

Southeast Asia's story of globalization began in the 1970s. By the early 2000s, the region provided a perfect complement to the dramatic growth of highly competitive assembly industries in China. This section examines four characteristics of Southeast Asia's globalization and the respective roles of China and the United States: trade dependence, foreign direct investment, development finance and sovereign debt, and cross-border migration patterns.

Trade Dependence

At more than 100%, the trade-to-GDP ratio of Southeast Asia today is the highest of any region in the world, including the European Union.[4] Southeast Asia's trade-to-GDP ratio, however, peaked in 2005 (at 156%) and has since seen a decline on account of growing protectionist tendencies and resource nationalism in the region's "big four" economies (Indonesia, Malaysia, the Philippines, and Thailand).

Two notable features stand out in Southeast Asia's international merchandise trade over the past two decades. The first is the emergence of complex value chains led by multinational enterprises that allowed the region's factories to supply inputs to China for further processing, assembly, and final sale. The second feature is China's trade with Southeast Asia, which rose from being a mere one-fifth of the United States' in 1995 to almost twice as large today (see **Figure 1**).[5] These trends are likely to be reinforced by the Regional Comprehensive Economic Partnership (RCEP), which is a trade agreement that includes the Association of Southeast Asian Nations (ASEAN) as well as China and four other Asia-Pacific economies, and the withdrawal of the United States from the Trans-Pacific Partnership (TPP).

---

[4] Data is from the World Bank's World Development Indicators. The numerator in the trade-to-GDP ratio includes imports and exports of goods and services.

[5] This finding is based on data from the UNCTAD Direction of Trade Statistics.

FIGURE 1 China, the EU, the United States, and intra-ASEAN trade as shares of ASEAN's total trade

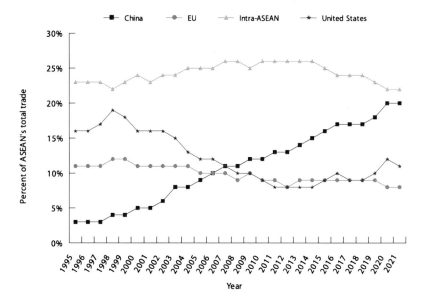

SOURCE: UNCTAD Department of Trade Statistics, UN Comtrade database, https://comtradeplus.un.org.

Tourism is Southeast Asia's largest service export, with Thailand being the most visited country and China the origin of most of those visitors. Apart from tourism, however, the rest of Southeast Asia's trade in services remains embryonic.[6] A shortage of skilled labor and numerous trade and regulatory restrictions are largely responsible for this situation. But this is changing rapidly, as the high costs of services trade, associated with face-to-face contact, decline with advances in digital technology and artificial intelligence. Southeast Asia's digital economy is growing at over 20% a year—primarily in fintech (financial technology), e-commerce, food delivery, transportation, and online media—giving rise to the region's growing number of unicorns and decacorns and its first homegrown multinational companies.[7]

---

[6] Singapore is a notable exception. This tiny state of five million people is a services powerhouse, trading services equivalent to 114% of GDP in 2021.

[7] In 2014, there were just three unicorns (startup companies with valuations over $1 billion) in Southeast Asia, mainly in Indonesia and Singapore. Now there are twenty, in addition to five decacorns (startup companies with valuations over $10 billion). All operate in the digital economy.

Foreign Direct Investment

FDI has helped Southeast Asia become an economic powerhouse by bringing scarce capital, market access, and spillovers of new product and process technologies. Investors have been attracted to the region by its comparative advantage in cheap but disciplined labor as well as its natural resource endowments. Today, China is the only developing country that receives more FDI than Southeast Asia.[8]

Singapore plays a unique conduit role for the region's FDI inflows.[9] Many, if not all, multinational investors prefer to register their local operations in Singapore, thus making their contracts subject to its laws and enforceable by its courts. By locating in Singapore, investors also partially protect their assets from capricious, and sometimes corrupt, court decisions in other Southeast Asian countries where their operations may be located but where judicial systems are less well developed.

Just as China has come to dominate trade with Southeast Asia, U.S. businesses have been the region's dominant foreign investors (see **Figure 2**). Flows of U.S. FDI into Southeast Asia contribute almost a quarter of total FDI flows to the region. If FDI from Singapore-located U.S. multinational companies is included, the share of U.S. FDI is even higher. The current stock of U.S. FDI in Southeast Asia exceeds $350 billion, more than U.S. investment in China (excluding Hong Kong), India, Japan, and South Korea combined, and accounts for over a third of U.S. FDI in the entire Indo-Pacific.[10]

The top-three sectoral destinations of FDI into Southeast Asia—finance, manufacturing, and domestic trade—reflect not only the most dynamic parts of the region's economy but also the competitive advantage of U.S. companies.[11] FDI in finance is focused mainly in Singapore. Although FDI in manufacturing is more broadly diversified across the region, the most preferred destination has been Vietnam. Owing to its relatively open trade and investment policies, productive and skilled labor force, and excellent logistics, Vietnam has successfully attracted

---

[8] These findings are based on 2021 data from the World Bank's World Development Indicators.

[9] Singapore is also the biggest foreign investor in both India and China (if one excludes round-tripping from Hong Kong).

[10] "ASEAN Matters for America/America Matters for ASEAN," 5th ed., East-West Center, 2021, https://www.eastwestcenter.org/publications/asean-matters-americaamerica-matters-asean-0.

[11] Singapore is benefiting from the migration of financial institutions and Chinese wealth from Hong Kong. See "Is Singapore Replacing Hong Kong as Asia's Financial Hub?" Squadron Lending, July 29, 2022, https://squadronlending.com/asia-business-news/is-singapore-replacing-hong-kong-as-asias-financial-hub; and Frederik Kelter, "China's Rich Flee Crackdowns for 'Asia's Switzerland' Singapore," Al Jazeera, March 27, 2023, https://www.aljazeera.com/economy/2023/3/27/chinas-rich-flee-crackdowns-for-asias-switzerland-singapore.

FIGURE 2 Top sources of FDI to Southeast Asia, 2021 ($ millions)

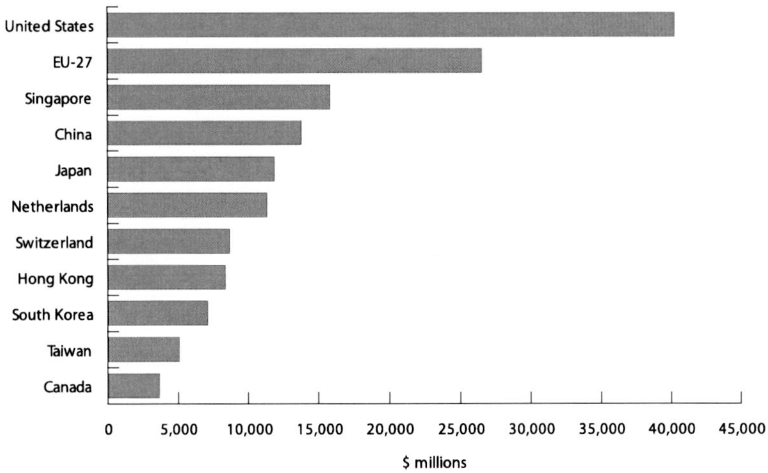

United States
EU-27
Singapore
China
Japan
Netherlands
Switzerland
Hong Kong
South Korea
Taiwan
Canada

$ millions

SOURCE: ASEAN Statistics Division, ASEANStatsDataPortal, https://data.aseanstats.org.

manufacturers leaving the Chinese mainland on account of rising real wages and U.S. trade barriers affecting exports from China to the United States.[12]

Development Finance and Sovereign Debt

China is Southeast Asia's largest source of development finance but offers mainly nonconcessional loans. The United States ranks only seventh, but most of its financial support is provided as grants.[13] Commitments of U.S. development finance to Southeast Asia have averaged slightly over $2.3 billion a year, less than one-tenth of China's ($24.2 billion a year) (see **Figure 3**).[14]

Notwithstanding the pandemic's impact on Southeast Asia's fiscal and external balances, the debt indicators of most economies in the region are in

---

[12] Japan, South Korea, and Singapore (the lattermost being a conduit for multinationals) have been the three largest foreign investors in Vietnam.

[13] Lowy Institute, "Southeast Asia Aid Map," available at https://seamap.lowyinstitute.org.

[14] Figures are in real 2021 prices averaged over 2015–21 and include official development assistance and other official finance. Official development assistance is provided by official agencies and administered primarily to promote the economic development and welfare of developing countries. Other official finance incorporates non-concessional lending, lending to the private sector from official sources, bilateral military assistance, and other components of formal bilateral relationships that are not captured in official development finance.

FIGURE 3 Official financial commitments to Southeast Asia, 2015–21 (annual average in real 2021 terms)

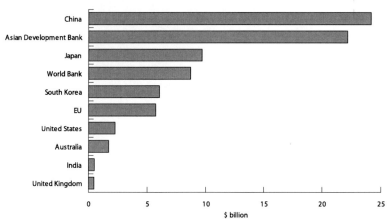

SOURCE: Author's estimates based on Lowy Institute, "Southeast Asia Aid Map," available at https://seamap.lowyinstitute.org.

sound shape. The one exception is Laos.[15] But official data can be misleading. Unlike traditional official creditors—the International Monetary Fund (IMF), World Bank, and Organisation for Economic Co-operation and Development (OECD) members of the Paris Club—China often does not disclose the amounts and terms of its loans and also prevails upon its borrowers to keep such details secret.[16] One estimate indicates that around half of Chinese lending is not reported to the World Bank or IMF.[17]

The case of Laos is instructive. Over the last decade, the government increased public investments sharply (including through state-owned enterprises), financing most of them with external loans from China.[18] Within a decade, China accounted for over half of Laos's total external debt stock. The loans mostly financed investments in energy and transportation, such as the Kunming-Vientiane railway, which alone is estimated to cost around

---

[15] The "official" debt statistics refer to those reported to and recorded by the World Bank.

[16] See Anna Gelpern et al., "How China Lends: A Rare Look into 100 Debt Contracts with Foreign Governments," Peterson Institute for International Economics, Kiel Institute for the World Economy, Center for Global Development, and AidData at William & Mary, March 2021, especially section 3.1.

[17] See Sebastian Horn, Carmen M. Reinhart, and Christoph Trebesch, "China's Overseas Lending," National Bureau of Economic Research, Working Paper, no. 26050, July 2019.

[18] China's loans to Laos climbed from $100 million in 2007 to $3.8 billion in 2018 (over 20% of the country's GDP).

$6 billion.[19] Not only were these projects large, but their cash flow was insufficient to cover their external debt service. Thus, when the pandemic hit in 2020, and Russia's invasion of Ukraine in 2021 compounded the challenges faced by low-income economies, Laos's capacity to service external debt (primarily government revenues and export earnings) fell precipitously just when its debt-servicing burden was peaking. In the past, such cases of debt distress in low-income countries were resolved through a well-established cooperative approach led by the IMF and World Bank. But in this case, China has been unwilling to participate in any multilateral arrangement, preferring instead to negotiate bilaterally in secret with the Laotian government.[20] This has stalled any resolution of Laos's debt crisis, just as happened in Sri Lanka and Pakistan—two other countries facing an acute debt crisis where China is the largest external creditor. Laos's other official creditors are unwilling to restructure their loans without the participation of China for fear that it would be a "free rider" in such an arrangement.

Cross-border Migration Patterns

Southeast Asia's globalization has not been restricted to trade and finance. It extends to the cross-border movement of people. North America, Europe, and the Middle East have been important destinations for many Southeast Asian migrants, but the majority of the 23.6 million who have left their Southeast Asian country of birth remain in the region. Of all Southeast Asian countries, the Philippines has by far the largest number of migrants abroad, estimated at over 6 million.

Intraregional migration is driven by the interaction between proximity, economic opportunity (proxied by differences in per capita income), and population size.[21] The region has two main migration corridors—Cambodia, Laos, and Myanmar to Thailand, and Indonesia to Malaysia.[22] The origin and destination countries are close in distance, culture, language, and history. Some of these migrants are refugees fleeing violence, mainly from Myanmar. In September 2022, the UN High Commissioner for Refugees registered 183,430 refugees and asylum seekers in Southeast Asia, most of whom were from Myanmar (86%), comprising Rohingya, Chin, and other ethnic groups.[23]

---

[19] Unfortunately, the terms of China's loans have not been made public, and international organizations such as the IMF and World Bank rely on the government's external debt service projections.

[20] Anne O. Krueger, "A World of Debt," Project Syndicate, May 23, 2023, https://www.project-syndicate.org/commentary/debt-restructuring-china-spanner-in-the-works-by-anne-o-krueger-2023-05.

[21] Eric Fong, Kumiko Shibuya, and Xi Chen, "Migration among East and Southeast Asian Economies," *International Migration* 58, no. 4 (2020): 69–84.

[22] Malaysia also hosts migrants from outside Southeast Asia, including Bangladesh and India.

[23] The Rohingya group makes up 58% of the total refugee population in Malaysia.

Remittance flows from migrants have been a key foreign exchange earner in the Philippines, Vietnam, and Indonesia, contributing to poverty reduction in these countries. The Philippines, by far, receives the region's largest amount of remittances, followed by Vietnam, Indonesia, and Thailand. Philippine remittances totaled nearly $35 billion in 2020 and are estimated at $38 billion in 2022, equaling around 9.6% of GDP and 34% of exports. The pandemic squeezed remittances to the region, but they are once again set to grow at their pre-pandemic annual rate of around 5% a year.

Southeast Asia's cross-border movement of goods, services, finance, and people can be captured by two composite indicators. The first is the convergence of per capita incomes within the region. Despite rapid globalization, the per capita incomes of Southeast Asian economies have converged less than economies in some other regions or groupings, such as the EU.[24] This suggests that intraregional cross-border flows remain subject to substantial restrictions. The second indicator is the "global connectedness index"—an imperfect but nevertheless useful index that aggregates many facets of globalization into one convenient measure (see **Tables 1** and **2**).[25] The index underlines Southeast Asia's enormous diversity. Singapore, for example, is among the most globalized economies in the world (ranking second only to the Netherlands). At the other extreme, Myanmar is among the least globalized. The rankings for components of globalization reveal where countries possess deep connections with the global economy and where they fall short.

The Forces Shaping Southeast Asia's Globalization

The degree to which Southeast Asian economies have globalized and the direction of these trends can be considered as outcomes. Causing them are four forces: geography, regional trade agreements, national trade and investment policies, and the interaction between comparative advantage, technological change, and resource nationalism.

Geography

The force that initially drove Asia's trade integration was geography; the supportive effects of policies and international trade agreements arrived

---

[24] The measure used is the coefficient of variation.

[25] Steven A. Altman and Caroline R. Bastian, "DHL Global Connectedness Index 2022," New York University, Stern School of Business, Center for the Future of Management and DHL Initiative on Globalization, 2022, https://www.dhl.com/content/dam/dhl/global/delivered/documents/pdf/dhl-global-connectedness-index-2022-complete-report.pdf.

TABLE 1 Global connectedness by overall rank, 2021

Global percentile in overall connectedness	Country	Trade (% of GDP)					FDI		Portfolio equity outflows and inflows		People	
		Total trade	Merchandise exports	Merchandise imports	Services exports	Services imports	Stock (% GDP)	Flow (% of GFCF)	Stock (% of mkt cap)	Flow (% mkt cap)	Tourists (per capita)	Immigrants (% of population)
99	Singapore	331	115	102	58	56	506	108	199	10	0.35	43
92	Malaysia	159	80	64	6	10	50	16	47	2	0.13	10
86	Thailand	125	29	34	5	13	55	10	29	3	0.56	5
71	Brunei	153	79	59	4	11	52	5	–	–	0.14	25
67	Philippines	64	19	31	9	5	29	12	12	–	0.01	–
64	Vietnam	190	93	91	1	5	53	14	–	–	0.04	–
55	Cambodia	181	67	104	2	8	152	50	–	–	0.08	–
35	Indonesia	40	19	17	1	3	22	6	15	1	0.01	–
26	Laos	80	40	35	2	3	65	17	–	–	0.11	1
18	Myanmar	59	24	23	7	5	57	11	–	–	0.02	–

SOURCE: Altman and Bastian, "DHL Global Connectedness Index."

NOTE: GFCF is gross fixed capital formation.

TABLE 2 Global connectedness by overall rank, 2021

Global percentile in overall connectedness	Country	Global percentile in:						
		Internet bandwidth (global percentile in bits per sec per internet user)	International phone calls (global percentile in mts per capita)	International competitiveness	Shipping connectivity	Tariffs	Logistics performance	Capital account openness	Trade agreements (% GDP)
99	Singapore	99	99	100	99	97	95	100	100
92	Malaysia	61	64	80	96	49	74	45	95
86	Thailand	56	49	71	84	50	79	45	78
71	Brunei	65	69	59	11	98	46	–	93
67	Philippines	36	41	53	52	67	60	49	84
64	Vietnam	58	61	51	91	89	75	45	98
55	Cambodia	53	14	22	30	35	35	99	51
35	Indonesia	43	54	63	58	60	71	45	82
26	Laos	19	29	17	–	92	46	37	89
18	Myanmar	32	72	–	23	64	11	5	50

SOURCE: Altman and Bastian, "DHL Global Connectedness Index."

later. In particular, China's size, location, and dynamism have created a strong gravitational force that is drawing into its orbit all the economies within close proximity. ASEAN's merchandise trade with China has grown at a blistering pace (29% a year from 2001 to 2021). Predictably, the economies of Southeast Asia that are geographically closer to China—those on the mainland of the continent—have seen their trade with China grow faster than those of maritime Southeast Asia (Indonesia and the Philippines).[26]

The economic distance between Southeast Asia and China has been further shrunk by transportation, energy, and communications infrastructure investments linking the two. Oil and gas pipelines run through Myanmar from the Bay of Bengal to southern China. New highways from China to Southeast Asia and from Vietnam's east coast to Thailand's west coast have cut transportation costs. Likewise, high-speed rail is reducing freight times from China all the way to Malaysia; and port construction is proceeding apace throughout the region. Launched in 2013, China's Belt and Road Initiative (BRI) financed a significant acceleration in these infrastructure investments, largely in Cambodia, Indonesia, Laos, the Philippines, and Vietnam.[27] In the first three years, the focus was on physical connectivity—mainly transportation and energy infrastructure. BRI investments later diversified to include special economic zones and, during the pandemic, protective health equipment and vaccine production. More recently, BRI's focus has shifted to digital connectivity through telecommunications infrastructure and digital platforms—the so-called Digital Silk Road—which, on account of their low cost and rapid rollout, have proved to be popular in most Southeast Asian countries, notwithstanding the security risks they may involve.

Regional Trade Agreements

The integrative force of geography and connective infrastructure has been buttressed by a regional institutional architecture that, in its scope and depth, is unrivaled by any other developing region. All ten Southeast Asian nations are members of ASEAN, which was founded in 1967 and has as one of its principal goals the establishment of a single market for goods, services,

---

[26] For the purposes of this analysis, mainland Southeast Asia comprises Laos, Cambodia, Malaysia, Myanmar, Thailand, and Vietnam; maritime Southeast Asia only includes Indonesia and the Philippines. Trade-to-GDP ratios are much higher for mainland Southeast Asia than they are for Indonesia and the Philippines. In stark contrast, intra-ASEAN trade during 2001–21 averaged around 7.5% a year. This growth rate is impressive, but still only about a quarter of the growth rate of trade between Southeast Asia and China. A key reason is that, despite their close physical proximity to each other, many Southeast Asian economies have broadly similar factor endowments.

[27] For further information on this trend, including a breakdown of BRI projects by year, country, and status, see International Institute for Strategic Studies (IISS), *Asia-Pacific Regional Security Assessment: Key Development and Trends, 2023* (London: IISS, 2023), 95.

TABLE 2 Global connectedness by overall rank, 2021

Global percentile in overall connectedness	Country	Internet bandwidth (global percentile in bits per sec per internet user)	International phone calls (global percentile in mts per capita)	Global percentile in:						
				International competitiveness	Shipping connectivity	Tariffs	Logistics performance	Capital account openness	Trade agreements (% GDP)
99	Singapore	99	99	100	99	97	95	100	100
92	Malaysia	61	64	80	96	49	74	45	95
86	Thailand	56	49	71	84	50	79	45	78
71	Brunei	65	69	59	11	98	46	–	93
67	Philippines	36	41	53	52	67	60	49	84
64	Vietnam	58	61	51	91	89	75	45	98
55	Cambodia	53	14	22	30	35	35	99	51
35	Indonesia	43	54	63	58	60	71	45	82
26	Laos	19	29	17	–	92	46	37	89
18	Myanmar	32	72	–	23	64	11	5	50

SOURCE: Altman and Bastian, "DHL Global Connectedness Index."

later. In particular, China's size, location, and dynamism have created a strong gravitational force that is drawing into its orbit all the economies within close proximity. ASEAN's merchandise trade with China has grown at a blistering pace (29% a year from 2001 to 2021). Predictably, the economies of Southeast Asia that are geographically closer to China—those on the mainland of the continent—have seen their trade with China grow faster than those of maritime Southeast Asia (Indonesia and the Philippines).[26]

The economic distance between Southeast Asia and China has been further shrunk by transportation, energy, and communications infrastructure investments linking the two. Oil and gas pipelines run through Myanmar from the Bay of Bengal to southern China. New highways from China to Southeast Asia and from Vietnam's east coast to Thailand's west coast have cut transportation costs. Likewise, high-speed rail is reducing freight times from China all the way to Malaysia; and port construction is proceeding apace throughout the region. Launched in 2013, China's Belt and Road Initiative (BRI) financed a significant acceleration in these infrastructure investments, largely in Cambodia, Indonesia, Laos, the Philippines, and Vietnam.[27] In the first three years, the focus was on physical connectivity—mainly transportation and energy infrastructure. BRI investments later diversified to include special economic zones and, during the pandemic, protective health equipment and vaccine production. More recently, BRI's focus has shifted to digital connectivity through telecommunications infrastructure and digital platforms—the so-called Digital Silk Road—which, on account of their low cost and rapid rollout, have proved to be popular in most Southeast Asian countries, notwithstanding the security risks they may involve.

Regional Trade Agreements

The integrative force of geography and connective infrastructure has been buttressed by a regional institutional architecture that, in its scope and depth, is unrivaled by any other developing region. All ten Southeast Asian nations are members of ASEAN, which was founded in 1967 and has as one of its principal goals the establishment of a single market for goods, services,

---

[26] For the purposes of this analysis, mainland Southeast Asia comprises Laos, Cambodia, Malaysia, Myanmar, Thailand, and Vietnam; maritime Southeast Asia only includes Indonesia and the Philippines. Trade-to-GDP ratios are much higher for mainland Southeast Asia than they are for Indonesia and the Philippines. In stark contrast, intra-ASEAN trade during 2001–21 averaged around 7.5% a year. This growth rate is impressive, but still only about a quarter of the growth rate of trade between Southeast Asia and China. A key reason is that, despite their close physical proximity to each other, many Southeast Asian economies have broadly similar factor endowments.

[27] For further information on this trend, including a breakdown of BRI projects by year, country, and status, see International Institute for Strategic Studies (IISS), *Asia-Pacific Regional Security Assessment: Key Development and Trends, 2023* (London: IISS, 2023), 95.

investment, and skilled labor by 2025. This and other goals, however, remain aspirational, as the region is far from reaching them. For example, Southeast Asian economies may have lowered their tariff barriers, but they have at the same time raised non-tariff barriers.[28] ASEAN's agreements to promote trade in services tell the same story. They include commitments to reduce restrictions on services trade, yet Southeast Asian countries have some of the most restrictive policies on services trade in the world. The authorities have been unable to confront domestic vested interests supporting such protections and have been unwilling to adopt the requisite domestic laws and regulations consistent with these international commitments. As a result, the contribution of services to trade and growth in the region has been muted.

ASEAN's ten members have also agreed to promote the cross-border movement of skilled professionals through the mutual recognition of professional qualifications across member states and collaborative research among universities. Just as in the case of services trade, domestic laws and regulations supported by strong domestic lobbies have ensured that barriers remain in place to shelter domestic service providers from foreign competition. Equally, virtually every Southeast Asian country has tough border restrictions for unskilled migrant workers. As a result, illegal migration has proliferated, exposing migrants to potential abuse, human trafficking, forced labor, sexual exploitation, and bodily harm.

When it comes to trade with non-ASEAN partners, Southeast Asian economies—individually or as a group—have crafted 59 regional trading arrangements with their main trading partners.[29] As protectionism appears to be spreading globally, this web of agreements places pressure on the region's policymakers to maintain, and perhaps even increase, openness in trade and investment policies.

The most important regional trading arrangement for Southeast Asia is the RCEP, which came into force in 2022.[30] It includes every member of ASEAN together with five of its major trading partners—Australia, China, Japan, New Zealand, and South Korea.[31] Together, these fifteen economies

---

[28] These include trade and investment licensing, procurement restrictions, pre-shipment and post-shipment inspection, restricted ports of entry, sanitary and phytosanitary standards, technology transfer requirements, differential excise taxes, fiscal subsidies, loans with below-market interest rates, duty drawback schemes, undervalued exchange rates, quantitative restrictions, and procurement restrictions, among others.

[29] Data from UN Economic and Social Commission for Asia and Pacific, "List of Trade Agreements Covered by the UNESCAP Regional Trade Agreement Analyzer," February 2023, https://www.unescap.org/kp/2023/list-trade-agreements-covered-unescap-regional-trade-agreement-analyzer.

[30] To enter into force, the RCEP agreement required ratification by a minimum of six ASEAN members and three non-ASEAN signatories. This condition was met after Australia and New Zealand ratified the agreement in November 2021. Myanmar is now the only signatory that has yet to ratify the deal.

[31] India participated in the initial negotiations but eventually withdrew.

account for about a third of global GDP and a third of global exports, making the RCEP the world's largest regional trading agreement. Notwithstanding criticisms that it is a "low ambition" agreement, the RCEP also contains some important provisions, including common rules of origin that are expected to boost trade among its members.[32] The agreement also requires all member countries to adopt a "negative list" for FDI,[33] provide foreign investors national treatment, and ensure that openness to foreign investment, once granted, cannot be reversed. Encouragingly, the RCEP also includes rules governing intellectual property rights, investment, competition policy, government procurement, small and medium-sized enterprises, and e-commerce. Finally, its coverage extends to the formulation of an entire range of digital economy rules.[34]

The next most important regional trading arrangement in Southeast Asia is the Comprehensive and Progressive Agreement for Trans-Pacific Partnership (CPTPP)—initially called the TPP—which includes only four of Southeast Asia's ten economies (Brunei, Singapore, Malaysia, and Vietnam). Arguably the gold standard of all regional trade agreements, the twelve-member TPP lost much of its luster when the United States withdrew from the negotiations in January 2017, inflicting not just economic but also strategic costs on the region.[35] Japan assumed leadership of the negotiations, and the remaining eleven members pressed on to finalize the CPTPP and bring it into force in December 2018. In July 2023, the United Kingdom formalized its accession to the CPTPP, subject to ratification by existing members. China and Taiwan have also formally applied to join the agreement, though their road to membership is likely to prove more challenging.

---

[32] Bin Sheng and Chenxin Jin, "An Evaluation of the Regional Comprehensive Economic Partnership Agreement: Market Access and Trading Rules," *China and World Economy* 30, no. 5 (2022): 49–74. The RCEP was characterized as "low ambition" by former Australian prime minister Malcom Turnbull when speaking to a U.S. audience in 2020. See Tim McDonald, "What Is the Regional Comprehensive Economic Partnership (RCEP)?" BBC News, November 16, 2020, https://www.bbc.com/news/business-54899254.

[33] A "negative list" contains sectors prohibited or restricted from foreign investment without special regulatory approval.

[34] These rules include paperless trade, electronic authentication and signatures, information security, consumer rights, online consumer protection, and a commitment to avoid duties on cross-border digital trade.

[35] The estimated benefits would have been three times as great if the United States had remained in the agreement. See Peter A. Petri et al., "The Economics of the CPTPP and RCEP: Asia Pacific Trade Agreements without the United States," in *The Comprehensive and Progressive Trans-Pacific Partnership: Implications for Southeast Asia*, ed. Cassey Lee and Pritish Bhattacharya (Singapore: ISEAS–Yusof Ishak Institute, 2021). See also Jeffrey J. Schott, "Overview: Understanding the Trans-Pacific Partnership," in *Trans-Pacific Partnership: An Assessment*, ed. Cathleen Cimino-Isaacs and Jeffrey J. Schott (Washington, D.C.: Peterson Institute for International Economics, 2016).

companies like Ola Cabs and Flipkart are just cloning Western techniques and lack technological innovation.[83]

India's cautious approach toward the RCEP indicates that the country is not yet ready to participate in Asia's economic rise. Influential opposition to this and other trade agreements from the Swadeshi Jagran Manch and Bharatiya Kisan Sangh, the two affiliates of Rashtriya Swayamsevak Sangh (RSS) has been an important factor in India's refusal to join the grouping. The RSS, which forms the backbone of the ruling BJP, is the foremost advocate of Swadeshi, emphasizing economic self-reliance. With such opposition to trade negotiations and investment treaties, it is difficult for India to play an important role in global value chains. Even in the global apparel trade, its share has stagnated at around 4%, despite India having the advantage of a large domestic market for scaling, a large domestic supply of cotton and other raw materials, and a large labor pool. Bangladesh and Vietnam are already bigger players than India on this front. Due to distortions in land and labor markets, as well as weaknesses in infrastructure and the banking sector, Indian companies continue to struggle in traditional areas.

Likewise, with a protectionist mindset, increasing income inequality, and a lack of resources available for public higher education and research, it is not easy for India to emerge as an important player in areas of high technology. Though a few centralized teaching and research institutions may be able to compete internationally, a large-scale technological transformation of the industry and society may not happen easily. A recent study by Sunitha Raju shows that "imports from China have a positive association with manufacturing output and exports."[84] China is a low-cost supplier in 30% of products, and in many sectors Chinese components are not easily substitutable. Raju concludes that a decoupling or self-reliance policy "will not be effective unless the domestic manufacturing is propelled to high technology products." Therefore, reforms in the public higher education sector are crucial for any new high-tech sector to take off.

Conclusion

The Indian economy is expanding and integrating with other Asian economies. Foreign trade in goods and services is becoming more important for the economy. These trends are likely to continue. India-China trading links

---

[83] S.A. Aiyar, "2010s: The Decade Is Ending on a Sour Note for Indian Economy," *Times of India*, September 7, 2019, https://timesofindia.indiatimes.com/blogs/Swaminomics/2010s-the-decade-is-ending-on-a-sour-note-for-indian-economy.

[84] Sunitha Raju, "Impact of Imports from China on Indian Manufacturing Performance: An Analysis of Trade Competitiveness," *International Journal of Emerging Markets* (2023).

have multiplied over the last two decades, and despite decoupling measures, China continues to be one of India's leading trade partners. Beyond imports, linkages in investment and connectivity are limited. Although Chinese imports threaten some domestic industries, they are useful in domestic manufacturing and exports and are critical for some sectors. However, economic ties are being adjusted to the realities of a contentious border and antagonistic political relations. As a result, the government has taken measures to reduce imports and the trade deficit, ban mobile apps, and screen investments, among other initiatives. Still, some crucial minority shareholding investment proposals are being cleared quietly. A serious effort is also being made to strengthen domestic manufacturing by easing rules and incentives. So far, the impact of these measures has been limited.

Most Asian economies are deeply engaged with the Chinese economy through trade, investment, supply chains, trading arrangements, and BRI projects. Despite apprehensions, they are still integrating with China. These supply chains are being strengthened through the participation of many countries in the RCEP and CPTPP and balanced by the U.S.-led IPEF. India will have to either become part of this emerging economic architecture or help create an entirely new economic architecture along with its Quad partners. Although India is reluctant to fully participate in any of these frameworks, its manufacturing troubles and stagnating exports underscore its economic vulnerabilities. The Indian economy will continue to be an attractive destination for foreign companies due to its size and growth potential. However, the current economic policy framework may not lead India to become an economic heavyweight in an integrated Indo-Pacific. Therefore, instead of framing future economic ties with China in terms of decoupling or de-risking, India should work to create an independent economic strategy to strengthen its linkages with the existing economic frameworks within the Indo-Pacific region, including with the Chinese economy. This strategy, however, will likely not be viable without de-escalation at the border with China.

In the meantime, a number of measures have been initiated to strengthen domestic manufacturing. Growing exports in the last two years seem to have given policymakers the confidence needed to push for new trade deals with countries such as Australia and the UAE. To improve connectivity with major trading partners, the IMEC was also announced in September 2023. Despite developing a global partnership with the United States, India's importance within the evolving Indo-Pacific economic architecture will depend on its own economic expansion and its linkages with neighboring regions. Even if reducing economic ties with China and not joining multilateral trade deals could make it "self-reliant," India must aim to be at the center of Indo-Pacific economic dynamism rather than outside it.

National Trade and FDI Policies

Although Southeast Asia is the world's most trade-dependent region, trade and FDI policies across its ten economies exhibit wide variation. Singapore's policies are the most liberal, Vietnam's are modeled on the interventionist export-orientation strategy of China, Indonesia's exhibit rising protectionism and resource nationalism, while Myanmar's economy is autarkic. In most cases, however, Southeast Asian trade policies tend to be quite interventionist. Nonetheless, virtually all the economies in the region have become part of global value chains to varying degrees and are all tightly integrated with the Chinese economy through forward and backward linkages.

While Southeast Asian economies have lowered import tariffs in line with their international commitments, most have introduced non-tariff barriers that continue to shelter domestic production against import competition. To be sure, some non-tariff measures are justified, such as requiring agricultural imports to meet sanitary and phytosanitary standards. But in Southeast Asia, the real motivation for these measures is often the protection of domestic producers. In particular, Southeast Asia's imports of manufactures tend to be subject to a wide variety of non-tariff measures. The effective rates of protection they provide are uniformly higher than nominal tariff protection, particularly for fabricated metal products and motor vehicle production. Worse, effective rates of protection for some products are negative, indicating that trade policies impose a disadvantage on them in the international marketplace.[36]

With some exceptions, Southeast Asian countries apply particularly restrictive policies to services trade, which accounts for the region's low level of services trade and the poor quality of domestically provided services. Nowhere is this more important than in health and education. Restrictive policies inhibit the import of foreign skills to relieve critical skills bottlenecks to the detriment of economic and social development. Policies are less restrictive on digital services trade, however, possibly because of the lack of government capacity. Singapore is a notable exception. Indeed, its regulations for digital services trade are regarded as exemplifying best practices internationally, and it has concluded cutting-edge agreements on digital services trade with New Zealand, Chile, Australia, South Korea, and the United Kingdom.[37]

---

[36] Ben Shepherd, "Effective Rates of Protection in a World with Non-tariff Measures and Supply Chains: Evidence from ASEAN," Economic Research Institute for ASEAN and East Asia, ERIA Discussion Paper Series, no. 394, 2020, https://www.eria.org/uploads/media/discussion-papers/FY21/Effective-Rates-of-Protection-in-a-World-With-Non-Tariff-Measures-and-Supply-Chains_Evidence-from-ASEAN.pdf.

[37] U.S. Department of State, "2022 Investment Climate Statements: Singapore," 2022, https://www.state.gov/reports/2022-investment-climate-statements/singapore.

Technological Change, Comparative Advantage, and Resource Nationalism

Technological change, interacting with trade and FDI policies, is rapidly reshaping the economic landscape in Southeast Asia. Nowhere is this more evident than in industries related to electric vehicles (EVs), where activities run from nickel mining and smelting to battery production to manufacturing. Indonesia and the Philippines are among the top-six countries that account for over 80% of global nickel reserves (nickel being a critical input for car batteries).[38]

Indonesia represents the epicenter of Southeast Asia's entry into the global EV value chain. Driven by concerns that Indonesian mineral wealth was enriching multinationals rather than Indonesians, the country started restricting mineral ore exports in 2009, encouraging domestic smelting and metals production, and increasing Indonesian ownership of foreign-owned mines. In 2014, Indonesia went a step further and banned the export of mineral ores. Today, just one Indonesian industrial park dedicated to nickel processing (among many) employs over 43,000 workers and includes, among other facilities, smelters, coal-fired power plants, a port, road links, an airport, and dedicated telecommunications facilities that include underwater cables linked to Chinese satellites. All these facilities were built by Chinese companies and financed by China's largest state banks. Over the last decade, China has invested more than $29 billion in Indonesia's underdeveloped nickel-rich regions.[39] By contrast, U.S. and European companies—including EV producers—have been late in recognizing the potential of Indonesia's reserves and are now playing catch-up. Ford recently announced investments in nickel processing in Sulawesi, as have Volkswagen, BASF, and Eramet.

Emboldened by its seemingly successful foray into industrial policy, Indonesia has already placed export bans on bauxite to encourage aluminum smelting onshore and is now considering placing restrictions on nickel exports, forcing firms to produce batteries in Indonesia. Policymakers could go even further and require battery manufacturers in Indonesia to sell only to EV manufacturers located in the country. Reading these tea leaves, East Asian companies have been quick to invest in battery production (e.g., Tsingshan) and even EVs (e.g., Hyundai).

Similar to developments in the nickel industry, the rapid growth in Southeast Asia's digital sectors (e-commerce, fintech, travel, transportation, digital media, and digital applications in manufacturing more generally) has

---

[38] There are also around 3,000 nickel-based alloys, with stainless steel being the most prominent among them. Continental, "Nickel & High Temp Alloys," https://continentalsteel.com/nickel-alloys.

[39] See Eliot Chen, "The Nickel Pickle," Wire China, May 7, 2023, https://www.thewirechina.com/2023/05/07/the-nickel-pickle-tsingshan-xiang-guangda-indonesia.

led to rapid development in telecommunications infrastructure. Southeast Asian countries have faced the choice of adopting technology platforms from the West (primarily Nokia and Ericsson) or China (primarily ZTE and Huawei). Apart from Vietnam, virtually every Southeast Asian country is exploring or has opted for much cheaper Chinese technology, which has been offered with few restrictions. Some countries have also backed domestic suppliers. The pace of digitalization accelerated after the outbreak of the pandemic, driven in large part by the expansion of 4G mobile networks. Progress in 5G deployment, however, varies. Singapore is the most advanced (with 95% of the population having access), Thailand is less so (with 80% having access), and Brunei is still at an early stage.[40] Vietnam has chosen to abjure Chinese involvement in its 5G development altogether and is instead pursuing domestic technology options while partnering with companies from the United States and Europe. Many Southeast Asian countries are still building their digital economies and telecommunications sectors and remain open to purchasing Western hardware and software if offered the right competitive mix of technology, price, and financing.

The Impact of U.S.-China Competition on Southeast Asia's Economic Trajectory

Economic tensions between the United States and China are effectively reversing the decades-long course of integration between the two economies. For four decades after China's "opening up" in 1978, these two economies had become increasingly interwoven, thanks to lower trade and investment barriers and increased cross-border investment and cooperation on technology development. In 2018, however, the United States started introducing tariffs, investment restrictions, export controls, and domestic subsidies, all aimed at reducing China's access to the U.S. market and technology. U.S. actions on tariffs have been met with retaliatory actions from China. U.S. tariffs cover around 70% of all U.S. imports from China, with an average rate of around 20%, while China's retaliatory tariffs cover around 60% of China's imports from the United States, with an average rate of around 21%.[41]

Both countries are focused on building their own technological capabilities independently of the other by introducing industrial policies designed to accelerate domestic innovation while keeping new technologies

---

[40] "5G in South East Asia and Oceania: A Closer Look," Ericsson, https://www.ericsson.com/en/reports-and-papers/mobility-report/closer-look/south-east-asia-and-oceania.

[41] Clark Packard and Scott Lincicome, "Course Correction: Charting a More Effective Approach to U.S.-China Trade," Cato Institute, Policy Analysis, no. 946, May 9, 2023, https://www.cato.org/policy-analysis/course-correction.

under tight security. The United States' foray into industrial policy for chip manufacturing is a recent development, but China's industrial policy has been a central feature of the Chinese economy for decades. It is driven by evolving strategies, objectives, and sectoral focus and uses a variety of state interventions, including fiscal subsidies, directed lending, joint-venture and technology-sharing requirements, market entry restrictions, and price controls.

The Biden administration has tried to make clear that U.S. policy is aimed at "de-risking" the U.S. economy rather than "decoupling" it from China. Whichever term is used, the implications for Southeast Asia, with its deep economic links to both economies, are likely to be complex, varied, and probably profound. The uncertainty generated by the unpredictable directions of U.S. and Chinese policies will affect investor sentiment and lower investment levels. Different rules, standards, and governance arrangements employed by the United States and China will potentially segment markets and prevent Southeast Asian economies from exploiting scale economies. Rising trade and investment barriers between the two giants are already disrupting regional and global value chains. Restrictions imposed on technology flows by both countries will inevitably reduce the ability of Southeast Asian economies to access the most efficient capital equipment to increase productivity growth.

Impact on Trade Flows

First and foremost, the erection of trade barriers between China and the United States has hurt both countries directly. China's share in U.S. imports and the United States' share in China's imports have both declined. At the same time, the value of exports from China to ASEAN and from ASEAN to the United States has increased, while U.S. exports to ASEAN and ASEAN's exports to China have also climbed. So far, therefore, Southeast Asia appears to have been a net beneficiary of the U.S.-China trade war.[42] Since August 2022, however, ASEAN's electronics and machinery exports have slowed in anticipation that the U.S. Inflation Reduction Act and the Chips and Science Act will link U.S. government subsidies to domestic content requirements for U.S. firms.[43]

Vietnam has gained the most. Not only has its share of U.S. imports climbed significantly, but so has its share of China's imports. Vietnam's exports of high-tech products and electronics to the United States

---

[42] World Bank, *Reviving Growth: World Bank East Asia and the Pacific Economic Update* (Washington, D.C.: World Bank, 2023), https://www.worldbank.org/en/publication/east-asia-and-pacific-economic-update.

[43] World Bank, *Services for Development: World Bank East Asia and the Pacific Economic Update* (Washington, D.C.: World Bank, 2023), https://www.worldbank.org/en/publication/east-asia-and-pacific-economic-update.

doubled after Washington imposed tariffs and restrictions on imports of telecommunications equipment, semiconductors, and other high-tech products from China.[44] Some of this export growth came from multinationals relocating from China to Vietnam to evade U.S. tariffs. But Chinese firms benefited too. In fact, Chinese firms were among the largest investors of newly registered FDI in Vietnam after 2019.[45]

Indonesia is another Southeast Asian country that has benefited in the last five years from U.S.-China rivalry. As noted above, growth in Indonesia's nickel exports to China was the product of a scramble by Chinese nickel producers to relocate their production from the Chinese mainland to Indonesia. Their decision in part was caused by Indonesia's export ban on nickel ore, but another factor was their desire to gain an early-mover advantage by seizing nickel ore supplies ahead of potential competitors from the United States and other Western battery manufacturers.

A simulation analysis of the world economy in which 43 high-income economies, on one side, and China, Russia, and Belarus, on the other, raise tariffs by an additional 25% shows that the participating countries incur the worst negative impacts. By contrast, Southeast Asia, which does not participate in the simulated decoupling, is one of the beneficiaries (with the automobile sector benefiting the most).[46] The simulation also shows that if ASEAN were to participate in the trade war, it would be negatively affected. A key implication is that Southeast Asia's established supply chains are likely to benefit from disruptions in U.S.-China trade relations, and it is hardly surprising that there appears to be little appetite in Southeast Asia to restructure them.[47]

Going forward, as the economics of production fragmentation reach their limits and the full effects of recent U.S. protectionist legislation become apparent, growth in intra-industry merchandise trade between Southeast Asia and its major trading partners should be expected to slow. At the same time, growth in cross-border flows of services, data, and digital finance should be expected to increase, as should the cross-border flow of energy supplies.[48] The United States and China have their respective advantages in capitalizing on

---

[44] As noted in the previous paragraph, more recent U.S. legislation in support of domestic high-tech production has affected Vietnam's exports of these products over the past year. But this effect has so far been small in relation to the country's overall export growth in recent years.

[45] Euihyun Kwon, "The U.S.-China Trade War: Vietnam Emerges as the Greatest Winner," *Journal of Indo-Pacific Affairs*, August 1, 2022, https://www.airuniversity.af.edu/JIPA/Display/Article/3111127/the-uschina-trade-war-vietnam-emerges-as-the-greatest-winner.

[46] Ikumo Isono and Satoru Kumagai, "ASEAN's Role in the Threat of Global Economic Decoupling: Implications from Geographical Simulation Analysis," ERIA, Policy Brief, no. 2022-10, February 2023.

[47] Minoru Nogimori, "ASEAN Is Reluctant to Join the U.S.-Led Decoupling/De-risking Strategy for China," *JRI Research Journal* 6, no. 5 (2023).

[48] This flow could include blue hydrogen, solar energy, and hydropower.

this trend. The United States enjoys an unassailable comparative advantage in high-end services (such as health, education, design, finance, marketing, and entertainment), while China has gained a first-mover advantage in installing much of Southeast Asia's digital infrastructure and could benefit from imports of energy from Southeast Asia. Viewed from this perspective, Southeast Asia will remain an important market and investment destination for both the United States and China and will benefit from maintaining close trading relations with both countries.

Impact on Flows of Infrastructure Finance

Financing Southeast Asia's huge infrastructure needs is another area of keen rivalry between the United States and China. The United States and its partners are responding to China's BRI with infrastructure-financing initiatives of their own. BRI's earlier focus on financing hard infrastructure has been replaced by the Digital Silk Road, with an emphasis on financing digital connectivity and the rollout of next-generation information and communications technology (ICT) networks. Recently announced U.S. controls on the export of advanced semiconductor chips might delay, but not derail, these Chinese initiatives.[49] U.S. warnings about the potential data security and surveillance risks of Chinese ICT systems appear to have gained little traction in Southeast Asia.

Not to be outdone, the United States and its G-7 counterparts have responded with a range of initiatives of their own to provide Southeast Asia alternative financial resources to meet its infrastructure needs. Japan was the first. In 2016, it launched the Expanded Partnership for Quality Infrastructure and allocated $200 billion to be delivered through the Japan Bank for International Cooperation (JBIC). In 2018, the U.S. Congress passed the BUILD Act, creating the U.S. International Development Finance Corporation with a lending capacity of $60 billion. More recently, in 2022 the G-7 launched the Partnership for Global Infrastructure and Investment (PGII), pledging $600 billion in infrastructure financing for developing countries.[50] So far, the U.S. government has announced that of its $200 billion pledge to the PGII, $30 billion in grants, federal financing, and private sector funding has been mobilized, and other G-7 members are expected to follow suit.

Viewed broadly, however, not only do these G-7 initiatives fall far short of the funding that China has provided, but their implementation has also

---

[49] Cheng Ting-Fang, "Huawei to Restart 5G Mobile Chip Output as Early as This Year," *Nikkei Asia*, July 27, 2023, https://asia.nikkei.com/Business/Tech/Semiconductors/Huawei-to-restart-5G-mobile-chip-output-as-early-as-this-year.

[50] Of the $600 billion pledged, the United States pledged $200 billion, the EU pledged $317 billion, and Japan pledged $65 billion.

been slow. Some have not even financed a single project.⁵¹ Yet, if they do get off the ground, these initiatives will be welcomed by Southeast Asia for two important reasons. First, the demand for infrastructure in the region far exceeds the total financing currently available. Second, G-7 financing could compensate partly for a further slowdown in BRI-related financing, as China's faltering economy and the growing nonperforming loan portfolio of its banks begin to impinge on the lending capacity of the Chinese financial system.

Impact on Technology Standards

Tariffs and finance are not the only instruments that have been used in the trade war between the United States and China. Other tools include technical standards, applied principally to imports of agricultural and high-tech products. If the United States and China had adopted harmonized standards, lower costs of trade, information, and design would have allowed Southeast Asian firms to capture scale economies in production. With fragmented standards, on the other hand, Southeast Asian firms will face increased costs, lowering their international competitiveness and inhibiting them from adopting new technologies.

When it comes to setting technology standards for the digital economy, China is responding quickly to the United States' Clean Network program.⁵² It is building on its Southeast Asian investments in ICT by advancing new proposals promoting fresh norms and standards that cover data security and storage, as well as e-commerce, and claiming to adopt principles of multilateralism, fairness, and justice.⁵³ China's close trade ties and participation in the RCEP and various ASEAN-related organizations provide it a seat at the table to engage Southeast Asian countries on developing common standards for the burgeoning e-commerce sector and cross-border provision of digital services, including digital payment systems. Indeed, China's interventionist approach toward governance of cross-border flows of digital goods, services, and data and its penchant for surveillance resonate with the preferences of Southeast Asian policymakers.

---

[51] In contrast, by 2021, 90 BRI projects had been completed in Southeast Asia, 25 were ongoing, and 16 were planned.

[52] Launched by the Trump administration, this program was designed to safeguard system security, sensitive information, and privacy from aggressive intrusions by malign actors.

[53] These issues are covered in China's Global Data Security Initiative, which is a complement to China's Global Development Initiative and Global Security Initiative.

Impact on Technology Acquisition

Partial technological decoupling between the United States and China will allow Southeast Asia to continue its hedging policy and thereby retain access to the latest technology from both countries. Given its limited technological capacity, the region is highly dependent on the availability of knowledge and technology embedded in products, processes, capital equipment, and patents created in the advanced economies and China. While the United States continues to dominate most dimensions of technological innovation, China is expanding its technological capacity and becoming an increasingly important source of knowledge for Southeast Asia.[54] It is using these capabilities to expand commercial opportunities throughout the world in a range of industries, most notably in transportation and renewable energy infrastructure. China's high-speed rail projects in Laos and Indonesia, for example, may be commercially risky, but they demonstrate that Chinese technological capabilities in some industries are close to the technological frontier in areas of strategic importance to Southeast Asian economies.

ICT is another area where China is at or near the technological frontier. It has formal agreements with Laos, Malaysia, and Myanmar to deliver digital and technology infrastructure and has ongoing initiatives related to the Digital Silk Road with other Southeast Asian economies. Chinese digital infrastructure is becoming increasingly embedded in Southeast Asia, and the accumulation of these legacy assets will make any future switch to Western ICT systems and equipment increasingly costly (but not impossible).

The emergence of China as a source of critical technological know-how in competition with the United States places Southeast Asian countries in a quandary. In the event of a full-scale technological decoupling between the United States and China, on which technological power would Southeast Asian countries likely rely? Or would they hedge their bets and seek access to technology from wherever they can find it, while also honoring restrictions on sharing these technologies with third parties? Surveys and interviews suggest that Southeast Asian countries are likely to hedge their bets for as long as possible, seeking to gain the best technologies and prices that their suitors (China, the United States, and the rest of the OECD) have to offer.[55] And they are unlikely to disrupt their relationship with China on existing projects and initiatives when the United States has yet to offer equally attractive alternatives.

---

[54] World Bank, *Reviving Growth*, 53.

[55] Sharon Seah et al., *The State of Southeast Asia: 2023 Survey Report* (Singapore: ISEAS–Yusof Ishak Institute, 2023). The survey, conducted between late 2022 and early 2023, included 1,308 respondents throughout Southeast Asia from academia, think tanks, and research institutes; business and finance; civil society, NGOs, and the media; government; and regional and international institutions.

As the technology rift between China and the United States grows, however, Southeast Asia's policy space for hedging shrinks. Southeast Asian governments might choose Chinese technology suppliers purely based on cost, efficiency, or quality, despite any risks to their own system security.[56] In that scenario, the United States could consider such action as jeopardizing the security of its systems, withdraw from defense or economic cooperation, and restrict access to its latest technologies. Conversely, if concern with security were to drive Southeast Asian governments to exclude Chinese technology suppliers, the former would risk economic retaliation from Beijing.

By reducing access to the full range of available technology options, a full-scale U.S.-China decoupling would hurt every Southeast Asian economy. In the event of such a rupture, Southeast Asian countries would need to choose with which technological hub to align. Singapore, Brunei, and Vietnam, with closer economic ties to the United States and the West, would probably opt for Western technologies and remain within the CPTPP. This choice would grant Singapore the additional benefit of becoming a preferred destination for Western technology companies seeking to relocate their research and development facilities from China. Laos, Cambodia, and Myanmar, largely locked into economically dependent relationships with China, would most likely opt to continue with their reliance on Chinese trade and technology. Finally, the large middle-income countries of Indonesia, Malaysia, Thailand, and the Philippines, which have equally close economic ties with China and the United States, could go either way. Their decisions would likely be based on pragmatic considerations of cost, security concerns, and ease of access to new technologies. Much will depend on the assurances they receive from either side and their assessment of which technology hub will prevail over the long term. The United States' ban on exports of advanced chips to China and China's retaliatory export restrictions on key precious metal compounds used in manufacturing semiconductor wafers would undoubtedly have to be factored into their final decisions.[57]

---

[56] Despite statements by U.S. policymakers to the contrary, there are reasons to believe that U.S.-China technological decoupling is likely to escalate. See James Crabtree, "U.S.-China De-risking Will Inevitably Escalate," *Foreign Policy*, August 20, 2023, https://foreignpolicy.com/2023/08/20/derisking-decoupling-us-china-biden-economy-trade-technology-semiconductors-chips-supply-chains-ai-geopolitics-escalation.

[57] While the Chinese retaliatory decision to place export restrictions on certain gallium and germanium compounds (critical in the production of semiconductor wafers) will have little impact on global supplies of these precious metals, it will raise U.S. production costs and provide a warning that other retaliatory actions could be taken by China.

Impact on Public and Elite Opinion in Southeast Asia

In addition to how U.S. and Chinese hard power works through economic channels, it is important to ask whether soft power is leaving an imprint on Southeast Asian public and elite opinion. This is an important question because public and elite opinion have the power to shape future domestic and foreign policy in ways that would have differential effects on Southeast Asia's economic relations with the United States and China.

A comprehensive measure of the relative economic influence of the two countries in Southeast Asia shows China well ahead of the United States in every Southeast Asian country, albeit by varying degrees (**Figure 4**).[58] Moreover, over the last five years (2018–23), China's economic influence has grown, while that of the United States has waned. Economic influence, however, does not translate to soft power. A recent analysis of public and elite opinion polls in Southeast Asia confirms that most people see China as the dominant economic power, but this does not appear to have garnered the country much favor among the public or the elite.[59] In fact, the United States is more popular than China across most of Southeast Asia.

A deeper analysis of the most authoritative survey in Southeast Asia, conducted by the ISEAS–Yusof Ishak Institute in Singapore, provides the underpinning for these findings.[60] According to nearly 60% of respondents, China is the most influential economic power in the region, while only 10% of respondents held this view of the United States.[61] As one would expect, Southeast Asians worry about China's influence (65%) and welcome greater U.S. influence (66%). Similarly, China is viewed as having more political influence (42%) than the United States (32%). Southeast Asians do not consider any global power as a champion for free trade (United States, 22%; EU, 18%; China, 15%). Yet, even though respondents' endorsement of the United States and the EU as leaders for a rules-based international order was not overwhelming (United States, 27%; EU, 23%), their endorsement of China in this regard was even less so (5%).

More broadly, many more respondents felt that the United States would "do the right thing" (50%) than China (30%). Southeast Asians trust the United States because of its vast economic resources, its military power, and

---

[58] See Lowy Institute, "Asia Power Index 2023," 2023, https://www.lowyinstitute.org/publications/asia-power-snapshot-china-united-states-southeast-asia. The index on economic influence measures economic size, international leverage, technological capability, and connectivity. Underlying these categories are a total of 21 measures.

[59] For an overview, see the table titled "Southeast Asian Public and Elite Opinion toward the United States and China" in Gregory B. Poling and Andreyka Natalegawa, "Assessing U.S. and Chinese Influence in Southeast Asia," Center for Strategic and International Studies, August 2023, 2.

[60] Seah et al., *The State of Southeast Asia*.

[61] Results are rounded to the nearest percent.

FIGURE 4 Economic influence of China and the United States, 2022

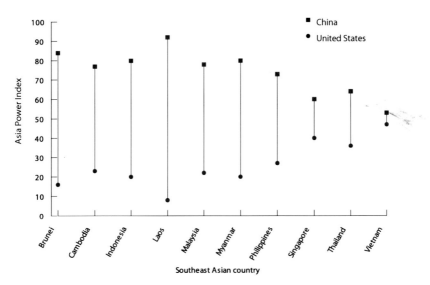

SOURCE: Susannah Patton and Jack Sato, "Asia Power Snapshot: China and the United States in Southeast Asia," Lowy Institute, 2023.

its actions as a "responsible stakeholder." Those who distrust it believe that the United States is distracted by its internal affairs, its military could pose threats to national sovereignty in Southeast Asia, and it is an unreliable partner. Respondents, however, were more distrustful of China. China's increasingly aggressive posture in the South China Sea, sheer economic and military dominance in the region, and unclear strategic intentions make Southeast Asians nervous about the country's economic power and how it could be used.

Impact on Economic Policies in Southeast Asia

The survey results analyzed above notwithstanding, Southeast Asia's domestic or international economic policies have seen little change since the escalation of the U.S.-China trade war in 2016. Countries with foreign policies "bandwagoned" to China (Cambodia, Laos, and Myanmar) have little agency or inclination to rebalance their policies toward other powers or diversify their economic relations. If anything, since 2016, they have become even more dependent on China, driven not by U.S.-China economic rivalry so much as by domestic forces. For example, following Myanmar's military coup in 2021, a combination of autarkic policies adopted by the new regime and economic sanctions applied by the advanced economies deepened the economy's isolation from the rest of the world and increased its dependence on China. Similarly, Laos's unsustainable external debt burden, owed mostly to China, has made it more vulnerable than ever to Chinese economic coercive power.[62] As for Cambodia, its recent generational change in regime leadership provides an opportunity for reducing the economy's almost total dependence on China, but the new leadership's patrons (inside both Laos and China) will unlikely grant agency for such change in foreign policy direction.

The remaining Southeast Asian countries have hedged their economic relations between the United States and China to varying degrees, balancing their economic interests (which increasingly lie with China) against their security concerns (increasingly driven by China). Many have frequently expressed concern about China's increasingly aggressive actions in the South China Sea, sought new or better security arrangements with the United States, and endorsed U.S. initiatives to maintain freedom of navigation along the important sea lines of communication. But their international economic policies since 2016 do not appear to have been altered substantially in response to the trade and technology tensions between the United States and China or to counter China's growing economic influence in the region. Their membership in the RCEP and openness to Chinese trade, investment, and technology have been balanced by initiatives to negotiate new trade agreements with the EU and participation in the Indo-Pacific Economic Framework (IPEF). As noted earlier, four Southeast Asian countries have also joined the CPTPP.

There are few signs that Malaysia and Thailand are shifting the balance of their policies away from China and toward the United States and its allies. Indonesia also appears unwilling to change its receptive attitude to Chinese trade, investment, and technology. Nonetheless, it has expressed an interest in a limited trade agreement with the United States that would allow nickel and other critical commodities used in EV production to be exported to the U.S. supply chain and benefit from U.S. tax credits. The United States, troubled by Indonesia's ban on nickel (and other mineral) ore exports, has been reluctant to respond positively to this approach. Vietnam and the Philippines, on the other hand, are threatened more directly by China's actions in the South

---

[62] Laos is fully aware of its weak bargaining position vis-à-vis China. For example, in a 2021 agreement to restructure its debt owed to China, Laos's state-owned electric power company ceded control of the country's power grid to a Chinese state-owned power company for 25 years, effectively giving China control of the country's electricity trade. The current debt crisis could once again force Laos to surrender some of its economic sovereignty to its powerful neighbor. See Anjali Bhatt, "Laos Is Not in a Chinese 'Debt Trap'—but It Is in Trouble," *Diplomat*, April 27, 2023, https://thediplomat.com/2023/04/laos-is-not-in-a-chinese-debt-trap-but-it-is-in-trouble.

China Sea and increasingly driven by domestic anti-Chinese sentiment. They thus would be open to exploring new economic arrangements with the United States that would reduce their dependence on China and protect their long-term economic security. For example, to balance the recent surge in Chinese FDI to Vietnam, Vietnamese policymakers might consider incentives to attract investors from other countries, especially the United States, to overcome their lack of competitiveness vis-à-vis Chinese firms.[63] The Philippines could adopt a different approach and seek a trade agreement with the United States as a national security priority. The question is whether a protectionist United States would be prepared to reciprocate.

Implications for U.S. Policy

A review of U.S. policy must start with the clear-eyed assessment that while the United States still enjoys a significant advantage over China in Southeast Asia in terms of both hard and soft power, China's economic ascendancy is shifting the balance of power in the region in a way that may compromise the long-term stability and economic prosperity of Southeast Asia as well as the long-term interests of the Indo-Pacific region.

U.S. influence in Southeast Asia waned during the Trump administration, thanks to its "America first" vision, downgrade of the region in its economic priorities abroad, emphasis on trade protection, and withdrawal from the TPP. Earlier, the Obama administration missed a key opportunity when it refused to join the China-led Asian Infrastructure Investment Bank (AIIB), signaling that fears of engaging China overrode any possible benefits such institutions could have for the common prosperity of the region.

The United States has made strenuous efforts to engage Southeast Asian countries through myriad other initiatives, however, which have been accelerated and strengthened under the Biden administration. Over the last decade, it has developed strategic partnerships with countries in Southeast Asia, emphasizing U.S. interest in the region. A significant recent development was the launch of the U.S.-ASEAN Comprehensive Strategic Partnership in 2022, which elevates U.S.-ASEAN relations and emphasizes greater intensity in strategic cooperation. Prior to the launch, President Joe Biden announced an allocation of $102 million to new initiatives in support of the partnership. An array of U.S.-ASEAN programs and initiatives promote cooperation, training, and capacity building on maritime cooperation; measures to counter human trafficking

---

[63] It is unclear, however, whether Vietnam has the agency to offer differentiated incentives without incurring Chinese economic retaliation.

and other transnational crime; nonproliferation and disarmament; intra-parliamentary cooperation; digital economy; trade, investment, and financial stability; micro, small, and medium-sized enterprises; energy security; climate-friendly transportation technologies, including development of EV ecosystems; smart cities; sustainable infrastructure and connectivity; subregional cooperation and support for the Initiative for ASEAN Integration; regional health resilience; environment, climate change, agriculture, and food security; education and people-to-people initiatives; youth and women empowerment; sustainable development; and bio-circular and green economy.[64]

This extremely broad range of mostly governance-related support suggests that the United States' partnership with Southeast Asia is more aspirational than practical, lacks focus and strategic coherence, has neither clear end goals nor agreed-on milestones to track progress, gets chopped and changed every four to eight years with each new incoming administration, and is difficult to coordinate. Strategic partnerships with individual Southeast Asian countries—such as Indonesia, Malaysia, and the Philippines—are equally broad and similarly aspirational. These partnerships have undoubtedly strengthened and deepened the U.S. relationship with the region, creating a reservoir of goodwill. But they differ starkly in approach from the more strategic, focused, financial, and technical support provided by other regional powers, especially China.

Against a backdrop of bipartisan alarm in Washington at Beijing's growing influence in Southeast Asia, the Biden administration has stepped up efforts to respond to concerns in Southeast Asian capitals that the United States is disengaging from the region and to demonstrate U.S. commitment to the region. High-level visitors and delegations from the president and vice president to lower-level officials have visited the region to emphasize Washington's interest in supporting its development ambitions and strategic interests. But handicapped by bipartisan opposition to trade agreements, hobbled by congressional deadlock on budgetary issues, and restricted by a deeply polarized political climate, the Biden administration has found it difficult to back words with a large, fully funded, durable program of support that will survive successive administrations.

---

[64] The array of U.S. programs and initiatives focused exclusively on ASEAN include the U.S.-ASEAN Smart Cities Partnership, U.S.-ASEAN Universities Connection Initiative, U.S.-ASEAN Connect, Young Southeast Asian Leaders Initiative, U.S.-ASEAN Institute for Rising Leaders, USAID Southeast Asia Smart Power Program, U.S.-ASEAN Electric Vehicle Initiative, International Visitor Leadership Program, Southeast Asia Youth Leadership Program, IPEF Upskilling Initiative, Just Energy Transition Partnership, U.S.-ASEAN Health Futures Initiative, U.S.-ASEAN Climate Futures Initiative, U.S.-ASEAN Platform for Infrastructure and Connectivity, and U.S.-ASEAN Science, Technology, and Innovation Cooperation Program, among others.

To its credit, however, the Biden administration has crafted a new initiative that is bold in its vision despite being financially constrained—the IPEF. That fourteen economies have already joined the initiative (including seven in Southeast Asia) signals a demand for U.S. leadership on economic issues.[65] The IPEF is worth examining carefully because, with some small changes, it could help focus, structure, and manage a strategic vision to secure and protect an international economic order that would bring peace and prosperity to the Indo-Pacific region (including Southeast Asia as an important constituent part).

The IPEF has four supporting pillars: trade, supply chains, clean economy, and fair economy.[66] They seek to advance integration, economic resilience, environmental protection, and good governance—all consistent with advancing the interests of Southeast Asia. The question is whether these elements of the IPEF address the central development concerns of the Southeast Asian economies. To be sure, the region's diversity implies that each country has its own development priorities. But there are three broad development challenges that are common to all Southeast Asian economies (except for Singapore): human capital shortages, climate change and the consequences of extreme weather events, and large deficits in energy and transportation infrastructure. The following discussion examines how the IPEF—and U.S. engagement in the region more broadly—could more effectively deal with these three central concerns.

Human Capital

Many Southeast Asian countries face shortages of skills and substantial human capital deficits. Continued rapid growth in Southeast Asia will depend on how effectively these countries fill these deficits by boosting human capital. Human capital, after all, is the "new wealth of nations" and accounts for more than two-thirds of Southeast Asia's total wealth.[67] To some extent, the IPEF recognizes this. The U.S. Department of Commerce recently announced the IPEF Upskilling Initiative for women and girls, under which U.S. companies will provide over seven million digital training and education opportunities

---

[65] The IPEF's members are Australia, Brunei, Fiji, India, Indonesia, Japan, Malaysia, New Zealand, the Philippines, Singapore, South Korea, Thailand, the United States, and Vietnam. Excluded Southeast Asian nations are Cambodia, Laos, and Myanmar.

[66] The trade pillar is the IPEF's most complex component, comprising nine subsections: agriculture, competition policy, digital economy, environment, inclusivity, labor, trade facilitation, transparency and good regulatory practices, and technical assistance and economic cooperation.

[67] World Bank Group, *The Changing Wealth of Nations 2021* (Washington, D.C.: World Bank, 2021), 154, table 7.3. For further discussion of human capital as the new wealth of nations, see Surjit S. Bhalla, *The New Wealth of Nations* (New Delhi: Simon and Schuster, 2018).

to women and girls in IPEF countries.[68] This is a laudable initiative. All the evidence shows that investments in health and education, especially among young girls and poor communities, yield impressive social and economic returns. U.S. financial and technical support to Southeast Asia for building skills and advancing literacy, including digital literacy, will increase the region's growth potential while also building the reputational stock of the United States.

The IPEF's fair economy pillar could, however, be tasked with taking up the broader challenge of improving education quality in Southeast Asia and ensuring a more efficient allocation of skills across the region. In addition to digital upskilling, the IPEF could encourage region-wide mutual recognition of academic and technical credentials to permit the cross-border flow of skilled workers throughout Southeast Asia.[69] At the same time, it could expand foreign investment in higher education, including from U.S. institutions.

Climate Change

A second long-term binding constraint—and arguably even an existential threat—is climate change. The clean economy pillar of the IPEF prioritizes energy security while transitioning to clean energy sources; lower greenhouse gas emissions in key sectors; sustainable land, water, and ocean solutions; scaling up innovative technologies for greenhouse gas solutions; and incentives to enable the clean energy transition. While this pillar has yet to be negotiated among IPEF members, another G-7 initiative—the Just Energy Transition Partnership (JETP)—is proceeding apace. The JETP involves an international partnership group of several advanced economies—formed under the leadership of the United States and co-chaired by Japan—that provides financial commitments in exchange for pledges by partner developing countries to reach net zero by 2050 (among other energy transition goals). So far, the group has signed JETP agreements with South Africa, Indonesia, and Vietnam and offered substantial financial support to assist in the transition to clean energy sources.

One way to lend the United States' climate change engagement greater strategic coherence in Southeast Asia would be to make the JETP a part of the IPEF's clean economy pillar and coordinate its actions with the pillar's other components. In addition, the partnership focuses exclusively on mitigation, when most Southeast Asian economies are small contributors to

---

[68] Fourteen U.S. companies—Amazon Web Services, American Tower, Apple, Cisco, Dell, Edelman, Google, HP, IBM, Mastercard, Microsoft, PayPal, Salesforce, and Visa—have agreed to each provide 500,000 upskilling opportunities to women and girls in the IPEF's emerging economies by 2032.

[69] Mutual recognition agreements are already a part of the ASEAN Framework Agreement on Services.

global greenhouse gas emissions but are among the world's most vulnerable to climate-induced extreme weather events.[70] It is critical that adaptation be included as part of the effort to promote a just energy transition in these countries. Finally, the financial commitments underpinning the JETP agreements may appear substantial, but they need to be increased significantly to have a realistic chance of achieving the program's objectives.[71]

Infrastructure

A third binding constraint for many Indo-Pacific developing countries is infrastructure, especially in energy, transportation, and telecommunications. McKinsey Global Institute estimates that Southeast Asia will need to invest hundreds of billions of dollars each year in infrastructure for the region to maintain rapid growth well until 2035.[72]

As noted earlier, the United States, together with key OECD partners such as Japan, is trying to fill part of this gap. Since 2015, the United States and its Quad partners have provided $48 billion in official finance for high-quality infrastructure in countries in the Indo-Pacific, including Southeast Asia.[73] The United States also supports infrastructure development with concessional finance from multilateral development banks (MDBs) and the International Development Finance Corporation.[74] Even so, taken in its entirety, U.S. support for infrastructure financing in Southeast Asia will need to increase by multiples, perhaps even by an order of magnitude, if it is to make a meaningful contribution to the region's infrastructure needs.

In stark contrast, China is by far the largest source of infrastructure finance to Southeast Asia.[75] Unfortunately, China neither provides reliable

---

[70] These extreme weather events include typhoons, hurricanes, rising sea levels, and volatile precipitation (with consequences for agricultural productivity and food security).

[71] For example, the World Bank estimates that Vietnam's costs of mitigation and adaptation total about $700 billion. The international partnership group, however, has offered only $15.5 billion, with half coming from official sources and the other half from the Glasgow Financial Alliance for Net Zero—a group of private sector financial institutions. Similarly, the International Renewable Energy Agency estimates that Indonesia would need $163.5 billion for limited transition investments in renewable energy technology, grid expansion, and storage needs alone through 2030, whereas the international partnership group has offered only $20 billion. See Victoria Milko, "Indonesia Submits Plan on How It Will Spend $20 Billion on Clean Energy Transition," *Diplomat*, August 17, 2023, https://thediplomat.com/2023/08/indonesia-submits-plan-on-how-it-will-spend-20-billion-on-clean-energy-transition.

[72] See Jonathan Woetzel et al., "Bridging Infrastructure Gaps: Has the World Made Progress?" McKinsey Global Institute, Executive Briefing, October 13, 2017, https://www.mckinsey.com/capabilities/operations/our-insights/bridging-infrastructure-gaps-has-the-world-made-progress.

[73] See "Marking One Year since the Release of the Administration's Indo-Pacific Strategy," U.S. Department of State, Fact Sheet, February 10, 2023, https://th.usembassy.gov/marking-one-year-since-the-release-of-the-administrations-indo-pacific-strategy.

[74] The key MDBs for Southeast Asia are the World Bank and the Asian Development Bank.

[75] Lowy Institute, "Southeast Asia Aid Map."

data on the substantial amounts it invests in Southeast Asian infrastructure nor the financial terms of its loans (which are usually nonconcessional). But the debt crisis faced by Laos gives cause for concern. Its problems can be traced to recent sharp increases in debt-servicing requirements on Chinese loans, which are accelerating shifts in the power dynamics of Southeast Asia. Unless the United States, together with other OECD economies, can provide significant alternative funding sources, other countries in the region may well meet the same fate.

The Way Forward

The preceding discussion on U.S. policy toward Southeast Asia points to four important challenges facing U.S. economic policy. The first challenge is the widespread perception that the United States' economic engagement with Southeast Asia has faltered and been eclipsed by a more dynamic China, especially in trade and development finance. Second, the United States' economic initiatives in Southeast Asia are scattered across too many programs and institutions, which dilutes their strategic coherence. Third, U.S. bilateral assistance programs in Southeast Asia lack continuity and durability across administrations, with each new administration starting new initiatives at the expense of those inherited from the past. Fourth, U.S. economic engagement in Southeast Asia lacks sufficient fiscal and financial support to ensure that programs are executed swiftly and to a high standard.

Addressing these four shortcomings will require the United States to rethink its economic policy strategy toward Southeast Asia. Two key dimensions of the strategy that require special focus are improving strategic coherence and increasing strategic effectiveness.

Improving Strategic Coherence

Although the IPEF is arguably one of the most significant U.S. policy initiatives in recent years that affects Southeast Asia, it falls short of providing an overall framework that lends strategic coherence to U.S. bilateral economic policy and assistance. With some imaginative retooling and strengthening, however, the IPEF could provide that framework, promoting stability, resilience, and economic security, while also serving U.S. long-term interests in Asia.

The United States should use the momentum gained from the successful conclusion of negotiations on the IPEF's supply chain pillar to address the more complex issues contained in the IPEF's trade pillar. Progress here may be slow, but it is important to use these discussions as an avenue for U.S. officials to re-engage on trade issues with their Southeast Asian counterparts with the ultimate goal of fashioning a trade agreement that would be an improvement over the CPTPP.[76] In addition, during its IPEF negotiations, the United States should consider win-win limited trade agreements with individual Southeast Asian countries. For example, EV tax credits, available under the Inflation Reduction Act to battery producers that add value within the United States or with free trade partners, could be extended to U.S. battery producers located in Indonesia and the Philippines.[77] This would reduce the United States' dependence on battery imports from China while also reducing the dependence of Indonesia and the Philippines on Chinese battery producers.

On climate change, it makes little sense for the IPEF to negotiate its clean economy pillar when a group of international advanced countries led by the United States and Japan are, in parallel, advancing the JETP. Quite apart from avoiding duplication, the JETP would bring to the IPEF an operationally and institutionally viable approach to implementing energy transitions in the Indo-Pacific. Learning from the experience of the JETP negotiations with Indonesia and Vietnam, IPEF negotiations could be expanded to include not just mitigation actions in partner countries but also the significant investments in adaptation that will be needed to manage the costs of climate change.

The IPEF's strategic coherence could also be enhanced if it included a human development component within the fair economy pillar. This component could include not only the Upskilling Initiative but also programs to increase foreign investment in tertiary education (especially by U.S. universities) and policies to ensure that the regional labor market for skilled and unskilled workers operates more efficiently.

Increasing Strategic Effectiveness

Irrespective of the strategic framework that is ultimately adopted by the United States, other critical steps still need to be taken to ensure that bilateral assistance programs are maximally effective. Foremost among these is the need for more, and more sustained, financing.

---

[76] Even if there were political will in the United States to join the CPTPP, China's application for membership will significantly complicate any U.S. entry bid. The IPEF, however, could provide a fresh start for U.S engagement on trade with Southeast Asia and build on lessons learned from the CPTPP, the U.S.-Mexico-Canada Agreement, and the RCEP.

[77] There is a precedent for this recommendation. The Biden administration has negotiated a mineral deal with Japan that allows Japanese mineral exporters to access tax credits under the Inflation Reduction Act, and it is in the process of negotiating one with the EU.

Ensuring that signature programs in Southeast Asia are properly funded will require a substantial increase in U.S. bilateral aid.[78] To match rhetoric with reality, additional funds will need to be contributed to the multilateral programs in which the United States is a signatory, most notably the PGII, which remains largely unfunded. U.S. contributions will also be needed to leverage MDBs—especially the World Bank and the Asian Development Bank—through a capital increase. In this regard, an independent expert group, commissioned by the G-20 presidency to examine the future of MDBs, has called for a tripling of their sustainable lending levels by 2030 to meet the challenge of climate change and accelerate progress toward the Sustainable Development Goals, a target that cannot be reached unless the capital base of these institutions is increased substantially.[79] In addition, the United States should reconsider its stance toward membership in the AIIB. Joining the institution would boost financing for infrastructure in Southeast Asia, and the United States would be better positioned to shape that support.

Unless the United States commits to an ambitious agenda of reform, China's economic influence in Southeast Asia will continue to grow, leaving a lasting imprint on the rules and norms that will govern international economic relations in the region. There is bipartisan support in Congress for a muscular response to these developments that will accelerate U.S. economic engagement and ensure that any future economic order in Southeast Asia serves the broader interests of the Indo-Pacific, including the United States. Increasing the strategic coherence of bilateral economic assistance programs and improving their effectiveness will form critical first steps in this direction.

---

[78] Many U.S. development programs rely on funding promised by private sector agencies (the Upskilling Initiative and the JETP being two such examples), even when there is little clarity on whether the private sector will be forthcoming with its contribution and on what terms these funds will be provided.

[79] Independent Experts Group, "Strengthening Multilateral Development Banks: The Triple Agenda," vol. 1, 2023, https://www.cgdev.org/sites/default/files/The_Triple_Agenda_G20-IEG_Report_Volume1_2023.pdf.

EXECUTIVE SUMMARY

This chapter examines how Australia is grappling with the trade-offs of deep economic interdependence with China and the real—albeit so far limited—impacts that emerging national security concerns are having on how policymakers and economic actors think about and manage bilateral exchange.

MAIN ARGUMENT

For decades, Australia insisted it could enjoy a relatively clean separation between economics and national security. However, three shocks—the discovery of China's growing influence in its domestic politics, Beijing's economic sanctions campaign, and pandemic-induced supply vulnerabilities—triggered a major perceptual shift. Actors across Australian society now believe that interdependence with China carries sustained geopolitical risk. Despite this shift and clear changes in government policy, the bulk of exchange between the two economies remains robust. The only evidence of meaningful and potentially enduring decoupling has manifested in narrow domains, such as information and communications technology infrastructure and critical mineral supply chains.

POLICY IMPLICATIONS

- While Australia's commitment to deepening security and economic cooperation with the U.S. is beyond doubt, U.S. policymakers must understand the Australian government's and business sector's interests in engaging with China economically while upholding a rules-based order.

- Concrete security-based economic cooperation should be focused on bringing new production online to build new supply chains; thus, the Biden administration's policies supporting the development of new mining and processing facilities are welcome.

- Australia's balancing of its economic and security interests gives it much in common with other states in the Indo-Pacific and underscores the need for the U.S. to develop models of economic cooperation that can complement the region's interests in broad-based economic engagement with China.

Australia

Australia's Reassessment of Economic Interdependence with China

Darren J. Lim, Benjamin Herscovitch, and Victor A. Ferguson

In contemporary debates about the extent to which the forces of great-power rivalry, weaponized interdependence, and technology competition will restructure the patterns of trade and investment in the global economy, Australia's position often appears to be a difficult circle to square. Having been the first country to ban Huawei from its national 5G network in 2018 and redirected a wide range of its exports away from China while navigating a sanctions campaign initiated by Beijing in 2020, Australia is sometimes held up as an exemplar of decoupling in action.[1] On the other hand, despite those developments, the country's monthly exports to China reached an all-time high in March 2023,[2] leading some commentators to argue that any talk of decoupling is at odds with the "economic reality" that China is Australia's most important trading partner and will likely remain so for decades to come.[3]

Darren J. Lim is a Senior Lecturer in the School of Politics and International Relations at the Australian National University. He can be reached at <darren.lim@anu.edu.au>.

Benjamin Herscovitch is a Research Fellow in the School of Regulation and Global Governance at the Australian National University. He can be reached at <benjamin.herscovitch@anu.edu.au>.

Victor A. Ferguson is a JSPS Postdoctoral Research Fellow in the Research Centre for Advanced Science and Technology at the University of Tokyo. He can be reached at <victor.ferguson@anu.edu.au>.

[1] See, for example, Jeffrey Wilson, "Australia Shows the World What Decoupling from China Looks Like," *Foreign Policy*, November 9, 2021, https://foreignpolicy.com/2021/11/09/australia-china-decoupling-trade-sanctions-coronavirus-geopolitics.

[2] "Australia's Exports to China Hit Record Highs as Barriers Ease," Reuters, May 3, 2023, https://www.reuters.com/markets/australias-exports-china-hit-record-highs-barriers-ease-2023-05-04.

[3] See James Laurenceson, "Australian Reliance on Chinese Exports an Economic Reality," East Asia Forum, February 22, 2023, https://www.eastasiaforum.org/2023/02/22/australian-reliance-on-chinese-exports-an-economic-reality; and James Laurenceson, "They Want Our Lithium, We Want Their Cars. No, We're Not Decoupling from China," *Sydney Morning Herald*, June 22, 2023, https://www.smh.com.au/world/asia/they-want-our-lithium-we-want-their-cars-no-we-re-not-decoupling-from-china-20230619-p5dhq6.html.

This chapter seeks to reconcile these competing narratives by examining whether and to what extent Australian policymakers and economic actors have embraced the logic of decoupling—the gradual unwinding of economic exchange with China—in recent years. As a medium-sized, open economy heavily reliant on international trade and investment, Australia has for several decades been an advocate for and beneficiary of a rules-based order where economic exchange is shaped by market forces rather than geopolitical considerations. Internationally, its policymakers have promoted liberalization, actively participated in regional and global economic institutions, and embraced the belief—popular in scholarly and policymaking circles in the post–Cold War era—that deep economic interdependence is a stabilizing force in world politics. Domestically, market-oriented structural reforms to enhance productivity and competitiveness since the 1980s have led to a focus on primary resource and service exports, a reliance on global supply chains for many essential goods, and a shrinking domestic manufacturing base.[4]

While such economic policies may have served Australia well for decades, the logic that underpins them has recently come under scrutiny. Unlike some other Western democracies where similar reassessments have in part been prompted by domestic political pressure from reactionary populist movements or other groups opposed to free trade, Australia's reassessment has been overwhelmingly driven by international factors. Among them are the resurgence of protectionism abroad, supply shocks during the Covid-19 pandemic, trade sanctions by China, and emerging expectations that Canberra will participate in Washington's "friendshoring" initiatives.[5] These trends have forced Australian policymakers to reconsider how they ought to balance the relative costs and benefits of deep economic engagement with China, economic interdependence, and the rules-based trading system. In a dramatic turnaround, Australia's minister for trade and tourism openly conceded in November 2022 that "it is no longer possible…to insulate our trade policy from geo-politics" and that emerging pressures require "diversifying not just who we trade with, but what we trade and how we trade," as well as "using effective industry policy."[6]

To what extent are those words translating into economic reality? In this chapter, we argue that any economic decoupling between Australia and

---

[4] Stephen Bell, *Ungoverning the Economy: The Political Economy of Australian Economic Policy* (Melbourne: Oxford University Press, 1997).

[5] Christopher Condon, Heejin Kim, and Sam Kim, "Yellen Touts 'Friend-shoring' as Global Supply Chain Fix," Bloomberg, July 18, 2022, https://www.bloomberg.com/news/articles/2022-07-18/yellen-touts-friend-shoring-as-fix-for-global-supply-chains.

[6] Don Farrell, "Trading Our Way to Greater Prosperity and Security," Australian Minister for Trade and Tourism and Special Minister of State, November 14, 2022, https://www.trademinister.gov.au/minister/don-farrell/speech/trading-our-way-greater-prosperity-and-security.

China has been limited and will likely remain so for the foreseeable future. While there has been a marked shift in Canberra's tone regarding the need for businesses to be sensitive to the benefits of diversification and a broader change in the government's willingness to conduct market interventions to advance national security objectives,[7] the deep complementarities between the two economies have meant that both policymakers and business leaders continue to see China as a vital economic opportunity. Prime Minister Anthony Albanese summarized this reality in May 2023 when he stated that "trade with China is worth more than the trade combined with the United States, Japan, and South Korea." He added that "we are working cooperatively wherever we can, we'll disagree where we must, but we are engaging in our national interests."[8] This suggests that the current government would prefer that the contours of Australia's economic interdependence with China—in the absence of a major political crisis or war—be closer to business as usual, albeit with some sensitive areas of trade and investment carved out.

The chapter proceeds in four additional sections. The first main section sketches a general picture of Australia's position in the global economy in the years leading up to the exogenous shocks driving the decoupling debate by detailing the structure of the country's foreign exchange in 2018 to provide a benchmark against which we can draw comparisons in future years. The following section investigates Australia's reassessment of its deepening economic interdependence with China and considers three drivers. The chapter then evaluates whether and to what extent this reassessment has manifested in shifts in government policy and economic activity in three domains, which we treat as separate case studies: trade, market access and investment screening, and industrial policy. The subsequent section synthesizes the findings from the case studies and evaluates the breadth and depth of any changes. The chapter concludes by considering the implications of our analysis for policy and debates about decoupling and the emergent notion of de-risking in Australia and the wider Indo-Pacific region.

Australia's Trade, Investment, and Industrial Policy Settings

Australia is a wealthy, industrialized country with the thirteenth-largest GDP (approximately US$1.5 trillion) and the eighteenth-highest GDP per

---

[7] Victor A. Ferguson, Darren J. Lim, and Benjamin Herscovitch, "Between Market and State: The Evolution of Australia's Economic Statecraft," *Pacific Review* (2023): 1–33.

[8] Anthony Albanese, "FiveAA Mornings with Matthew Pantelis," Prime Minister of Australia, May 15, 2023, https://www.pm.gov.au/media/fiveaa-mornings-matthew-pantelis.

capita (approximately US$60,000).[9] With trade accounting for roughly 40% of GDP since the late 1990s, the country's economic growth and tax earnings are dependent on reliable access to overseas markets. Australia has a service-intensive economy, with the service industry employing nearly 90% of workers and accounting for approximately 80% of GDP.[10] Despite this, merchandise trade dominates exports.

Trade

Merchandise exports accounted for approximately 89% of Australia's total exports and just over 50% of its total trade in 2021.[11] Australia is among the largest sources globally for minerals and energy, including iron ore, coal, natural gas, and lithium. In 2022, coal, iron ore, and natural gas alone accounted for approximately 60% of the total value of its goods exports. Service exports, which in 2021 accounted for some 11% of total exports, were dominated prior to the Covid-19 pandemic by education and tourism. As a net exporter of agricultural commodities, mining products, and energy, Australia's primary imports are services, manufactured goods, and refined liquid fuels.

Australia was an active participant in the construction of the post–World War II multilateral trading regime. Yet for several decades it remained a reluctant trade liberalizer, maintaining high tariff rates and eschewing reciprocal trade liberalization in a bid to develop domestic industry and protect local jobs.[12] The shift away from protectionism toward internationalizing the Australian economy began when the center-left Labor Party government unilaterally reduced all tariffs by 25% in 1973. Following Labor's re-election in 1983, the government embarked on a widespread program of economic liberalization, including privatizing large state-owned businesses, further reducing tariff rates, opening the economy to more foreign investment, and floating the Australian dollar. Such reforms were followed by decades of ongoing trade liberalization as Australia pursued a range of bilateral, regional, and multilateral free trade agreements (FTAs).[13]

---

[9] World Bank, World Bank Open Data, https://data.worldbank.org.

[10] Productivity Commission (Australia), "Things You Can't Drop on Your Feet: An Overview of Australia's Services Sector Productivity," 2, https://www.pc.gov.au/ongoing/productivity-insights/services/productivity-insights-2021-services.pdf.

[11] Department of Foreign Affairs and Trade (Australia), "Australia's Direction of Goods and Services Trade—Calendar Years from 1989 to Present," updated June 2023, https://www.dfat.gov.au/sites/default/files/australias-direction-of-goods-services-trade-calendar-years.xlsx.

[12] Ann Capling, *Australia and the Global Trade System: From Havana to Seattle* (Cambridge: Cambridge University Press, 2001).

[13] Jeffrey Wilson, "Adapting Australia to an Era of Geoeconomic Competition," Perth USAsia Centre, February 16, 2021, https://perthusasia.edu.au/our-work/geoeconomics-report.

Since 2000, Australia has inked bilateral FTAs with all of its largest trading partners except Taiwan, including China, Japan, South Korea, and the United States; been a strong supporter of trade liberalization led by the World Trade Organization; and actively participated in the construction of new regional FTAs, including the Comprehensive and Progressive Agreement for Trans-Pacific Partnership (CPTPP) and the Regional Comprehensive Economic Partnership (RCEP). This embrace of trade openness, together with an ongoing bipartisan liberal reform agenda for the domestic economy, has contributed to Australia's increasing reliance on overseas markets for many manufactured goods and seen the emergence of Asian economies—and especially China—as the primary destination for Australia's top exports.

On the back of surging demand for iron ore, coal, natural gas, and other Australian mineral and energy exports, China became Australia's largest two-way trading partner in 2007. China also eclipsed the United States to become Australia's largest source of imports and overtook Japan as Australia's biggest export destination in 2009. Simultaneously, as China's middle class grew, its tourists and students became the most lucrative sources of Australia's biggest service exports in the late 2000s and early 2010s. By the time Canberra and Beijing signed an FTA in 2015, China accounted for 27% of Australia's total exports, greater than the combined value of Australia's next three-largest export markets.[14] By 2018, Australia's trade interdependence with China had deepened further.[15] With trade accounting for 43% of Australia's GDP and China accounting for more than 25% of Australia's total trade, trade with China alone equated to approximately 11% of Australia's GDP. Although China and Hong Kong were among the top-five sources for five of Australia's top-ten imports (see **Table 1**), trade interdependence with China was most pronounced among the markets for Australian exports. Of Australia's top-ten exports, China and Hong Kong were among the top-five destinations for eight of them (see **Table 2**). Moreover, China was either the first or second destination for the top-five exports by value. This market concentration in China was especially acute in some cases. For instance, more than 81% of the value of Australia's iron ore exports (its second most valuable export in 2018) went to China, while China consumed more than 33% of Australia's largest service export (education).

---

[14] Department of Foreign Affairs and Trade (Australia), "Australia's Direction of Goods and Services Trade."

[15] We have selected 2018 as our baseline for evaluating the extent of decoupling because it is the final year before each of the drivers of Australia's reassessment come fully into operation and begin to meaningfully shape the decision-making of actors in Australian government and industry. This process is examined in detail in section three of this chapter.

TABLE 1 Top-ten imports by top-five sources and rest of world (ROW), 2018

Product	Country					
Tourism $45.6b	U.S. 17.3%	UK 9.1%	NZ 8.0%	Indonesia 7.7%	Japan 5.5%	ROW 52.4%
Refined petroleum $25.2b	Singapore 32.5%	ROK 24.3%	Japan 12.5%	China 8.2%	Malaysia 7.0%	ROW 15.5%
Passenger vehicles $22.4b	Japan 36.9%	Germany 13.1%	ROK 12.2%	Thailand 10.8%	U.S. 9.1%	ROW 17.9%
Transport* $18.5b	Singapore 11.1%	Germany 9.6%	Hong Kong 7.7%	Japan 5.8%	NZ 3.9%	ROW 61.9%
Telecom equipment $14.4b	China 59.2%	Vietnam 11.2%	U.S. 8.2%	Mexico 3.2%	Malaysia 2.7%	ROW 15.5%
Crude petroleum $13.7b	Malaysia 33.7%	UAE 14.4%	Indonesia 8.1%	Brunei 5.5%	Algeria 5.3%	ROW 9.2%
Business services** $13.4b	U.S. 23.6%	Singapore 11.6%	UK 11.6%	NZ 8.4%	Hong Kong 6.2%	ROW 38.6%
Commercial vehicles $10.7b	Thailand 51.7%	Japan 18.6%	U.S. 6.8%	Germany 5.7%	Spain 2.4%	ROW 15.8%
Computers $9.7b	China 66.9%	U.S. 7.5%	Malaysia 7.4%	Singapore 3.7%	Taiwan 2.3%	ROW 12.2%
Medicaments $7.2m	Germany 15.7%	U.S. 14.1%	Switzerland 9.7%	Ireland 7.5%	UK 7.1%	ROW 45.9%

SOURCE: Author calculations from the Department of Foreign Affairs and Trade (DFAT) (merchandise) and the Australian Bureau of Statistics (ABS) (services) at Standard International Trade Classification (SITC) 3-digit level.

NOTE: Dollar figures represent total value of exports to all markets in Australian dollars (A$). Percentages represent percentage of total value. Asterisk indicates that the ABS reports most service import data at the country level in an aggregated form (2-digit level). This figure includes "freight" (A$10.1 billion), "passenger (b)" (A$7.3 billion), "other" (A$8.8 million), and "postal and courier services (c)" (A$1.3 million). Double asterisk indicates that this figure is also presented in aggregated form (2-digit level) and includes "research and development services" ($2.2 million), "professional and management consulting services" ($7.4 billion), and "technical, trade-related, and other business services" ($5.7 billion).

TABLE 2   Top-ten exports by top-five destinations and ROW, 2018

Product	Country					
Coal $66.8b	Japan 28.4%	China 21.4%	India 16.4%	ROK 10.9%	Taiwan 7.7%	ROW 15.2%
Iron ore $63.3b	China 81.2%	Japan 8.1%	ROK 6.0%	Taiwan 2.2%	India 0.8%	ROW 1.7%
Natural gas $43.2b	Japan 44.2%	China 31.5%	ROK 10.6%	Singapore 6.3%	Taiwan 2.8%	ROW 4.6%
Education $35.2b	China 33.3%	India 13.0%	Nepal 6.1%	Malaysia 4.0%	Vietnam 3.8%	ROW 39.8%
Tourism $22.2b	China 18.5%	UK 10.3%	NZ 8.1%	U.S. 7.3%	Japan 4.6%	ROW 51.2%
Gold $19.1b	Hong Kong 36.5%	China 30.2%	UK 8.2%	Thailand 8.1%	Singapore 6.0%	ROW 11.0%
Bauxite/alumina $11.3b	China 11.3%	South Africa 8.1%	Mozambique 5.9%	NZ 3.5%	Norway 0.5%	ROW 70.7%
Beef $8.6b	Japan 26.2%	U.S. 20.3%	ROK 15.9%	China 15.0%	Indonesia 3.7%	ROW 19.1%
Crude petroleum $8.1b	Thailand 24.5%	Singapore 19.8%	Malaysia 11.9%	Indonesia 10.2%	ROK 9.8%	ROW 23.8%
Copper ores $6.1b	China 44.0%	Japan 28.6%	India 10.7%	ROK 7.5%	Philippines 4.4%	ROW 4.8%

SOURCE: Author calculations from DFAT (merchandise) and ABS (services) at SITC 3-digit level.

NOTE: Dollar figures represent total value of exports to all markets in A$. Percentages represent percentage of total value. Due to the way the ABS reports trade in services data, this figure for education does not capture students who continued to pay fees to Australian universities while studying remotely due to Covid-19 travel restrictions. Education exports to geographically remote students totaled $4 billion ($2.4 billion of which went to China) in 2022, compared with $837 million ($116 million of which went to China) in 2018.

Investment

Though Australia has been a net exporter of capital in recent years, it was a net importer for much of its modern history.[16] The most dominant sources of investment have traditionally been the United Kingdom and the United States. In the early 2000s, they accounted for more than 60% of the total value of foreign investment in Australia. Despite China's rapid industrialization from the late 1970s onward and its emergence as Australia's largest two-way trading partner in 2007, it was only in 2013–14 that the country emerged as Australia's top source of new foreign investment flows.[17] During the resources boom, Chinese investment primarily went into energy, metals, and agriculture, but it diversified over time to include other sectors like healthcare and commercial real estate. China remained Australia's top source of new direct investment between 2013–14 and 2015–16, but by 2017–18, it had fallen back behind the United States (see **Figure 1**). In 2018, 74 major investments were made by China-based actors, representing approximately US$6.2 billion.[18]

FIGURE 1   Flow of FDI in Australia by top-five source countries and ROW, 2017–18

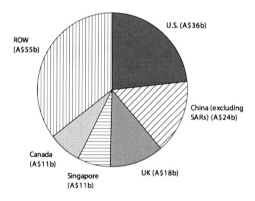

SOURCE: Foreign Investment Review Board (Australia), *Annual Report 2017–18* (Canberra, January 2019), https://foreigninvestment.gov.au/sites/firb.gov.au/files/2019/02/FIRB-2017-18-Annual-Report-final.pdf.

---

[16] See, generally, Productivity Commission (Australia), *Foreign Investment in Australia* (Canberra: Commonwealth of Australia, 2020), https://www.pc.gov.au/research/completed/foreign-investment/foreign-investment.pdf.

[17] Peter Drysdale, "A New Look at Chinese FDI in Australia," *China & World Economy* 19, no. 4 (2011): 54–73.

[18] See Figure 3 later in the chapter.

Notwithstanding a relative decline, the United States and the UK together still accounted for more than 45% of the value of total foreign investment stock in Australia in 2018, while China accounted for less than 2% (see **Figure 2**).[19] Of the top-ten investors that year, six were Western European or North American. Thus, Australia's economic interdependence remained geographically uneven. With the United States and Germany being the only North Atlantic economies among Australia's top-ten trading partners in 2018, its trade interdependencies were firmly centered on the economies of Asia. Meanwhile, North Atlantic economies continued to be Australia's largest sources of investment.

Industrial Policy

Australia's sustained shift to market-based approaches to economic management had significant consequences for domestic industry and import dependencies. With successive governments from the 1980s onward eschewing industrial policy and exposing domestic industry to the rigors of international markets, Australia's manufacturing capacity declined precipitously, while

FIGURE 2 Stock of investment in Australia by top-four partners, China, and ROW, 2018 (% of total)

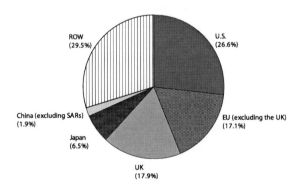

SOURCE: Author calculations from ABS.

---

[19] Perceptions of risk have not stemmed from China's overall importance as a source of capital to fund Australia's current account deficit. Rather, as discussed below, concerns revolve around potential security externalities arising from direct investment in specific companies and assets.

dependence on foreign markets for consumer goods, advanced manufactured goods, and essential material inputs increased.[20] Australian manufacturing peaked in the 1960s, when it accounted for approximately 30% of both GDP and employment.[21] By 2020, it had declined to less than 10% of the Australian economy, and its share of GDP has continued to fall in a pattern broadly similar to other wealthy, industrialized economies that are dominated by the services sector.[22]

Australia's deepening dependence on foreign markets for automobiles and refined petroleum is emblematic of these shifts. In the postwar period, successive Australian governments provided wide-ranging assistance for the domestic automobile industry for many decades, including tariffs, quotas, purchasing arrangements, and budgetary support. From the 1980s onward, however, those policy measures were progressively unwound. Although Australia still produced more than 200,000 automobiles annually in 2013, the three remaining automobile manufacturers ceased operations in 2016–17.[23] With declining state support and increasing competition from carmakers in Asia and Latin America, Australia went from meeting the majority of domestic demand for automobiles through local production in the 1980s to being entirely dependent on imports by the 2020s.[24]

Similar dynamics lie behind a deepening dependence on imported liquid fuels. As recently as the early 2000s, Australia had eight oil refineries capable of meeting nearly all of its petroleum demand. However, the growth of mega-refineries in the Middle East and Asia progressively made Australia's refining industry less competitive, with only two remaining in operation by 2022.[25] Among International Energy Agency member countries, Australia continues

---

[20] Stephen Bell, *Australian Manufacturing and the State: The Politics of Industry Policy in the Post-War Era* (Cambridge: Cambridge University Press, 1993); and *The Australian Manufacturing Industry* (Canberra: Commonwealth of Australia, 2022), https://www.aph.gov.au/Parliamentary_Business/Committees/Senate/Economics/REFSManufacturing/Report.

[21] Productivity Commission (Australia), *Australia's Automotive Manufacturing Industry* (Canberra: Commonwealth of Australia, 2014), 4, https://www.pc.gov.au/inquiries/completed/automotive/report/automotive.pdf.

[22] Australia, however, has maintained robust resource industries, especially during times of high commodity prices. Mining has been the largest sector of the Australian economy by share of total GDP in recent years, although it represents a small share of total employment (around 2%).

[23] Department of Industry, Innovation and Science (Australia), "Australian Automotive Industry: Transition Following the End of Australian Motor Vehicle Production," January 2020, 7, https://www.industry.gov.au/sites/default/files/2022-08/australian-automotive-industry-transition-following-the-end-of-australian-motor-vehicle-production.pdf.

[24] Productivity Commission (Australia), *Australia's Automotive Manufacturing Industry*, 8.

[25] Gareth Hutchens, "Australia Loses Another Oil Refinery, Leaving Our Fuel Supply Vulnerable to Regional Crises," ABC News (Australia), February 10, 2021, https://www.abc.net.au/news/2021-02-11/australia-loses-another-oil-refinery-risking-fuel-supply/13139648.

to be the only oil importer that does not maintain the required 90-day reserve, with only 61 days in stock as of February 2023.[26]

Australia's Reassessment of Economic Interdependence with China

Drivers

As outlined in the previous section, between the 1970s and the mid-2010s, the Australian economy became one of the most open in the world. Policymakers believed that economic openness and deep interdependence with the outside world were central to the country's prosperity,[27] as well as a stabilizing force in international politics. China occupies a central place in this narrative. Despite growing reliance on the Chinese market,[28] few in Canberra entertained the notion that this entailed meaningful risk, let alone that it might need to be managed via diversification or other initiatives. Instead, leaders in government and industry maintained that the trading relationship could continue to flourish unrestricted and remained sanguine that the mutual benefits of "hot economics" would insulate the relationship with China from any "cold politics" stemming from occasional political and foreign policy disagreements due to the two countries' divergent values, strategic preferences, and political systems.[29]

In November 2014, President Xi Jinping addressed the Australian parliament, celebrating the completion of a wide-ranging FTA that would be signed the following year and declaring that the "relationship [had] reached a new and higher starting point."[30] Yet, while economic exchange continued to expand in the following years, at least three drivers prompted a gradual transformation in the Australian government's assessment of the costs and benefits that come from relatively unmanaged economic interdependence: (1) perceptions of China's rising assertiveness and influence, both in world

---

[26] International Energy Agency, "Oil Stocks of IEA Countries," https://www.iea.org/data-and-statistics/data-tools/oil-stocks-of-iea-countries.

[27] Few would disagree that openness was indeed central to Australia's prosperity in recent decades. See Adam Triggs and Peter Drysdale, "Complex Trade-offs: Economic Openness and Security in Australia," in *Navigating Prosperity and Security in East Asia*, ed. Shiro Armstrong, Tom Westland, and Adam Triggs (Canberra: Australian National University Press, 2023).

[28] See, for example, Australian Trade and Investment Commission (Austrade), "How Dependent Are Australian Exports on China?" February 2015.

[29] Victor Ferguson and Darren J. Lim, "Economic Power and Vulnerability in Sino-Australian Relations," in *China Story Yearbook: Crisis*, ed. Jane Golley, Linda Jaivin, and Sharon Strange (Canberra: Australian National University Press, 2021).

[30] Xi Jinping, "Address by the President of the People's Republic of China," Parliament of Australia, November 17, 2014, https://parlinfo.aph.gov.au/parlInfo/search/display/display.w3p;query=Id:%22chamber/hansardr/35c9c2cf-9347-4a82-be89-20df5f76529b/0005%22.

politics and especially within Australia, (2) China's imposition of trade restrictions on Australian exports following a political dispute in early 2020, and (3) specific supply chain vulnerabilities identified during the Covid-19 pandemic.

Perceptions of Chinese Assertiveness and Influence

Beginning in the early 2010s, a growing number of researchers and commentators began voicing concerns that China was becoming more assertive as its power grew and its interests expanded.[31] This narrative was especially prevalent in discussions of China's actions in the South China Sea,[32] but was also seen in other areas of Chinese foreign policy, including the country's use of economic statecraft and approach to bilateral diplomacy.[33] Such discussion occurred against the backdrop of the Obama administration's "rebalance to Asia" and the gradual shift in the United States' security focus away from transnational terrorism and the Middle East toward competition with China. These developments fed into Australia's own debate about how to navigate its relationship with China.[34] While policymakers expressed concern about the country's international behavior, such as China's rejection of the 2016 arbitral tribunal award regarding its maritime claims in the South China Sea,[35] the major inflection point was driven by events at home.

Beginning in 2017, the tone of Australia's conversation about China's actions and intentions began to change. This was especially true after a national scandal in which a high-profile senator allegedly engaged in inappropriate dealings with Chinese and Chinese-Australian donors and businesspeople, prompting broader investigations and a vigorous debate about the Chinese Communist Party's influence in Australian politics.[36] These developments ultimately led the government to introduce a suite of new laws

---

[31] See, for example, Michael D. Swaine, "Perceptions of an Assertive China," *China Leadership Monitor*, 2010; and Alastair Iain Johnston, "How New and Assertive Is China's New Assertiveness?" *International Security* 37, no. 4 (2013): 7–48.

[32] Andrew Chubb, "PRC Assertiveness in the South China Sea: Measuring Continuity and Change, 1970–2015," *International Security* 45, no. 3 (2021): 79–121.

[33] See, for example, Thomas J. Christensen, "The Advantages of an Assertive China: Responding to Beijing's Abrasive Diplomacy," *Foreign Affairs*, March/April 2011; and Gregory T. Chin, "China's Bold Economic Statecraft," *Current History* 114, no. 773 (2015): 217–23.

[34] On the history of this debate in the 2000s, see James Curran, *Australia's China Odyssey: From Euphoria to Fear* (Randwick: University of New South Wales Press, 2022).

[35] "Australia Supports Peaceful Dispute Resolution in the South China Sea," Department of Foreign Affairs and Trade (Australia), Press Release, July 12, 2016, https://www.dfat.gov.au/news/news/Pages/australia-supports-peaceful-dispute-resolution-in-the-south-china-sea.

[36] Jamie Smyth, "Australian MP Quits in Chinese Influence Scandal," *Financial Times*, December 12, 2017, https://www.ft.com/content/7ac14e70-ded8-11e7-a8a4-0a1e63a52f9c; and Andrew Chubb, "The Securitization of 'Chinese Influence' in Australia," *Journal of Contemporary China* 32, no. 139 (2023): 17–34.

targeting foreign interference in June 2018. This marked the beginning of a series of policy initiatives through which Canberra would seek to "reset" the terms of its engagement with Beijing.[37] Though these initial events did not yet prompt the government—let alone businesses—to reassess economic relations with China, they did draw attention to potential security risks stemming from different types of engagement.

The 2020 Sanctions Campaign

In 2018 the Australian government effectively banned Huawei from its 5G network, and in 2019 it issued statements of concern regarding the Hong Kong authorities' suppression of protests and the treatment of Uighur Muslims in Xinjiang.[38] However, even as Beijing complained bitterly about these decisions and political and diplomatic relations rapidly deteriorated, trade continued to go from strength to strength.[39] That changed when in April 2020 the Australian government called for an international inquiry into the origins of Covid-19 and for giving World Health Organization officials new powers akin to those of "weapons inspectors."[40] In response, the Chinese government began introducing a wide range of restrictions on Australian exports in what officials in Canberra deemed to be a campaign of "economic coercion."

The restrictions on Australian exports came in a variety of different forms. China's approach to implementing and enforcing economic sanctions differs from that of Western actors like the United States and the European Union. Rather than announcing sanctions publicly and enshrining them in legal instruments, the Chinese government often relies on informal mechanisms—blocking trade by weaponizing health, safety, and customs laws or creating unofficial blacklists where companies understand that commerce should not be pursued with target countries—while publicly denying that

---

[37] John Garnaut, "Australia's China Reset," *Monthly*, August 1, 2018, https://www.themonthly.com.au/issue/2018/august/1533045600/john-garnaut/australia-s-china-reset.

[38] Eryk Bagshaw, "China's Ambassador Expects Australian Relations to 'Return to Normal' after 'Mixed Year,'" *Sydney Morning Herald*, December 19, 2019, https://www.smh.com.au/politics/federal/china-s-ambassador-expects-australian-relations-to-return-to-normal-after-mixed-year-20191219-p53lir.html.

[39] There were several incidents in the years leading up to 2020 where irregular, if minor and short-lived, trade disruptions were reported and alleged to be linked to political disagreements between Beijing and Canberra (dairy in 2016, beef in 2017, and wine and coal in 2019). However, we are not aware of any evidence that these experiences prompted actors in Australia's government or industry to seriously reconsider the prevailing approach to economic exchange with China.

[40] Eryk Bagshaw, "'Australia Brutus to China's Caesar': Chinese Embassy Explains Hurt," *Sydney Morning Herald*, August 26, 2020, https://www.smh.com.au/world/asia/australia-brutus-to-china-s-caesar-20200825-p55p84.html.

sanctions are being imposed.[41] The campaign against Australia was broader than previous episodes involving other countries but otherwise followed a familiar playbook. Beijing targeted products that were relatively substitutable for China so that costs would fall asymmetrically on the Australian side. At least nine industries were affected within the first year of the campaign. Barley and wine were hit with anti-dumping tariffs; beef, timber, and lobster were blocked due to phytosanitary and labeling concerns; coal and cotton were blacklisted; and animal feed exporters were refused export-license renewals. In addition, Beijing issued travel warnings, which might have affected tourism and education had the pandemic not already closed international borders.[42] Importantly, Australia's lucrative iron ore exports were left untouched, suggesting a limit to how much pain Beijing was willing to endure to make its point.[43]

The sanctions campaign was a major turning point for Australia's assessment of its economic relationship with China and reverberated not only with political leaders and the policy community but also with the wider Australian public. It provided concrete evidence that the trade links underpinning decades of economic prosperity could also be a source of coercive vulnerability. Canberra framed the dispute as evidence of Beijing's "bullying," and public attitudes toward China, already souring, hit record polling lows.[44] Despite misgivings in some business quarters about Australia's handling of bilateral ties, the Australian corporate sector also took a broadly dim view of China's campaign. As Australia's leading financial publication opined in June 2022, China should end its "'tremble and obey' economic coercion that Australia has been singled out for."[45] In addition to driving a broader reassessment of the costs and benefits of economic interdependence, the experience prompted several economic policy responses from the government and led some in the business community to revisit their assumptions about the balance of opportunities and risks in the Chinese market.

---

[41] Darren J. Lim and Victor A. Ferguson, "Informal Economic Sanctions: The Political Economy of Chinese Coercion during the THAAD Dispute," *Review of International Political Economy* 29, no. 5 (2022): 1525–48.

[42] Victor A. Ferguson, Scott Waldron, and Darren J. Lim, "Market Adjustments to Import Sanctions: Lessons from Chinese Restrictions on Australian Trade, 2020–21," *Review of International Political Economy* 30, no. 4 (2023): 1255–81.

[43] While China took approximately 83% of Australian iron ore exports in 2020, it relied on Australia for 66% of its supply, such that the significant costs of disruption would fall more evenly across both sides.

[44] Stephen Dziedzic, "Australians' Trust in China Has Fallen to Record Low, Latest Lowy Institute Annual Poll Reveals," ABC News (Australia), June 22, 2021, https://www.abc.net.au/news/2021-06-22/trust-china-fallen-record-lows-lowy-institute-annual-poll-/100232258.

[45] "China Reset Should End Economic Coercion," *Australian Financial Review*, June 2, 2022, https://www.afr.com/policy/foreign-affairs/china-reset-should-end-economic-coercion-20220531-p5aq21.

Pandemic-Era Supply Shocks

The third driver was only indirectly related to China. During the early months of the Covid-19 pandemic, as the world went into lockdown, Australia briefly experienced some of the downsides of offshoring manufacturing and relying on "just-in-time" supply chains. To take one example, at the time the pandemic broke out, Australia had only one medical mask manufacturing company, with just seventeen staff members and two machines that relied entirely on foreign raw materials for production.[46] The interruption of sea and air logistics, the closure of production facilities (especially factories in China), and overseas export restrictions (e.g., India restricting some pharmaceutical component exports) led to key shortages, notably in medical and pharmaceutical products, and delays in vaccine access.

The pandemic was the first time an Australian government had to grapple with meaningful supply shocks in decades. Indeed, the country had emerged relatively unscathed from other major supply disruptions in the postwar period. The 1973 oil crisis, for example, had minimal impact because Australia at that point did not rely heavily on foreign oil.[47] The Covid-19 pandemic spurred the government to commission a review into the country's potential vulnerability to global supply chain disruptions for essential goods and services.[48] The review found that less than 5% of imports should be deemed "vulnerable," many of which are not considered essential (such as Christmas lights, toys, and textiles) or are substitutable. The authors found that the main supply chain risks lie in the use of vulnerable chemical imports in the health (human medicine manufacturing), energy (petrol and coal product refining), and water treatment industries.[49]

A few months after the commission issued its findings, the vulnerability of the energy supply chain was illustrated when Australia experienced shortages of a diesel fuel additive, AdBlue, which is made from urea and controls harmful emissions in diesel engines. Australia had offshored most domestic urea manufacturing in recent decades, with imports of the chemical overwhelmingly sourced from China. In late 2021, China reduced urea (also used in fertilizer) exports for domestic reasons. Australian importers were

---

[46] Grace Tobin, "Coronavirus Fires Up Production at Australia's Only Medical Mask Factory," ABC News (Australia), March 26, 2020, https://www.abc.net.au/news/2020-03-27/inside-australias-only-medical-mask-factory/12093864.

[47] Michael Wesley, *Power Plays: Energy and Australia's Security* (Canberra: Australian Strategic Policy Institute [ASPI], 2007), https://www.aspi.org.au/report/power-plays-energy-and-australias-security.

[48] "Productivity Commission Review into Australia's Supply Chain Stability," Department of the Treasury (Australia), Press Release, February 19, 2021, https://ministers.treasury.gov.au/ministers/josh-frydenberg-2018/media-releases/productivity-commission-review-australias-supply.

[49] Productivity Commission (Australia), *Vulnerable Supply Chains* (Canberra: Commonwealth of Australia, 2021), https://www.pc.gov.au/inquiries/completed/supply-chains/report.

caught off guard, and rising prices and supply shortages threatened the country's domestic freight and logistics industries, which are critical for the food industry.[50] In the wake of pandemic-related shortages, the realization that a shortage of a particular fuel additive could result in empty supermarket shelves had the impact of amplifying calls for a comprehensive reassessment of Australia's reliance on foreign markets in critical sectors of the economy.

The following sections explore how the three drivers of Australia's reassessment of economic interdependence with China have affected government policy and economic activity in three domains: trade, market access and investment screening, and industrial policy and sovereign capability.

Trade

Government Policy

It was not until 2020, with the dual shocks of China's economic sanctions campaign and pandemic-induced supply shortages, that Australia's reassessment of interdependence came to include what and how the country exported and imported. Prior to that, the benefits to the Australian economy were simply too great, and the belief, or hope, was that trade relations with China could be kept separate from political or security differences. The sanctions campaign highlighted that under certain conditions—namely, when Beijing deemed that the need to send a political signal outweighed the potential economic and reputational costs of disrupting trade—high export dependence gave Beijing leverage to signal its displeasure by imposing commercial pain. As summarized by then-treasurer Josh Frydenberg in a September 2021 speech, roughly fifteen months into the trade sanctions campaign:

> Many have worked hard to access the lucrative Chinese market. This has brought great benefits to them and to Australia overall. And they should continue to pursue these opportunities where they can. But going forward, businesses also need to be aware that the world has changed. And that this creates greater uncertainty and risk. In this respect, they should always be looking to diversify their markets, and not overly rely on any one country. Essentially adopting a "China plus" strategy.... The world we operate in has fundamentally changed.... This will see our economic and security interests increasingly overlap.[51]

---

[50] Joanna Prendergast and Lucinda Jose, "AdBlue Supply Fears as Clock Ticks on Australian Production," ABC News (Australia), July 3, 2022, https://www.abc.net.au/news/2022-07-04/adblue-fears-with-australian-manufacturing-to-cease/101197454.

[51] Josh Frydenberg, "Building Resilience and the Return of Strategic Competition" (speech, Melbourne, September 6, 2021), https://ministers.treasury.gov.au/ministers/josh-frydenberg-2018/speeches/building-resilience-and-return-strategic-competition.

This speech was notable for its explicit recognition of the overlap between economic and security interests and the emerging logic of "China plus" trade diversification.

As a policy agenda, promoting diversification and encouraging Australian companies to rely less on China took two main forms. First, policymakers accelerated negotiations to secure access for industries affected by the sanctions, resulting in new or improved access to 46 agricultural and fisheries export markets. They also sped up the negotiation of new FTAs with India, the UK, and the EU.[52] Second, policymakers established programs to support exporters looking to grow existing or develop new markets. To cite one example, the A$85.9 million Agri-Business Expansion Initiative, launched in December 2020, enhanced existing mechanisms for exporters to receive tailored advice, training opportunities, and additional assistance from short-term agricultural counselors who are posted in foreign missions to cultivate connections in local markets.[53]

More broadly, the China-plus concept can be observed in public statements from political leaders and officials regarding the bilateral economic relationship. Previously, even where bilateral political relations were strained, political leaders never publicly contemplated diversification. As recently as 2015, a report from the Australian Trade and Investment Commission argued that while Australian dependence on China was real, the risks were low.[54] By contrast, in February 2021 the Joint Standing Committee on Trade and Investment Growth explicitly recommended "that the Australian government develop and release a plan for trade diversification," which included "enhanced diplomatic capability to identify and secure new supply chains and markets."[55] This recommendation was endorsed by the government, albeit with the recognition that "the private sector remains the ultimate decision-maker."[56] Diversification was also debated during the 2022 federal election campaign, with the opposition Labor Party launching a "trade diversification plan" and criticizing the government for not adequately addressing dependence on

---

[52] Department of Agriculture, Fisheries and Forestry (Australia), "Agricultural Export Markets Continue to Diversify," August 2022, https://www.agriculture.gov.au/sites/default/files/documents/august-2022-agricultural-export-markets-continue-diversify.pdf.

[53] See Ferguson, Lim, and Herscovitch, "Between Market and State."

[54] Austrade, "How Dependent Are Australian Exports on China?"

[55] Parliament of Australia, *Pivot: Diversifying Australia's Trade and Investment Profile* (Canberra: Commonwealth of Australia, 2021), 69, https://www.aph.gov.au/About_Parliament/House_of_Representatives/About_the_House_News/Media_Releases/~/link.aspx?_id=39BD8633ECBD4509B27FFBED27BEDDBD&_z=z.

[56] Australian Government, "Australian Government Response to the Joint Standing Committee on Trade and Investment Growth Report: Pivot: Diversifying Australia's Trade and Investment Profile," July 2021, 3, https://www.dfat.gov.au/sites/default/files/government-response-joint-standing-committee-trade-investment-growth-report.pdf.

China. Since Labor has become the ruling party, diversification has been described as the "first principle" of its trade policy.⁵⁷

Notwithstanding this focus, after taking office in May 2022 the Labor government achieved modest but consistent success over the next year in reversing the decline in relations with Beijing. Ministers resumed meetings in June 2022, and, concurrent with a gradual thaw in political ties, reports in the first half of 2023 indicated that several Australian products—coal, copper, cotton, and timber—were again passing through Chinese customs.⁵⁸ Beijing also agreed in August 2023 to remove its anti-dumping duties on Australian barley in exchange for Canberra discontinuing its WTO complaint regarding the restrictions.⁵⁹

Following a virtual meeting in February 2023, Australia's trade minister, Don Farrell, reported his Chinese counterpart saying that the "freeze is over and we're moving to a warm spring."⁶⁰ Yet even as this process was unfolding, Labor ministers maintained a consistent focus on diversification. Ahead of a historic meeting with her counterpart in Beijing, Foreign Minister Penny Wong said in December 2022 that "Australian business has done an outstanding job in diversifying its markets, and it's always going to be in our interest to continue to prioritize that diversification."⁶¹ In April 2023, also ahead of a trip to Beijing, Trade Minister Farrell described the government's plan as "let's solve our problems with China, but also let's diversify our trading relationships."⁶² This consistent public messaging on diversification at a time of cautious optimism regarding bilateral ties with China is indicative of a

---

[57] Madeleine King, "Labor Launches Trade Diversification Plan," May 5, 2022, https://madeleineking.com.au/news/portfolio-releases/labor-launches-trade-diversification-plan.

[58] Michael Smith and Peter Ker, "China Resumes Australian Coal Imports: Reports," *Australian Financial Review*, February 2, 2023, https://www.afr.com/world/asia/china-resumes-australian-coal-imports-reports-20230202-p5chio; Lewis Jackson, Siyi Liu, and Melanie Burton, "Australia Exports First Copper to China since 2020, Industry Hopes End to Ban Near," Reuters, May 10, 2023, https://www.reuters.com/markets/commodities/chinese-buyers-anticipate-end-soft-ban-australian-copper-2023-05-10; Lewis Jackson and Dominique Patton, "Australian Cotton Clears Chinese Customs on Bets Sanctions Will End," Reuters, February 21, 2023, https://www.reuters.com/markets/commodities/australian-cotton-clears-chinese-customs-bets-sanctions-will-end-2023-02-21; and Lewis Jackson, "China to Resume Australian Timber Imports, Talks Under Way for PM Visit," Reuters, May 18, 2023, https://www.reuters.com/markets/commodities/china-resume-australian-timber-imports-talks-under-way-pm-visit-2023-05-18.

[59] Penny Wong, "Step Forward to Resolve Barley Dispute with China," Australian Minister for Foreign Affairs, Press Release, April 11, 2023, https://www.foreignminister.gov.au/minister/penny-wong/media-release/step-forward-resolve-barley-dispute-china.

[60] Don Farrell, "Interview with Patricia Karvelas, ABC Radio National," February 24, 2023, available at https://www.trademinister.gov.au/minister/don-farrell/transcript/interview-patricia-karvelas-abc-radio-national.

[61] Andrew Tillett and Michael Smith, "Wong Warns of 'Hard Issues' amid Signs of Trade Draw," *Australian Financial Review*, December 20, 2022, https://www.afr.com/politics/federal/hard-issues-with-china-will-take-time-to-resolve-wong-20221220-p5c7o7.

[62] Daniel Hurst, "Australia's Trade Minister Hopeful China Bans Will End but Warns against Putting 'All Our Eggs in One Basket,'" *Guardian*, April 13, 2023, https://www.theguardian.com/australia-news/2023/apr/13/australia-trade-minister-don-farrell-interview-china-bans-exports-tariffs.

Economic Activity

Despite China's sanctions and Australia's shifting policy, the everyday trading relationship remained relatively robust. Whereas China was the destination for more than 31% of Australia's total goods and services exports in 2018, this had decreased to less than 28% in 2022.[63] In terms of Australia's top-ten exports in 2018, China remained the first- or second-largest export destination for six of them in 2022 (see **Table 3**). The major shifts between 2018 and 2022 concerned coal, copper, and tourism. China's share of coal and copper exports declined from 21.4% to 0% and 44% to 0.9%, respectively, due to trade barriers, while tourism decreased from 18.5% to 1.5% due to Covid-19 travel restrictions. Apart from these exports, China's share actually increased for other products, including beef, which had faced restrictions in the Chinese market.[64] Looking at specific industries gives a more accurate sense of where any shifts in the structure of trade are occurring.

Actors in industries affected by sanctions (whether partially like beef or fully like coal) pursued a variety of strategies, depending on the characteristics of their products and the structure of the markets in which they were traded. These included redirecting trade to other markets, circumventing sanctions via gray trade, or, where possible, shifting into the production of alternative products.[65] With the exception of beef, trade with China decreased dramatically for most sanctioned products. Price movements in global commodity markets saw the value of total trade for some sanctioned products increase in 2022, mostly notably coal and barley. But even after redirection to third markets, many industries traded at lower volumes than they would have had China been open (see **Table 4**).[66]

Though industries are now alert to the potential political risks of export concentration, it is unclear whether shifts away from the Chinese market

---

[63] Due predominantly to the steep rises in the price of iron ore during the peak of the sanctions campaign, the value of Australia's trade with China actually increased in 2021 (to 36.4% of total exports), obscuring the fact that large volumes of trade in some products had decreased significantly.

[64] In 2022, Australia's exports of tourism ($7 billion) and copper ore ($7.5 billion) fell, whereas wheat ($14.5 billion) and crude minerals ($12.2 billion) rose. China was the top destination for both wheat and crude minerals (20.4% and 96.7%, respectively).

[65] Ferguson, Waldron, and Lim, "Market Adjustments to Import Sanctions."

[66] Discrepancies between value and volume reflect several trends, including how effectively exporters were able to redirect to third markets, shifting global commodity prices, overall supply levels, and lost premiums. See Mike Adams and Ron Wickes, "Standing Up to Chinese Economic Coercion: Is Australia a Model of Economic Resilience?" University of Adelaide, Institute for International Trade, Working Paper, no. 13, June 13, 2023, https://iit.adelaide.edu.au/news/list/2023/05/17/standing-up-to-chinese-economic-coercion-is-australia-a-model-of-economic.

TABLE 3 Top-ten exports (2018) by top-four destinations, China, and ROW, 2022

Product	Country					
Coal $142.3b	Japan 40.1%	India 16.2%	ROK 12.1%	Taiwan 9.6%	China 0.0%	ROW 22.0%
Iron ore $124.1b	China 83.4%	Japan 6.9%	ROK 5.6%	Taiwan 1.9%	Vietnam 1.0%	ROW 1.2%
Natural gas $90.3b	Japan 38.9%	China 20.6%	ROK 14.4%	Singapore 10.1%	Taiwan 9.9%	ROW 6.1%
Education $26.5b*	China 22.4%	India 16.6%	Nepal 9.7%	Vietnam 4.4%	Indonesia 3.2%	ROW 43.7%
Tourism $7.0b	NZ 20.1%	UK 11.9%	U.S. 8.9%	Singapore 8.4%	China 1.5%	ROW 49.2%
Gold $23.5b	China 30.8%	Hong Kong 21.2%	Singapore 12.4%	Switzerland 9.2%	India 6.5%	ROW 19.9%
Bauxite/alumina $9.8b	China 16.6%	Bahrain 15.2%	UAE 11.7%	South Africa 7.1%	Qatar 6.9%	ROW 42.5%
Beef $10.2b	China 20.2%	Japan 19.6%	ROK 18.0%	U.S. 16.9%	Indonesia 3.8%	ROW 21.5%
Crude petroleum $10.1b	Singapore 28.0%	ROK 7.3%	Indonesia 6.9%	Malaysia 6.0%	China 1.0%	ROW 49.2%
Copper ores $7.5b	ROK 17.4%	India 7.3%	Finland 2.8%	Spain 1.2%	China 0.9%	ROW 70.4%

SOURCE: Author calculations from DFAT (merchandise) and ABS (services) at SITC 3-digit level.

NOTE: Dollar figures represent total value of exports to all markets in A$. Percentages represent percentage of total value.

will endure as barriers are removed.[67] The easing of China's restrictions in early 2023 was widely welcomed by industry leaders, who were "delighted"—as a representative from the timber sector put it—to have regained access to a market that offers scale and premium pricing.[68] Representatives from

---

[67] After all, temporarily redirecting trade to third markets while locked out of one market is not a reliable indicator of genuine diversification. See Laurenceson, "Australian Reliance on Chinese Exports an Economic Reality."

[68] Scale is a consideration for cotton, barley, lobster, timber, and wine. Premium pricing is especially relevant for barley, beef, and wine. See Ferguson, Waldron, and Lim, "Market Adjustments to Import Sanctions."

TABLE 4 Value and volume of nine Australian exports sanctioned by Beijing to China and ROW, 2018 and 2022

Product	China		ROW	
	2018	2022	2018	2022
Beef	$970.3 (15.0%) 175.7 kg	$1,447.3 (20.2%) 179.0 kg	$5,504.4 (85.0%) 1,001.1 kg	$5,703.3 (79.8%) 751.8 kg
Lobster	$453.1 (80.6%) 7.7 kg	$0.366 (0.2%) 0.009 kg	$109.1 (19.4%) 2.2 kg	$217.4 (99.8%) 5.8 kg
Barley	$1,054.4 (75.6%) 4,708.5 kg	$0 (0%) 0 kg	$339.6 (24.4%) 1,414.8 kg	$2,322.9 (100%) 8,002.4 kg
Forages	$75.8 (18.6%) 286.2 kg	$56.4 (9.9%) 158.6 kg	$332.5 (21.4%) 1,106.0 kg	$514.2 (91.1%) 1,442.0 kg
Wine	$676.7 (40.6%) 117.5 lt	$4.7 (9.5%) 0.7 lt	$992 (59.4%) 252.1 lt	$1,039.8 (99.5%) 223.1 lt
Timber logs	$446.7 (93.2%) 4,016.8 kg	$0 (0%) 0 kg	$32.7 (6.8%) 281.3 kg	$79.6 (100%) 754.6 kg
Cotton	$223.6 (12.2%) 101.1 kg	$73.8 (2.4%) 29.1 kg	$1,605.9 (87.8%) 796.3 kg	$2,946.8 (97.6%) 1,086.9 kg
Copper ores	$1,990.4 (44.4%) 1,237.7 kg	$0 (0%)* 0 kg	$2,490.4 (55.6%) 834.9 kg	$4,936.3 (100%) 1,591.7 kg
Coal	$10,590.8 (21.3%) 89,322.5 kg	$0 (0%) 0 kg	$39,140.1 (78.7%) 297,494.9 kg	$98,238.2 (100%) 339,192.2 kg

SOURCE: Author calculations from UN Comtrade. Dollar figures represent U.S. dollars in millions. Percentages represent percentage of total value. Volume figures represent net million kilograms/liters, with the exception of timber which represents gross million kilograms.

NOTE: We note the discrepancy between ABS (Table 3) and UN Comtrade data on copper ores and concentrates.

several industries emphasized that while they are looking to increase exports to new markets, they are simultaneously eager to return to China at similar levels as prior to the dispute.[69] As one beef industry expert had quipped earlier, "Tell business to diversify? It is just naive. We can't just give

---

[69] See, for example, Glenda Korporaal, "Meat Industry Primed for New China Talks," *Australian*, December 21, 2022, https://www.theaustralian.com.au/business/economics/how-will-china-reengage-with-the-world-after-three-years-of-covid-shutdown/news-story/e204cdf819a258df000ea55090475c97; Matt Brann, "China the 'Natural Home' for Australian Cotton, but How Long Will Industry Have to Wait for Trade to Resume?" ABC News (Australia), August 19, 2022, https://www.abc.net.au/news/2022-08-20/china-the-natural-home-for-australian-cotton-how-long-to-wait/101349688; and Michael Smith, "China Moves to Wind Back Aussie Beef and Timber Trade Sanctions," *Australian Financial Review*, February 13, 2023, https://www.afr.com/world/asia/china-moves-to-wind-back-aussie-beef-and-timber-trade-sanctions-20230213-p5ck60.

up premium."[70] Some exporters in the industries that suffered most due to limited alternatives—such as wine and lobster—appeared somewhat more cautious about a return to pre-sanction trade levels,[71] but the degree of hesitancy appears to vary.[72] Other sectors might look for a middle ground. As one barley farmer put it, "We'll make a gradual increase, but probably won't go back to the levels we were [at] before."[73]

Beyond the sanctioned industries, it is difficult to detect significant shifts away from China in Australia's major exports. In fact, Australia's export dependence on the Chinese market deepened in some cases. For example, not only did the absolute value of iron ore exports to China more than double between 2018 and 2022—driven by surging prices—but China also increased its percentage share of Australia's total exports. Aside from small-scale examples like Australia's replacement of China as a source of the fuel additive urea, there is little evidence of meaningful shifts away from reliance on China as a source of major imports. Indeed, China's share of the total value of Australian goods and services imports increased from 19% in 2018 to 22% in 2022.[74]

Market Access and Foreign Investment

Market Access

Australia's restrictions on market access for Chinese firms have focused on information and communications technology (ICT) companies. Although Canberra placed narrow limits on market access for select Chinese technology companies in 2023, these restrictions affected only a small number of government customers. Such limited restrictions contrast with two earlier decisions that dramatically curtailed the access of Chinese ICT companies to the Australian market. Based on advice from the Australian Security Intelligence Organisation—Australia's domestic security and intelligence agency—the center-left Labor government in 2011 determined that it would not accept any bids from Huawei for contracts for Australia's A$38 billion

---

[70] Richard McGregor, "Chinese Coercion, Australian Resilience," Lowy Institute, October 20, 2022, https://www.lowyinstitute.org/publications/chinese-coercion-australian-resilience.

[71] See, for example, Glenda Korporaal, "Exporters Wary on China," *Australian*, December 22, 2022.

[72] Some wine exporters, for example, intend to "hit the ground running" if barriers are removed. See Eden Hynninen, Kellie Hollingworth, and Emile Pavlich, "Chinese Wine Importers Looking to Re-sign Contracts with Australian Growers amid Government Talks," ABC News (Australia), April 13, 2023, https://www.abc.net.au/news/rural/2023-04-14/china-wine-importers-look-to-buy-rumours-trade-freeze-to-end/102219466.

[73] Dan Holmes, "Hope Grows for Barley Farms," *Rural*, April 27, 2023.

[74] Department of Foreign Affairs and Trade (Australia), "Australia's Direction of Goods and Services Trade."

national broadband network. Although not publicly announced at the time, this decision was revealed in 2012 and justified on national security grounds. Citing concerns about cybersecurity and infrastructure resilience, Attorney General Nicola Roxon said that the determination was "consistent with the government's practice for ensuring the security and resilience of Australia's critical infrastructure more broadly."[75]

In 2018 a more expansive policy excluded Huawei and ZTE from the construction of Australia's 5G network on national security grounds. The decision, taken by the center-right Coalition government, excluded "vendors who are likely to be subject to extrajudicial directions from a foreign government that conflict with Australian law."[76] Although the government was taciturn about the national security rationale for this decision at the time, it was subsequently revealed that China's 2017 National Intelligence Law, which compels all Chinese organizations and citizens to assist national intelligence efforts, was the decisive motivation.[77] The prime minister at the time, Malcolm Turnbull, described his government's concerns after he left office: "If the Chinese Communist Party called on Huawei to act against Australia's interests, it would have to do it. Huawei says, 'Oh no, we would refuse.' That's laughable. They would have no option but to comply."[78]

If the 2011 decision on the national broadband network reflected an early example of Australia's unease about the potentially adverse national security implications of technological interdependence with China, the 2018 decision on 5G signaled a dramatic intensification of these concerns. Whereas the 2011 decision only excluded one Chinese company (Huawei) from one, albeit large, government ICT infrastructure project, the 2018 decision excluded both Huawei and ZTE from the Australian business market more broadly. Although both companies could still sell directly to Australian consumers, they were subjected to a blanket ban on selling their equipment to Australian telecommunications carriers building ICT infrastructure. The decision departed from Australia's long-standing liberal approach of providing nondiscriminatory access to foreign companies. It also set an international

---

[75] Maggie Lu-YueYang, "Australia Blocks China's Huawei from Broadband Tender," Reuters, March 26, 2012, https://www.reuters.com/article/us-australia-huawei-nbn-idUSBRE82P0GA20120326.

[76] "Government Provides 5G Security Guidance to Australian Carriers," Parliament of Australia, August 23, 2018, https://parlinfo.aph.gov.au/parlInfo/download/media/pressrel/6164495/upload_binary/6164495.pdf;fileType=application%2Fpdf#search=%22media/pressrel/6164495%22.

[77] Simeon Gilding, "5G Choices: A Pivotal Moment in World Affairs," ASPI, Strategist, January 29, 2020, https://www.aspistrategist.org.au/5g-choices-a-pivotal-moment-in-world-affairs.

[78] Peter Hartcher, "Huawei? No Way! Why Australia Banned the World's Biggest Telecoms Firm," *Sydney Morning Herald*, May 21, 2021, https://www.smh.com.au/national/huawei-no-way-why-australia-banned-the-world-s-biggest-telecoms-firm-20210503-p57oc9.html.

precedent, making Canberra the first capital to formally exclude Chinese companies from its ICT infrastructure market.

Investment Screening

Although Australia has been a net importer of foreign capital for much of its modern history, in the 1960s and 1970s it pursued a more restrictive approach via foreign exchange controls and foreign investment policy levers. Consistent with Australia's overarching embrace of economic liberalization from the 1980s onward, the trend until the mid-2010s was toward a more welcoming approach to foreign investment.[79] Australia maintained a legislatively mandated screening process throughout this period, but foreign investment still boomed, including a dramatic increase from China in the 2000s and 2010s. In the early 2010s, however, public concern grew about the scale of investment from China after the country emerged as Australia's largest source of new flows. This was an unprecedented development, given that the largest source of foreign investment had always previously been liberal democracies.[80]

The late 2010s onward saw a series of high-profile rejections of Chinese investments because of, among other reasons, assessed national security risks. In 2016 the government blocked a 99-year lease and acquisition of a controlling stake in Ausgrid (Australia's largest electricity network) sought by two bidders: China's government-owned State Grid Corporation and Hong Kong–based Cheung Kong Infrastructure (CKI). The bid was reportedly rejected due to concerns about critical infrastructure supported by the grid, including a U.S.-Australian joint defense facility at Pine Gap.[81] Meanwhile, a 2018 decision rejected CKI's A$13 billion acquisition of the APA Group, which ran more than half of Australia's gas pipeline network, on the grounds that it would be "contrary to the national interest." Having been approved by Australia's competition regulator, this rejection was seen by many as being motivated by national security considerations.[82] Finally, the Australian treasurer blocked China Mengniu Dairy Company's proposed A$430 million acquisition of Lion Dairy and Drinks by declaring it contrary to national

---

[79] Department of the Treasury (Australia), "Foreign Investment Policy in Australia: A Brief History and Recent Developments," 1999, https://treasury.gov.au/sites/default/files/2019-03/round5-4.pdf.

[80] Productivity Commission (Australia), *Foreign Investment in Australia*.

[81] Peter Hartcher, "Why Power Sale Was Vetoed," *Canberra Times*, May 29, 2018.

[82] Peter Jennings, "Australia Can Learn from Josh Frydenberg's Rejection of CK Group," ASPI, November 10, 2018, https://www.aspi.org.au/opinion/australia-can-learn-josh-frydenbergs-rejection-ck-group; and John Kehoe, "CKI's Bid for APA Group Officially Rejected by Treasurer Josh Frydenberg," *Australian Financial Review*, November 21, 2018, https://www.afr.com/policy/foreign-affairs/ckis-bid-for-apa-group-officially-rejected-by-treasurer-josh-frydenberg-20181120-h1850d.

interests, despite the deal having been endorsed by the Australian Treasury and the Foreign Investment Review Board.

Following these decisions, the Australian government in 2020 announced significant reforms to the foreign investment review regime. Among other changes, it introduced a new national security test for foreign investments that applied in cases that fell beneath the screening threshold for the national interest test, a mandatory notification measure with respect to proposed foreign investment in a "sensitive national security business," and a "last resort" review power to reassess approved investments where subsequent national security risks emerge. Just as these reforms were being implemented in January 2021, the treasurer blocked China State Construction Engineering Corporation (CSCEC) from purchasing Probuild, a South African–owned construction company, on national security grounds. Concerns were raised about the A$300 million deal because of CSCEC's supposed connections with China's defense industry and Probuild's involvement in the construction of two projects deemed sensitive: a state police department headquarters and the headquarters of a company involved in the production of Covid-19 vaccines.

Australian opinion was divided on the costs and benefits of blocking investment from China.[83] But regardless of the true scale of the foregone economic opportunities or the severity of the national security risks avoided, these rejections underscore the shifting Australian assessment of interdependence with China. A growing range of Chinese investments are now seen as potential proxies for China's statecraft and thereby potential national security risks. Treasurer Frydenberg acknowledged as much in 2021: "I have increasingly seen foreign investment applications that are being pursued not necessarily for commercial objectives but strategic objectives, and as you know I have said no to applications that in the past may have been approved."[84]

Summary

The above developments indicate that the trend toward more restrictive and securitized governance of market access for Chinese investors and firms, which began in the early 2010s, has continued under recent governments.

---

[83] John Durie, "Josh Frydenberg Must Explain Why Chinese Deals Are Being Blocked," *Australian*, January 13, 2021, https://www.theaustralian.com.au/business/economics/josh-frydenberg-must-explain-why-chinese-deals-are-being-blocked/news-story/809f88a1e5c952c58d4e55933fe122a9; and John Lee, "Why Banning China from Buying Probuild Is Justified Discrimination," *Australian Financial Review*, January 17, 2021, https://www.afr.com/policy/foreign-affairs/why-banning-china-from-buying-probuild-is-justified-discrimination-20210113-p56tvz.

[84] Josh Frydenberg, "Doorstop Interview, Parliament House, Canberra," Treasurer of Australia, July 7, 2021, https://ministers.treasury.gov.au/ministers/josh-frydenberg-2018/transcripts/doorstop-interview-parliament-house-canberra-46.

It is worth noting, however, that the current Labor government appears to be tactically finessing how it delivers adverse determinations to Beijing. The government is still restricting market access for both Chinese investors in sectors deemed sensitive (e.g., critical minerals) and firms that are judged to pose a potential security risk (e.g., technology companies). Yet in both cases, it also appears to be seeking to minimize the negative impact on the bilateral relationship. In the case of critical minerals, the government has twice announced the rejection of investments from Chinese or China-linked companies at the same time as it announced the approval of investments from China in less sensitive sectors like iron ore and nickel.[85] Meanwhile, Australia's decision to remove TikTok from government devices came after many other countries had already imposed similar bans, thus ensuring that Canberra did not attract Beijing's ire as a result of first-mover status, as happened with the 2018 5G decision.[86]

The net effect on investment flows of these shifts in Australia's approach remains unclear. Since 2018, the value and number of completed deals have continued to decline (see **Figure 3**),[87] with the result that flows from China now make up a smaller share of Australia's new foreign investment.[88] Although shifts in Canberra's approach to assessing Chinese investments have no doubt contributed to the downward trend, it is likely also a function of global trends in China's foreign investment flows. After reaching a peak of US$216 billion in 2016, China's foreign investments suddenly fell in 2017, and by 2019 they had fallen to 63% of their 2016 high.[89] This suggests that a decline in the value of Chinese investments in Australia may have occurred even in the absence of Canberra adopting a more cautious approach.

---

[85] Based on authors' conversations with Australian officials. See also Benjamin Herscovitch, "Chinese Mining Investments in Australia and Darwin Port Permutations," Beijing to Canberra and Back, March 5, 2023, https://beijing2canberra.substack.com/p/chinese-mining-investments-in-australia; and Benjamin Herscovitch, "Tactically Timed Investment Rejections, a Leader-Level Visit to China, and Barley Exports," Beijing to Canberra and Back, July 27, 2023, https://beijing2canberra.substack.com/p/tactically-timed-investment-rejections.

[86] Benjamin Herscovitch, "Competing CPTPP Bids, Canberra's Contentious China Policy Choices, and TikTok Turbulence," Beijing to Canberra and Back, March 22, 2023, https://beijing2canberra.substack.com/i/110113968/tiktok-turbulence.

[87] While we have focused on inbound Chinese investment, it is notable that Australian investment in China has also declined in the years since 2018. See Nicole Adams et al., "China's Evolving Financial System and Its Global Importance," Reserve Bank of Australia, September 16, 2021, https://www.rba.gov.au/publications/bulletin/2021/sep/chinas-evolving-financial-system-and-its-global-importance.html.

[88] China's share of Australia's total stock of investment remained relatively unchanged in 2022 at 2.2%.

[89] Organisation for Economic Co-operation and Development, "FDI Flows," https://data.oecd.org/fdi/fdi-flows.htm#indicator-chart.

FIGURE 3 Value of Chinese overseas direct investment in Australia and number of completed deals, 2014–22

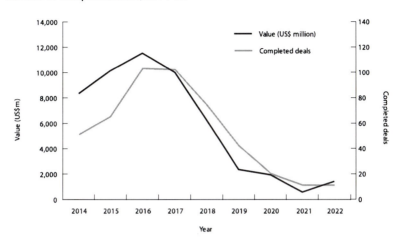

SOURCE: Doug Ferguson et al., "Demystifying Chinese Investment in Australia: April 2023," KPMG and University of Sydney, April 2023, https://kpmg.com/au/en/home/insights/2023/04/demystifying-chinese-investment-in-australia-april-2023.html.

Industrial Policy

Given the history of Australian economic policy, perhaps the most surprising policy shift has been in the domain of industrial policy. In the wake of major structural economic reforms in the early 1980s, successive governments maintained a consistent market-based approach to domestic economic policy, eschewing a major role for the state and promoting competitive markets as the optimal way to organize economic activity.[90] Economic policy orthodoxy in Australia tracked the dominance of "neoliberal" and "rationalist" economic thinking (albeit with a strong social safety net), and as a commodity-rich country, it was structurally well-positioned to take advantage of the era of rapid globalization. The government was uninterested in industrial policy during this reform era; indeed, the dominant trends were the privatization of state-owned enterprises and the outsourcing of labor-intensive manufacturing as high wages made local production unprofitable. The limited size of Australia's internal market was also a barrier to achieving

---

[90] Michael Pusey, *Economic Rationalism in Canberra: A Nation-Building State Changes Its Mind* (Cambridge: Cambridge University Press, 1989).

economies of scale, underscoring the prohibitively high cost of state-sponsored production. During this period, government reports explicitly rejected industrial policy. The Industry Commission argued in 1995 that "normal market forces…will be the determinants of change," in a report on the production and use of new materials, further asserting that "most of this activity will be undertaken by larger, established companies" and "there is little influence that the government can or should have."[91]

Since 2018, a reassessment of that logic has begun to occur. Australians were shocked by certain key shortages in the early months of Covid-19, which caused the government to embrace the concept of "sovereign capability"—previously only applied to Australia's defense industrial base—to justify state intervention in industries such as pharmaceuticals, personal protective equipment, and vaccines. The logic was explained by a parliamentary committee: "to support some critical national systems, Australia must develop and maintain the sovereign capability to design, manufacture and certify enabling components of the system."[92]

Given China's dominance of global manufacturing, it is unsurprising that imports from the country are important to many of the systems that the Australian government now assesses as requiring greater sovereign capability. However, there is no strong evidence that Beijing limited any of its exports to Australia as part of the sanctions campaign.[93] Accordingly, while such restrictions remain conceivable, the public narrative around sovereign capability has not specifically identified China as a threat. Instead, it has focused on a broader argument that Australia requires certain domestic production capacities in critical national systems in an era when cross-border supply chains have revealed structural fragilities.

Changing perceptions of China have also motivated a shift in industrial policy through another channel. Given the overwhelming dominance in Australia's economic profile of exports of primary resources and internal service trade, Australia is not a major producer in critical technology industries. Accordingly, China's actual (e.g., solar cells) or potential (e.g., semiconductors) market dominance of such industries does not pose a direct threat. It is, however, a concern for Australia's allies and partners, especially the United States and Japan. The assessment that "economic security is national security" that first appeared in the Trump administration's 2017 National

---

[91] Industry Commission (Australia), *New and Advanced Materials* (Melbourne, March 1995), 99, https://www.pc.gov.au/inquiries/completed/new-advanced-materials/42newmat.pdf.

[92] Joint Standing Committee on Foreign Affairs, Defence and Trade (Australia), *Inquiry into the Implications of the COVID-19 Pandemic for Australia's Foreign Affairs, Defence and Trade* (Canberra: Commonwealth of Australia, 2020), 113.

[93] The AdBlue shortage, for example, appeared credibly motivated by domestic considerations.

Security Strategy has become bipartisan policy orthodoxy in both Washington and Tokyo and involves the formation of "secure" technology supply chains that exclude Chinese producers.[94] Accordingly, the depth of shared security interests with Washington and Tokyo has motivated Canberra to look for ways to contribute to this novel form of economic cooperation. Australia's interests are as much about "alliance management" and wanting to contribute to joint security initiatives as they are a direct response to a geoeconomic threat.

How can Canberra contribute to supply chain security initiatives? The answer lies upstream, given Australia's outsized role as a commodities exporter, and specifically in the supply of critical minerals such as lithium, cobalt, titanium, and rare earth elements. These are essential inputs for a wide range of renewable and defense industrial technologies and are thus central to an economic security agenda. At present, China dominates the midstream refining stage of production and therefore exerts an outsized influence on global supply.[95] Accordingly, increasing extraction of raw minerals and investing more in midstream refining are tangible ways that Australia could play its part in the establishment of supply chains that are less susceptible to China's influence.

Critical minerals are thus becoming the core plank of a new targeted industrial policy in Australia.[96] In 2019 the government released its first Critical Minerals Strategy and established a Critical Minerals Facilitation Office to support the growth of the country's extraction and refining capacities. While these include standard economic objectives like job creation, the government also frames these efforts as enhancing the security of Australia and its allies and partners. In 2022, Industry Minister Angus Taylor observed about one package of loans that "China currently dominates around 70% to 80% of global critical minerals production and continues to consolidate its hold over these supply chains. This initiative is designed to address that dominance."[97]

---

[94] See, for example, Jake Sullivan, "Remarks by National Security Advisor Jake Sullivan at the Special Competitive Studies Project Global Emerging Technologies Summit," White House, Press Release, September 16, 2022, https://www.whitehouse.gov/briefing-room/speeches-remarks/2022/09/16/remarks-by-national-security-advisor-jake-sullivan-at-the-special-competitive-studies-project-global-emerging-technologies-summit; and Yasutoshi Nishimura, "Building a New Order after Overcoming an Illusion" (address given at the Center for Strategic and International Studies, January 5, 2023), https://www.csis.org/events/japans-2023-g7-priorities-and-future-economic-order.

[95] Rodrigo Castillo and Caitlin Purdy, "China's Role in Supplying Critical Minerals for the Global Energy Transition," Brookings Institution, August 1, 2022, https://www.brookings.edu/articles/chinas-role-in-supplying-critical-minerals-for-the-global-energy-transition-what-could-the-future-hold.

[96] Llewelyn Hughes, "Securing Critical Mineral Supply Chains in the Indo-Pacific: A Perspective from Australia," National Bureau of Asian Research, NBR Special Report, no. 102, December 1, 2022, https://www.nbr.org/publication/securing-critical-mineral-supply-chains-in-the-indo-pacific-a-perspective-from-australia.

[97] Angus Taylor, "Supercharging Critical Minerals Manufacturing," Department of Industry, Science and Resources (Australia), Press Release, March 16, 2022, https://www.minister.industry.gov.au/ministers/taylor/media-releases/supercharging-critical-minerals-manufacturing.

In tandem, Australia has refreshed and bolstered its export credit agency, Export Finance Australia (EFA), which some had argued should be abolished in 2014.[98] In recent years, EFA has not only provided larger loans but also taken equity investments—financial support designed to de-risk new critical minerals projects. A specific A$2 billion Critical Minerals Facility was established, and a A$1.25 billion non-recourse loan contributed to financing Australia's first dedicated rare earths plant in 2022.[99] Through other government programs, over half a billion Australian dollars have been pledged to ten other critical minerals projects since 2021.[100] This departure from standard policy, represented by a willingness to underwrite emerging industries that are not yet considered commercially viable, is dramatic. Less than a decade prior, when Lynas Rare Earths, the first firm to extract rare earth elements in Australia, was experiencing difficulties, Canberra did not step in to help. Instead, it was investments of US$250 million from Japan that helped the company survive and offer an alternative to Chinese supply.[101]

Notwithstanding some domestic debate about how readily Australia should embed itself in friendshoring arrangements with its allies,[102] the government has so far shown a significant willingness to buttress its new industrial policy at home with cooperation from security partners abroad via minilateral and bilateral agreements. The South Korean president's trip to Australia in December 2021 yielded the Memorandum of Understanding on Cooperation in Critical Mineral Supply Chains and several other deals

---

[98] Robert Potter, "Shark Bay Salt Hits Up EFIC—Again and Again," *Australian Financial Review*, May 9, 2014, https://www.afr.com/policy/economy/shark-bay-salt-hits-up-efic-again-and-again-20140509-itsk1.

[99] "Strategically Significant Government Loan Enables Development of Australia's First Fully Integrated Rare Earths Refinery," Department of Industry, Science and Resources (Australia), Press Release, April 4, 2022, https://www.industry.gov.au/news/strategically-significant-government-loan-enables-development-of-australias-first-fully-integrated-rare-earths-refinery.

[100] Department of Industry, Science and Resources (Australia), *Critical Minerals Strategy 2023–2030* (Canberra, June 2023), https://www.industry.gov.au/data-and-publications/2022-critical-minerals-strategy.

[101] Eugene Gholz and Llewelyn Hughes, "Market Structure and Economic Sanctions: The 2010 Rare Earth Elements Episode as a Pathway Case of Market Adjustment," *Review of International Political Economy* 28, no. 3 (2021): 622.

[102] Those calling for caution highlight that, rather than supporting Australian industries sanctioned by China, commercial actors in some key partner states capitalized on Australia's exclusion to expand their own market shares. See, for example, Jane Golley and James Laurenceson, "The Future of Australian Wine: Fabulous Friends or Dedicated Diplomacy?" Australian Institute of International Affairs, Australian Outlook, May 18, 2023, https://www.internationalaffairs.org.au/australianoutlook/the-future-of-australian-wine-fabulous-friends-or-dedicated-diplomacy. Compare with Naoise McDonagh, "Responding to Economic Coercion: Can Allies Be Trusted to Cooperate?" Australian Institute of International Affairs, Australian Outlook, May 25, 2023, https://www.internationalaffairs.org.au/australianoutlook/responding-to-economic-coercion-can-allies-be-trusted-to-cooperate.

between Australian companies and their South Korean counterparts.[103] In 2022, Australia and its Quad partners (India, Japan, and the United States) mapped critical minerals capacity and vulnerabilities in global semiconductor supply chains as a step in reducing dependence on China.[104] Australia and India also launched the Critical Minerals Investment Partnership, which emphasizes Australia's role as a "trusted supplier" of resources and energy to India and jointly funds studies into Australia's lithium and cobalt deposits.[105]

Potentially the most consequential deal was made in May 2023 when President Joe Biden and Prime Minister Albanese signed the Climate, Critical Minerals and Clean Energy Transformation Compact. Key to the compact is Biden's plan to request that the U.S. Congress designate Australia as a "domestic source" pursuant to the 1950 Defense Production Act. The designation would remove barriers to U.S. investment in the Australian sources of listed critical minerals, which could further enable Australian critical minerals producers to access U.S. loan and guarantee programs and other incentives.[106] While not yet complete, this action would effectively incorporate Australian critical minerals into U.S. industrial and national security policies, furthering Washington's friendshoring objective.

Evaluating Continuity and Change

Australia represents one of the most interesting and informative case studies of how states have managed complex bilateral relations with China over the past decade. The open and democratic nature of Australian society means that the country's "China debate" has been relatively transparent.[107] Political leaders frequently speak on the topic, and a vibrant civil society that engages media, business, think tanks, and academia sees many voices contribute to the discussion. There is, however, no consensus. There are

---

[103] Elouise Fowler, "Miners Sign Critical Mineral Deals with South Korea," *Australian Financial Review*, December 15, 2021, https://www.afr.com/companies/mining/miners-ink-critical-mineral-deals-with-south-korea-20211215-p59hmz.

[104] Denham Sadler, "Quad Countries Finish Mapping Critical Minerals Vulnerabilities," InnovationAus.com, May 25, 2022, https://www.innovationaus.com/quad-countries-finish-mapping-critical-minerals-vulnerabilities.

[105] Madeleine King, "Building Stronger Critical Minerals Cooperation with India," Australian Minister for Resources and Minister for Northern Australia, Press Release, July 4, 2022, https://www.minister.industry.gov.au/ministers/king/media-releases/building-stronger-critical-minerals-cooperation-india.

[106] "Energy Transition Insights: Australia—United States Climate, Critical Minerals and Clean Energy Transformation Compact," Sullivan and Cromwell LLP, May 25, 2023, https://www.sullcrom.com/insights/memo/2023/May/Australia-US-Compact.

[107] Darren J. Lim and Nathan Attrill, "Australian Debate of the China Question: The COVID-19 Case," *Australian Journal of International Affairs* 75, no. 4 (2021): 410–31.

those who argue that economic interdependence with China is a resounding strategic vulnerability that must be urgently addressed.[108] Others maintain that the enduring complementarities of the two economies mean that there is often no good alternative to the Chinese market.[109] In terms of measuring the breadth and depth of Australia's reassessment of its interdependence, the cacophony of voices risks lowering the signal-to-noise ratio. This task is complicated further by the country's domestic politics. The current center-left Labor government has argued that its center-right predecessor, the Liberal-National Coalition, adopted an unnecessarily provocative tone toward Beijing for electoral reasons.[110]

Moreover, even if one were able to pin down a precise point on a spectrum between "openness" and "closure" that reflected the average assessment of the ongoing opportunities and risks of interdependence with China, Australian policy would oscillate within a band around that point over time. While it is true that domestic political differences drive fluctuations within that band, the band itself is narrow because those same forces serve to homogenize policy. Neither side wants to invite criticism by straying too far from the centrist consensus. For example, the Labor Party is sensitive to the "soft on China" criticism, and during the 2022 election campaign, it backed all major planks of the Coalition government's China policy. Since becoming the governing party, Labor has sought to finesse the implementation of China policy to avoid antagonizing Beijing, but there do not appear to be substantive partisan policy differences in terms of appetite for "openness" to China.

Notwithstanding different opinions on how to manage the relationship, there has been an undeniable bipartisan shift in tone on the merits of deep interdependence with China. In the words of Foreign Minister Penny Wong in January 2023:

> We're not going back to where we were fifteen years ago. We know that we want a more stable relationship with China, but we know we're not going to be able to continue to separate our economic and our strategic relationship. So what does that mean? It means Australian producers…are going to have to look to

---

[108] See, for example, Alan Dupont, "Beijing Rapprochement: We Should Trade Very Carefully," *Australian*, January 28, 2023, https://www.theaustralian.com.au/commentary/beijing-rapprochement-we-should-trade-very-carefully/news-story/71d8bb8b494341d6a5d7c94805e47277.

[109] See, for example, Peter Drysdale and Shiro Armstrong, "How Australia Can Find Common Purpose with China," East Asia Forum, June 27, 2022, https://www.eastasiaforum.org/2022/06/27/how-australia-can-find-common-purpose-with-china.

[110] Richard Marles, "News Corp's Defending Australia, Australian War Memorial," Defence Australia, May 22, 2023, https://www.minister.defence.gov.au/speeches/2023-05-22/news-corps-defending-australia-australian-war-memorial.

diversify markets, and that's one of the things the government is working on with industry.[111]

In June 2023, Trade Minister Don Farrell, fresh from talks in Beijing and optimistic about the removal of China's trade restrictions, noted that "one of our biggest priorities has been to work to stabilize our relationship with China—by far our largest trading partner. We've been clear on our position with China from day one. We want a stable and prosperous trading relationship, and the full resumption of trade." Nevertheless, earlier in the same speech, he reiterated the foreign minister's line: "Overreliance on any single trading partner comes with risks. Across the private sector, any business that relied on a single client, would be destined for failure, so too for global trading economies. We've learnt valuable lessons over the last few years, and I encourage all Australian businesses to continue with their diversification plans."[112]

How important is this tonal shift in practice? The challenge of managing the evolving trade-offs of economic interdependence is that governments do not control markets the way they control the political domain. Rather, they coexist with private economic actors who conduct the vast majority of international exchange. This is especially true in liberal economic systems. Businesses have a voice, and the incentives offered by the Chinese market remain powerful. Moreover, the private sector may be more comfortable bearing political risk than the government. Simply encouraging or easing the process of diversification is unlikely to bring about decisive shifts without hard legal mandates or strong financial incentives. Short of this, profit-seeking actors will chase the promise of higher returns.

This logic is borne out in recent macroeconomic data on the trade relationship. Despite heightened concerns about the risks of economic interdependence and Beijing's sustained restrictions, Australia's exchange with China remained robust between 2018 and 2022. Indeed, China consolidated its position as Australia's most valuable export destination across a wide range of goods and services. As a result, while China's risk profile has settled at a higher level in recent years, this does not mean that the alternatives are necessarily so appealing as to justify large-scale diversification for the bulk of Australian exports. There remains variation across and within industries on the premiums available in the Chinese market, on the availability of alternatives, and in appetites for political risk. Still, many of those exporters

---

[111] Penny Wong, "TV Interview, Today Show," Australian Minister for Foreign Affairs, April 12, 2023, https://www.foreignminister.gov.au/minister/penny-wong/transcript/tv-interview-today-show.

[112] Don Farrell, "National Press Club Address, Canberra," Australian Minister for Trade and Tourism and Special Minister of State, June 1, 2023, https://www.trademinister.gov.au/minister/don-farrell/speech/national-press-club-address-canberra.

most adversely affected by China's sanctions remain eager to re-enter the Chinese market despite their experiences. For those industries relatively untouched by the economic coercion campaign, including education, tourism, iron ore, and natural gas, many actors intend to deepen their already extensive exposure to the Chinese market. The dominant concern for these and other China-exposed industries is slowing economic growth rates in China rather than future coercion by Beijing.

The practical state of play for foreign investment is less confounded by market incentives because of the gatekeeping role played by Canberra. Here, a longer-term trend toward closing off Chinese investment in certain sensitive industries—especially technology, critical infrastructure, and critical minerals—seems patent. Indeed, polling data supports continued or increased restrictions on Chinese technology, giving the government latitude to further restrict the involvement of Chinese companies like TikTok.[113] However, foreign investment might also be a policy domain where, at the margins, different governments adopt different settings. Labor's approval of Baowu Steel's investment in the Western Range iron ore project might be one example.[114] This could therefore be evidence of a relatively greater degree of openness to Chinese investment under the current Labor government, motivated by a slightly different assessment of the risks, an alternative domestic political calculus, and/or a decision to accommodate Beijing's prioritization of greater investment access as a relatively low-cost approach to improving the bilateral relationship.

The outlook for industrial policy and the issues of supply chain diversification is more complex. Because Australia is a net exporter of critical minerals, decoupling from China in the sector would have a slightly different meaning for it than for those states whose concerns stem from their reliance on China for imports. Policy steps to secure supply chains with like-minded partners would include reducing reliance on Chinese finance for Australian critical minerals projects, developing greater domestic capacity for midstream processing and manufacturing,[115] and potentially redirecting some exports away from China to other (presumably "friendlier") markets. In doing so, Australia could simultaneously satisfy the expectations of its allies and

---

[113] Miah Hammond-Errey, "Technology Distrust the Most Pressing Decoupling Issue," United States Studies Centre, February 27, 2023, https://www.ussc.edu.au/analysis/technology-distrust-the-most-pressing-decoupling-issue.

[114] For criticism of the decision, see Peter Jennings, "Show Some Steel on China's Investments in Our Critical Assets," *Australian*, February 23, 2023, https://www.theaustralian.com.au/commentary/show-some-steel-on-chinas-investment-in-our-critical-assets/news-story/0944b543572b173067ac83356d86edfe.

[115] See Madeleine King, "Speech to the ASPI Darwin Dialogue," Australian Minister for Resources and Minister for Northern Australia, April 13, 2023, https://www.minister.industry.gov.au/ministers/king/speeches/speech-aspi-darwin-dialogue.

partners in the economic security cooperation domain, while also deriving greater returns from its geological endowments. However, if pursued, each of these tasks will take time and effort and involve extensive costs.

Evidence of any of the three indicators of decoupling from China is tentative. In terms of reducing reliance on Chinese finance, the Australian treasurer in February and July 2023 rejected two separate investments from Chinese or China-linked companies in rare earth elements and lithium miners, respectively. Consistent with these data points, Resources Minister Madeleine King implied in March 2023 that Australia would prioritize working with like-minded countries on critical minerals deals into the future.[116] Meanwhile, as outlined above, Japan, South Korea, and the United States are all increasing their involvement. The development of further midstream processing is also underway. A rare earths processing plant under construction in Kalgoorlie by Lynas Rare Earths is due to come online in 2023, and the (Canberra-financed) Iluka processing plant is expected to be working by 2025. China-linked actors, however, continue to play a central role in some initiatives to move up the value chain, such as in the production of battery-grade lithium.[117] Finally, the third and perhaps most important indicator of economic separation—physically redirecting minerals exports away from China—is not yet on the horizon.

The development of new critical minerals supply chains oriented toward trade with like-minded partners is arguably the economic policy domain in which there is the greatest compatibility between the government's reassessment of the geopolitical risks from interdependence with China and the commercial incentives of companies. However, doing so will be costly. These costs must be borne either by partner countries, if they are willing to pay premium prices and enter into offtake agreements, or by Australian taxpayers, if government subsidies are required to build production networks consistent with geopolitical priorities.

Nevertheless, across Australia's trade, investment, and industrial policy, there is little evidence of the kind of wholesale economic separation from China that decoupling implies. Some may wonder if the narrower (albeit more ambiguous) concept of "de-risking," which has recently come to rhetorical

---

[116] Herscovitch, "Chinese Mining Investments in Australia and Darwin Port Permutations"; and King, "Speech to the ASPI Darwin Dialogue."

[117] Australia's first battery-grade lithium was produced by Chinese-owned Tianqi Lithium in 2022. See James Bowen, "Australia Needs to Be Economically as Well as Strategically Like-minded on Critical Minerals," ASPI, Strategist, May 4, 2023, https://www.aspistrategist.org.au/australia-needs-to-be-economically-as-well-as-strategically-likeminded-on-critical-minerals.

prominence in Western policy circles, is a more accurate characterization.[118] Given that Australia does not compete with China in advanced technologies or export the dual-use products that drive much of the de-risking discussion, Australia might not be the right case to litigate that conceptual debate. Nevertheless, it is clear that any separation Australia seeks from its economic relationship with China will likely be limited—in terms of both the breadth of domains and the absolute volume of exchange. Above all, what the Australia case seems to suggest is that even countries with stark geopolitical differences with China may wish to retain the bulk of their economic relationship for the foreseeable future.

Finally, it should be noted that regardless of Australia's preferences, a certain amount of economic separation may be initiated by China. This may be because Beijing does not consider Australia a reliable long-term supplier, as is said to be especially true of iron ore,[119] or because it has a domestic policy that prioritizes greater self-reliance. For example, China has long been focused on diversifying food imports as part of a broader food security strategy, raising the possibility that trade restrictions on barley were in part motivated by a desire to reduce import dependence on Australia for that grain, which had averaged 65% of all Chinese imports in 2008–18, with spikes up to 80%.[120]

Implications

In reassessing its interdependence with China, Australia is being pushed and pulled in opposing directions. The factors pushing Canberra away from Beijing are headlined by perceptions of a growing threat arising from China's increased influence in Australia's domestic affairs and the ordeal of being on the receiving end of economic sanctions. These push factors are complemented by forces pulling Canberra toward a limited decoupling or de-risking agenda via its interest in participating in new forms of economic cooperation with its closest security partners, initially in the critical minerals industry.

Yet there are countervailing factors. As highlighted by the economic data, for many Australian industries, the economic opportunities presented

---

[118] Whereas "decoupling" implies largely separating two economies, "de-risking" is promoted as a more surgical separation of specific forms of risky exchange while the remainder continues unhindered. The term, first used by president of the European Commission Ursula von der Leyen in April 2023, was subsequently picked up by the United States and other countries.

[119] McGregor, "Chinese Coercion, Australian Resilience."

[120] Scott Waldron, "The Exposure of Australian Agriculture to Risks from China: The Cases of Barley and Beef," Asian Cattle and Beef Trade Working Papers, 2020, available at https://espace.library.uq.edu.au/view/UQ:8287be9.

by China's internal market in terms of size and price premiums remain unparalleled. Even many of those businesses directly in the firing line of Beijing's sanctions appear to have calculated that the potential risk of politically motivated disruption recurring in the future does not justify the economic costs of a permanent exit from the trading relationship. Moreover, Australia's historical commitment to free markets, open trade, and the rules-based order, as well as its modest economic size, push the government away from adopting overtly nationalistic positions, notwithstanding rhetoric about sovereign capability. Australia's industrial policy efforts remain modest and narrowly focused on areas of comparative advantage (e.g., critical minerals mining).

Nevertheless, the narrative shift is stark. Leaders across the political spectrum, business executives, and the wider policy community all appear to recognize that the glory days of relatively unfettered trade with China are over. Geopolitical risk is now a nearly permanent feature of Australia's trade profile, and there are no influential domestic political forces pushing for a reversal of the trend toward selective decoupling or de-risking from China. While the economic gravity generated by the two countries' complementary trade profiles currently sustains deep levels of interdependence, the dark clouds of growing geopolitical rivalry are observable to all.

It is therefore worth emphasizing the extent to which future separation may well be out of Australia's hands. Yes, Canberra has made independent decisions to exclude Chinese providers from critical infrastructure and technology systems, but these are relatively marginal in the broader interdependence picture. Arguably, the most important factor prompting deep, if temporary, cleavages in the economic relationship to date has been Beijing's trade restrictions. As China under President Xi Jinping continues its assertive statecraft and seeks greater economic and technological self-sufficiency, Australia may well find itself unwillingly pushed by forces in Beijing toward a greater unwinding of the interdependent relationship.

The other external force to monitor is the United States. To date, Australia has largely been able to watch the most consequential aspects of the geoeconomic competition between Washington and Beijing from the sidelines. With only a small advanced manufacturing industry and exports dominated by commodities and services, Australia has not been drawn into the United States' efforts to maintain its lead (and thus constrain China's development) on the technology frontier.[121] But how viable is this approach in the long term? Might future U.S. policymakers demand that Australia cease supplying Chinese industry with certain critical minerals? U.S.-China

---

[121] Andrew B. Kennedy and Darren J. Lim, "The Innovation Imperative: Technology and U.S.-China Rivalry in the Twenty-First Century," *International Affairs* 94, no. 3 (2018): 553–72.

technology competition could constrain Australia's options and render untenable its desire to keep China as a customer for those commodity exports that will power 21st-century innovation in vital policy domains like climate change.

The possibility of direct military confrontation in the Taiwan Strait or elsewhere requires this line of thinking to be extended. Could a demand from the United States extend to iron ore? Russia's invasion of Ukraine and China's determination to unify with Taiwan are causing policymakers in Washington to consider how to enhance deterrence of China via both military and economic means. Part of this effort must inevitably involve engaging with Canberra about when and how Australia—an essential supplier of energy, food, and raw materials for China—might join any effort to punish and deter Beijing should it escalate its actions against Taiwan. Such a scenario would generate impossible dilemmas for Australia, caught between the nation's sustained commitment to economic openness and its desire to preserve the regional security status quo, as well as between its deepening security cooperation with the United States and its efforts to stabilize and repair relations with China.

In the short term, Beijing's attempted accession to the CPTPP will provide an indication of how the current government might manage some of these trade-offs. Canberra will face political pressure to reject accession unless all of China's trade barriers are removed. But if that happens, the economic benefits from China's membership and the damage that blocking its bid could do to bilateral relations would generate significant pressure for Australia to drop its opposition. Yet the original geopolitical goal of the trade agreement (at least from Washington's perspective) is to counterbalance China's regional economic leadership. The longer Washington is unable or unwilling to provide such leadership in the form of market access to Asian economies, the weaker the geopolitical argument for excluding China from the CPTPP will become.

More pointedly, Canberra and other CPTPP capitals face an acute geopolitical test, given the competing entry bids from Beijing and Taipei. China strongly opposes Taiwan's entry, even though nothing in the CPTPP precludes Taiwanese membership. China's sanctions campaign against Australia, despite a bilateral FTA and shared WTO membership, underscores issues with the argument that binding Beijing to CPTPP rules and procedures would constrain its noncommercial activities and other objectionable behavior in the future. By contrast, Taiwan is a reliable trade partner and already Australia's fourth-largest goods export destination. Nonetheless, public Australian support for Taiwan's entry could prompt China's ire and jeopardize the so-far incomplete removal of Beijing's trade restrictions. Such support might also be futile, given that China is likely to prevail on at least some CPTPP members to ensure that the necessary consensus support for Taiwan's bid is never achieved. Given these vexing trade-offs, Canberra may well push for Beijing and Taipei to accede at the same time.

Beyond the geopolitical gymnastics of the CPTPP, Australia's longer-term approach to economic interdependence with China will continue to be buffeted by contradictory forces. Spurred by concerns about perceived security threats from China and efforts by allies and partners to securitize supply chains, Australia will maintain interests in furthering a targeted decoupling agenda in the fields of ICT infrastructure and critical minerals. But at the aggregate trading level, the commercially irresistible embrace of economic interdependence with China will endure. Even as Australia's security relationship with the United States reaches new heights and Beijing's external policy grows more assertive, the Chinese market is highly likely to remain indispensable for Australia's prosperity.

About the Contributors

Victor A. Ferguson is a JSPS Postdoctoral Research Fellow in the Research Centre for Advanced Science and Technology at the University of Tokyo. He studies issues at the intersection of international political economy, global governance, and international security. He received his PhD from the School of Politics and International Relations at the Australian National University's Research School of Social Sciences.

Benjamin Herscovitch is a Research Fellow in the School of Regulation and Global Governance at the Australian National University (ANU). His primary areas of research are Australia-China relations, China's economic statecraft, and Australian foreign and defense policy. Prior to joining ANU, Dr. Herscovitch was an analyst and policy officer in the Australian Department of Defence, specializing in China's external policy and Australia's defense diplomacy. He was previously a researcher for Beijing-based thank tanks and consultancies.

Hyo-young Lee is an Associate Professor at the Korea National Diplomatic Academy (KNDA). Before joining the KNDA in March 2017, she worked as a research fellow at the Korea Institute for International Economic Policy in the Division of International Trade from 2013 to 2016 and as assistant secretary for trade, industry, and energy at the Presidential Office from 2014 to 2015. Her research interests span various issues in international trade, with a particular interest in trade rules on industrial subsidy policies, trade and national security, and digital trade. Dr. Lee's recent publications include the reports "Economic Security: Concept and Recent Trends" (2022), "Evolution and Evaluation of International Rules on Digital Trade" (2021), "Current Trends and Prospects for Asia Regional Economic Integration: Comparison of RCEP and CPTPP" (2021), and "Regulation of Subsidies and U.S.-China Strategic Competition" (2020). She obtained her PhD in international studies at the Seoul National University, majoring in international trade law and policy.

Darren J. Lim is a Senior Lecturer in the School of Politics and International Relations at the Australian National University. His major research interests focus on geoeconomics (including economic coercion and technology competition), grand strategy in the context of power transitions and international order, and the Indo-Pacific region. He also hosts a podcast on Australian foreign policy called *Australia in the World*. Dr. Lim received his PhD from the Princeton School of Public and International Affairs at Princeton University. Initially trained in law and economics, he previously worked as associate to the Chief Justice of the Federal Court of Australia, a corporate lawyer, and a researcher at the International Crisis Group.

Syaru Shirley Lin is Founder and Chair of the Center for Asia-Pacific Resilience and Innovation, Research Professor at the Miller Center of Public Affairs at the University of Virginia, Adjunct Professor at the Chinese University of Hong Kong, and a Nonresident Senior Fellow in the Foreign Policy Program at the Brookings Institution. Previously, she was a partner at Goldman Sachs, responsible for private equity investments in Asia and led the first round of institutional investments in Alibaba and Semiconductor Manufacturing International Corporation. She currently serves as a director of Langham Hospitality Investments, Goldman Sachs Asia Bank, TE Connectivity, and MediaTek. Dr. Lin is the author of *Taiwan's China Dilemma: Contested Identities and Multiple Interests in Taiwan's Cross-Strait Economic Policy* (2016), which was also published in Chinese (2019). She is currently writing a book about economies in the Asia-Pacific caught in the high-income trap, facing problems such as inequality, demographic decline, financialization, climate change, political polarization, and inadequate policy and technological innovation. She earned an MA in international public affairs and a PhD in politics and public administration at the University of Hong Kong and graduated *cum laude* from Harvard College.

Vikram Nehru is Senior Fellow at the Foreign Policy Institute, Johns Hopkins University School of Advanced International Studies (SAIS), and Honorary Fellow in Exeter College, Oxford University. Between 2016 and 2023, he was distinguished practitioner-in-residence at SAIS, where he taught courses on political economy and development economics with a focus on East, South, and Southeast Asia. Between 2011 and 2016, he served as the chair in Southeast Asian Studies at the Carnegie Endowment for International Peace in Washington, D.C. Prior to that, Dr. Nehru worked at the World Bank, including in a number of senior management positions. His last position there was chief economist and director for poverty reduction, economic management, and private and financial sector development for East Asia and the Pacific. In this capacity, he advised East Asian governments on economic and governance issues, including macroeconomic management, public sector and public financial management, financial and private sector development, sovereign debt management and debt restructuring, and poverty reduction. His articles have appeared in numerous journals, he has contributed to several books, and he has written many op-eds for leading newspapers, journals, and think tanks.

William J. Norris is an Associate Professor of Chinese Foreign and Security Policy in the Bush School of Government and Public Service at Texas A&M University, where he leads the school's Economic Statecraft Program and supervises the China Studies concentration. His broad research interests include international relations of East Asia, business-government relations, Chinese foreign and security policy, grand strategy, and international relations theory, particularly the strategic relationship between economics and national security. He earned his PhD from the Security Studies Program in the Department of Political Science at the Massachusetts Institute of Technology and graduated *summa cum laude* from Princeton University, concentrating in economics and politics.

Gulshan Sachdeva is a Professor and Jean Monnet Chair at the Centre for European Studies in the School of International Studies at Jawaharlal Nehru University in New Delhi. He is also coordinator in the Jean Monnet Centre of Excellence and the editor of the book series *Europe-Asia Connectivity* (Palgrave Macmillan). Between 2016 and 2021, he was editor-in-chief of the journal *International Studies*. He headed the Asian Development Bank and Asia Foundation projects on regional cooperation at the Afghanistan Ministry of Foreign Affairs in Kabul. He was also consultant with the International Labour Organization. Dr. Sachdeva has been Indian Council of Cultural Relations Chair on Contemporary India at the University of Leuven, as well as visiting professor at the University of Antwerp, University of Trento, University of Amsterdam, Autonomous University of Barcelona, University of Warsaw, Pompeu Fabra University (Barcelona), Mykolas Romeris University (Vilnius), Corvinus University of Budapest, Institute of Oriental Studies (Almaty), and Institute of Oriental Studies (Moscow). He has contributed more than one hundred research papers in academic journals and edited books. Some of his recent publications include *Challenges in Europe: Indian Perspectives* (2019) and *India in a Reconnecting Eurasia* (2016). He holds a PhD in economics from the Hungarian Academy of Sciences in Budapest.

Yul Sohn is a Professor in the Graduate School of International Studies (GSIS) and the Underwood International College at Yonsei University and President of the East Asia Institute in Seoul. He served as president of the Korean Association of International Studies in 2019. He also served as dean of the GSIS from 2012 to 2016 and president of the Association for Contemporary Japanese Studies in 2012. Before joining the faculty at Yonsei, Dr. Sohn taught at Chung-Ang University and was a visiting scholar at the University of Tokyo, the University of North Carolina–Chapel Hill, and the University of California–Berkeley. He also was a senior fellow of the Fulbright Foundation, MacArthur Foundation, Japan Foundation, and Waseda University's Institute for Advanced Studies. Dr. Sohn currently serves as a policy adviser for South Korea's Ministry of Foreign Affairs, the Northeast Asian History Foundation, and the Korea Foundation. He has written extensively on East Asian international relations, Japanese and East Asian political economy, and public diplomacy. He received his PhD in political science from the University of Chicago.

Alison Szalwinski is Vice President of Research at the National Bureau of Asian Research (NBR). She provides executive leadership to NBR's policy research agenda, oversees research teams in Seattle and Washington, D.C., and is a member of the *Asia Policy* journal's editorial advisory committee. She is the author of numerous articles and reports and a co-editor of seven volumes in the *Strategic Asia* series along with Ashley J. Tellis and Michael Wills. Prior to joining NBR, Ms. Szalwinski spent time at the U.S. Department of State and the Center for Strategic and International Studies. Her research interests include U.S. policy toward Asia, especially U.S.-China relations and the importance of great-power competition for U.S. alliances in the region. She holds a BA in foreign affairs and history from the University of Virginia and an MA in Asian studies from Georgetown University's Edmund A. Walsh School of Foreign Service.

Ashley J. Tellis is the Tata Chair for Strategic Affairs and a Senior Fellow at the Carnegie Endowment for International Peace. He has also served as Research Director of the Strategic Asia Program at the National Bureau of Asian Research (NBR) and co-editor of the program's annual volume since 2004. While on assignment to the U.S. Department of State as senior adviser to the undersecretary of state for political affairs, Dr. Tellis was intimately involved in negotiating the civil nuclear agreement with India. Previously, he was commissioned into the Foreign Service and served as senior adviser to the ambassador at the U.S. embassy in New Delhi. He also served on the U.S. National Security Council staff as special assistant to President George W. Bush and senior director for strategic planning and Southwest Asia. Prior to his government service, Dr. Tellis was a senior policy analyst at the RAND Corporation and professor of policy analysis at the RAND Graduate School. He is the author of *Striking Asymmetries: Nuclear Transitions in Southern Asia* (2022), *Balancing Without Containment: An American Strategy for Managing China* (2014), and *India's Emerging Nuclear Posture* (2001); the co-author of *Interpreting China's Grand Strategy: Past, Present, and Future* (2000); and the co-editor of *Getting India Back on Track* (2014). He holds a PhD in political science from the University of Chicago.

Kristin Vekasi is an Associate Professor in the Department of Political Science and the School of Policy and International Affairs at the University of Maine. Her research focuses on trade and investment strategies in changing geopolitical environments and the political risk management of supply chains. Dr. Vekasi specializes in Northeast Asia and has spent years conducting research in China, Japan, and South Korea. Her book *Risk Management Strategies of Japanese Companies in China* (2019) explores how Japanese multinational corporations mitigate political risk in China. Her current research examines how Japan, China, and the United States cooperate and compete to manage complex supply chains in Southeast Asia, focusing on industries essential for the transition to green energy. Dr. Vekasi is a member of the Mansfield Foundation's U.S.-Japan Network for the Future and was a 2019 National Asia Research Program Fellow with the National Bureau of Asian Research, where she is currently a nonresident fellow. In 2021–22, she was an academic associate at the Harvard University U.S.-Japan Program. She received her PhD in political science from the University of Wisconsin, Madison.

Michael Wills is Executive Vice President at the National Bureau of Asian Research (NBR). He manages all aspects of NBR's financial and business operations and serves as secretary to the Board of Directors. His research expertise includes geopolitics, international security, and the international relations of Asia, with a particular interest in China's relations with Southeast Asia. Mr. Wills is a co-editor of thirteen *Strategic Asia* volumes as well as *New Security Challenges in Asia* (2013, with Robert M. Hathaway). Before joining NBR, he worked at the Cambodia Development Resource Institute in Phnom Penh, and prior to that with Control Risks Group, an international political and security risk management firm, in London. He holds a BA (Honors) in Chinese studies from the University of Oxford.

About Strategic Asia

The **Strategic Asia Program** at the National Bureau of Asian Research (NBR) is a major ongoing research initiative that draws together top Asia studies specialists and international relations experts to assess the changing strategic environment in the Asia-Pacific. The program combines the rigor of academic analysis with the practicality of contemporary policy analyses by incorporating economic, military, political, and demographic data and by focusing on the trends, strategies, and perceptions that drive geopolitical dynamics in the region. The program's integrated set of products and activities includes:

- a series of edited volumes written by leading specialists
- an executive brief tailored for public- and private-sector decision-makers and strategic planners
- briefings and presentations for government, business, and academia that are designed to foster in-depth discussions revolving around major public policy issues

Special briefings are held for key committees of Congress and the executive branch, other government agencies, and the intelligence community. The principal audiences for the program's research findings are the U.S. policymaking and research communities, the media, the business community, and academia.

Previous Strategic Asia Volumes

Now in its 21st year, the *Strategic Asia* series has addressed how Asia functions as a zone of strategic interaction and contends with an uncertain balance of power.

Strategic Asia 2021–22: Navigating Tumultuous Times in the Indo-Pacific assessed the impact of three major trends on the geopolitical environment of the Indo-Pacific region: intensifying strategic competition between China and the United States, growing pushback against globalization, and the Covid-19 pandemic.

Strategic Asia 2020: U.S.-China Competition for Global Influence offered a forward-looking assessment of how the rivalry between China and the United States is playing out around the globe and drew implications for U.S. policymakers.

Strategic Asia 2019: China's Expanding Strategic Ambitions assessed Chinese ambitions in a range of geographic and functional areas and presented policy options for the United States and its partners to address the challenges posed by a rising China.

Strategic Asia 2017–18: Power, Ideas, and Military Strategy in the Asia-Pacific identified how Asia's major powers have developed military strategies to address their most significant challenges.

Strategic Asia 2016–17: Understanding Strategic Cultures in the Asia-Pacific explored the strategic cultures of the region's major powers and explained how they inform decision-making about the pursuit of strategic objectives and national power.

Strategic Asia 2015–16: Foundations of National Power in the Asia-Pacific examined how the region's major powers are building their national power as geopolitical competition intensifies.

Strategic Asia 2014–15: U.S. Alliances and Partnerships at the Center of Global Power analyzed the trajectories of U.S. alliance and partner relationships in the Asia-Pacific in light of the region's shifting strategic landscape.

Strategic Asia 2013–14: Asia in the Second Nuclear Age examined the role of nuclear weapons in the grand strategies of key Asian states and assessed the impact of these capabilities—both established and latent—on regional and international stability.

Strategic Asia 2012–13: China's Military Challenge assessed China's growing military capabilities and explored their impact on the Asia-Pacific region.

Strategic Asia 2011–12: Asia Responds to Its Rising Powers—China and India explored how key Asian states have responded to the rise of China and India, drawing implications for U.S. interests and leadership in the Asia-Pacific.

Strategic Asia 2010–11: Asia's Rising Power and America's Continued Purpose provided a continent-wide net assessment of the core trends and issues affecting the region by examining Asia's performance in nine key functional areas.

Strategic Asia 2009–10: Economic Meltdown and Geopolitical Stability analyzed the impact of the global economic crisis on key Asian states and explored the strategic implications for the United States.

Strategic Asia 2008–09: Challenges and Choices examined the impact of geopolitical developments on Asia's transformation over the previous eight years and assessed the major strategic choices on Asia facing the incoming U.S. administration.

Strategic Asia 2007–08: Domestic Political Change and Grand Strategy examined internal and external drivers of grand strategy on Asian foreign policymaking.

Strategic Asia 2006–07: Trade, Interdependence, and Security addressed how changing trade relationships affect the balance of power and security in the region.

Strategic Asia 2005–06: Military Modernization in an Era of Uncertainty appraised the progress of Asian military modernization programs.

Strategic Asia 2004–05: Confronting Terrorism in the Pursuit of Power explored the effect of the U.S.-led war on terrorism on the strategic transformations underway in Asia.

Strategic Asia 2003–04: Fragility and Crisis examined the fragile balance of power in Asia, drawing out the key domestic political and economic trends in Asian states supporting or undermining this tenuous equilibrium.

Strategic Asia 2002–03: Asian Aftershocks drew on the baseline established in the 2001–02 volume to analyze changes in Asian states' grand strategies and relationships in the aftermath of the September 11 terrorist attacks.

Strategic Asia 2001–02: Power and Purpose established a baseline assessment for understanding the strategies and interactions of the major states within the region.

Research and Management Team

The Strategic Asia research team consists of leading international relations and security specialists from universities and research institutions across the United States and around the world. A new research team is selected each year. To date, more than 150 scholars have written for the program. The research team for 2023 is led by Ashley J. Tellis (Carnegie Endowment for International Peace), Alison Szalwinski (NBR), and

Michael Wills (NBR). Aaron Friedberg (Princeton University, and Strategic Asia's founding research director) and Richard Ellings (NBR, and Strategic Asia's founding program director) serve as senior advisers to the program.

Attribution

Readers of *Strategic Asia* and visitors to the Strategic Asia website may use data, charts, graphs, and quotes from these sources without requesting permission from NBR on the condition that they cite NBR and the appropriate primary source in any published work. No report, chapter, separate study, extensive text, or any other substantial part of the Strategic Asia Program's products may be reproduced without the written permission of NBR. To request permission, please write to publications@nbr.org.

Index

advanced technology, 12, 20, 130–32, 136, 138–39, 142–47, 151, 159–62, 271

Africa-China, 46, 48

artificial intelligence (AI), 21, 139, 147, 161

Asia-Pacific Economic Cooperation (APEC), 77

Asian Infrastructure Investment Bank (AIIB), 108–9, 234

Association of Southeast Asian Nations (ASEAN), 76, 99, 212–13

ASEAN-China, 60, 106, 138

ASEAN-India, 170, 174

ASEAN-Japan, 220, 264–65

ASEAN–South Korea, 105–6

ASEAN-Taiwan, 138

ASEAN–United States, 39, 205–6, 220, 222–34, 264–67

Australia: domestic politics, 268; economy, 238–40, 247, 252, 263–64; energy, 240–41, 246, 274; security, 161, 274; trade, 238, 240–41, 253, 271–73

Australia-China, 30–31, 44, 238, 241, 247–50, 252, 255, 269, 272–74

Australia-India, 170, 253, 267

Australia-Japan, 241

Australia–South Korea, 241

Australia-Taiwan, 274

Australia–United States, 31, 241, 273–75

Belt and Road Initiative (BRI), 46, 56, 63, 175, 212, 220

BRICS (Brazil, Russia, India, China, South Africa), 57, 63, 174

Central Asia–China, 46

China: agriculture, 36, 52; Anti-Foreign Sanctions Law, 38; Anti-Monopoly Law 38; Cybersecurity Law, 38; demographics, 41, 50–51, 63, 166; domestic politics, 37–38, 50, 54, 61, 62, 138, 144; dual circulation strategy, 25, 36–37, 42, 51, 55–57, 60–62, 66, 110, 144; economy, 35–59, 106, 117, 130, 133, 138–39, 142–43, 146, 148, 160, 213; energy, 50, 56, 59, 64; espionage, 42, 64, 143; exports, 4, 39, 40, 43, 55–56; foreign policy, 248; great-power status, 38; imports, 36, 39, 45–48, 52; indigenous production and innovation, 38, 43, 51–53, 64, 133, 144; investment, 20–21, 29–31, 40–42, 50–51, 55, 64, 144–48, 260–62, 270; Made in China 2025, 28, 38, 42, 54, 133; maritime disputes, 62; military strategy, 52, 62–63, 149, 151–53, 163; national rejuvenation, 38; national reunification, 149, 151, 162; nationalism, 58, 62–63, 66; "one country, two systems," 131, 151, 162; regional security, 52, 62–63, 66; rise, 4–6, 8, 11–17, 22, 31–32, 62–66, 82, 122–23, 142, 151, 247–48; strategic

culture, 58, 63, 66; territorial disputes, 52, 58; 20th Party Congress, 38, 54
China-Africa (*see* Africa-China)
China-ASEAN (*see* ASEAN-China)
China-Australia (*see* Australia-China)
China–Central Asia (*see* Central Asia–China)
China-EU, 43–44, 49, 54, 125
China–global South, 46, 48–49
China-India: economic relations, 177–78, 183–90, 194, 198; geopolitical and strategic relations, 193; security relations, 186–87; territorial disputes, 29, 62, 110, 186, 198; trade, 28, 178–82
China-Indonesia, 36, 216
China-Japan: economic relations, 26, 44–46, 49, 69, 76–77, 85, 92, 147; security relations, 26; territorial disputes, 69, 77; trade, 26, 44–46, 49, 54, 69, 73, 77–78, 92
China–Latin America, 43–44, 46, 48, 52
China–Middle East, 43–44
China-Russia: economic relations, 57; geopolitical and strategic relations, 35; trade, 36, 44–45, 59
China-Singapore, 54
China–South Korea: economic relations, 27, 46, 101, 106–10, 116, 125, 147; geopolitical and strategic relations, 100–11; trade, 46, 52, 54, 103–6, 111–16
China–Southeast Asia, 43–44, 54, 183, 203, 206, 212, 215, 221–25, 231–32
China-Taiwan, 36, 43–44, 60–62, 65; economic relations, 43, 129–39, 141, 146–48, 150, 153, 155–56, 160–61, 163; geopolitical and strategic relations, 139, 148–49, 151–53, 157–58, 160–63; historical relations, 131–39, 160; security relations, 28, 70, 139, 144, 149, 152, 157–58, 160, 162; trade, 28, 36, 131–38, 143–45, 150, 161

China–United States: competition, 5–6, 13, 16, 19–20, 24, 30–33, 70, 84, 137–38, 147, 158–60, 162, 220–22, 248, 273; economic relations, 33–39, 41–44, 46, 49–51, 65–67, 137, 142, 147, 162, 217; geopolitical and strategic relations, 35, 37–38, 66–67, 100, 109–10, 131, 138, 142, 147–49; historical relations, 37; security relations, 37–38, 65, 137, 149; trade, 9, 19, 24–25, 36–39, 41–46, 49–51, 66, 118, 217–18
China–Vietnam, 36
Chinese Communist Party (CCP), 248, 259
Cold War, 3–4, 8, 13, 18
Comprehensive and Progressive Agreement for Trans-Pacific Partnership (CPTPP), 75–76, 138, 150, 173, 194–195, 198, 214, 241, 274
Covid-19 pandemic, 9, 17–18, 31, 36, 38, 49–50, 60, 70, 73, 78–79, 86, 117, 130, 133, 137–38, 141–42, 145, 153, 155–56, 160, 238, 240, 248–49, 251, 255, 264
critical minerals, 41–42, 48, 52, 59, 69–70, 80–81, 89–91, 95–96, 121–25, 141, 166, 262, 265–67, 270–73, 275
currency, 35, 56–57

decoupling, 5–6, 14–15, 18, 24–30, 33, 35–36, 45, 52–54, 58–61, 65–66, 70–72, 80, 83, 86–89, 91–94, 96–97, 100–11, 117, 125–26, 129–31, 136, 139, 155, 160, 162, 194, 198, 222–23, 237–39, 270–73, 275
de-risking, 18–19, 23, 31, 36, 39, 62, 65–66, 70, 88–92, 94, 97, 100, 125–26, 194, 198, 218, 239, 271–73
Digital Silk Road, 212, 220–22

electric vehicle (EV), 64, 121–22, 139, 216, 233
energy, 251, 267
EU-China (*see* China-EU)

foreign direct investment (FDI), 53, 56, 73–74, 115, 166, 188–89, 205, 214, 244–45

free trade agreement (FTA), 75, 99, 108, 137–38, 150, 155, 170–73, 240–41, 247, 253, 274

friendshoring, 22–23, 238, 266–67

G-7, 81, 126, 220, 230

General Agreement on Tariffs and Trade (GATT), 7–11

global financial crisis, 9, 37, 40

globalization, 3–4, 6–15, 17–18, 21–23, 28–31, 70, 76, 96, 129–30, 209, 263

hegemony, 6–7, 13, 15, 17, 19, 31

Hong Kong, 131, 133–34, 142, 151, 162, 178–81

India: demographics, 166; domestic politics, 197; economy, 165–68, 190, 192–98; energy, 173–74, 177, 184, 195; foreign policy, 175, 192–93; trade, 167–69, 170–74, 177–78, 182, 190–91, 197–98

India-ASEAN (*see* ASEAN-India)

India-Australia (*see* Australia-India)

India-China (*see* China-India)

India-Japan, 81

India–Southeast Asia, 182–83

India–United States, 39, 195

Indian Ocean, 62

Indo-Pacific, 3, 62, 195

Indo-Pacific Economic Framework (IPEF), 29, 32, 76, 81, 150, 173, 195, 198, 229–30, 232–33

Indonesia, 123, 216, 219

Indonesia–China (*see* China-Indonesia)

industrialization, 8–9, 20, 32, 244

information and communications technology (ICT), 10, 28, 31, 122, 130–33, 138–39, 153, 222, 258–60, 275

intellectual property (IP), 9, 12, 16, 80, 83, 130, 142–44, 147

Japan: business, 72–77, 80–87, 95–97; domestic politics, 75–76, 151; economy, 70–72, 75, 79, 86, 94, 97, 151; foreign policy, 70, 75; investment, 73–74, 78, 81–82, 93, 96, 140; military strategy, 80; territorial disputes, 69, 77; trade, 71–76, 91–92, 96–97

Japan-ASEAN (*see* ASEAN-Japan)

Japan-Australia (*see* Australia-Japan)

Japan-China (*see* China-Japan)

Japan-India (*see* India-Japan)

Japan–South Korea, 91, 116

Japan–Taiwan, 91, 141–42

Japan–United States: alliance, 81, 96, 147; economic relations, 72–74, 76, 81; security relations, 81, 96; trade, 72–73, 76,

Just Energy Transition Partnership (JETP), 230–31, 233

Korea (*see* South Korea)

Laos, 207–8

Minerals Security Partnership, 124–25

nuclear energy, 154–57

Pacific Islands, 62–63

Philippines, 203, 208–9, 216, 226–28

Quad, 82, 192–93, 231, 267

raw materials 35, 42, 64

Regional Comprehensive Economic Partnership (RCEP), 29, 75–76, 137, 173, 194–95, 198, 203, 213–14, 241

Russia,18, 102, 158, 169, 177, 219

Russia-China (*see* China-Russia)

Russia-Ukraine, 18, 70, 78, 166, 274

semiconductor, 20–22, 27–28, 41–43, 53–54, 60, 70, 79–81, 89–91, 95–96, 102, 111–19, 130–33, 136–48, 154, 159, 162, 264, 267

Shanghai Cooperation Organisation (SCO), 174

Singapore, 141–42, 205, 215

Solomon Islands, 62

South China Sea, 58, 225–26, 248

South Korea: demographics, 151; domestic politics, 151; economy, 27, 101, 110, 119–20, 123–26, 151; security, 109, 126; trade, 101–3, 106–8, 141

South Korea–United States: alliance, 27; economic relations, 118, 147; trade, 39, 106

Southeast Asia, 29–30, 202; domestic politics, 215; economy, 204, 209, 218–19, 226; energy, 230; geography, 209; migration, 208–9, 213; technology, 216–17; trade, 203, 213, 215, 219

Southeast Asia–China (*see* China–Southeast Asia)

Southeast Asia–India (*see* India–Southeast Asia)

Southeast Asia–Taiwan, 135–36, 155

supply chain, 9, 14, 18–19, 22, 25–26, 32, 35–36, 39, 41, 43, 49, 51, 54, 60, 69–71, 74–76, 78–81, 84, 86–88, 91–92, 94–97, 110–11, 116–19, 123–24, 129–30, 132, 134, 138–41, 143, 145, 147, 160–61, 193, 238, 248, 251, 253, 264–67, 270–71, 275

Taiwan: Cross-Strait Service Trade Agreement, 135, 155; Democratic Progressive Party (DPP), 131, 135, 148, 150–58; demographics, 132, 141–42, 150, 153–56, 161–62; domestic politics, 28, 131, 135, 151–58, 161–63; 129–63; Economic Cooperation Framework Agreement (ECFA), 135, 150, 155; economy, 28; energy, 132, 153–54, 157; foreign direct investment, 132–36, 144; Kuomintang (KMT), 131, 135, 147, 151–52, 155–58; military, 149–51, 153, 156, 160; one-China policy, 131; security policy, 139, 149, 157; Sunflower Movement, 135; Taishang, 133–34, 136–38, 148, 159; Taiwan People's Party (TPP), 155–58; trade, 28, 160

Taiwan Strait, 19, 130, 133, 142, 151, 156, 158, 273

Taiwan-ASEAN (*see* ASEAN-Taiwan)

Taiwan-China (*see* China-Taiwan)

Taiwan–Southeast Asia (*see* Southeast Asia–Taiwan)

Taiwan–United States: economic relations, 39, 130–34,140, 144, 146–50,159–60, 163; geopolitical and strategic relations, 130–31, 140, 145, 148–52, 155–63; historical relations, 132–34, 149, 162; security relations, 145, 150–52, 156, 159, 162; trade, 134, 144–45, 148, 160–61

Terminal High Altitude Air Defense (THAAD), 109–110

Trans-Pacific Partnership (TPP), 32, 75, 99, 108, 214

Ukraine, 18, 35, 59, 156, 166, 274

United States: economy, 17, 22, 41–42, 57, 118, 140, 143, 146–47, 159; foreign policy, 142, 147, 158–59, 227, 232; imports, 39, 42; military strategy, 248, 274; security, 43, 62, 137, 142, 144, 149, 160, 248

United States–ASEAN (*see* ASEAN–United States)

United States–Australia (*see* Australia–United States)

United States–China (*see* China–United States)

United States–India (*see* India–United States)

United States–Japan (*see* Japan–United States)

United States–South Korea (*see* South Korea–United States)

United States–Taiwan (*see* Taiwan–United States)

value chain, 37, 43, 53, 61, 65, 130, 140, 146, 159, 168, 216

Vietnam, 105–6, 111–13, 117, 197, 205, 217–19

World Trade Organization (WTO), 7, 9, 11–12,16, 32, 37, 72, 92, 137, 241, 254, 274

World War II, 7–9